AF757944

THE SACRED LAW OF ISLAM

The Sacred Law of Islam

A Case Study of Women's Treatment in the Islamic Republic of Iran's Criminal Justice System

HAMID R. KUSHA
Associate Professor of Criminal Justice
Texas A&M International University
Laredo, Texas, USA

Routledge
Taylor & Francis Group
LONDON AND NEW YORK

First published 2002 by Dartmouth Publishing Company Limited
and Ashgate Publishing

Published 2017 by Routledge
2 Park Square, Milton Park, Abingdon, Oxfordshire OX14 4RN
711 Third Avenue, New York, NY 10017, USA

First issued in paperback 2017

Routledge is an imprint of the Taylor & Francis Group, an informa business

Copyright © Hamid R. Kusha 2002

All rights reserved. No part of this book may be reprinted or reproduced or utilised in any form or by any electronic, mechanical, or other means, now known or hereafter invented, including photocopying and recording, or in any information storage or retrieval system, without permission in writing from the publishers.

Notice:
Product or corporate names may be trademarks or registered trademarks, and are used only for identification and explanation without intent to infringe.

British Library Cataloguing in Publication Data
Kusha, Hamid R.
The sacred law of Islam : a case study of women's treatment in the Islamic Republic of Iran's justice system
1.Women - Legal status, laws, etc. (Islamic law) - Iran
I.Title
340.5'9'082'09055

Library of Congress Control Number: 00-135336

ISBN 13: 978-1-138-26888-3 (pbk)
ISBN 13: 978-1-84014-729-2 (hbk)

Contents

List of Tables

Preface

Islam is a simple and coherent religion. It requires submission to one God Who is the epitome of sublime values. This God is the Creator Who has sent prophets for guidance to human kind – prophets who have brought messages of peace, tranquillity and observance of God's Law. Be it Abraham, Moses, Noah, Janus, Ud, Thamud, David, Jesus or Muhammad, all are prophets of God who have been vouchsafed with the same message albeit in different formats. In Islam, this message is contained in the text of the Qur'an, a message in whose divinity Muslims entertain no doubt. It is in the Qur'an that God's message is reiterated: live, prosper, do good, avoid evil and leave your legacies for your offspring, for the earth is a temporary abode designed by Allah to test our resolve in the face of social injustice. These are the essential points of Islam's Sacred Law, the Sharia, whose primary source is the Qur'an and whose injunctions have eternally been exemplified in the words and deeds of Muhammad Ibn Abd Allah, a simple and yet righteous man who appeared at a proper time in history to inculcate the message of submission to God's message once again. Within a generation after Muhammad, the primordial Islam and its message of submission to Allah had spread to the four corners of the Old World. Thus, Islam and its Sacred Law developed as Muslims created a world religion throughout fourteen centuries. This book is a humble attempt to give the lay reader a synopsis of Islam's Sacred Law.

The book also concerns itself with the manner in which women have been treated in the Islamic Republic of Iran's justice system which emerged after Iran's now famed Islamic Revolution in 1979. This system is based on Islam's Sacred Law that replaced Iran's secular justice system established under the Pahlavi monarchy (1925-1979). Although there is a natural historical gap between the two parts of the book, thematically, this gap is bridged by the claim of the new regime in Iran – namely, that Iran's Sacred Law system emulates Prophet Muhammad's style of adjudication. As grandiose as it sounds, this claim is challenged in this book through an analysis of the Qur'an and the legacies of the Prophet Muhammad, as they are applied to Iranian women. Because of the ideological nature of the Islamic government in Iran and because Iran's Islamic justice system claims adherence to the Prophet Muhammad's application of the Sacred Law (both procedurally and substantially), the justice system has remained *terra incognita* to the Western audience in both the fields of criminology and criminal justice. This book is an attempt to fill this gap.

On Transliteration

Because this is for general readership, transliteration of the Arabic words cited from original sources has been kept to a minimum. The reason for this is quite simple. The expert in the field is cognizant of those Arabic words, and the general reader would not be interested in the exact pronunciation of such words other than knowing their proper meanings for which explanations have been provided in the text. Names of places are pronounced in the manner they appear in common English parlance as, for example, Tehran, Istanbul, Macca and Madina.

Acknowledgements

I started working on this book when I was appointed Associate Professor of Criminal Justice at Minot State University in North Dakota in August 1997. I would like to thank my then Department Chair, and now my colleague and friend at Texas A&M International University, Professor Dean J. Champion for his constant encouragement of this writing project. The same goes for my friend and the Chair of the Department of Social Sciences, Professor Nasser Momayezi, the Dean of our College, Dr. Jerry D. Thompson, a gentle giant in his field and a constant source of academic encouragement for novices like me. The same applies to my friend Dr. Faridoun Farrokh, Associate Provost at Texas A&M International University for his encouragement and the enlightening discussions that we had about Iran and Islam. During the course of writing this book at Texas A& M International University, I received two mini-grants from the University and one from the Center for Middle Eastern Studies at the University of Texas at Austin. These mini-grants helped defray the cost of research and therefore I express my thanks to the Mini Grants Committee at Texas A&M International University, and to the Director of the Center for Middle Eastern Studies at UT Austin, Abraham Marcus.

My special thanks also go to my colleague and friend Dr. Jeffrey Cass, whose professional editing improved the quality of the book immeasurably even though he was meagrely remunerated for his invaluable assistance. The credit goes to all of these colleagues. All the pitfalls of this book fall upon the shoulders of the author. I am also greatly indebted to Valerie Saunders, the anonymous editors and especially Pauline Beavers who meticulously went through the the pages of the manuscript and suggested ways to improve the overall quality of the text.

Finally, this work would not have reached the completion stage had it not been for the love, patience and understanding of my beloved wife Farah. She is the Almighty's cherished reward to me for some spectacular thing that I must have done in my life, of which I have yet to discover. I hope, my newly born baby boy whom we named Arman Reza, will one day read these pages about his parents' beloved country, Iran, the *Sarzamin-e Afsanehi*.

1 Introduction

The Sacred Law of Islam, commonly known by its Arabic name as the *Sharia*, is a complex and intertwined admixture of principles of law (*qaanun*), justice (*adala, qist*), and morality (*akhlaaq*). Until very recent times, the Sharia constituted the base of the legal system and social relations in Islamic societies. At present, only two Middle Eastern states, the Islamic Republic of Iran and the Kingdom of Saudi Arabia, adhere to a Sharia-based legal system. Other Islamic societies have adopted secular laws and systems. The Sharia, however, is a very important constituent of the tradition-based social relations in many Islamic societies, and a call to a return to the Sharia has become an integral part of the Islamic revivalist movements since the 1980s.

The Etymology of the Sharia

The term *sharia* stems from the Arabic root word *shar* which means "the road to the watering place, the clear road to be followed, as a technical term, the canon law of Islam...."[1] Other variations are *shari* (based on the *Sharia*) and *mashru* (legitimated by the *sharia*), all of which connote a premise and legitimated status within the Sacred Law. The technical field that has historically concerned itself with the study of the Sharia is known as the science of jurisprudence (*ilm al-fiqh, usul al-fiqh*), which will be dealt with later in this study.

The Sources of the Classical Sharia Law

In the formation of what a number of Muslim and Western scholars have characterized as the "classical theory of Islamic jurisprudence which has dominated all the orthodox schools of law since the third century of the Muslim era,"[2] four principal sources can be enumerated as follows:

(1) The *Qur'an* Kitaab, or the "Book" in jurisprudential vernacular
(2) The *Sunna* traditions of the Prophet Muhammad
(3) The *Ijma* consensus of the community; and interpreted in some quarters as the consensus among Muslim Jurists

(4) The *Qiyaas* analogical deductions from these three sources concerning a jurisprudential issue.

In Shii Islam, besides the first two principal sources (Qur'an and Sunna), the so-called News (*Akhbaar, s. khabar*) pertaining to the lives and deeds of the Shii Imams has played a significant role in the formation and canonization of the Shii version of the Sharia Law. In essence, the two versions are identical to each other except for procedural differences that separate the Sunni version of the Sharia Law from its Shii version. Below, a short description of each source is provided. In addition, the significance of human rationality and interpretation to the study of the Classical Sharia Law will become a focus of these investigations.

The Qur'an

The Qur'an is the most important source of the Sharia Law for the text is believed to represent the verbatim word of God gradually revealed to the Prophet Muhammad within a period of twenty-three years (610-632 CE). The revelation (*wahy*) of the Qur'an is a cardinal belief in Islam, begun in 610 CE on Mount Hira, near Macca, and concluded in 632 CE. The Prophet died in the summer of the same year in the City of Madina. There are one hundred and fourteen chapters in the Qur'an. Each chapter, known as a *surah*, consists of a number of rhyming verses (known as the *ayah*). Some chapters are very short (e.g., cxiv which has 6 verses; cxi which has 5 verses etc.), and some are very long (e.g., ii which has 286 verses; iii which has 200 verses; or iv which has 176 verse etc.). As a general rule, the shorter verses belong to the Maccan, and the longer ones to the Madinan, periods of the Prophet's life. The content of the Qur'an, the text itself maintains, has been inscribed in a Heavenly Protected Source (*Luh Mahfuz*) implying that the Qur'an is a divine text. It is a cardinal belief in Islam that the Qur'an is not a human-created collection of words of wisdom; neither is it a collection of poetry or soothsaying. It is the word of the living God (*Kalam Allah*), revealed for guidance, salvation and for peace of mind in this world and the next to come. Naturally, it contains what is known as God's Commandments (*Ahkam Allah*) and God's Boundaries and Punishments (*Hudud Allah*). Together, the *Ahkam* and the *Hudud* comprise one-third of the Qur'an, which together have given a complex and detailed system of law, justice and morality. This system includes the Qur'anic view that some acts are evil in themselves, the so-called *mala in se*. Next to these, the Qur'an has provided a mechanism for dealing with acts known as the *mala prohibita* in Western criminology. These are acts deemed anti-social or of a law-infracting nature that run against the prevailing norms of society. Altogether, the Commandments, the Boundaries and the Punishments in the Qur'an historically provide the bases for the Sharia's notion of penology as well as the principles from which a Sharia-based legal theory has been extrapolated. The field of study that has historically concerned itself with the Qur'an is known as the "science" of the Qur'anic Interpretation (*Ilm al-Tafsir al-Qur'an*), and the field that has concerned itself with the Islamic notions of law, justice and punishment (penology) is known as the "science of Judgement" (*Ilm al-qaza,* or *qizaawat*). I shall specifically deal with various aspects of the Qur'an with regard to the formation of the Sharia Law in Chapters 2 and 3 of this study.

The Sunna: The Tradition of the Prophet Muhammad

The Tradition (the *Sunna*) of the Prophet Muhammad constitutes the second most important source of the Sharia (and therefore of classical theory of Islamic jurisprudence). These traditions are composed of: (1) the authentic Prophetic utterances, as well as those utterances that later generations of Muslim writers of Hadith attributed to him; and (2) the authentic Prophetic deeds as well as those that later generations of writers attributed to him. Both are grouped under the term Sunna. Naturally, from the time of the Prophet to the present, the question as to what constitutes an authentic Hadith has required a methodology by means of which those involved in the study of the Tradition could answer this important question. This methodology, known as the authentication of evidence (*isnaad),* gradually emerged in the post-Muhammad period (632-661CE) and played a significant role in the formation of the classical view of the Sharia Law, for authentication had to follow a certain interpretive-deductive method of reasoning with regard to the issue of the Qur'anic Commandments and Prohibitions. Therefore, the Islamic Sharia Law has been open to a certain degree of purge and re-positioning. These changes have occurred despite the contentions of scholars who argue that by the tenth century CE the four Sunni orthodox schools of jurisprudence had reached their established format. The schools became closed to interpretive process through what is known as the "Closure of the Gates of Interpretation". This closure implies that Sunni Jurisprudence reached its fundamental format by the tenth century CE and, since then, no Sunni jurist has been able to point to a jurisprudential issue that needs reinterpretation. This premise, of course, is a Western view. Muslim legal scholars argue that the Sharia Law has never become a closed system.

The situation of Shii Islam is to some extent different, for although the Sixth Shii Imam, Jafar as-Sadiq (699-765), as most scholars agree, systemized the Shii principles of jurisprudence, the Shii notion of the Sharia Law has never been subjected to the closure process in the manner of the Sunni schools. Not only did other Shii Imams, who followed As-Sadiq, build further upon the Shii juristic thought, so did a number of prominent medieval and even Safavid Shii jurists. The field of study that has historically concerned itself with the Prophet Muhammad's and Shii Imami Traditions is known as the Science of Tradition (*Ilm as-Sunna/al-Hadith/al-Khabar*).

The Ijma: The Communal/and or Juristic Consensus

The communal and/or juristic consensus on jurisprudential matters constitutes the third source in the construction of Sharia Law. The rationale for utilizing this source stems from a Hadith attributed to the Prophet: "My community (*umma*) will not agree on an error." C. Snouk Hurgronje has taken this Hadith as to mean that "...whatever my community agrees on, is the truth."[3] Whether this meaning was intended by the Prophet or not, what is certain is that with the passage of time, the communal consensus ought to have been replaced by a consensus among the learned men of the law (the *fuqaha*) because Sharia Law underwent an elaborate and sophisticated process of canonization making it a far too specialized field of knowledge on which the community could reach consensus. In the course of this process, a much needed juristic *esprit de corps* evolved among jurists as they felt the need to set themselves as the only legitimate corporate body who had the requisite knowledge and methodology to interpret, and authenticate the evolving Sharia as the Law of God; this process has helped them to defend themselves and their professions against the charges of heresy, innovation and falsification.

Qiyaas: The Analogical Reasoning

Based on inductive reasoning, *qiyaas* means analogy, a term in daily usage in both Persian and Arabic. David Santillana takes this term to mean the exact opposite of the *ijma* in so far as the fallibility of human judgment is concerned, whereas *qiyaas*, according to Santillana "...is not the purely personal judgement, the application of personal opinion, but an inductive process governed by the rules of logic."[4] The importance of analogy as a juristic device stems from the fact that a jurist may not find in the Qur'an and the Sunna the requisites for a decision concerning a case. In such cases, the jurist, writes Santillana, "...has to search whether a rule cannot be deducted...from what has been decided in similar cases."[5]

Why Study the Sharia Law?

The Sacred Law of Islam, as I shall explore briefly in this study, emerged gradually as primordial Islam reached the status of a world religion during the first three centuries of Islam (650-950 CE). The Sharia Law itself was an evolutionary process in which the two primary sources of the Law, the Qur'an and the Tradition of the Prophet Muhammad, were utilized, first by the Prophet's Deputies (the *Caliphs*) and, subsequently, by a cadre of learned men of Islam in the canonization of the Law's principles. This complex and historical process, which entailed a gradual prohibition of old Arab bedouin norms and their replacement by Islamic ones, came to its maturity by the tenth century of the Christian Era (CE); it led to the formation of four orthodox Sunni and three mainstream Shii, jurisprudential schools. From this time until the middle of the nineteenth century, the Sharia Law has been adhered to in its capacity to regulate family, tort, contract and criminal matters throughout the Islamic world. The study of Sharia Law, as complex as it is, gives us a much needed background for understanding the turmoil that many Islamic countries face as they enter the twenty-first century.

Another important reason for studying Sharia Law has a lot to do with the issues of democracy, human rights, and improvement in women's social and legal status in many Islamic societies. This is especially important in the face of the profound challenges that Islamic societies face as our world becomes what some sociologists term a "global village". The world of Islam, composed of approximately one billion people, is one of the important constituents of this global village; Islam is a dynamic religion and is finding many new converts in Europe, Africa and the Americas. For these new converts, Islam is an attractive religion in the face of the moral decay that some conservative Western thinkers are now attributing to Western civilization. Accordingly, the Western crisis of civilization and culture has both economic and moral bases to its development and propagation. The enormous differences that separate the northern hemisphere from the southern hemisphere where most Islamic societies are located, have given this urgent feeling that something has to be done to bridge the gap between the two. Does post-industrial Western civilization have the moral strength to bridge this gap? There are those on the both sides of the aisle who doubt this and are now looking elsewhere for this moral strength.

Can a new and democratic version of Islam provide this much sought-after model of morality? If so, could a better understanding of the Sharia Law help to better assess the strengths and weaknesses of Islam? It is no exaggeration to suggest that, from the mid-nineteenth century to present, a powerful Western modernist challenge has been directed against Islam's Sacred Law with regard to its relevance as a rational system of conflict resolution. Many Islamic societies have gradually modernized their society and economy in the course of which they have been forced to adopt modern, semi-secular man-made laws and systems of conflict resolution and, therefore, they have shoved aside the Sharia-based legal system. This said, it should be remembered that Islam's Sacred Law has traditionally been regarded as more than just a code of law and morality. The Sharia has been looked upon as an integral part of a way of life, of one's faith, as a route to the Faithful's peace of mind and tranquillity, and as a moral and just way of living in this world and, finally, as a means to eternal salvation. Whereas most Islamic societies have desired social progress and economic development, these processes have confronted a bulwark of Islamic traditions that are represented by the Sharia Law. The profound power of these traditions stems from the fact that they permeate the core of social structures in most Islamic societies, providing epistemological meaning to a wide range of social actions based on the Sharia Law.

To give an example of this epistemological meaning, take the power of daily prayer in Islam. The prayer gives to the average believer a personal eschatological connection to Allah Who has given meaning to the Islamic notion of *tavakkul,* a concept that has a very powerful Qur'anic connotation: pray to Allah, and ask Allah's guidance only for your moral and social needs, for it is only Allah Who is the Kindest of all; it is Allah who gives you strength in the face of life's calamities; have faith in Allah and ask only for Allah's pity on you against despair and fright; have confidence in Allah. All these mean having *tavakkul* in Allah! At the same time, however, the Qur'an reminds us that every believer should do their personal utmost to achieve their legitimate (*mashru*) goals for Allah does not help those who do not strive. In other words, besides *tavakkul* in Allah, a true believer should work hard for his/her legitimate goals in this life and in the next world to come. The Sharia Law facilitates one's achievement of these goals provided that one is not striving for illegitimate ones. In other words, the Sharia Law ought not be utilized as an instrument of power for illegitimate, but for legitimate, goals and for their eventuation.

The Question of Women's Social and Legal Status: Another Reason to Study the Sharia Law

The question of the Sharia Law's stance on the social and legal status of women has emerged in social, political, and academic circles of most modern Islamic societies. In its most abstract context, the question has been as follows: how can women's social and legal status be improved in spite of the Sharia Law and its extensive web of social relations? Three general answers have been provided.

Islamic societies ought to abandon the Sharia Law once and for all and replace it with modern and secular laws. Categorized under the umbrella term of modernization, this emerging force, in many Islamic countries, has argued that the Sharia Law impedes any attempts to improve women's status because no matter how approached, the Sharia Law embodies a medievalist, sexist and patriarchal ethos.

Strict defenders of the Sharia Law have argued that women have historically enjoyed a privileged status in Islamic societies based upon the various rights (*huquq*) and responsibilities (*masuliyat*) that the Sharia Law has recognized for women. The problem of today's Islamic societies is that they have become too Westernized at the expense of Islam and the Sharia Law. The remedy is not to abandon, but, in fact, to return (*rija*), to the Sharia Law in its purity.

Reform-minded politicians, academicians and segments of the clergy argue that the Sharia Law is in dire need of reform. The reformers argue that both the Qur'an and the Prophet Muhammad have advised believers that the Law of God is for humankind's prosperity, social tranquillity and peace of mind. It is open to time and culturally bound interpretive nuances. The Sharia Law is not, and has never been, a closed system, they propose further. They reject the "Closure" of the gates of

Interpretation argument that is an invention of the Western scholarship and accordingly has no historical base in the development of the Sharia Law.

In general terms, the secular modernizers belong to the upper-class echelons in many Islamic societies. These are highly educated men and women (both at home and abroad), usually having received their education from prestigious colleges and universities in Europe and North America. As academicians, governmental bureaucrats, industrialists, and entrepreneurial capitalists and politicians, they have gained a sophisticated view of postmodern industrial societies (e.g., Western Europe, North America or Japan) and their mindset is one of progress and development within a capitalist system. From the time of the Ottoman Reform Movement (e.g., *the Tanzimat)* in the mid-nineteenth century to the Iranian Constitutional Revolution of 1906-1911, to the Nassirite Arab Nationalism in the mid-1950s, to the present, the secular modernizers, whether Mustapha Kemal Ataturk in Turkey, Reza Shah in Iran, Jamal Abdul Nassir in Egypt, Muhammad Ali Jinnah in Pakistan, Anwar al-Sadat in Egypt, or King Hasan in Morocco, have all adhered to this rationale that the Sharia Law has to be abandoned altogether so that social, economic and legal relations can be based on secular laws. Their views on women's social and legal status are relatively progressive within the context of what these modernizers have attempted to transform their constituent societies – into modern capitalist societies.

The strict defenders of the Sharia Law mostly belong to a social force that is composed of three social layers, comprising what one may characterize as the backbone of "Islamic traditionality" (*sunnati, sunnatgarai, sunnatcilik*): the Islamic clergy (*ruhaniyyah*), the Middle Eastern Bazaar-based middle and lower-middle class, as well as the Bazaar-based working class. These segments have been, and remain, a powerful force in many Islamic societies in regard to both economics and politics so that the Sharia Law – especially as it applies to the status of women – can hardly be ignored by those who opt for its total abandonment. It suffices to remind the reader at this juncture that as recently as 1979, these segments of Iranian society could claim to have spearheaded a powerful revolution, the Islamic Revolution, against a relatively well entrenched quasi-modernized and secular state and regime, the Pahlavi monarchy (r.1925-1979). Iranian women, from almost all walks of life, participated wholeheartedly in that revolution, one of whose main aims was to institutionalize an Islamic Republic. As the title of this study indicates, I shall explore Iranian women's treatment at the hands of the

Islamic Republic's justice system that has been restructured on the Sharia Law.

Next to the strict defenders, we have yet another defender of the Sharia Law in many Islamic societies, a force that, because of the "Islamic Revolution," has entered the political arena, representing a social psychology based on anti-modern, anti-secular and anti-Western thoughts and influences. This force, generally characterized as Islamic Fundamentalism, has embarked upon a political campaign of total "return" to the time of Prophet Muhammad, as well as to the ideal of emulating the Prophet's model of the application of the Sharia Law in its purest form during his reign in the City of Madina (622-632 CE). This demand underscores an Islamic *Weltanschaung* whose power stems from its idealized view that the Sharia Law ought to be adhered to in its strict totality.

With the rise of the Ayatullah Ruhullah Musavi Khumaini in Iran, and with his theocratic state system based on the Shii version of the Sharia Law, Muslim fundamentalist forces have found a strategic anchor in the region for their political agenda which is based on the argument that all Islamic countries ought to emulate the model of Iran's Islamic Republic in order to rid themselves of social and political dependency on the West. For these forces, Iranian women belong to the larger Islamic community (the *Ummat-e Islami)* and, therefore, Iranian women's social and legal status under the Sharia Law in Iran's Islamic Republic is an ideal model for all Muslim women to follow throughout the Islamic world. The Taliban movement in Afghanistan, the Islamic Front in Algeria, and various Islamic Jihadi type of movements throughout the Middle East and North Africa support this as an ideal Islamic model for women.

Finally, from the mid-1960s, there has been a new modern Islamic movement that first came to the world's attention in Algeria, as this French colony in North Africa sought her independence from France. The Algerian patriots used Islam as a unifying force against the French colonialists, by arguing that Islam made it a duty for all Algerians to fight against a foreign occupier of Muslim soil. Such participation in the independence struggle was a duty irrespective of whether one believed in Islam, or not. In other words, Islam gave to Algeria a powerful view of struggle (*al-jihad*). It was incumbent upon all Algerians to wage *jihad* against French infidels for the sake of Islam as well as for the sake of the Motherland. Naturally, Algerian women (e.g., Jamilah Bupasha) contributed to this cause. The success of the Algerian revolutionaries in their interpretation of the *jihad* as a unifying force and their effective utilization of women's energies in the success of the revolution made Islam a suitable alternative for women's emancipation in the Islamic world. In Iran, for example, the Algerian model of the use of Islam inspired a number of modern Islamic-nationalistic movements such as the Freedom Movement of Iran (*Nehzat-e Azadi-ye Iran*, from now on FMI), the Revolutionary Movement of Iranian Muslims (*Junbesh-e Inqilabi Muslmanan-e Iran*, from now on JAMA), and the People's Mujahedin Organization of Iran (*Sazman-e Mujahedin-e Khalq-e Iran*, that I shall refer to as PMOI).

The main characteristics of these modernist-Islamic movements have been that all have adhered to a relatively modern view of Islam, of the Qur'an, and of Prophet Muhammad's Traditions. The status of women in these movements has been approached from a relatively egalitarian perspective. From a class perspective, these types of modern Islamic movement are capable of attracting segments from a wide range of social strata because they adhere to a forward-looking Islam, rather than to a strategic return to a certain period of Islam as Muslim fundamentalists propose. In so far as the question of women's social and legal status is concerned, we have to differentiate between the Islamic traditionalist, fundamentalist and reformist forces that we have delineated above.

In sum, if the Sacred Law is to remain as a viable system of conflict resolution as has been advocated by Muslim fundamentalists and traditionalists, it has to go through systematic change so as to apply to the substantive and procedural aspects of the Law – in the same manner that constitutional laws do – resolving the many social, economic and political conflicts that modern Islamic societies face. This, again, is another reason why the study of the Sharia Law is important.

The Islamic Sharia Law and the Revolution in Iran

It has been observed time and again that the Islamic Revolution in Iran has focused on the role of religion as an important instrument of social change. At the same time, there are scholars and social critics who argue that this revolution has presented Islam as an alternative way to organize Iran's society and economy, based on a return to Islam. Some scholars have argued that the most profound among these changes relates to the manner in which the social and legal status of women have been determined in the

Islamic Republic's Constitution and the manner in which the emerging Islamic justice system is treating Iranian women. This system of justice operates on the Ayatullah Khumaini's view of Islam which, most scholars agree, has its theoretical foundation in Khumaini's doctrine of the *Wilayat-e Faqih* (Mandate of the Jurist).

Iran adheres to Twelve Imami Shii Islam. The Constitution of the Islamic Republic of Iran makes this brand of Islam Iran's official religion. The Constitution is a religiously-based legal document that recognizes Khumaini's doctrine of the Jurist Council as a "pure" representation of Islam and therefore gives primacy to this doctrine as the basis of present Iran's justice system. This premise of the Constitution, of course, is a very controversial issue because the Islamic origin of this doctrine has been challenged in different Islamic countries and among both Iranian opposition quarters and Shii men of the cloth. At the same time, there are scholars who have argued that the Constitution has sought to transform Iran into a Sharia-based ideal Islamic community of believers. It is within this community that the formation of an ideal woman's legal status has been envisaged. It is no exaggeration to propose that there lies the heart of the problematic: the Constitution, at the same time that it seeks to transform Iran – one of the earliest converts to Islam – into a re-Islamized religious community, strives to adhere to principles of modern nationhood. In other words, while the Constitution resurrects the Sacred Law of Islam as the only valid legal base on which to organize the Iranian economy, justice system and social relations, it also attempts to create a modern, parliamentarian and republican form of governance based on a very doctrinaire ideology. I shall explore this doctrine, its impacts upon Iran's Islamic system of justice, and the manner in which women have been treated there in some detail in this study.

Notes

1. Joseph Schacht,"Sharia", pp. 524-529 in *The Shorter Encyclopedia of Islam*, eds, H.A.R. Gibb and J.H. Kramers, (Ithaca, New York, Cornell University Press, 1961), p. 524.

2. Herbert, J. Liebesny, *The Law of the Near & Middle East: Readings, Cases & Materials*, (Albany, New York, State University of New York Press, 1975), p.12.

3. Liebesny, quoting C. Snouk Hurgronje's "Le Driot Musluman", pp. 225-227, *ibid.*, p.17.

4. Liebesny, quoting David Santillana's "Istituzioni di Diritto Musulmano Malichita", vol. I, p.46, *ibid.*, p.18.

5. Liebesny, quoting Santillana, *ibid.*

2 The Sharia Law's Genesis: A Brief History

It is commonly observed by Muslim legal scholars that the Sharia Law's genesis was formed during the tenure of the Prophet Muhammad (610-632). This premise is based on the fact that it was during this period that the Qur'an, the most important primary source of Sharia Law, was revealed to the Prophet urging him to spread God's Law among his people. Muslim scholars have observed further that the Prophet applied Sharia Law's injunctions in both Macca and Madina. This chapter gives a synopsis of the formation of the Sharia Law's genesis during the Prophet Muhammad's tenure. By the Law's genesis I mean the general principles of the Law and not the technical field whose development has been attributed to Imam Shafii's *Risala* (767-820 CE).

The Revelations of the Qur'an, 610-632

It is a cardinal belief in Islam that the Qur'an was revealed to the Prophet Muhammad in 610-632. The revelations covered a wide range of social issues including the question of law. These revelations descended gradually upon Muhammad on occasions that necessitated such revelations. Some of these related to daily affairs of believers in Macca and later in Madina; at the same time, there were others that seem to concern Muhammad's personal affairs (e.g., his marriages, and conjugal relationships), as Western Orientalist scholars have observed.

The Role of the Two Revelatory Periods in the Formation of the Sharia Law's Genesis

The Qur'an, as previously mentioned, is the primary source of the Sharia Law, a premise that is universally agreed upon by both the Sunni and Shii creeds. This premise, in fact, has attained the status of a dogma in the Islamic jurisprudence. It has been customary in the study of the Qur'an, and in the study of the rise of the Sharia Law, to divide the Prophet Muhammad's tenure into the Maccan (610-622), and the Madinan (622-632) periods. The rationale for this division has been that each period's revelations played different roles in Muhammad's life, in the progression of his divine mission, and in the development of the Sharia Law's genesis. This division is also important because there are discernible differences in the tone and thrust of the Maccan and Madinan revelations as we touched upon in Chapter 1. These differences which I shall explore shortly, naturally impacted on the Sharia Law's formation process. The Maccan revelations established the moral tone of the Law, whereas the Madinan ones established the Law's social dimensions as well as enhancing its general moral tone and disposition toward crimes, law, justice and punishment.

Both Muslim and Western scholars have observed that the Maccan revelations are mostly of a warning (*nizar*) nature and are quite powerful in their composition, structure, tone and rhythmic poetic flow. Unlike the Madinan verses, which are long, detailed in nature, and concerned with many social and legal issues, the Maccan verses confront the eschatological aspects of Islam, questions to which Islam, as a new divine faith had to respond. Examples include the nature of the Deity, the nature of the Creation, and the nature of life after death. Maccan verses of the Qur'an provided the moral and eschatological dimensions to the Sharia Law. This aspect of the Maccan verses had a lot to do with the fact that Muhammad, as the Last among Allah's Chosen Prophets according to the Qur'an, had not only to lay out the base of the Sharia Law as he gradually received the revelations of the Qur'an in Macca (and subsequently in Madina), but also had to apply the Law. But he could not apply the injunctions of the Law unless he gained political power. In the absence of actual power, Muhammad could only attend to the moral and eschatological aspects of the revelations in Macca, the city of his birth.

It has often been observed that the Madinan verses provide solutions for various social and legal issues that the first Community of Believers had to face in Madina. The best example of this is the Qur'anic chapter "Women," wherein many social issues (e.g., marriage, divorce, inheritance, and family and its dynamics) are addressed. Or, take the chapter of "The Cow," that, again, provides the *modus operandi* that the new faith was to act as arbiter between Muslims and followers of other faiths in Madina. It was, however, in Madina that Muhammad rose to the position of the enforcer of Islam's divine law upon which his precedents in adjudication were to find both moral and legal expression in the community. In Madina, Muhammad acted in the capacity of a political and religious leader as well as a judge in whose powers of mediation and sound judgment the community trusted. In this capacity,

Muhammad provided a set of procedures to determine the guilt or innocence of the parties involved in tort or in crime litigations.

The Maccan revelations (*ayati Makki*), are believed to have been revealed between 610 and 622 CE, a period during which Muhammad ibn Abd Allah (Muahmmad the son of Abd Allah), the future Prophet of Islam, lived in Macca as someone who had arisen from orphan status to that of a respected man of good standing in the community. All reputable classical commentators on the Qur'an are unanimous about the gradual nature of the revelations even while they argue that the Qur'an was first revealed *in toto* upon the Prophet's heart in accordance with the Maccan chapter (xcvii), which is known as The Night of Power (*al-Qadr*). This totality, which comprises the totality of the Qur'an, was nonetheless subjected to a piecemeal re-revelation throughout 610-632. Muslims believe that Muhammad received the Qur'an in its totality and then, as the need arose, enunciated the relevant parts of that totality. Muslim scholars have also argued that the Maccan-Madinan division of the revelations does not mean that the division ought to be looked at in a strictly chronological order. Instead it has an event-based logic to its enunciation (the *shani nuzul, asbabi tanzil* argument).[1] Some parts of the Maccan revelations were revealed a second time in Madina for the simple reason that Muhammad in Macca was in no position to enforce them.[2] This situation especially applies to those aspects of the Sharia Law that a political authority had to enforce.

Muslims believe that Muhammad's divine mission commenced in 610 CE, as he was meditating in the cave Hira near Macca. Imam Bukhari reports in the *Sahih al-Bukhari* and on the authority of Aishah, one of Muhammad's most beloved wives, that the Archangel Gabriel (*Jibrail*) appeared to Muhammad and commanded him to "Read." It is yet another cardinal belief in Islam that the Prophet was illiterate. The same Hadith reports that upon Muhammad's wonder at his ability to read despite his illiteracy, the Angel grabbed Muhammad and urged him to: "Read in the name of your Lord, who has created (all that exists) has created man from clot. Read! And your Lord is the Most Gracious...."[3] This is known as the *al-Alaq* (the Clot) chapter in the Qur'an, and all classical Islamic sources agree that this revelation informed Muhammad that he had been chosen as the awaited Messenger of God.

It is noteworthy that, based on the Qur'an, Muslims believe that both Moses and Jesus informed their followers that another Prophet by the name of Muhammad (or Ahmad which is a derivative of the same) would appear in due time and would bring joy and salvation to the world. Muhammad's prophecy, therefore, was of much interest to Rabbinic Jews. This interest in Muhammad's career, classical commentators of the Qur'an have observed, had a lot to do with the fact that the Jews of Hijaz thought that the awaited Prophet was to promote Judaism. Once they found out that Muhammad was to proclaim Islam as the one and only true faith, they started to denigrate Muhammad, accusing him of being a false prophet. Imam Bukhari, for instance, cites a Hadith on the authority of Khadijah that Muhammad, prior to his appointment as Allah's Messenger, was in search of God and used to go to Hira' to meditate regularly. The *al-Alaq* and other early Maccan revelations were, perhaps, Allah's answer to Muhammad's search for the true God. In fact, the Qur'an bears witness to the fact that Muhammad's search was taking place in a social medium that was not devoid of the concept of a monotheistic and universal God, but that these concepts had been corrupted by two developments: (1) the practice of idolatry among Maccans; (2) by the insertion of falsity in Judaism and Christianity. The Rabbinic Jews and Christians priests had falsified their Scripture by attributing anthropocentric characteristics to God by arguing that God had got a son (Jesus), or that God was a Jealous God who belonged to one nation, the Jews, and no one else. The True God, proclaimed the Qur'an, was neither begotten nor had offspring, as in the Maccan chapter *al-Ikhlas* (The Sincerity) (cxii: 1,2,3,4): "Say: He is Allah, the One! Allah, the eternally Besought of all! He begetteth not nor was begotten. And there is none comparable unto Him."[4]

This translation of the verse contradicts the literalist meaning because it genders Allah at the same time that it says Allah neither begets, nor has begotten. Allah ought to be considered as an entity that is gender-neutral. However, in the classical source, Allah is by and large described by its "masculine" epithet. In any case, this Allah comprises the concept of a Universal Deity that the Qur'an proclaims Allah represents. This Universal Deity does not belong to one group of people, has no human attributes, and is not afflicted by any human desires, shortcomings and attributes. This Allah is beyond reproach. It exists for the good of humanity, creation, the cosmos and everything that inhibits it. Allah, however, has given humanity rationality, choice, freedom and foresight by means of which believers may discern between good and evil. Allah has given us life and its bounties, one of which is the Law.

The classical sources agree on a period of forty days that they report having elapsed between the first revelation and the next one. This is known as the Interregnum Period in the revelation process and early Muslim commentators, including Imam Bukhari, have advanced various explanations for it. The thrust of the classical view, by and large, has been that the Interregnum was perhaps part of Allah's divine plan for Muhammad – a plan that our fallible human logic is incapable of comprehending – or that the period was to give to Muhammad sufficient time to appreciate adequately the magnitude of this encounter with the Heavens and to prepare him for subsequent encounters with the Archangel Gabriel in which Gabriel reassured Muhammad that he was indeed the awaited chosen messenger (e.g., xciii:1-11).

The classical sources also give the impression that the Maccan revelations of the Qur'an profoundly changed Muhammad's view about many aspects of life, including his notion of Deity. Although of a monotheistic nature, Muhammad's notion was not yet pure. This profound change in Muhammad's soul occurs despite his rational disposition towards life, his gentle mannerism, and his simple and righteous life style in Macca. He was known as *al-Amin* (the Honest) among the Maccans; they all knew that he had refrained, throughout his youth and adult life, from those vile traditions for which Maccans were infamous. There is one Hadith that purports that, in his youth, Muhammad was tempted to visit a place of ill repute but was stopped by Heavenly intervention. Yet another Hadith purports that when Muhammad, in his youth, was about to receive a small portion of a sheep slaughtered as a sacrifice to one of the grand idols of Macca, he was miraculously prevented from doing so. Other Hadiths give testimony to Muhammad's generosity, bravery and concerns for the less privileged.

In both the Maccan and Madinan revelations, Muhammad has been characterized as Allah's Messenger (*Rasul Allah*) as, for instance, in the Madinan chapter "The Clear Proof" (xcviii,2) or in the Maccan chapter "The Sun" (xci,13). Muhammad is sometimes portrayed as the Prophet of God (*Nabi*) and sometimes as Warner (*Nazir*). In these highly exalted positions, he is portrayed as neither a ruler, nor as a soothsayer, nor a poet, but as an illiterate who has the highest moral qualities (*uswah hasanah*). He has been chosen by Allah to receive and to convey the same message that Allah had sent to other prophets (e.g., Abraham, Noah, Lot, Uad, Thamud, Janus, Moses, David and Jesus). This eternal message, maintains the Qur'an, has been engraved in the "primary scroll" (*al-suhaf al-awwali*); it is by this mechanism that Allah sends to whomever "He" wishes part of "His" everlasting message of guidance for humanity, as He did with pre-Muhammad prophets, be it Abraham or Moses (lxxxvii, 18,19). This is one of the most powerful claims of the Qur'an and it gives a powerful ontological dimension to Islam as part of Allah's grand design. These verses have had an eternal impact on the Muslim social and legal mind because Allah's Creation has a divine plan of which the law is one of the most important ingredients.

Western Orientalist Scholarship's View on the Revelation Process

These premises of the Qur'an, however, have been countered by Western Orientalist scholars who have argued that the reason that the Qur'an characterizes Muhammad in different capacities – sometimes as a Prophet of the doomsday, sometimes as a unitarian sage, sometimes as God's Messenger, and sometimes as God's prophet – is because of Muhammad's worldly ambitions and his vocation as the "author" of the Qur'an. Ignaz Goldziher, a pioneer of this school of thought, first tries to establish what Islam is and how Muhammad is the builder of Islam and the author of the Qur'an. He opines that:

> The Arab Prophet's message was an eclectic composite of religious ideas and regulations. These ideas were suggested to him by contacts, which had stirred him deeply, with Jewish, Christian, and other elements, and they seemed to him suited to awaken an earnest religious mood among his fellow Arabs. [5]

This premise of Goldziher, of course, means that Muhammad is the creator of Islam, a man-made religion whose divinity is quite suspect in the eyes of Western Orientalist scholars. This view has categorically been rejected by Muslim lay people and intellectuals on the premise that the divinity of the Qur'an is a not open to any middle-ground argument. For Muslims, the text is divine in its origin because the text claims unequivocally that it is a divine text authored by God, not by Muhammad, or by any other mortal being.

To explain Muhammad's zeal for concocting a new religion based upon conscientious trial and error, Goldziher follows Alfred von Harneck's observation about the "pathology of superman" to establish this view that Muhammad was a "superman" afflicted with diseases that, accordingly, "...strike supermen who then draw from them new life never before suspected, energy that levels all hindrances in its path...."[6] It is within this "pathology" that Goldziher analyses the Maccan and the Madinan revelations including the reasons as to why these revelations characterize Muhammad differently. Reading the Maccan revelations in the context of Muhammad's actual attempts to create Islam based on his patchwork of learning from other religions, Muhammad is portrayed as a zealot, as one who was drawn to meditation and "hallucination"[7] so that what he had heard here and there, he could put them in the context of his divine call to Maccans. All these concocted efforts were for a worldly purpose accordingly:

> Thus, it was with borrowed blocks that Muhammad built his eschatological message. He made use of Old Testament history (mostly in haggedic form), citing from it admonitory examples of the fate of ancient peoples who opposed and scoffed at the warners sent to them. Muhammad now placed himself at the end of this chain of prophets; he was its final link. [8]

Goldziher takes this position in spite of the fact that the Qur'an, time and again gives the unequivocal impression to the reader that Muhammad was an illiterate person with no knowledge of the past scripture as evinced by the Maccan chapter (xlii, 52) which reads:

> And thus We inspired in thee (Muhammad) a Spirit of our command. Thou knewest not what the Scripture was, nor what the Faith. But we have made it a light whereby We guide whom We will of our bondman. And lo! Thou verily dost guide unto a right path. [9]

The Maccan and Madinan revelations give this distinct impression that Muhammad was indeed a passive receiver, rather than a creator, of the Qur'an and of its contents. Every chapter of the Qur'an starts with a benediction to Allah; nowhere do we find any evidence to the contrary. Nowhere does the Qur'an suggest that Muhammad possessed any divine attribute, or was a superman and of any special significance other than deserving to be chosen by Allah as the Messenger because he exemplified a righteous man in his words and deeds. It is indeed amazing that Goldziher and other Orientalist scholars of his ilk, although superb Arabists and highly schooled in various Middle Eastern languages (e.g., in Hebrew, Aramaic, Persian and Turkish), have ignored this distinct tone of the Qur'an at the expense of a hypercritical deconstruction of the Qur'an to "prove" that the text is but a "creation" of Muhammad. This depiction of Muhammad as the author of the Qur'an exists in spite of the fact that, on the one hand, Muhammad is depicted to have been "afflicted" by the pathological power of the belief that he was receiving messages from some divine sources, and yet, on the other, he is as a very rational and calculating politician who produces self-serving revelations. Based on this approach, the general thrust of Orientalist scholarship is that there are discernible differences between the Maccan and Madinan revelations. These differences are explained in terms of Muhammad's plans to create a religion for Arabs. This premise, of course, runs against the very Qur'an that reminds believers that the only true faith is Islam, which means submitting to the Will of Allah, the one and only universal Deity whose message, adamantly states the Qur'an, has been the same and vouchsafed to Allah's Prophets, be it Abraham, or Moses, or Jesus or Muhammad. This is the gist of the Qur'an, the heart of the Qur'anic claim as to what Islam is and what the charge of Muhammad has been: not to create a "new" religion for Arabs, but to resurrect the one and only religion that is the true faith. Judaism and Christianity are but versions of Islam forgotten and/or corrupted by those who received Allah's Message through the Abrahamic line of Prophets, to borrow Louis Massignon's famous phrase and conception of Islam.

Goldziher ignores this very powerful claim of the Qur'an and tries to explain these differences in terms of Muhammad's worldly ambitions. These verses, accordingly, contain the learning that Muhammad acquired from contact with Rabbinic Jews, Christian monks, and Zoroastrian (Mu`beds?) and Unitarian Hanifs (sages). He is sometimes kind and conciliatory towards Rabbinic Jews and Christian monks, and sometimes quite harsh towards them. Likewise, to win over the Maccans, Muhammad, "produces" verses that sometimes are conciliatory and sometimes threatening to Maccan idols. These are tactics, opines Goldziher, that have implications for the style of the Qur'an: "The change in Muhammad's prophetic character unavoidably left its mark on the style and rhetoric of the Qur'an."[10] This premise, again, means that it is the Qur'an that, as a creation of Muhammad, is influenced by his political schemes and plans and not the other way around. After thirteen years of futile efforts, Muhammad realizes that his creation is but a total failure and therefore he "flees" from Macca to find refuge in Yathrib, the arch rival of Macca. The "flight" again, is depicted by Goldziher as a calculated political move because the two cities are rivals and enemies to each other, a premise that is not without its merits, but hardly explains the fact that Muhammad's flight to Yathrib (Madina) takes place on behest of an invitation extended to him by the Madinan who sought his wise judgment in a number of disputes that they had with each other. This invitation, of course, debunks the conspiratorial schemes and calculations that the likes of Goldziher intimate in their depiction of Muhammad's self-serving moves.

In Madina, Muhammad continues to produce verses that show him to be an ambitious full-fledged politician ready to wheel and deal with every lever of power for the sake of achieving his old dream of unifying Arabs under the banner of a concocted religion that at best is a vapid replica of Judaism, Christianity and Zoroastrianism.

Muslim Scholarship's View of the Revelation Process

Muslim scholars do not agree with this type of approach to the Qur'anic revelations based on the political motivation argument of Western Orientalist scholars. Most agree that there are discernible differences between the tone and thrust and purpose of the two period's revelations. But these differences, they argue, ought to be posited in the context of the occasions of the revelations that I mentioned above rather than within the context of power politics. Muslim theologians take a more deterministic position, arguing that these differences ought to be posited in the context of Allah's preordained divine plan for Muhammad, a plan that was designed to guide Muhammad against his cunning and ruthless enemies. This premise, of course, reflects faith rather than a rigorous historical-sociological analysis of the Qur'an and of the two periods' revelations.

My approach in this study is based on the very text of the Qur'an whose contents have to be analysed based on the methodology that the text itself has provided for us in dealing with its contents. As I shall expound in Chapter 4 of this study, the advice of the Qur'an is that its contents ought to be explicated by reference to the very text and the occasion of the revelation. Because of space limitations, I won't be able to follow this methodology for every citation of the Qur'an that I have utilized here. I also follow the Islamic view that considers Islam as a revelatory and monotheistic faith whose principal beliefs start with Judaism, continues through Christianity and finds its most evolved form under the mantle of Islam. This view of Islam, as I mentioned above, does not mean that Islam is "better" than other religions, it simply means that, from an evolutionary perspective, the Qur'anic notion of the Sacred Law has to be analysed in the context of a much more evolved plane of social relations that existed in the Old World during the time of Islam's appearance and spread.

Based on the argument so far, it is no wonder that the Maccan verses do not advise Muhammad to actively enforce any Qur'anic injunctions in the context of an enforceable legal doctrine of law, but to receive the contents of these scrolls which, of course, contain Allah's Commandments (*Ahkam Allah*) and Allah's Boundaries (*Hudud Allah*). In other words, reading the Maccan and Madinan verses suggests that the revelations position Muhammad to challenge the prevailing traditions and mores of the Maccans first, and then replace them with those of Islam. That is why these revelations have a very powerful moralistic tone and disposition against the Maccans and their way of life as, for instance, (cvi) which maintains that Allah had given all the bounty to the Quraysh of Macca so that they would worship the one and true Deity that Abraham had introduced to them, but the Quraysh had long since forgotten this Deity and had reverted to the worship of idols. The Quraysh represented a powerful federation of tribes to one of which Muhammad belonged.

The Qur'an advises the Maccans to heed Muhammad's warnings, and to take a lesson from the fate of those who arrogated themselves against Allah's might in past. The chapter (cv) titled "The Elephant," for example, reminds the Maccans of the miraculous defeat of Abraha of Abyssinia. Abraha attempted to conquer Macca (around 560) in order to destroy the House of Kaba that stood as a witness to the monotheistic legacy of Abraham albeit long since forgotten. Abraha, the Qur'an reminds us, could not achieve his goals because Allah protected Macca against Abraha's mighty force, a force that included warriors mounted on African elephants. The Qur'an maintains that by the order of Allah the "*flying ababil*" (locusts?) attacked this mighty force and pelted them with stones made of "baked clay" (*sajjil*). The moral of this and similar Maccan verses (e.g., xcix, ci, cvi, cvii) is that the Quraysh did not recognize that the same force that had rescued Macca from the wrath of Abraha, was now protecting Muhammad – a force whose might, declares the Qur'an, is unlimited.

The Methodology in the Study of the Qur'an and of the Sharia Law

As previously mentioned, the revelation of the Qur'an was of a gradual nature based on what is known as the occasions of the revelation (*asbabi tanzil, shani nuzul*) as, for instance, the example of "The Elephant" given above. These occasions, together with the contents of the Qur'an, have been studied extensively by a wide range of disciplines in the past so that together they have comprised the Classical Science of the Qur'an (known as the *Ilm al-Qur'an*). It includes various branches such as:

Ilm al-Tafsir wa al-Tabyin	Concerned with the commentaries on the Qur'an
Ilm al-Hadith wa al-Sunna	Concerned with the Prophet's words and deeds
Ilm al-Qir'a	Concerned with the correct recitation of the Qur'an
Ilm al-Lugha	Concerned with word counts and sentence structures of the Qur'an
Ilm al-Rijal	Concerned with the life and deeds of those involved in the interpretation of the Qur'an and of Hadith
Ilm al-Nahv wa al-Sarf	Concerned with the grammar of the Qur'an
Ilm al-Gharaib	Concerned with esoteric aspects of the Qur'an
Israil'iyat wa Masihiyat	Concerned with the question of Judaic and Christian concepts in the Qur'an.

These classical disciplines, to which some reference will be made as the occasion arises, have provided us with a classical methodology for the study of the Qur'an, as the primary source of the Sharia Law in the past. This methodology and its written sources, if approached systematically, enable the researcher to form an idea about the relation of the revelations to the formation of the Sharia Law's genesis during the Prophet's tenure. What are some of these rules?

The first rule, developed throughout the centuries, has been that the Qur'an comprises the most authentic source on Muhammad's life, on his divine mission, and on the legal principles out of which the Sharia Law's genesis was formed during Muhammad's tenure. This rule means that any investigation on the Sharia Law ought to start with the Qur'an and its revelation during Muhammad's tenure. That is why in both Sunni and Shii juristic schools and texts, it is the Qur'an that comprises the first and the most important source of the Sharia Law. No reputable Sunni, or Shii jurist, has ever argued against this cardinal principle. It is the Qur'an which has provided the general frame of the "Knowledge" (*Ilm*) that the issue of lawful and/or unlawful raises. This rule means that one ideally reaches the status of an Islamic judge and jurist by learning thoroughly the so-called "Science of the Qur'an," *Ilm al-Qur'an*, of which, the "Science of the Jurisprudence," *Usual al-Fiqh*, is a very important constituent. It is the *Fiqh* that concerns itself with the legal and technical aspects of the Sharia Law.

The second rule has been that the Qur'an is the Sublime Word of Allah; it carries no falsehood, no contradictions, and no apology for Muhammad's deeds. The implications of this rule have been enormous for the Muslim legal mind. Muslims believe that the contents of the Qur'an are of an everlasting validity that ought to be reflected upon, studied and adhered to with regard to any aspects of crime, justice and punishment. It is through the tripartite acts of reflection, study and adherence that believers create in their inner self a powerful preventive mechanism against the sin/crime (*maasi*) duality, giving the Sharia Law a very powerful individualistically validated dimension of responsibility in that a true believer has to follow the Law's injunctions covering personal, social and communal obligations. For example, a believer has to perform his/her duties toward his/her parents, spouse and children at the same time that he/she has to perform his/her religious obligations (prayer, fasting, paying taxes and defending the honour and integrity of the community). In short, the Sharia Law, it has been observed time and again, links the individual with the community and the state in terms of a collective and anti-criminogenic responsibility that the Law elicits from the three constituents of the society: individual, community and state. It is through this linkage that order, justice and tranquillity are maintained in the realm of *Dar al-Islam*, a highly idealized Islamic utopia that has its counterparts in Judaism and Christianity.

Because it reflects the Divine Logic of Allah expressed in the Sublime Qur'an, the Sharia Law imparts three levels of responsibility: individual, communal and statist. In both Sunni and Shii juristic texts, therefore, the Sharia Law has assumed the status of the most perfect system of law whose first and foremost objective has been to lead humanity to a better life in this world and salvation in the next world to come. That is why all classical juristic texts present a complex and yet logical connection between the Sharia Law (*Qanun-e Shar*) and the principles (*usul, aadaab*) of a prescribed moral way of life. In other words, the study of the Law is intrinsically linked to the *aadaab* of daily life in a particular social and cultural setting. The Sharia Law is *sui generis* and can go into a dizzying array of complexity as it relates to various social acts in terms of their legality/illegality in both Sunni and Shii jurisprudential versions. This aspect of the Sharia makes the Law complex in scope, procedure and substance.

The third rule has been that the Sharia Law reflects the righteous and the just path (*shira`*) that the Prophet Muhammad traversed in his capacity as Allah's Messenger during his lifetime. To implement the Sharia Law, believers ought to follow Muhammad's Tradition (deeds, words and mannerisms) which, as Muhammad's historical heritage, reflects his view and interpretations of the Qur'an and therefore of the Sharia Law. This rule implies that it is Muhammad's life and events that any researcher ought to concentrate on in order to form an idea about the manner of, and the correct procedures in, the application of the Law's injunctions. Therefore, next to the Qur'an, Muslim believers have to study the Prophet's Tradition and even memorize them in order to adhere to Islam's Sacred Tradition. This studying of the Prophet's life is especially important in one's understanding of the application of the Law's injunctions to cases, whether they are to civil law and cases (family, inheritance, marriage and divorce, rituals, etc.), or to criminal and tort laws. This aspect of the Sharia, again, adds to the complexity of the Law in scope, procedure and substance. However, this aspect also allows the judge to go to the second source of the Law in case a legal issue or principle is hard to find by reference to the Qur'an.

The fourth rule has been that Islam is the most complete among other revelatory religions of scripture. This means that the Sharia Law, having emanated from the Qur'an based on Muhammad's Tradition, not only has elevated the Mosaic-Davidic laws, as well as those put forth by the Gospel of Jesus of Nazareth, but in fact, has perfected them. That is why the Qur'an advises Muhammad that Allah does not legislate against those good laws that have already been revealed (to previous Prophets of Allah), but makes improvements upon them (through the Qur'anic revelations). This rule means that the similarities between the laws of Islam and other revelatory religions are natural, for Allah has revealed similar laws in "His" divine message to pre-Muhammad Prophets, but since Muhammad is designated as the "Last" among the Chosen Prophets of Allah (*Khatam al-Anbiyin*), the Sharia Law contains the Everlasting and Universal Deity – i.e., Allah's most perfect and complete set of laws. I should caution my Western readers that this premise should not be construed as a value judgment on my part, but one that aims to posit Islam and its laws in the social and historical evolutionary perspective, a point which we will explore in some detail later as we expound on the development of the Sharia Law.

The Islamic Legal Discipline (Usul al-Fiqh)

This is the main branch or discipline (*usul*) Muslim jurists have derived from the Qur'an and from the Prophet's Tradition, which deals with the Sacred Law's legal principles. In both Sunni and Shii creeds, the *usul* reflects a certain consensus as to the following questions and answers that Muslim jurists have raised:

(1) What is law? A: It is a socially contracted necessity.
(2) Where does law come from? A: From Allah.
(3) Why law is important? A: It resolves conflicts, serves the cause of justice and imposes a legitimate social order.
(4) What is the range of law? A: All-inclusive.
(5) What happens if law is infracted upon: A:A sin/crime is committed that needs to be redressed in order to prevent society falling into anarchy and disorder.
(6) What shall be done with those who infract law? A:They should be punished, but punishment ought to be swift, certain and of a redemptive nature while at the same time deterring others from wishing to commit the sin/crime.
(7) Whose responsibility is it to uphold law? A: The individual, community and the state.
(8) What is to be done in confronting new law-infracting situations? A: The bases of the Sharia Law ought to be consulted.
(9) What is to be done with ancestral law? A: If they are not anti-Sharia they ought to be respected and followed.
(10) Who is the proper authority to apply law? A: Those who are knowledgeable about the Sharia, its sources and its interpretation, and are pious, God-fearing and just.
(11) Who is the proper authority to enforce law and deal with malcontents? A: The state and its organs.

Whereas these issues have been extensively dealt within the *usul al-fiqh* literature to which reference will be made, the Sharia Law's actual application has been covered under the so-called *Hukm wa Qaza* which can be characterized as the Islamic criminal justice system. The Sharia Law not only has an elaborate view of what we may call a general legal theory of law, but also of crime and of punishment which in essence means Sharia-based penology.

Muslim jurists, like all other seekers of the "Science of the Knowledge of the Qur'an" believed that the ultimate "Knowledge" of everything resides with Allah; nonetheless, they also believe that Allah has provided human beings with faculties to discern the knowledge of the Qur'an and its laws. We find this view in all branches of Islamic sciences ranging in diversity from the most rational – i.e., *Ilam al-Tarikh* (History) – to the most eschatological in nature – such as *Hikma* (Gnosticism). The following quotation from Ibn Khaldun (1332-1406), the Maghrebi historian, may shed some light on this view of the source of knowledge in Muslim thinking. Writing on Islamic jurisprudence, he states that:

> Jurisprudence is the knowledge of the classification of the laws of God, which concern the actions of all responsible Muslims, as obligatory, forbidden, recommendable, disliked, or permissible. These [laws] are derived from the Qur'an and the Sunnah [traditions], and from the evidence the Lawgiver [Muhammad] has established for knowledge of [the laws]. The laws evolved from the [whole] of this evidence "jurisprudence" (*fiqh*).[11]

Next, Ibn Khaldun goes on to explain the role of the Prophet Muhammad in interpreting the revelations, how Muhammad's Companions (*Sahabah*) recorded the revelations (by committing them to memory or by writing them down), how some of them differed in their understanding of the Prophet's interpretations as well as how different jurisprudential schools developed in Macca, Madina, Kufa and Basrah. Ibn Khaldun has been characterized as the one of the most profound rationalists among the medieval Islamic historians.[12] The same rational approach applies to most Muslim jurists who, from the very inception of the Islamic jurisprudence as a branch of Islamic Sciences (*Ulum*), were quite cognizant of the fact that their field required a rigorous methodology – one that could logically deal with the contents of the Qur'an.

The general thrust of Western scholarship of the Sharia Law is that the Law does not develop until the second century of Islam. Muslim jurists, under a number of Umayyad Caliphs in the second century of Islam, start to systematically study other legal systems of other civilizations and especially those of the of the Byzantine Rome and of Sasanid Iran, accordingly.

The Methodological Thrust of this Study

The thrust of this study is that in a systematic study of the Sharia Law's rise and elaboration, besides the text of the Qur'an and primary sources available to us, there are logical reasons to propose that the Sharia Law's genesis developed during the Prophet's tenure. One simple and yet logical reason is that if we follow the Western premise that Muhammad was the "author" of the Qur'an and therefore of its laws, then his tenure ought to be looked upon as the period for the enforcement of such laws. It is also logical to argue that Muhammad, as the would-be lawgiver, was bound to enforce his own enunciated laws in order to give legitimacy to the idea that he was a lawgiver, even if such a regime were of a rudimentary nature. Therefore, Muhammad's tenure ought to be considered as the exemplar of the Sharia Law's penology in the context of both procedure and substance. In other words, following the Western view, the most logical starting point for the study of the development of the Law and of its penology is Muhammed's tenure, rather than the Umayyad Caliph's tenure.

Next to these logical conclusions, there are authentic Hadiths that purport that Muhammad does, in fact, enforce those injunctions of the Qur'an to be dealt with later in this chapter.

Muhammad's Personality and its Impacts on the Sharia Law's Genesis

From an Islamic belief system and perspective, Muhammad is not the founder of the Sharia Law *per se*, but from a sociology of law perspective, it could be argued that Muhammad's personality deeply influenced the Sharia Law's development from the very beginning. In the Islamic belief system, Muhammad is looked upon as the noblest person, whose deeds, words and personality embody Islam in its purest form. That he received Allah's Commandments and applied them in the most just manner is the gist of this belief. This application, Muslim jurists have argued, had a lot to do with Muhammad's unique personality which developed in the social atmosphere of Macca and under the most difficult conditions, especially after he started preaching Islam openly. These conditions can be summarized in terms of: (1) Muhammad's orphan status, (2) Muhammad's destitute conditions, and (3) Muhammad's abilities to face calamities and yet remain steadfast in his resolve. These conditions influenced the development of the Sharia Law's genesis, reflecting Muhammad's personality and concerns both in the letter and in the spirit of the laws that the Qur'an enunciates.

Muhammad's Orphan Status

Early sources are unanimous that Muhammad was brought up as an orphan (*yatim*). The Qur'an reminds us of Muhammad's orphan status in the Maccan chapter (cvii); it also reminds Muhammad that Allah had protected him as an orphan among Maccan idolaters in an urban setting that was renowned for its abusive practices with regard to the less powerful and less privileged. The Qur'an gives Muhammad the solace of his future accomplishments at a time in which such accomplishments appeared impossible. In its later Madinan chapters, the Qur'an advises Muhammad of the importance of dealing fairly with orphans. This advice has two dimensions: (a) from the standpoint of morality as, for instance, (ii, 220) which maintains that: "Upon the world and the Hereafter. And they question thee concerning orphans. Say: To improve their lot is best. And if ye mingle your affairs with theirs, then (they are) you brothers...."[13]; (b) from the standpoints of the social and economic well-being of the orphans as exemplified by (iv, 2) which states: "Give unto orphans their wealth. Exchange not the good for the bad (in your management thereof) nor absorb their wealth into your own wealth. Lo! That would be a great sin."[14] Naturally, the Qur'an's emphasis on fair dealings with orphans found an important place in the Sharia Law to the effect that, to this date in many Islamic societies, it is one of the most admonished and loathsome acts to abuse an orphan and to abscond with his/her wealth. Interestingly, the Qur'anic advice of fair conduct towards orphans also applied to women (*al-nisa*), as well as indigent and destitute persons. For example (iv, 6) states:

> Prove orphans till they reach marriageable age; then, if ye find them of sound judgement, deliver unto them their fortune; and devour it not by squandering and in haste lest they should grow up. Whoso (of the guardians is) rich, let him abstain generously (from taking of the property of orphans); and whoso is poor let him take thereof in reason (for his guardianship). And when ye deliver up their fortune unto orphans, have (the transaction) witnessed in their presence. Allah sufficeth as a Reckoner.[15]

The importance of these types of Qur'anic declaration has to be understood in the context of the pre-Islamic bedouin Arab stance towards the disenfranchised – a subject to be dealt with shortly.

Muhammad's Destitute Status

Early sources are adamant that, although Muhammad was brought up in relatively destitute conditions, first by his grandfather Abd al-Muttalib and then, after his death, by his parental uncle, Abi Talib, Muhammad never reverted to unsavory practices that destitute lads of his generation would have done. This aspect of Muhammad's life, perhaps, had a lot to do with his noble personality and the good seed genealogy (in contrast to the concept of bad seed in Western criminology). Ibn Saad's *Tabaqat* informs us that Muhammad belonged to a relatively high-class Maccan family of Hashim which, in turn, was related to Abd Manaf.[16] Early sources also inform us that Muhammad lost his father, Abd Allah, even before his birth. He also lost his beloved mother Aminah bint Whahb at the age of six. In spite of these early setbacks, Muhammad, from very early childhood, showed signs of high intelligence, charisma, a gentle and yet passionate soul and a certain noble shyness (*hujb*) that is highly valued in the Qur'an, according to Ibn Saad. This quality made the young Muhammad especially attractive to those who were bothered by the social demeanour of their fellow Maccans. By and large, Maccans were known for their crass and aggressive manner.

Ibn Saad depicts some aspects of Muhammad's childhood in miraculous terms, as for instance Muhammad's encounter with a Christian monk named Bahirah. In this encounter which apparently took place in Bahirah's monastery around 582 CE, putting Muhammad at age twelve, Bahirah, immediately recognized the many extraordinary qualities of the young boy (as the promised Prophet of God of Abraham) and warned Muhammad's guardian, Abu Talib, to safeguard the youngster against any harm that might come to him from the Jews. This possibility was due to the fact that Muhammad's appearance as the "Last of the Revelatory Prophets" had been known to both Jews and Christian. The Qur'an refers to this in (xlvi, 10) and in (lxi, 6). This literature depicts Muhammad's life in Macca (570-622) as one of the tribulations that Allah placed in his path in order to gauge Muhammad's noble personality; he was an orphan who was forced to earn his living as a shepherd, one of the lowliest of professions in Macca.

Later, Muhammad was employed by Khadijah bint Khuwaylad, a widowed lady of high standing in Macca involved in the long-distance caravan trade. Early sources inform us that Khadijah had heard of Muhammad's honesty and integrity and took him into her employment, subsequently asking Muhammad to marry her even though she was in her forties whereas Muhammad was in his early twenties. This marriage, the same sources inform us, gave Muhammad happiness, contentment and financial security as well four daughters (Fatimah, Zaynab, Um-Kulthum and Ruqayyah) and a number of boys all of whom died in early infancy. This happy and monogamous marriage lasted for about a quarter of a century (595-619) until Khadijah's death in 619. Early sources indicate that Muhammad's grief over Khadijah's death was so intense that the Heavens had to intervene to ameliorate it. The historian Al-Tabari narrates a Hadith on the authority of Aishah bint Abu Bakr that it was the Archangel Gabriel who, in one of his many appearances to the Prophet, urged him to marry Aishah to lessen this grief.[17] It was after Khadijah's death that Muhammad married a number of wives, some of whom played important roles in his life as well as playing roles in the progression of Islam and even in the progression of the Sharia Law (e.g., Aishah, Hafsah, Swada, Umm Salama, Mariah and Zaynab bint Jahsh).

Muhammad's Resolve in Confronting Calamities

Reading early sources, one gets the distinct impression that Muhammad was resolute in confronting calamities. According to several Hadiths, he endured being an orphan, but never reverted to unsavoury practices. These Hadiths portray Muhammad as honest, upright, brave, generous, gentle, caring and yet firm in his stance against those things that the Qur'an has condemned in the Maccan way of life. One of the most vile among these was the worship of idols, a practice that, by the time of Muhammad, had developed into a complex system of religious rituals with Macca as its centre. It had evolved with the long-distance trade and commerce that had its own laws, notions of crime, justice and penology. Muhammad's biggest challenge as a preacher of divine law was to stand up against this power bloc in Macca, challenge this system, and defeat it through the Teachings of Islam encapsulated in Sharia Law's genesis. In other words, Muhammad's personality reflected the essence of the Law in that he lived a simple and righteous life in Macca in the same manner that he continued a simple and righteous life after he attained the status of the God's Last Chosen Prophet to receive God's Commandments. This centrality of Muhammad's simple and yet righteous life, in the Muslim legal mind, has put its imprint on to the purpose of the Sharia Law – namely, that God's Law is for the sublime purpose revealed to Muhammad and other messengers of God for the good of the individual and the community.

The Hijaz region is a part of the Arab Peninsula, where Islam originated. The Arab Peninsula is a vast stretch of land that separates the African continent from Asia. Covering modern Iraq, Saudi Arabia, Yemen, as well as Syria, Jordan and the Levants, this huge land mass is located between the Red Sea to the west, the Indian Ocean to the south and the Persian Gulf to the east. Despite being surrounded by large bodies of water, it is an arid and hostile land, especially in the interior known as the *Rub al-Khaali* (the Empty Quarter). Alongside a pastoral mode of existence in the interior, there had developed sophisticated settled cultures on the coastal exteriors of the Peninsula, as for example in Yemen. Macca, the city where Islam originated, was located on an important and historical trade route that linked Yemen to the Eastern Mediterranean centres of trade and civilization. This route started at Aden in the south and followed a number of commercial centres such as Maraib, Najran, al-Taif to reach Macca and then to link to Yathrib (Madina), Khaibar and Daydan all the way to the Levant coast. By the time of Muhammad's appearance, this settled mode of existence based on long-distance trade had created a relatively sophisticated view of law, justice, crime and punishment based on the sanctity of private property and its social dynamics (inheritance laws, tort and property-related crimes).

Arab nomads although living in the desert, had nonetheless developed a symbiotic relationship with the coastal settlements. They visited these centres to sell or exchange their tribal wares and products as well as to pay homage to their idol gods. The most important among these was, of course, Macca, which housed the grand and lesser idols in the House of Kaba. Over a long period there had evolved a complex tribal system that linked various groups of people to one another as Ashirah, Taifah and Qabilah. These were different human groups in so far as numbers, blood and non-blood affiliations were concerned. The development of this complex arrangement had much to do with survival in a hostile desert environment. As observed by De Planhol, "The Muslim faith drew the essence of its initial drive from the very setting in which it arose."[18] Noting the symbiotic relationship between the two, De Planhol argues that Arab tribal life was socially and politically unstable, aggressive and strife-ridden. This structure of tribal life had given rise to contradictory social and moral characteristics in bedouin Arabs: on the one hand, they were courageous, free-spirited and bizarrely generous; on the other hand, they were also unruly, quarrelsome, vengeful and violent. Muhammad had to give some semblance of order and morality to these unruly elements within the context of the Sharia Law. To expound further on this point, I have to provide some preliminary information about the pre-Islamic notions of law, justice, crime and penology, the purpose of the next section.

Pre-Islamic Social Norms and their Relationship to the Sharia Law

Bedouin Arabs were renowned for their generosity towards strangers who sought their protection. Some have argued that the harsh conditions of the desert was the prime cause of this generosity.[19] With the passage of time, this aspect of the pastoral life led to the development of traditions that sought to protect one's life from adversaries. Based on this tradition, one's blood (*thaar*) became protected if one could find refuge (*jawaar, hilaf*) in a bedouin's tent, which, in turn, would link the seeker of refuge with the bedouin's immediate larger social units (*ashirah, taifah, and qabilah*).

The same principle of protection applied to those who sought refuge in religious sanctuaries, be it in Macca, in Nakhlah or in al-Taif and others. This tradition had its strength in the bedouin Arab concept of *asabiyah*, roughly corresponding to *esprit de corps*. According to Ibn Khaldun, what separates the bedouin people from the settled people is the fact that the former possess *asabiyah,* whereas the latter lacks it due to the civilizing impacts of settled life.[20] Those who sought refuge in any tribal affiliation became a ward of that tribe under its protection – and the *asabiyah* applied to them. The laws of blood and refuge did not bode well for the development of an adjudicatory system in which one's guilt or innocence could be determined based on a rational system of appeal to a central authority for justice. Muhammad, in Madina, put a decisive end to this arbitrary system. The Constitution of Madina, as I shall explore in this chapter, was the main legal-political document for this purpose.

The Arbitrary System of Punishment

As a general rule, the tribal system of punishment was to some extent arbitrary. Although punishment was imposed on those found guilty of law-infracting behaviour, the social standing of a person weighed heavily in the process and the fact that the arbiters' decision could be subjected to all kinds of extralegal consideration in favour of powerful persons. Persons of means and power could, if they could not buy the favour of the arbiter, employ various stratagems to mitigate their punishment(s), including the substitution process whereby slaves would be forced to bear the burden of actual punishment. That is why the Qur'an directed believers to punish (in the case of murder) a free man for a free man, a woman for a woman and a slave for a slave according the law of *al-Qisaas wa al-Diyaa* expressed in (ii, 179). The verse states that:

> O ye who believe, *equitable* retaliation in the matter of slain is prescribed for you; the free man for the free man, and the slave for the slave, and the female for the female. But if one is granted any remission by one's brother, then pursuing *the*

> *matter for the realization of the blood-money* shall be done with fairness and *the murderer* shall pay him the blood-money in a handsome manner. This is an alleviation from your Lord and a mercy. And whoso transgresses thereafter, for him there shall be a grievous punishment.[21]

Imam Bukhari narrates a Hadith on the authority of Ibn Abbas that the Law of Retaliation (*al-Qisaas*) was originally prescribed to the Israelites but not the Law of Blood Money (*al-Diyaa*) until the appearance of Islam. According to the Hadith,[22] this was a "Concession and a Mercy" from Allah. As we will explore in some detail, one important aspect of the Qur'anic system of legislation is the fact that the text attempts to improve other monotheistic religions' (e.g., Judaism and Christianity) view of the law and punishment, such as the position of disenfranchised, the subject of the next section.

The Position of Disenfranchised in the Pre-Islamic Hijaz Region

Prior to Islam, unless women, destitute youths, the mentally deranged and slaves were linked to the powerful persons, families or kinship groups, they could face arbitrary treatment, especially in cases in which they were involved in law-infracting behaviours or crimes. The pre-Islamic tribal Arab traditions sought, by and large, to redress various forms of wrongs and crimes through mediation *(hakamiyah*), and other forms of informal conflict resolution. At the same time, various forms of personal and collective punishments existed that were meted out by the tribal chieftain authorities.

There were, however, various sanctuaries into which a felon could take refuge from the aggrieved parties' wrath and punishment. The powerful could take into custody the relatives of the accused, or of the felon, as hostages to punish them instead of the fleeing felon. This power-related arbitrary form of punishment could initiate blood feuds (*thaar*) necessitating blood vengeance, a disruptive process that would usually cause further retribution. Naturally, the Qur'an, as the primary base of the new faith and its divine law, could not remain indifferent to these types of arbitrary punishment that could initiate blood feuds; neither could it remain indifferent to various abusive traditions with regard to the position of the weak and the oppressed. Therefore, the Qur'an called attention to what it characterized as the "vile" nature of pre-Islamic abusive traditions among bedouin Arabs, and especially to the manner in which such traditions dealt with the weakest segment of the society, whether orphans, slaves, women, the poor, or even the mentally deranged. One such vile tradition was female infanticide that occurred especially during times of drought. As we will explore in some detail, not only did the Qur'an admonish bedouin Arabs against these practices, but it enunciated a number of important rights and responsibilities for women and other social weaklings.

The Qur'an can also be looked on as a blueprint for a moral and just way of life in a sedentary setting. It has been customary in classical sources, as well as in the Qur'an, to characterize pre-Islamic life among bedouin Arabs as one based on "ignorance," of the period of *Jahiliyah.* The term *Jahiliyah* stems from the root word *jahl* which, maintains Muhammad Qarib, is unanimously agreed by etymologists to represent a state of ignorance, or lack of knowledge.[23] Its derivations appear in *al-Baqarah* (ii, 273), *al-Nisa* (iv, 17), *al-Maidah* (v, 50), *al-Araf* (vii, 138), and *al-Ahzab* (xxxiii, 72).[24] The central concern of these Qur'anic verses is that sin and crime are due to societal or individual ignorance, a view expressed in (vii, 138), in which the Prophet Moses admonishes the Israelites for their ignorance – an ignorance that the Qur'an maintains is due to their inability to comprehend God's majesty. In spite of the fact that it was God who had delivered the Israelites from bondage, the freed Israelites kept putting Moses in an embarrassing position by making all kinds of unreasonable demand on God. According to Muhammad Qarib, this Qur'anic notion of ignorance can be one of three types: (1) ignorance that is due to lack of knowledge; (2) ignorance that is due to one's mistaken belief about the nature of something; and (3) ignorance that is deliberate, such as not performing one's religious duties (e.g., prayer, fasting, paying alms).

Thus, the *Jahiliyah* was a state of mind in which bedouin Arabs existed prior to Islam, a state that is meant to be of the first type of ignorance – not having knowledge about that Allah despite the appearance of other prophets.[25] By contrast, Islam brought knowledge (*ilm*) and, therefore, enlightenment to the Hijaz region and replaced *Jahiliyah* traditions with Islam's moral ways. The most important among *Jahiliyah* social and legal institutions include: (1) the system of idolatry (*asnam*), (2) the legal system based on ancestral law (*sunna*) and tribal customs (*urf wa adaat*), (3) the commercial system based on usury (*ribaa)* and various land-, water- and slave-based exploitative practices coupled with various debt-financing and long-distance trade, and (4) a system of marriage and family that recognized various types of polygamous (both polygyny and polyandry) practices.

A synopsis of the first three institutions is provided below. I will explore the system of marriage and family and its dynamics in subsequent chapters of this study as I embark upon explaining women's legal status in the classical view of the Sharia Law.

The Institution of Idolatry (Asnaam)

Prior to Islam, a complex system of worship of idols known as the *Asnaam* prevailed among both tribes and settled population centres of the Hijaz region (roughly corresponding to today's modern Kingdom of Saudi Arabia). The term stems from the root word *sanam* connoting worship and love. In common parlance *sanam* means a female lover. This word appears in the Qur'an in *al-Araf* (vii, 138), in its plural format as *asnaam* and in relation to the term *akf* which means "to stay or settle in a place, to bow in reverence to something."[26] The verse concerns the Israelites' tendency to return to idol worship even after the God Almighty has rescued them from the wrath of the Pharaoh and has brought them to the Promised Land. The Qur'an bears witness to the Prophet Moses's abuse at the hands of the Israelites who wish to return to idolatry in spite of the miracles that God performs in their deliverance from bondage to freedom; instead of submitting to the will of true God, they revert to idol worship, thereby committing a grave sin. In the Qur'an, reference is made to those who reside in cities as *al-aakif* as for instance in *al-Hajj* (xxii, 25).[27] The verse, further argues Qarib, seems to suggest that those who reside in cities (e.g., Macca and Jerusalem) become ignorant of the true faith and even become an impediment to those who want to attend to the true faith. The verse also seems to indicate that those who reside in Macca and Jerusalem, although they have been exposed to the true faith twice (Judaism and Christianity), have abandoned the true faith and instead have reverted to the worship of idols (including its norms, mores and laws). In fact, the city of Macca has become the nerve centre of a complex system of *Asnaam*, housing the tribal idols in the sanctuary of *Kaaba*.

The tradition traces the building of *Kaaba* to Abraham, a central figure to Judaism, Christianity and Islam. Abraham is a righteous man vouchsafed with the everlasting message of Allah. The Qur'an (iii, 67), states that: "Abraham was not a Jew, nor yet a Christian; but he was an upright man who had surrendered [to Allah], and he was not of the idolaters."[28] With the passage of time, Abraham's monotheistic message becomes falsified and corrupted, so that the God of Abraham has to send a number of prophets, including Noah, Lot, `Ud, Thamud, Janus, Moses and Jesus to resurrect Allah's true message. But by the time of Muhammad, the region had long since reverted to idol worship as the main expression of religiousness.

Although Rabbinic Judaism and Eastern Christianity existed among Hijazi Arabs, the Qur'an maintains that both creeds had deviated from God's true message, and that it was thus now Muhammad's duty to resurrect Allah's message among the idolaters as well as among the People of Book in the region. That is why the Qur'an warns the "People of Scripture" that they should not deny Muhammad's mission and his authentic message in (iii, 69 through 72). This warning was directed against Jews and Christians. The Maccans, however, believed in the supremacy of their three grand idols, Lat, Manat and Uzza. These grand idols were looked upon as the protectors of Macca and of its complex system of long-distance trade linking Macca to other trade centres, from Yemen in the south, to Syria and Levant in the north, and to Byzantine Rome and Sasanid Persia. Macca was also the site of a yearly pilgrimage (*haj*) the origin of which is again traced by Muslim scholars of the Qur'an to Abraham.

In these yearly pilgrimages, thousands of idol worshippers would assemble in Macca to perform their religious duties as well as to conduct trade and commercial activities. Macca had long thrived on this system linking commerce to the worship of idols so, naturally, various power blocs in Macca were quite aware of the importance of this system and did their utmost to protect it. They did not approve of those who questioned the authenticity of idolatry, let alone those who characterized it as a vile and corrupt practice.

The Pre-Islamic View of Allah among Maccan Idolaters

Some scholars have argued that the concept of Allah as a deity existed among Maccans. D. B. Macdonald, for instance, writes: "That the Arabs, before the time of Muhammad, accepted and worshipped, after a fashion, a supreme god called Allah – '*ilah*' or 'the god', if the form is of genuine Arabic origin; if of Aramaic, from *alaha*, 'the god '– seems absolutely certain."[29] Citing the works of similar-minded scholars like Wellhausen, Noldke and Brockelmann in so far as non-Arabic sources are concerned,[30] Macdonald cites a number of Qur'anic chapters (e.g., xiii, 16; xxix, 61, 63; xxxi, 25; xxxix, 380 etc.,) to argue that the Qur'an itself attests to the fact that pre-Islamic Maccans did indeed worship Allah as a supreme god. In addition, Macdonald attributes to Muhammad a "doctrine of Allah" encapsulated in the famous Qur'anic formula "*La ilalaha illa illah* (There is no god save Allah)."[31] From the premise that both Muhammad and the Maccans had the same name for God (Allah), Macdonald argues that the Maccans nonetheless had differing notions as to what this Allah represented. The Maccans, accordingly, had no fear of

Allah, but Muhammad added the concept of fear to the notion of Allah.[32] In other words, Muhammad resurrects Allah through his authorship of the Qur'an, and not the other way around. From this perspective, Muhammad is not a Prophet in the manner of Moses or Jesus, but an ambitious political leader.

The Qur'anic view of Allah The Qur'anic view of Allah is quite original and positively anti-idolatrous. In both the Maccan and Madinan revelations the concept of Allah has been elevated to an unprecedented sublimity and majesty, expressed in such eschatological notions as, for instance, Allah's Realms of Knowledge (*Ilm*) which is unlimited. The same majesty applies to Allah's Might (*Qahr*) which is overbearing beyond our comprehension. Allah is endowed with an Everlasting Existence (*Hayat*) that has no beginning and no ending. At the same time, Allah has been characterized as the "Cherisher" (i, 2; vi, 64), as a "Guardian on a Watch-Tower" (lxxxix, 14), as "Guardian-Lord" (ii, 21-22), as "Helper" (i, 150; iv, 45), as "Creator of all" (ii, 29, 117; vi, 73), as one "to Him belongs the heritage of the heavens and earth" (iii, 180; xv, 23; xix, 40), and as the "Lord of Bounties" (iii, 174), as the "Most Bountiful" (xcvi, 3), as "Merciful" (iv, 26; v, 77; vi, 12, 54, 133) to name but a few epithets for Allah. Life, Death, the Day of Judgment, Paradise, Hell, and the Secrets of Creation and the Cosmos are under the purview of Allah. Naturally, this Allah personifies an omnipotency and includes what Muslim philosophers have characterized as a Totality of Contradictions (*Jam al-Azdad*). If this eschatological notion of Allah existed prior to Islam, why did the Maccans not find this god worthy of more attention? In fact, why would such a mighty god be secondary to the likes of Laat, Manaat and Uzza? And, finally, if the Maccans were in a position to accept Muhammad's view of Allah, why did they reject so vociferously the Qur'an and its teachings? Even if these questions can be explained in terms of politics of power, the question remains: how does Islam remain one of the fastest growing monotheistic religions in the modern world?

In Islam Allah has always been looked up to as the Source (*Marja*) of the *Nomos*, a concept that corresponds to the integrity (*Namus*) of Nature (*Tabiat*) and Creation (*Khilqat*). That is why, in both classical and modern Muslim legal thinking, nothing is haphazard, nothing comes into being arbitrarily, and nothing happens without Allah's permission (*izn*). Naturally, this view of Allah's omnipotency has led to the rise of a predeterministic fatalism in seeing Allah as the source of all good if not of evil, regardless of the will of the social actor. At the same time, however, this perception that there is a God Ordained Order (*Nizami Ilahi*) in the cosmos that ought to be discovered has led to the progression of positive sciences such as medicine, astronomy, physics, surgery, chemistry, geography and even advances in the medieval Islamic agriculturalist mode of existence in the past centuries as Islam became a world civilization during the Umayyad (r.661-749) and `Abbasid empires (749-1258). Naturally, the law has been one of the most important branches among these medieval Islamic disciplines.

Some of these characteristics of Allah were revealed in Macca and some others in Madina, as previously mentioned. Early sources indicate that some Maccans were so impressed by this new concept of Allah that they decided to convert. Khadijah bint Khuwaylad, `Ali ibn Abi Talib, Abu Bakr, `Umar ibn Khattab, `Uthman ibn `Affan, Bilal Habashi, and Abu Zar Ghaffari, were among the first converts. At the same time, there were those Maccans who were so horrified by Muhammad's teachings and claims that they decided to confront Muhammad and his followers, questioning Muhammad's source of revelations.

As previously mentioned, Muhammad was not operating in a social medium devoid of the idea of Deity, but the *Jahiliyah* concept of Deity had been entrenched in the institution of idolatry. Classical sources reveal that the strength of Muhammad's claim to prophecy was never shaken by such hostile confrontations of the idolaters in Macca because Muhammad believed unequivocally that he communicated with the Heavens; the many revelations of the Qur'an present Muhammad as the Prophet of Allah. These revelations seem to inform Muhammad how to respond to such provocative questions concerning idolatry, Allah's might, knowledge, and whereabouts (civ, 1 through 9; cv, 1 through 7; cix, 1through 6). This Qur'anic concept of Allah was not only quite different from that of the Maccan idolaters, it also represented a level of both social and eschatological authority.

Imam Bukhari maintains that Muhammad was instructed by the Heavens to invite his Maccan relatives to denounce idolatry and to submit to Islam. For the first three years (610-613), Muhammad carried out his mission clandestinely and was able to convert some to Islam. Later, Muhammad was instructed by the Qur'an to openly preach Islam's teachings. The majority of the Maccans, however, neither heeded Muhammad's invitation to denounce idolatry and submit to this "new" Allah's will, nor seemed to fear Muhammad's new religion and its universal message.

Ibn Saad's narrations give the distinct impression that this attitude changed drastically once Muhammad started to openly chastise the Maccans' grand idols. Ibn Saad narrates a Hadith whereby Muhammad warned prominent Quraysh families that unless they heeded Allah's message and declared their allegiance to Allah, he could not guarantee their wellbeing in this world and in the next. Upon hearing this unprecedented warning, Abd al-Uzza, known by his nickname of Abu Lahab, an uncle to Muhammad and yet one of the fiercest opponents of Islam, cursed Muhammad for having wasted their time, whence the chapter *Al-Lahab* (xci) was revealed. This chapter is the only one in the Qur'an that denounces the Prophet's opponent by name and sets the tone for Muhammad's irreconcilable and deepening challenge to Macca's most cherished institution, idolatry.[33]

To the question as to what had happened to the souls of those Maccan ancestors, including Muhammad's, who had died as idolaters, Muhammad's answer was straightforward: they all had perished in vain and were in Hell.[34] In the eyes of the Maccan idolaters, this proclamation was an unforgivable affront to both ancestral worship and to the traditions that required respect for the deceased. As a result of this answer, the Maccan idolaters, headed by Abu Lahab and Abu Jahl, started to openly harass Muhammad and his growing band of Muslim converts. They accused Muhammad and his followers of heinous crimes and in particular, accused the Prophet of violating the prevailing law *(sunna)* upon which the Quraysh, to which Muhammad belonged, had built its most venerable social and legal foundations.

The Maccan idolaters also plotted to kill Muhammad, although to no avail, because the Qur'an maintains that Muhammad was under the protection of Allah. Historically, Muhammad was protected by his uncle, Abu Talib, a well-respected man among the Maccans who mustered tribal respect and affiliation to protect Muhammad and his followers against harm. Ironically, he never converted to Islam and died as an idolater. Nevertheless, the hostility of the Maccan idolaters forced a group of Muslim converts to emigrate to Abyssinia. In 622, Muhammad emigrated to Madina. This date is cherished in the history of Islam because it represents the beginning of the Islamic calendar. Muhammad's emigration (*hijra*) from Macca to Madina inaugurates a new phase in the development of the Sharia Law.

Ibn Saad narrates a story that is known as the Qaraniq Affair – a story that recounts the first migration of Muslims to Abyssinia. Distressed that his declarations had resulted in the schism in Macca and the migration of some of his followers to foreign lands (Africa), and wishing to mend the schism, the chapter *Al-Najm* was revealed to the Prophet. Ibn Saad, like other narrators of Muhammad's life events, maintains that this revelation, which aimed to chastise the three grand idols (Laat, Manaat and Uzza), turned into a praise of these because "Satan" intervened and put the praise words (*telka al-Qaraniq al-ula wa inn shafaathan laturtaja*) in the Prophet's thought. This conciliatory revelation led Maccans to believe that Muhammad had changed his position and now considered the grand idols as worthy of praise and worship. With the spread of the news of the Qaraniq, those Muslims who had emigrated to Abyssinia, decided to return to Macca, thinking that Muhammad had come to some kind of truce with the idolaters. Ibn Saad, however, narrates a Hadith purporting that the Archangel Gabriel appeared to Muhammad and read the revelation to him again, this time without the praise words. Seeing Muhammad's distress, Allah revealed the verses 73 through 75 of the chapter (xvii) of the Qur'an. These verses warn Muhammad that there were some unbelievers who were attempting to beguile him and make him stray from the truth, which Allah had inspired. The verses gave a stern warning to the effect that had Allah not made his messenger firm in his belief and stance towards the idolaters, his reward would have been a double punishment in life and in the afterlife.

In some Western scholarly circles, the Qaraniq affair has been taken as a proof that Muhammad was an astute politician who knew how to wheel and deal with his opponents. Other scholars hold the view that perhaps Allah wanted to test Muhammad's resolve in the face of the Maccan idolaters' ever-increasing hostility. Most modern Muslim commentators on the Qur'an have argued that the Qaraniq does not have a base in the Qur'an or in the aforementioned *Sirah* literature. In any case, the returning Muslims found themselves in a difficult situation and appealed to the Prophet who allowed them a second migration to Abyssinia. This time, they carried with them a letter that called on Nejashi, the Emperor of Abyssinia, to convert to Islam. Ibn Sa`ad reports that Nejashi accepted this invitation and converted.[35] Thus, Islam found a peaceful foothold in Africa. From that time on, Muhammad realized that he could no longer safely preach Islam in Macca and had to find refuge elsewhere in the region. Yathrib, later known as Madina, was the only place where Muhammad could seek refuge from the wrath of the Maccan idolaters who now were determined to kill Muhammad and destroy the new faith.

Classical sources also give the distinct impression that although there came a time that the Maccan idolaters, including Abu Lahab, wanted to reach a modus vivendi with Muhammad, if he only would accept the authenticity of their idols, Muhammad never compromised on this central issue. The Qraniq affair has been looked upon as Muhammad's capitulation. The Muslim lay people's and intellectuals' position has been that even if there was such a temptation, Muhammad was protected by the Heavens and was directed to stand firm against the idolaters and their false deities. Later, when Muhammad conquered Macca in an almost bloodless campaign (June 8-11, 630), he ordered the total destruction of the idols in the House of Kaaba. Thus, the Maccan system of idolatry received its fatal blow at the hands of Muhammad – a blow that was also directed to its system of laws.

Pre-Islamic Crime and Crime Control Mechanisms

The bedouin Arab's system of law, crime, justice and punishment was complex, based upon a centuries-old system of private law whereby crimes committed by individuals against others were redressed through family and/or ancestral (*sunna*) laws. These covered capital crimes such as murder, theft, false witness and other lesser crimes that included bodily injuries, trespassing, and various types of property and agricultural crimes.

Pre-Islamic crime control mechanism Among both the bedouin and settled Arab population in the Hijaz region, crime was controlled through both informal and formal means. Procedurally, the testimony of those who had witnessed a crime, coupled with the taking of an oath, carried much weight in the formation of judgment of the arbitrating judge, or of the tribal chiefs, and/or of tribal counsels. During the pilgrimage season, for instance, no war and/or crime should occur due to the sanctuary nature of the Kaaba. As such, one of the most serious crimes was to show disrespect for the idols and especially to deny their divinity. Various types of punishment were meted out to those who violated the sanctity of this period. These included beheading, quartering, crucifying, stoning to death, exile, lashing and live burial in the desert sand. Another feature of the *Jahiliyah* penology had to do with the differential treatments that penalized the indigent disproportionally at the same time that it allowed bribery so that the powerful could escape punishment. Unsettled disputes, especially murders, could lead to blood feuds that might linger for generations.

In general, social and quasi-legal protections were extended to individuals through both horizontal and vertical social institutions. One received one's primary protection in the family. Every family was linked to its kin groups, which in turn linked the family to the clans and tribes and to their protective measures. This was a horizontal system of protection because it extended a certain degree of protection to all individuals regardless of their social standing. On the vertical level, one was also given protection through various group and community affiliations. Naturally, some communities were more powerful than others in the same manner that some individuals were more prominent than others – a situation that led to power differentials that found expression in the miscarriage of justice. Some cities (e.g., *Macca, Ta'if, Yathrib*), tribes (e.g., *Quraysh, Us, Khazraj*) and clans (*Bani Umayyah, Bani Hashim*) were richer, more populous and more diversified than others. Pride in one's genealogy, was followed by pride in one's family, in one's clan and/or tribal affiliations as well as by one's pride in the worship of the grand and lesser idols. Each clan and tribe had a certain place of access to the *Kaaba,* as the prime sanctuary in which asylum could be sought by those who wanted to escape the wrath of the powerful. Besides the ancestral laws among bedouin Arabs, the People of Scripture in the region adhered to their own canonic laws.

The Challenges Facing the Nascent Sharia Law

The biggest challenge facing the nascent Sharia Law was the question of how to replace this complex ancestral-canonic based system of law, crime and punishment gradually, without compromising the Qur'anic view that Muhammad was charged to bring back God's "true" divine laws and punishments. Imam Bukhari narrates a Hadith about the Prophet's judgment on the question of the propriety of the punishment for adultery, giving a clue to the complex nature of this challenge. Based on this narration, a group of Jewish residents of Madina appealed to the Prophet to adjudicate an adultery case between a Jewish man and a Jewish woman. The Prophet inquired about the customary manner in which adultery was punished among the Jews. The appealing Jews replied that it was customary to blacken the face of the accused with coal and subject him/her to a beating. Hearing this, the Prophet enquired about the punishment of *Ar-Rajam* (stoning) that the Torah had advised. The answer was that such a punishment did not exist in the Torah. Hearing this, Abd Allah bin Salam in the company of the Prophet accused the Jews of telling a lie. By forcing them to bring Torah to the session, and by showing the relevant verse in the Torah, Abdallah bin Slam showed that such punishment had indeed had been advised by the Scripture. Accordingly, the Prophet ordered the *Ar-Rajam* to be carried out on the two.[36] What makes this Hadith important is that it gives an idea about the Prophet's style of adjudication. After listening to the case, Muhammad, as the judge, first enquired about the prevailing custom among the Jews. Next, he also enquired the actual source of the law of Judaism, the Torah, with regard to punishment. I should add that, although the Hadith indicates that the Prophet ordered the punishment of *Ar-Rajam*, this order was due to the principle of adherence to the law of the Scripture that prevailed among the Jewish residents of Madina. This adherence does not mean that this Torah-based punishment for adultery has a basis in the Qur'an. As I shall explore in subsequent chapters of this study, the Qur'anic punishment for adultery is flogging (*jild*) of both male (*zaani*) and female (*zaaniyah*) involved in adultery and not stoning to death. Next to the Qur'an, the Prophetic Tradition prohibited other forms of cruel punishments such as mutilation (*muthlih*) and quartering (*shiqah*) that prevailed among bedouin Arabs.

Usury, Commerce and Trade-related Laws

The city of Macca occupied an important place in a caravan-based long-distance trade route. Maccan traders and shopkeepers were renowned for their commercial skills and negotiation tactics that included bargaining over prices as well as various deceptive tactics (taking false oath on the quality of merchandise, power-based bargaining and false negotiation, and imposing inordinate interest rates on the principle of the loan – a practice that is severely admonished by the Qur'an and which is known as *ribaa*). In Macca, Muhammad managed his wife-employer's commercial caravan in long-distance trade and was aware of these practices. Although Muhammad was advised by the Qur'an to challenge Maccan social traditions, it was only in Madina that he could indeed challenge these commercial relationships and traditions in order to weed out usury and other exploitative practices. That is why it is in the Madinan chapter, *al-Baqarah* (ii, 275) that Muhammad is advised to declare that the new faith is for trade but against exploitative practices. The verse reads: "But Allah has permitted trade and forbidden usury." Imam Bukhari cites the following Hadith on the authority of Aishah: "When the Verses of Surat al-Baqarah regarding usury (i.e., Ribaa) were revealed, Allah's Apostle recited them before people then he prohibited the trade, of alcoholic liquors."[37] According to Ibn Abbas, one of the most respected classical Hadith narrators, this was the last Qur'anic revelation in Madina before the Prophet passed away in June 632.

The fact that these and similar regulatory verses were revealed in Madina, rather than in Macca, had a lot to do with Muhammad's standing in Madina. In Macca, Muhammad could not forbid usury; neither could he forbid the trade of alcohol, both of which occupied an important place among Maccan traders. From an Islamic point of view, Muhammad, of course, neither consumed alcohol, nor was he known for any of the exploitative practices upon which the Maccan commercial establishment thrived.

The tradition also maintains that Muhammad was distressed over the fate of those who incurred debt but could not pay their indebtedness on time because of the inordinate amount of interest on the principal of the loan or other unforeseen events; in the *Jahiliyah* period, such people could face various forms of punishment that included enslavement to creditors. That is why the Qur'an advises Muslims to be fair in dealing with each other and to help those in financial distress. In the section about trade, the so-called *Kitab al-Buyu* of *Shahih al-Bukhari*, for example, we come across a number of Hadiths on the importance of fair dealing in trade and commerce.

One Hadith advises Muslims to be "...easy and generous in bargaining and whoever demands his debts back should do so in a modest manner."[38] Another Hadith implores the believers to be patient and to give enough time to each other in repaying their debts. Another one implores the buyer and seller to be honest in their descriptions of their wares. In the same section, Imam Bukhari quotes Hakim ibn Hizam who quotes the Prophet as saying:

> The seller and buyer have the right to keep or return the goods so long as they have not parted or till they part; and if both the parties spoke the truth and described the defects and qualities (of the goods), then they would be blessed in their transactions, and if they told lies or hide something, then the blessing of their transaction would be lost.[39]

Other Hadiths regulate various conditions under which either party could rescind (*faskh*) a commercial deal such as, for instance, if one party lied about the facts of the deal. Imam Bukhari opines that the Qur'an has not only prohibited what it has characterized as "eating usury" *(akl al-riba)*, it also warns those who witness the incurring of usury and recording of it as, for instance, (ii, 275) which reads: "Those who devour Riba (usury) Will not stand (on the Day of Resurrection) except like one who stands Similar to a person suffering from insanity."[40] Another verse (iii,130) admonishes the amount of usury, stating "O you who believe! Eat not usury (Riba) Doubled and multiplied. (But fear Allah: that you may be successful."[41] The Qur'an also enjoins believers of paying usury as, for instance, in (ii, 278-281) according to Imam Bukhari. The verses read: "O you who believe! Be afraid of Allah and give up What remains (due to you) from usury (Riba) (from now onwards) if you are indeed believers....”[42] Other dubious commercial practices, such as giving false oaths when selling goods and loan sharking, are also prohibited.

Incurring debt and payment of debt Known as (*al-Istiqraz*), anyone who incurs debt, argues the Qur’an, should do their utmost to repay. Repayment, however, has been regularized in the juristic texts under the so-called *Aada' al-Diyun.* Those who cannot truly repay may declare themselves as financial insolvents (*al-muflis*; the actual act is called *al-taflis*). According to Imam Bukhari’s narration of (iv, 58):

> Allah does command you
> To render back the trusts of the people,
> And when you judge
> Between persons,
> That you judge with justice,
> Verily, how excellent
> Is the teaching which He gives you, and indeed
> Allah is ever All-Hearer, All-Seer.[43]

The first verse implies that, because commerce is built upon mutual trust between the two parties who enter into a commercial venture based upon credit, it is incumbent upon them to adhere to their end of the bargain in good faith. In fact, a Hadith narrated by Abu Huraira reports the Prophet of having said that “Whoever takes the money of the people with the intention of repaying it, Allah will repay it on his behalf, and whoever takes it in order to spoil it, then Allah will spoil him.”[44] At the same time, the subsequent verses implore fair and impartial judgment where parties agree to the terms of indebtedness.

The Qur’anic term “trusts” used in the first verse is *al-amaanaat* which means anything that one party may give to another for safe keeping such as money, property, a will, or even the guardianship of juveniles, orphans and mentally insufficient persons. One who accepts the burden of trust is not only responsible to the party to whom the pledge of trust is made, but is also responsible to Allah Who is “All-Hearer (*Samian*) and “All-Seer” (*Basiran*). These warnings were later incorporated into both the letter and the spirit of Shari`a Law as Muslim jurists developed a very sophisticated and yet humanitarian view of the importance of trust in commercial relations as well as in the practices that concerned trust and guardianship of property and of real persons by a third party. Any infringement upon such trust would engender grave consequences from the standpoints of both the letter and the spirit of the Sharia.

Financial insolvency (al-taflis) Insofar as financial insolvency is concerned, in the *Jahiliyah* period insolvency could lead to one's enslavement. The Qur'an has prohibited various exploitative practices that may cause financial distress and insolvency. Among these, mention should be made of practices that lead to the pseudo-monopolization of the market by one group, of speculative business practices, of usury, or of gambling. At the same time, two distinct *Jahiliyah* types of transactions known as *Munabadha* and *Mulamasa* were prohibited by the Prophet himself. In the *Sahih Muslim,* Imam Muslim reports (based on the authority of Abu Huraira) that: "Allah's Messenger ...forbade...Mualamsa and Munabadha."[45] Both were of a speculative nature whereby the seller did not allow the buyer to actually examine the quality of the goods wrapped in a wrapping cloth. In *Munabadha*, the seller would throw the cloth to the buyer without allowing him/her to examine the contents of the bundle whereas, in *Mulamasa*, the buyer would allow the buyer to only touch the cloth as a way of examining the goods. With the passage of time, Muslim jurists prohibited other such transaction forms that they analogized as being of an speculative nature. These were systemized under the general category of the so-called Purchases (*al-Buyu*) that included the following in the classical juristic texts:

Bai al-Gharar	Purchase based on verbal or written contract
Bai al-Uryan	Purchase based on sight
Bai alal-Bai	Purchase on purchase (of something that has already been purchased)
Bai al-Mudlar	Purchase under stress (the seller is under financial stress)
Bai al-Hasal	Purchase based on speculation (by throwing a pebble at a bundle of merchandise).

These styles outline practices of buying and selling of agricultural products in which parties unjustly enrich themselves at the expense of other(s). That is why these practices were prohibited by both the Qur'anic revelations and the Prophetic Tradition.[46] In the case of financial insolvency, however, the believers were asked to show mercy to their brother/sister in distress and to be patient in recovering their debts; as a matter of Sharia Law, however, the creditors were prioritized in terms of receiving their debts. In time, a very sophisticated legal body of literature emerged in the Sharia Law spanning various aspects of commercial law, contracts and partnership.

In sum, Muhammad's tenure witnessed the rise of the Sharia Law's genesis. The Law covered a set of principles from which a specifically Islamic legal doctrine was constructed, based on the Qur'anic emphasis that humanity was too dear a creation of Allah to be left to its own devices; Allah, as the Creator, had blessed humanity with divine laws and had charged "His" Prophets, including Muhammad, with the mission of inaugurating such laws among their people. The divine laws that Allah had vouchsafed on "His" Prophets were in essence very similar, built upon one another to lead humanity to a honourable and bountiful life based on justice and social equity which, at the same time, guaranteed humanity's salvation. The next chapter further expounds on the development of the Sharia Law's genesis as well as its legal doctrines.

Notes

1. For further discussion see Muhammad Khazaeli, *Ilam-e Qur'an*,(Tehran, Iran, Intesharat-e Amir Kabir, 1371/1993), pp. 3-16.

2. For a classification of the Maccan and Madinan division of the Qur'an see *The Fihrist of al-Nadim*, vol.1, (New York, Columbia University Press, 1970), Bayard Dodge (translator and editor), pp. 48-85; see also *Fihrist Tafsir Kashf al-Asrar wa Udda I'labarar*, (Tehran, Iran, Amir Kabir, 1363/1985), Mohammad Jawad Shariat (ed.).

3. Imam Mumahmmad al-Bukahri, *Sahih al-Bukhari*, (Beirut, Lebanon, Dar al-Arabiyah, 1985), vol.1, Hadiths nos. 2 and 3, pp. 2-4, translated from Arabic to English by Muhammad Muhsin Khan.

4. *The Glorious Qur'an*, text and translation by Mohammad M. Pickthall, New York, (Mostazafan Foundation of New York, 1984), p. 737.

5. Ignaz Goldziher, *Introduction to Islamic Theology and Law*, (Princeton, NJ, Princeton University Press, 1981), p. 5, translated by Andras and Ruth Hamori.

6. *Ibid.*, p. 5. Goldziher cites this from Harnack's *Die Mission und Ausbreitung des Christentum in den ersten drei Jharhunderten* (Leipzig, 1902), p. 93 (4th edn), [(Leipzig, 1924) translated as the *Mission and Expansion of Christianity in the First Three Centuries* (London and New York, 1908), I, 126].

7. *Ibid.*, p. 7.

8. *Ibid.*, p. 8.

9. Pickthall, *The Glorious Qur'an*, p. 528.

10. Goldziher, *Introduction to Islamic Theology and Law*, p. 11.

11. Ibn Khaldun, *The Muqaddimah: An Introduction to History*, (Princeton, NJ, Princeton University Press), vol. 3., p. 3, translated from Arabic by Franz Rosenthal.

12. See Franz Rosenthal, *A History of Muslim Historiography*, (Leiden, E.J. Brill, 1968), second revised edn, p. 41.

13. Pickthall, *The Glorious Qur'an*, p. 33.

14. *Ibid.*, p. 74.

15. *Ibid.*, p. 75.

16. Muhammad Ibn Saad, *Tabaqat*, vol. 1, pp. 21-24, (Tehran, Iran, Nashr-e Now, 1365/1986), translated from Arabic to Persian by Mahmud Mahdavi Damghani.

17. For an historical account of this Hadith, see *The History of al-Tabari (Tarikh al-rusul wa'l-muluk): The Foundation of the Community*, (Albany, NY, SUNY Press, 1987), vol.vii, pp. 6-7, translated and annotated by W. Montgomery Watt and M.V. McDonald.

18. X. De Planhol, "The Geographical Setting" pp. 443-468, in *The Cambridge History of Islam, Volume 2, The Further Islamic Lands, Islamic Society and Civilization*, (Cambridge, Cambridge University Press, 1970), P.M. Holt *et al.* (eds), p. 469.

19. Muhammad H. Saket, *Nahad-e Dadrasi dar Islam* (Judicial Institutions in Islam), (Mashad, Iran, Intesharat-e Astan-e Qods-e Razawi, 1365/1986), pp. 28-30.

20. Ibn Khaldun, *The Muqaddmiah: An Introduction to History*, vol. 1, pp. 261-262.

21. Mirza Tahir Ahmad, *The Holy Qur'an*, vol. 2, (Islamabad, Pakistan, Islam International Publications Ltd., 1988) p. 229. The italics in the verse are original.

22. Imam Bukhari, *Shahih al-Bukhari*, vol. 6, Hadith no. 25, pp. 22-23.

23. Muhammad Qarib, *Tabyin al-Lughat lil-Bayan al-Ayaat: Yaa, Farhang-e Luqat-e Qur'an (Tehran, Iran, Intesharat-e Bunyaad, 1366/1987)*, vol. 1, pp. 292-294.

24. *Ibid.*

25. *Ibid.*, pp. 292-293.

26. *Ibid.*, vol. 2, p. 126.

27. *Ibid.*, p. 127.

28. Pickthall, *The Glorious Qur'an*, verse 67, p. 56.

29. D.B. Macdonald, the entry "Allah", pp. 33-42, in *The Shorter Encyclopaedia of Islam*, H.A.R. Gibb and J.H. Kramers (eds), (Ithaca, NY, Cornell University Press, 1961), p. 33.

30. Macdonald cites Wellhausen's *Reste Arabischen Heidentums*, 2nd edn, p. 117 *et seq.*; Noldke's article on Arabs (ancient) in Hesting's *Dictionary of Religion and Ethics*, i. 662 and Brockelmann in *Archiv für Religions-wissenschaft*, xx. 99-121. *Ibid.*, p. 33.

31. Macdonald, in *The Shorter Encyclopaedia of Islam*, p. 33.

32. *Ibid.*, p. 34.

33. Ibn Saad, *Tabaqat*, vol 1., pp. 196-197.

34. *Ibid.*, p. 197

35. *Ibid.*, pp. 203-205.

36. Imam Bukhari, *Shaih al-Bukhari*, vol. 6, Hadith no. 79, pp. 63-64.

37. *Ibid.*, vol. 6, Hadith no. 64, p. 49.

38. *Ibid.*, vol. 3, pp. 163-164.

39. *Ibid.*, Hadith no. 293, p. 166.

40. *Ibid.*, p. 168.

41. *Ibid.*, pp. 167-168.

42. *Ibid.*, p. 168.

43. *Ibid.*, p. 336.

44. *Ibid.*, Hadith no. 572, p. 336.

45. Imam Muslim, *Sahih Muslim*, (Beirut, Lebanon, Dar Al-Arabia, 1971), vol. 3, Hadith no. 3608, p. 797, translated from Arabic to English by Abdul Hamid S. Prisons Siddiqi.

46. *Ibid.*, p. 796. Siddiqi's explanatory notes to the book.

3 The Legal Theory of the Sharia Law

In this chapter, I briefly analyse the Sharia Law's general notion of legal theory followed by some observations on the nature of the Sharia Law during the Prophet Muhammad's tenure in Madina.

The Notion of Divine Authority in Islam and its Relation to the Sharia Law

Traditionally, it has been argued that Islam's Sacred Law represents a tripartite system of law, morality and justice, the core of which has emanated from a divine authority, Allah. The legal theory behind this tripartite system conceives the law as more than an abstract instrument of power, but also as a coherent and logical device that reflects Allah's eternal Wisdom and Will. This legal theory also becomes Allah's *raison d'être* of creation (*khilqat*), namely that Allah has created men and women for a lofty purpose: to live as Allah's deputies on earth (*khalifatallah fi al-ard*), to prosper, to multiply, to do good and refrain from evil, and to leave Allah's bounty for the next generation. The realization of this lofty purpose necessitates that we apply Allah's Commandments and Boundaries to every aspect of our social affairs. For this application to be legitimate, it has to be based on both the morality and justice of Allah's Will. In other words, the Qur'anic notion of God's Law is inseparable from morality and justice, and therefore the Sharia Law reflects a notion of God's Law which is only meaningful when it is at the service of morality and justice. As such, in so far as the concept of a "legal theory" of the law is concerned, such a concept has never been of a strictly anthropocentric nature to allow for a free revision of its contents although human rationality has historically played an important role in it; neither has it been of a strictly theocentric nature immune to time- and culture-based revisions.

This dualistic nature of a specifically Islamic legal theory is not only traceable to the very text of the Qur'an, but to a wide range of deeds and sayings that classical Muslim jurists have utilized in their structuring of the theory. For example, both the Sunni and the Shii jurisprudential (*fiqhi*) schools have stated that Allah is the one and only Universal Deity in existence.

He has revealed to the Prophet Muhammad His Commandments first and then has warned Muhammad, time and again, that those Commandments ought to be observed in the affairs of daily life. Moreover, they must be applied consistently to everyone without regard for race, creed, gender or station. The Qur'an admonishes Muhammad that those groups, tribes and nations who have not lived by Allah's Law, or have corrupted God's Commandments in the past, face calamities. It also warns humankind about the doomsday where the fate of those who have committed sins and crimes will be adjudicated next to those who sit in judgment of others' sins and crimes in this world (namely the judges); the punishment (*uqub*) of the latter group is indeed grave if they judge not in accordance with Allah's Balance (*al-Mizan*) and knowingly falsify Allah's Commandments and Punishments.

These and similar warnings of the Qur'an can be observed in various chapters as, for instance, in (iv, 58) which reads: "Lo! Allah commandeth you that ye restore deposits to their owners, and if ye judge between mankind that ye judge justly....";[1] or in (iv, 135): "O ye who believe! Be ye staunch in justice, witness for Allah even though it be against yourselves or [your] parents or [your] kindred, whether [the case be of] a rich man or a poor man....";[2] or in (lvi, 25) which states that: "We verily sent Our messengers with clear proofs, and revealed unto them the Scripture and the balance, that mankind may observe right measure...."[3] I shall deal with the impact of this view of the Qur'an on the Sharia Law's penological philosophy in subsequent chapters and as the occasion arises.

Western Scholarship's View of the Nature of the Sharia Law

Western legal scholars (and to some extent historians of Islam), argue, by and large, that Islam's Sacred Law represents a dual nature. As observed by Noel J. Coulson:

> The fundamental question of the nature of law is answered for Muslim jurisprudence, in terms that admit of no compromise, by the religious faith itself. Law is the divinely ordained system of God's commands. To deny this principle would be, in effect, to renounce the religious faith of Islam.[4]

Coulson further argues that: "Islamic law has been alternatively described as a divine law and as a jurist's law."[5] He concludes that these two contradictory descriptions of the law constitute an inherent tension that is bound to arise once we conceptualize the law as both revelation and a product of human reasoning.

Ignaz Goldziher and Joseph Schacht, two other influential scholars whose views of the Sharia Law have influenced a good number of scholars, argue that early Muslim jurists adopted, although quite unconsciously, various concepts, maxims and legal principles from various sources. Schacht, following Goldziher, defines these sources as from "...Roman and Byzantine law, from the Canon law of the Eastern Churches, from Talmudic law, from Sassanian law...."[6] It was in the second Islamic century that these incubating concepts and legal borrowings gave rise to what Schacht considers to represent a doctrine of law. In the same line of reasoning, J.N.D. Anderson argues that the distinctive characteristics of the Islamic law is in its religious nature,[7] a view that finds expression among some Muslim scholars as, for instance, in Fazlur Rahaman who observes that: "The Qur'an is primarily a book of religious and moral principles and exhortations, and is not a legal document. But it does embody some important legal enunciations issued during the community-state building process at Medina."[8] This view is also expressed in Parviz Saney's [9] and in Mustapha Azmai's[10] legal writings on this subject.

A Critique of the Western Scholarship on the Nature of the Sharia Law

There is no doubt that the Sharia Law went through a gradual process of canonization in order to respond to the social, economic and legal problems of an expanding Islam. This process was only natural considering that the Qur'an gives the distinct impression that Islam was destined, from its early inception, to become a world religion. Not only does it declare Islam as the last hope for humanity, insofar as salvation is concerned, it also proclaims that Islam is the most complete and perfect culmination of God's everlasting message that was revealed upon pre-Muhammad Prophets of God, such as Abraham, Noah, Lot, Ud, Thamud, Janus, Moses and Jesus. Naturally, it is not my argument that we are bound to accept this claim of the Qur'an within a social science perspective; however, it is my premise here that the thrust of the Qur'an in its "presentation of the self" (to use Ervin Gofmann's famous phrase) is that it is a Perfect Totality (*al-Kaamil*) – that is, nothing less than a Divine Miracle (*al-Ijaaz*), the inspired Sign(s) (*al-Ayah*) of God, and an Eternally Valid (*Sahih*) Revelation (*Wahy*) that reflects God's Will. The Qur'an dares both men and *jinnis* to produce a verse that may even remotely resemble the beauty and coherence of the Qur'anic verses even if it is impossible. One such verse (ii, 23, 24), reads: "And if you are in doubt concerning that which We reveal unto Our slave (Muhammad), then produce a Surah of the like thereof, and call your witnesses beside Allah if you are truthful." The next verse, however, finds it an impossible task, reading: "and if ye do it not – and ye can never do it – then guard yourselves against the fire prepared for disbelievers, whose fuel is of men and stones."[11]

From the inception of Islam, a central belief among Muslim believers and intellectuals has been that the Qur'an has remained inimitable at the same time that it has contained the Truth (*al-Haqiqah*) which has unfolded through Islam's fourteen centuries of evolution. Again, the point here is not that one can prove all these claims of the Qur'an, but that the thrust of the Qur'an gives to the text a profoundly majestic tone and purpose. That is why when Anderson writes that "...the Koran alone could never have provided an adequate source for any legal system. So in the traditional view it was augmented from the very first by the sunna or custom of the Prophet"[12] he observes that this is an idealized version concocted by the Sunni jurists. The true story of the Sharia Law is that which has been depicted by Joseph Schacht and his ilk. No matter how one approaches the issue of the Sharia Law's development, this characterization of the Qur'an as "inadequate" does not sit well with both traditional and modern Muslim legal thinkers, for arguing that the Qur'an is inadequate implies that God is inadequate, unless one accepts the argument that the text is anthropocentric and not teleological. Once reduced to this level, then all other claims of the Qur'an become meaningless, a premise that reduces Islam to the status of what nineteenth-century Western Orientalist scholars claimed it to be: a set of borrowings from other religions, especially from Christianity and Judaism.

Again, I would caution readers that, in Islam, it is the Qur'an which gives Muhammad and his prophecy an everlasting prophetic aura and legitimacy and not the other way around. In other words, it is not Muhammad who has ever been looked upon as the "creator" of the Qur'an in Muslim legal and social thinking, but the Qur'an and its unequivocal premise that it is Allah Whose Will is Supreme and Allah Who chooses any mortal being (Muhammad in this case) to receive Allah's Law. From this perspective, which takes the thrust of the text as one that has historically shaped the Muslim belief system to the present, the Qur'an becomes the principal source of Sharia Law. Naturally, this source has never been conceived of being "inadequate," as Anderson sees the Qur'an. In fact, as observed by many Muslim scholars, the Qur'an is not a legal text *per se*, but one that contains principles from which laws can be extrapolated. As Fazlur Rahman observes:

> The Qur'an is primarily a book of religious and moral principles and exhortations, and is not a legal document. But it does embody some important legal enunciation issued during the community-state building process at Medina.... The ban on consumption of alcohol affords an interesting example of the Qur'anic method of legislation and throws light on the attitude of the Qur'an to the nature and function of legislation itself. The use of alcohol was apparently unreservedly permitted in the early years. Then offering prayers while under the influence of alcohol was prohibited.[13]

It was only after this prohibition, as Fazlur Rahman suggests, that the specific Qur'anic injunctions about alcohol and gambling were revealed upon the Prophet in (ii, 219), followed by what Fazlur Rahman considers "a total ban" on the consumption of alcohol based on the authority of (v, 90-91). These injunctions have characterized gambling and alcohol as the evil instruments of Satan.[14]

In any case, despite the fact that the Sharia Law does indeed contain legal concepts and norms that existed in other systems of the past, the unequivocal claim of the Qur'an is that the Scripture contains Allah's revelations to Muhammad; that the Qur'an is the repository of every secret of the cosmos; that Allah is the source of all knowledge; and that there is no one single event in the cosmos of which Allah is unaware. From a purely eschatological approach to the claim of the Qur'an as the primary source of Sharia Law, such a divine source would hardly need what Goldziher and Schacht have characterized as "borrowing". How can Muslim jurists contemplate borrowing concepts and norms from sources other than the Qur'an? Even if the jurists did so, how could they have believed that such concepts were legitimate if they did not resonate harmoniously with the Qur'an and the Prophetic Traditions? Because the text is, and has presented itself as more than a strict "legal document" (to use Fazlur Rahman's phrase), it is plausible to suggest that the legal theory behind Islam's Sacred Law has to follow, and indeed does follow, an evolutionary yet self-contained logic. On the one hand, the evolving legal norms had to confront pre-Islamic norms, beliefs and customs prevailing among bedouin Arabs. On the other hand, as Islam expanded into other parts of the Old World as it became a world religion, various systems of laws, customs, traditions and mores that existed in the Old World came into contact with Islam's evolving doctrine of law. This evolving doctrine could neither become a strict man-made code of law such as that of Hamurabi, or Justinian, nor could it become one of strict theological doctrine such as that produced by medieval Christianity (e.g., Aquinas's *Summa Theologica)*.

The Sharia Law's View of Human Nature

Islam's Sacred Law took into consideration the issues of human nature in general. The Qur'an maintains that in creating human beings Allah has used the loftiest and the basest elements, implying that human beings are capable of both good and evil. When Allah finished creating Adam and Eve from the same source (*al-alaq*, a clot of blood), the Qur'an maintains that Allah asked all angels and jinns to give homage to "His" creation. All acquiesced except for *Iblis,* Satan, who raised objections to the baseness of Adam and Eve and contrasted it with his own angelic purity. The rationale of the Qur'an is that humanity is given a nature (*zaat, baatin*) that drags it between two poles of its nature which, in essence, means that the humanity suffers from opposing inner desires, thoughts and temptations. The social and legal implications of this representation is that human beings are given a choice (*khiyaar*) between good (*kahyr*) and evil (*shar*). This is not a cosmic dualism as in Zoroastrianism, but represents a complex state of development insofar as the Allah-humankind relationship is concerned: Allah, as the Creator, gives permission to its most beloved creation that essential element which makes us human, the element of choice. The Qur'an gives humanity the freedom to choose between good and evil. This is a Qur'anic state of mind that posits human action within a hierarchy. It gives a definite purposefulness to human social action based upon intentions and actions. One may intend to do harm to another, but it is the action, rather than the intention, that enters the realm of legality-illegality. In other words, in Islam's legal theory one cannot be tried for bad thoughts or bad intentions unless such intentions are accompanied by action (*fil-i haraam*). The Qur'anic notion of the so-called *corpus delicti* (the body of crime and criminality) is more relaxed when compared with the Western notion of it in that the guilty mind (*mens rea*) has to accompany the criminal act (*actus reus*). Incidentally, in early Islam, unlike medieval Islam, we do not come across an endless list of sins as crimes that one finds in Judaism or Christianity. As narrated by Imam Bukhari's *Sahih al-Bukhari*, the following constitutes the Prophet Muhammad's view of the three great sins (*akbar al-kabair*):

> Narrated Abu Bakra: Allah's Apostle (Peace Be Upon Him) said thrice, "Shall I not inform you of the biggest of the great sins?" We said, "Yes, O Allah's Apostle" He said, "To join partners in worship with Allah; to be undutiful to one's parents." The Prophet (Peace be Upon Him) set up after he had been reclining and added, "And I warn you against giving forged statement and forged witness....[15]

The same Hadith has been narrated on the authority of Anas bin Malik, one of the most authoritative sources of the Maliki (Sunni) school of jurisprudence. Other Sunni schools as well as Shii sources concur with the authenticity of this Hadith to the effect that it is one of the greatest sins in Islam to attribute a partner to Allah. It was only with the medievalization of Islam and that of Sharia Law that there emerged endless categories of thoughts and actions that were to gradually be deemed as sins and crimes.

From a purely legal perspective, the Hadith posits false witness as a grave sin, criminalized in Sharia Law. Attributing a partner to God is known as *shirk* and, in medieval times, a person charged with such crime was labeled a *mushrik* and could face harsh punishments unless he/she declared the *shadatain*, a verse from the Qur'an that declares one's witness for the Oneness (*Tawhid*) of Allah and the prophecy of Muhammad (*la ilaha illalah, Muahammad rasulallah*). In other words, although Islam is a natural religion on the surface, it has allowed for the criminalization of *mala in se* and the extrapolation of the *mala prohibita* by allowing the Prophetic Tradition as a secondary source of the Sharia Law. The former has been addressed through the Qur'an itself, based on the time-honoured premise that certain acts are inherently evil from the time of Adam to the Day of the Last Judgment – a concept that has its very Islamic portrayal in the *Youm al-Qiymah* (which literally means the "Day when the Dead will arise"). *Mala prohibita*, on the other hand, are addressed in Sharia Law through the gradual prohibition of a number of communal norms and deeds (*urf wa adaat*) that prevailed among bedouin Arabs of the Prophet's time. A majority of these deeds represent, in the eyes of the Qur'an, "ignorance" (*jahl*) of the pre-Islamic Arab life, deeds that had to be sanctioned against gradually so that, through time, they could be stamped out and replaced by a new set of pure and moral ones.

It is a commonly held view among Muslim legal scholars that the term Sharia means the social and political path (*shar*) that the Prophet Muhammad traversed himself in interpreting and enforcing the Qur'anic codes as they applied to both *mala in se* and *mala prohibita*. For example, the Qur'an advised believers to go to the Prophet Muhammad in the case of a dispute so that the Prophet could adjudicate the case through an old established Arab tradition, known as *hakamiyat* (conflict resolution through mediation). The Qur'an, however, advises that those who sit for such a practice ought to perform the mediation based on the principles of justice as well as righteousness. Prior to Islam, such practices were capable of being corrupted if the two sides had unequal social and political status. As narrated by Imam Bukhari and other classical sources (e.g., al-Waqidi, Ibn Saad, al-Tabari, Muslim) as well as by Shii sources, the Prophet observed this practice in the most impartial manner when he was invited by the people of Madina to resolve a dispute among them. Muhammad was known for his honesty and was nicknamed *al-Amin* (the Honest), a point to be dealt with later in this chapter.

The Sharia Law on Crime and Punishment

In the Qur'an, there is a multitude of concepts such as Allah's Judgment (vi, 51, 128; xxxiv, 3-5; xl, 59; li, 5-6, 12-14), Lesser Judgment (lxxv, 22-30; lxxviii, 40), Judgment Day (iii, 185;), Book of Deeds (xviii, 47-49), Scales of Justice (xxi, 47), Voice of Judgment (xxiii, 105-111), Regret of Wrong-doers (xxv, 27-30), Terror for Evil-doers and not for Good (xxvii, 83-90), Wrong-doers Questioned (xxxvii, 22-23), and Retribution for Evil (xxxvii, 33-36). Next to these, the Qur'an also speaks of justice, law, legitimacy, fairness, kindness, crime, sin, punishment, lowly inclinations of human beings and good intentions. Put together, these concepts and terms, appearing in the Qur'an, have allowed Muslim etymologists, jurists and legal scholars a wide latitude in deciphering the Qur'an's notions of law, justice, crime and punishment in the past.

These justice-related notions have found expression in the Sharia Law under three general categories. One category, known as *Hraam* denotes acts, deeds and intentions that are anti-Qur'anic and, therefore, are deemed anti-Sharia Law which by necessity denotes unlawfulness. The other category, known as *Halaal,* denotes the exact opposite. In between there are acts, deeds and intentions that occupy a middle ground and are termed *Makruh* which denotes reluctance. For example, Imam Bukhari narrates a Hadith concerning the revelation (v, 87):

> Narrated Abdullah...: We used to participate in the holy wars carried on by the Prophet...and we had no women [wives] with us. So we said [to the Prophet...], "Shall we castrate ourselves?" But the Prophet...forbade us to do that and thenceforth he allowed us to marry a woman [temporarily] by giving her a garment, and then he recited:-"O you who believe! Do not make unlawful the good things which Allah has made lawful for you."[16]

From this authentic Hadith one may see the Qur'anic view of legality and method of legislation. First, there is a principle enunciated in the revelation (v, 87) that there are "good" things that Allah has made "lawful" (*halaal*) that should not be made unlawful (*haraam*). Second, human needs ought to be attended to in an orderly and legal manner (for example, the sexual urges ought to be satisfied through lawful means).

Haraam and Halaal in the Sharia Law

The term *haraam* appears in various chapters of the Qur'an as, for instance, in (v, 57) cited above. The term used in the verse reads "*...la tuharrimawa tayyibati ma ahalla allahu lakum wa la taatadu...*" which means "do not make illegal or unlawful those good things which Allah has made legal, or lawful." The term *la tuharrimwa* stems from the root word *ha-ra-m* which connotes forbiddenness, something which is unprofitable or has been advised against.[17] Its derivations, argues Qarib, appear in: *al-Maidah* (v, 72, 95), *al-Anam* (vi, 139, [140]), *al-Araf* (vii, 157), *al-Nahl* (xvi, 116), *al-Hajj* (xxii, 30), and *al-Dhariyat* (li, 19).[18] In these verses, a number of acts have been characterized as forbidden by Allah, as, for example (vi, 140) that concerns the pre-Islamic pagan Arab's act of female infanticide. The term *ahalla* (made lawful) stems from the root word *ha-l-l* which means to resolve, to open, or to open a knot. The derivations of this term appear in *al-Baqarah* (ii, 168, 196, 275), *al-Madah* (v, 1, 2, 5), *al-Ra'd* (xiii, 31), Ibrahim (xiv, 28), *Ta-Ha* (xx, 81), and *al-Balad* (xc, 2).[19] These terms are important not only because they give us a clue about the Qur'anic view of legality and illegality, but because they also concern the Qur'an's attitude towards other divine scriptures law, expressed, for example, in verse 157 in *al-Araf* which reads:

> Those who follow the messenger, the Prophet who can neither read nor write, whom they will find described in the Torah and the Gospel [which are] with them. He will enjoin on them that which is right and forbid them that which is wrong. He will make lawful for them all good things and prohibit for them only the foul; and he will relieve them of their burden and the fetters that they used to wear. Then those who believe in him, and honor him, and help him, and follow the light which is sent down with him: they are the successful.[20]

The verse means that Muhammad's mission is not to invalidate the positive aspects of other scriptures (the Torah and the Gospel), but to build upon their positive points and to invalidate those aspects for which the social conditions no longer apply.

I have already explored the Qur'anic punishment for adultery. Where the Torah indicates stoning, the Qur'an demands flogging as an appropriate punishment. This, of course, does not validate adultery, but changes the thrust of punishment from one of stoning to death (if ever that had been the purpose of the Torah), to one of a lesser severity in terms of punishment; at the same time, the Qur'anic procedure for proof of adultery is quite stringent, requiring four reputable eye-witnesses of the actual penetration act. The Qur'an also makes false witness (*shahadti kizb*) of adultery a punishable crime. Put together, Muhammad's charge was not to invalidate the laws of Judiasm and Christianity, but to improve them.

Crime Categories

In both Sunni and Shii juristic texts, the legitimacy of an act has to be measured against the general thrust of the Qur'an as to whether such an act is prohibited by the principle of the *nas-i sarih* (the explicit word) of the Qur'an. For example, the Qur'an explicitly condemns murder. Likewise, it forbids adultery, thievery, aggression and mayhem, the consumption of alcoholic beverages and the consumption of mind-altering substances. We may argue that the more severe an act, the more severe the punishment for that behaviour. In general, the following classes of crime and undesirable acts have been classified in the juristic texts based on the above principle of the Qur'an:

(1)	*Qatl-i Nafs*	Unjustified homicide for which retributory (*Qisaas*) forms of punishment apply.
(2)	*Zinaa*	Adultery for which both stoning (*rajam*) and flogging (*jild*) apply.
(3)	*Sirqat*	Thievery for which the amputation (*qat'*) of from one to four finger(s) applies.
(4)	*Zarb wa jarh*	Battery and injury for which retribution in kind (*Qisaas-i Uzw*) and compensatory monetary punishments apply.
(5)	*Shahadat-i Kizb*	False witness, for which flogging applies.
(6)	*Khamr*	Drinking of alcoholic beverages for which flogging applies.
(7)	*Maysar*	The use of mind-altering substances for which flogging applies.

Another classification (the *Ifsaad)* describes acts that corrupt the soul and the body of the believer and the community. The most important among these has been the *Harb* crimes that involve rebellion against the state and/or rejection of Allah, the Qur'an and of Muhammad's Prophecy. For these crimes, the punishments have varied from no punishment (in the case of rebellious person(s) who repent (*tawbah*), to the most severe punishments that range from flogging, to beheading with a sword, or to the hanging and crucifixion of the unrepentant rebels. These punishments have their roots in the Qur'an and in the Prophet Muhammad's and the "Four Rightly Guided Caliphs's" (Abu Bakr, Umar, Uthman and Ali)' as well as in the Shaii Imams Traditions.

With the rise of the four Sunni and the three Shii jurisprudential schools in the second century of Islam, each school developed its own penological philosophy that allowed the judges to take into consideration the aggravating and mitigating circumstances. This consideration led the jurists to the recognition of the traditions and local customs (*urf wa adaat*) that prevailed among the many cultures and peoples that came under Islamic rule. It is beyond the scope of this study to give a synopsis of this aspect of the Law, other than reiterating the fact that the juristic consideration of the custom and traditions did not change the thrust of the Sharia Law in so far as the main categories of crime and law-infracting behaviours were concerned, but the incorporation of these local customs gave some leverage to the procedural aspect of each school of Law.

The Sacrosanct Nature of the Sharia Law: An Argument

One of the most difficult aspects of the Sharia Law derives from the fact that the Law has been considered sacred in the eyes of both classical and post-classical Muslim jurists. The reasons for this consideration of the Law as sacred can be enumerated as follows. First, in the Sharia Law, Allah is the Absolute Creator, the final source of guidance, of justice, of righteousness and the only supreme yardstick of true judgment as expressed in the Qur'an as for instance in (i, 1 through 7; ii, 1 through 19 etc.). These aspects of Allah have led to the belief that an Islamic judge must be impartial and of the highest moral integrity, schooled in prophetic precedents in the application of the Law. In the ideal Islamic system of adjudication, there is no such a thing as "legal guilt" versus "actual guilt"; Allah is always on the side of the righteous, a premise that has led to the popular belief that even if an innocent person were to be found guilty of a crime, he/she would not go to the hanging gallows, for Allah does not allow innocent persons to endure unjust punishments. There are a number of authentic Prophetic Hadiths that maintain that even if Muhammad were to judge wrongly, it is Allah who will redress the wrongs. In practice, however, the Islamic history of jurisprudence is filled with notorious judges whose style of arbitrary punishment was legendary to the effect that most modern Islamic societies have opted for various secular laws and Western systems of penology and adjudication processes.

Second, Allah has revealed, through the Qur'an, various dimensions of Islam's Sacred Law to Muhammad. These are expressed in various Qur'anic chapters:

ii, 178 about the law of retribution;
ii, 183 and 184 about the law of fasting and its duration;
ii, 187 about conjugal relations between husband and wife;
ii, 232 about the law of divorce;
ii, 238 about the five obligatory prayers;
ii, 275 about the law of bargaining and forbidding interest on loans.

These and similar ones, ought to be adhered to by all believers. This is the meaning of true belief, of being a good and decent Muslim follower of the Sharia Law.

Third, the purpose of Islam's Sharia Law is to show believers the straight path (*al-sirat al-mustaqim*) (i, 6; vi, 153) in order to enable them to opt for a moral and a bountiful life in this world and for salvation in the world to come. Because this path has been traversed by the lawgiver himself, Muhammad, it is logical to follow the path that has already been laid out. As previously mentioned, Imam Malik ibn Anas's famed *al-Muwatta* means the road that has already been traversed.

Fourth, believers, regardless of gender, creed, race or social class, are entitled to all the amenities of the Sharia Law and are advised to follow Allah's straight path. It is unbelievers who stray by not heeding the call to righteousness because Allah has sealed their hearts as expressed in (ii, 136, 142, 281, etc.,). This premise of the Qur'an has led to the view among some scholars that in Islam free will does not exist because one's fate has already been determined. Others, especially Muslim legal scholars, argue that free will is an important aspect of the Qur'anic notion of good faith (*imaan*), the lack of which may lead one to the commission of acts that may range from minor to major sins and crimes. Both the Shii and the Sunni classical juristic texts cover these under the so-called *al-Maasi* caption.

Fifth, believers are responsible to one another and to their communities because they are duty bound to call upon each other to do good and to enjoin each other from committing wrongs, a premise which finds expression in the Qur'anic formula of *al-amri bi'l-maruf wa al-nahy an al-munkar*.

Sixth, Sharia Law is more than just a system to discern the sacred from the mundane, it reflects the essence of Islam – an essence which finds expression in Islam's five pillars of belief. These pillars are as follows:

(1)	*Shadah*	To testify that there is no God, but Allah and that Muhammad is Allah's Messenger
(2)	*Salaa*t	To perform prayer five times a day
(3)	*Haj*	To perform a pilgrimage to Macca
(4)	*Zakaa*t	To give a certain amount of one's wealth to charity
(5)	*Saum*	To observe fasting during the month of Ramadan.

There are also three additional Principal Beliefs in Islam (*Usul al-Din*):

(6)	*Tawhid*	Belief in the Oneness of God
(7)	*Nubuvva*	Belief in the Messengers of God

(8)	*Ma`ad*	Belief in the Day of Judgment (*Yaum al-Qiymah*).

In Shii Islam, besides the above, there are three additional Principal Beliefs as follows:

(9)	*Adl*	Belief in the Justness of God
(10)	*Imama*	Belief in the authenticity of sinless (*masuum*) personalities, Imams (three In Zaidi, seven in Ismaili, and twelve in Ithana Ashari, Shiism)
(11)	*Rijaa*	Belief in the return of the Last Imam, al-Mahdi, to fill the earth with justice and righteousness.

All classical juristic texts, whether Sunni, or Shii, have suggested that a true believer ought to refrain from committing sin and/or crime because to do otherwise would not only entail unlawful behaviour but also un-Islamic behaviour. That is why all classical and post-classical Muslim jurists have taken these pillars as their starting point, arguing that Sharia Law reflects the ideals expressed in Islam's five pillars. These jurists have reached the following conclusions:

(1) One who earnestly believes in Allah's many qualities expressed in the Qur'an not only will refrain from the commission of sins or crimes but will advise others against such ungodly acts.

(2) One who shares his/her wealth with others will be immune to the criminogenic implications of absolute and/or relative depravity that modern criminology now recognizes as an important etiology of crime.

(3) One who prays on a daily basis to remind himself/herself of Allah's presence and might will refrain from the commission of crime or sin.

(4) One who is brought up in a family, educational system and community based on these values will refrain from committing sin or crime.

(5) It is incumbent upon the parents, educators, religious and community and state leaders to inculcate these values on the individual/community to combat sin/crime.

As a result, it can be argued that the elaboration and sophistication of Sharia Law can be explained by a centuries-long process whereby Muslim jurists have gradually extrapolated the implication of these pillars for every aspect of human affairs. This process, in turn, has led to the elaboration of the Law's procedural and substantial aspects. The jurists have taken each of these pillars to argue that the Prophet Muhammad applied them to his daily life and to the affairs of the state and polity. As a result, Muslim jurists came up with elaborate scenarios to apply these pillars to various aspects of daily life as well as to the correct manner of performing Islamic rituals (*ibadah*) and fulfilling personal responsibilities (*wazaaif*).

The Universalism of the Sharia Law

From a Muslim belief system, although Muhammad was a Maccan Arab his call to submission to Allah was of a universalistic nature, inviting humanity to submit once again to the Will of the Universal Deity, Allah, and to act in accordance with Allah's Law, a premise expressed in the Qur'an time and again. For example, (iii, 144) which reads: "Muhammad is but a messenger, messengers [the like of that whom] have passed away before him...."[21] In (v, 15), however, it is stated that: "O People of the Scripture! Now hath Our messenger come unto you, expounding unto you much of that which ye used to hide in the Scripture, and forgiving much. Now has come unto you Light from Allah and a plain Scripture."[22] The Qur'an admonishes Christians and Jews of the Hijaz for their claims that "Messiah, the son of Mary" is but God reincarnated in human form as, for instance, in verses 17 and 18 of *Al-Maidah*; the same chapter also reminds the Jews of their plight and of the manner in which Allah had helped them by sending the Prophet Moses in order to guide them into the Holy Land (v, 20, 21, 22, 23, 24, 25, 26).

The Sharia Law's Emphasis on the Sanctity of Life

Next to these reminders, this Qur'anic chapter also establishes part of what one may consider as the Qur'anic view of the sanctity of life which, of course, has found a cherished place in the Sharia Law's ideals of an Islamic adjudication style and philosophy. Life is too sacred in the eyes of Allah to be taken lightly in the adjudication of the cases that involve capital crimes and therefore require capital punishment. Starting with verse 27 in *al-Maidah*, which recalls the first killing on earth (Qabil's killing of Habil), the Qur'an argues in (v, 32) that:

> For that cause We decreed for the Children of Israel that whosoever killeth a human being for other than manslaughter or corruption in the earth, it shall be as if he had killed all mankind, and whoso saveth the life of one, it shall be as if he had saved the life of all mankind....[23]

In other words, the killing of one innocent person has been equated to the killing of all humanity in the same manner that the saving of one innocent life equates to the saving of all humanity. Verse 33, however, gives a stern warning to those who wage war against Allah and against Allah's Messenger, and spread corruption on earth:

> The only reward of those who make war upon Allah and His messenger and strive after corruption in the land will be that they will be killed or crucified, or have their hands and feet on alternate sides cut off, or will be expelled out of the land. Such will be their degradation in the world, and in the Hereafter theirs will be an awful doom.[24]

These and similar revelations assure Muhammad of his divine mission and the gradual imposition of the moral and legal foundations of this new order. Islam never remained a local religion because it spread by sheer force of conviction, sometimes by the sheer force of the sword, and sometimes by the combination of the two. It is an historical fact that Muhammad sent letters to kings and emperors and asked them to submit to Islam peacefully. Some did and some ridiculed him. They were subsequently subdued at the hands of Muslim warriors who waged Holy War in the path of Allah under Umar and Uthman. Once this was achieved, the next step was to institutionalize different aspects of the faith, including its divine law, the Sharia. The Law, besides having a divine purpose (critiqued above), also had a universal function, the subject of the next section.

The Functions of the Sharia Law

Traditionally, it has been argued by Muslim jurists that the main function of Sharia Law is to allow for the development of a community of believers who follow these aspects of the law in their daily conduct, at home and in the public. This adherence to the Law's injunctions is believed to have a long-term anti-criminogenic impact; this aspect of the Law has to be enhanced by the family, education and state-communal relationships, all of which ought to operate in unison in preventing and/or deterring believers from the commission of sin and/or crime.

The Sharia Law as an instrument of good The realization of this lofty purpose necessitates the application of the Sharia Law which contains Allah's Commandments *(Ahkam)* and Boundaries *(Hudud)* to every aspect of social affairs. For this application to be correct, it has to be legitimate, which means that the Law is too sensitive an issue to be left to arbitrary measures. That is why throughout the centuries, Muslim jurists have studied the Qur'an and the Prophetic Tradition (and those of the Shii Imams) in order to extrapolate the crime-related *Ahkaam* and *Hudud* of the Sharia Law. In juristic texts, these are covered under various captions such as:

(1)	*Kitaab al-Hudud*	Covers the *hadd* punishments
(2)	*Kitaab al-Qisaas*	Covers the retributory punishments
(3)	*Kitaab al-Qasama*	Covers the procedural laws concerning oath in adjudication
(4)	*Kitaab al-Diyaat*	Covers the procedural and substantive laws of blood money
(5)	*Kitaab al-Muharaba*	Covers the issue of rebellion against Islam, Muhammad and Allah.

Besides the general notion of appropriate norms of social conduct that the jurists extrapolated from these sources, they also came up with the specific notion of crime and appropriate punishment that I have already discussed above.

The notion of actus reus in the Sharia Law This Western juristic concept has its equivalence in the Sharia Law as the *fiil al-qabih,* and sometimes as the *fiil al-fahish.* These are acts of extremes, acts that go beyond normalcy and therefore transgress against Allah's norms and boundaries as expressed in the Qur'an. Comprising the Islamic notion of crime and misdemeanour, these acts have been categorized as follows:

(1) Any capital crime

(2) Any sinful act, thoughts and behaviour
(3) Any act that puts the family and the community to shame
(4) Any act that does not befit one's social status and responsibilities
(5) Any act that ignores the Qur'anic principle of moderation (*khayr al umurah awsatiha*)
(6) Any act that ignores in an egregious manner the good of the community
(7) Any act that is exploitative, unjust and improper
(8) Any act that transgresses against human dignity.

In other words, the Qur'anic notion of submitting to Allah's Will, as the first pillar of Islam, is inseparable from submitting to Allah's Law, both of which are inseparable from adhering to the Qur'anic principles of morality and justice. All these acts contravene the thrust, spirit and the letter of the Sharia Law and its sacrosanct nature. In other words, the sacredness of the Sharia Law is not due to its source alone, but to the fact that it has a sublime purpose. Neither is it the content or the form alone that makes the Sharia Law sacrosanct in the eyes of Muslim jurists, but a combination of the two. The same applies to those who sit in judgment of others' deeds, the so-called *qaazi* (Islamic judges). These judges have to purify their intentions first, and then apply the rationale and conventions of the Sharia Law.

The Principle of Consistency in Adjudication

Although the Sharia Law has its base in the Qur'an, it has incorporated concepts and conventions, the origins of which were attributed by classical Muslim jurists to the Prophet Muhammad as well as to the "Four Rightly Guided Caliphs" (Abu Bakr, Umar, Uthman and Ali) as they systemized the Sharia Law's legal base and its legal theory. For example, both the Sunni and the Shii jurisprudential schools have stated that Allah has revealed to the Prophet Muhammad His Commandments first, and then has warned Muhammad, time and again, that those Commandments ought to be consistently observed in daily life. This principle indicates, in my judgment, the Qur'anic base for the principle of consistency in the application of the Sharia Law – a principle that gives to any system of law its legitimacy without which the system loses its social and contractual base as well as its pretext of neutrality. In other words, the Qur'anic view of the law is that it is a God-ordained boundary, without which society falls into evil and anarchy. But the

Law has to be adhered to by all. Therefore, the Qur'anic view of the Law expresses a functional universality.

The Purpose of Punishment

The Qur'an also warns Muhammad that those groups, tribes and nations who did not live by God's law and corrupted God's Commandments in the past face calamities and even extinction; it warns humankind about the awful punishment awaiting those who commit crime and evil acts. It also reminds judges of the awful punishment that awaits those who sit in judgment but do not judge in accordance with God's Balance (*al-Mizaan*) and knowingly falsify God's Commandments. This Grand Judgment Day, however, is not only for evildoers, but also for those who do good. Allah's Balance, maintains the Qur'an in (xcix, 7,8), is so sensitive that it weighs the infinitesimal good (*faman yamal mithqala zarratan khayran yarrah*) as well as weighing the infinitesimal evil (*faman yamal mithqala zarratan sharran yarah*) in the Day of Judgment.

This Qur'anic stance has given the Muslim legal mind a view of deterrence and aversion towards sin and/or crime that has both personal and organizational import: those who beguile the community into committing sin or crime have to face Allah's Balance of Judgment sooner or later; those who beguile the community by deliberately misusing the law and its might (both judges and lawyers) will face the inescapable Day of Judgment and Allah's Balance as well.

The end result of this moral and legalistic attitude has been mixed. On the one hand, the Qur'an advises believers to be forgiving towards one another and to settle their disputes in a manner that would be pleasing to Allah's desire for the just resolution of conflicts. On the other hand, the Islamic world has been devoid, until very recent times, of a Western common law legacy that has led to the progression of the legal profession in the direction of serving an adversarial process centred on winning a case rather than serving the cause of truth and justice.

In sum, although the Qur'an is not a legal text *per se*, however, it contains important social and moral premises from which the principles of law (*qaanun*), jurisprudence (*hukm, qazaa*) and punishment (*hadd, taazir*) have been drawn. The main argument is that the Qur'anic revelations contained a wide spectrum of social and legal norms for the construction of a legal theory based on the notion that the crime and/or sin have both individual and social reasons behind their commission. On an individual level, a believer has to control his/her lowly inclinations by adhering to Islam's core values enunciated in the Qur'an.

From a societal perspective, the Qur'an gives the distinct impression that sin and crime are due to various social factors, including the manner in which power is utilized by those to whom Allah bestows, albeit temporarily, temporal power. This bestowal of power on groups, tribes and even nations, is quite deliberate and based on Allah's plan for gauging adherence to Allah's Law. It is therefore incumbent upon those in the position of authority to govern the affairs of the community based on justice, equity, piety and fear of Allah. This Qur'anic stance implies that in controlling the crime-sin duality, although power has to be utilized, this utilization has to be legitimate whether in the context of informal or formal means. The most important informal means are the family, education and mosque-community. The formal means are the Islamic state and its laws that by necessity are based on the Sharia.

Muhammad, the Ideal Judge and Political Leader

It is a commonly held view among Muslim legal scholars that Muhammad, through his deeds, words and interpretations, set examples as to how conduct the social and political affairs of a society as well as how to apply Allah's Commandments and Punishments. Muslim jurists later referred to Muhammad's style and precedents in their adjudication of cases. The Qur'an also maintains that Muhammad, like his predecessors, was a righteous man, one who was ready to heed Allah's call to righteousness. In the Qur'an, Muhammad is portrayed as the holy Prophet (vii, 158), as Allah's apostle (iii, 144), as one who was sent by Allah as a favour to believers (iii, 164). These stressed the fact that Muhammad was a mortal soul who never claimed to possess any divine attribute (e.g., the Trinity in Christianity) yet exemplified the high morals of Islam, and therefore his conduct exemplified what was desirable, correct, just and legal. The period 610-632 witnessed Muhammad in this capacity, and all classical sources have credited Muhammad with having been the exemplar of purity, faith, thought and action. The question is this: is it not logical to expect from a man of the highest station in Islam to have left his community of believers with a set of procedures in the application of the Sharia Law during his tenure, 610-632? The thrust of the Islamic view is that Muhammad did leave the community such a heritage.

Based on the Maccan revelations, it is a certainty that the Prophet Muhammad, and his followers, performed daily prayers as advised by *al-Asra* (xvii, 78, 79). They also observed fasting during the month of the *Ramadan* although it is in a Madinan chapter, *al-Baqarah* (ii,184-185, 187), that fasting and its injunctions were outlined. Nevertheless, it is improbable that Muhammad did not fast for thirteen years when he was in Macca and only started doing so in Madina. The Prophet and his followers also gave part of their wealth to the needy as it was advised by *al-Maun* (cvii, 1 through 7) and *al-Duha* (xciii, 9 and 10). Again, it is in (ii, 43, 110, 177, 277), (iv, 62) and in (v, 58) that the injunctions are established. For obvious reasons, they could not perform a pilgrimage (*al-haj*) in the manner that we understand the pilgrimage of today. The House of Kaaba was then a sanctuary to idols of the pre-Islamic period as previously mentioned. It was only after the conquest of Macca in 630 that Muhammad performed his pilgrimage, especially the most famed *Hajj al-Wida* (the Farewell Pilgrimage) in Macca based on a specifically Islamic content and procedure.

The question arises as to whether the Prophet of Islam who came up with a relatively coherent doctrine of law, justice and morality during these two periods left any written documents. Muslim legal scholars, basing their research on primary and classical sources, have argued that Muhammad, as he gradually received the revelations had them committed to memory, as well as having them written down on parchments, clay tablets and animal bones.[25] At the same time, Muhammad was in a unique position to interpret the contents of the revelation for his followers as well as to set precedents as to how these injunctions ought to be followed. In particular, Muslim scholars refer to the Constitution of Madina that has been preserved in the classical sources as the *Muahidah al-Madina,* the subject of the next section.

The Constitution of Madina

The Prophet Muhammad established governance in the city of Madina after he emigrated there in 622. This emigration was due to two factors. First, a group of people from Madina had met Muhammad in 620 or 621 in their annual pilgrimage to Macca and had been impressed by Muhammad's demeanour and reputation for honesty and integrity. They subsequently invited him to that city in order to resolve a dispute between various factions in the city. It was, however, in 622 that Muhammad decided to emigrate to Madina since he had lost all his temporal protection in Macca.

Muhammad's base of authority for establishing governance in the city of Madina derived from voluntary allegiances that the people of Madina made to him in accordance with a document, known as the Constitution of Madina. The first article of the Constitution establishes this authority:

> In the name of God, the Merciful, the Compassionate! This document is from Muhammad the Prophet, governing relations among the Believers and the Muslims of Quraysh and Yathrib (Madina) and those who followed them and joined with them and struggled with them.[26]

It should be noted that this article refers to two blocs of power in Madina: those who invited Muhammad to Madina, who have been designated as the Helpers (*Ansar*), and those Maccan followers of Muhammad who have been designated as the Immigrants (*Muhaijirun*) in the classical sources. These two groups played significant roles in Muhammad's life in Madina and in the immediate post-Muhammad period's political events that led to the rise of "the Four Rightly Guided Caliphs" (*Khulafa al-Rashidun*), a period that corresponded to 632-661 and has been of prime significance in the systematization of the Sharia Law. The voluntary allegiance included the allegiances of a number of Jewish clans to the Constitution. This voluntary allegiance of both Muslims and non-Muslim residents of Madina gives the document its unique status in depicting Muhammad's base of power in Madina.

The *biya* was an old bedouin Arab tradition for entering into a political alliance that usually took place between various clans, tribes or powerful personalities in the Hijaz region. Unlike other leaders to whom allegiances were made, based on their actual power factors (e.g., wealth, clan and tribal strength), Muhammad enjoyed none of these other than the fact that he claimed to be Allah's Messenger and his reputation as an honest and righteous person. The Constitution of Madina, through its various articles, departs drastically from the pre-Islamic practice of entering into political allegiance in which the power differentials played a central role in the process: the less powerful pledged his/her allegiance to the more powerful party and received, in turn, a pledge of protection.

Under the Constitution of Madina, it was a relatively powerful community in Madina that pledged its allegiance to Muhammad, not because of power considerations but because he had been invited to Madina to settle a conflict in his capacity of an honest arbitrator. Again, arbitration, known as *hakamiya*, was a pre-Islamic tradition whereby the parties to a conflict would agree to abide by the arbiter's judgment. Therefore, it is plausible to argue that, in Madina, Muhammad's base of political power drew upon the strength of his personal morality; at the same time, the two sides had entered into a written type of mutual agreement (*muahida),* the Constitution of Madian.

The term *muahida* stems from the Arabic root word *ahd* which means the earnest word of one party given to another party for an undertaking that can be of a one sided or of a mutual nature. Because it was mutually binding, the *muahida* of Madina can be looked upon as a mechanism that allowed Muhammad to establish a non-coercive style of governance in Madina, to resolve in his capacity as a leader-judge various conflicts that arose among Muslims and non-Muslim adherents of the Constitution, and therefore to set the Prophetic procedure in the application of the primordial Sharia Law. In other words, the Constitution of Madina could be looked upon as the political frame in the context of which Muhammad's style of conflict resolution framed its legitimate *Shari* base. The last point is of significance for our discussion, considering the fact that Muhammad was now in a position to gradually set in practice the moral, legal and justice considerations of Islam's divine law in Madina. In other words, where in Macca Muhammad could only object to those aspects of social and legal relations that he found vile and objectionable, it was only in Madina and in the context of the mutual *muahida* that Muhammad could move in the direction of changing the *Jahiliyah* practices.

In doing so, Muhammad had to implement a gradual and evolutionary plan. For example, Article 2 of the Constitution specifies that: "The emigrants of Quraysh shall pay the price of blood among themselves according to their present custom, and shall redeem their captives with the justice proper to true believers."[27] Although this article seems to stress the Maccan customary way of paying blood money, it is the second part of the article that emphasizes a new way of treating captives based on that which is expected of true believers. This new treatment regime of the captives, of course, means the implementation of the Qur'anic view of treatment, a view which states that captives ought to be treated fairly and freed upon their captors' receipt of a fair ransom. Likewise, Article 3 specifies that: "The Banu Awf shall pay the blood-price they paid before: every group shall redeem its prisoners with the justice proper to true believers."[28]

The same has been repeated in Articles 4 through 8 for other tribes (as, for example, *Banu al-Khazraj, Banu Saida, Banu Harith,Banu Jusham, Banu al-Najjar, al-Aws, Banu-Amr ibn Awf, Banu al-Nabit and Banu al-Aws*) that were signatories to the Constitution. The gist of these articles is to follow one's customs in so far as the *modus operandi* of blood money is concerned, but when it comes to treatment of captives, one should show them the spirit of the new faith. It should be noted that although some of these tribes adhered to Judaism, but perhaps because in the eyes of the Prophet Muhammad "fairness" and "justice" towards captives transcended the power of customs, none of these could treat captives but fairly. From a purely moral perspective, Muhammad, in these articles, suggests that the powerless (e.g., prisoners of war) ought to be given the most consideration because they lack any power and because they are at the mercy of those who have made a pact with Muhammad, the Messenger of Allah. Muhammad represented a Deity Who is the Most Merciful while being at the same time the Mightiest of All Tyrants (*al-Jabbar al-Qasimin*).

With this disposition towards the less privileged, the Constitution of Madina is a prime example of a doctrine of law, morality and justice. It could also be considered to be the first written document in Islam's history that exemplifies the Sharia Law's genesis. In other words, although the Qur'an is the primary source of Sharia Law, it is the Constitution of Madina that could be considered to be Islam's first written document in that it tries to enact a doctrine of law, morality and justice based on the injunctions of the Qur'an. This premise, of course, challenges the oft-repeated assertion of Western scholarship that the development of the Sharia Law took place in the second century of Islam. My argument here is that the Sharia Law's genesis not only took shape in the Maccan and Madinan periods, but it also had a procedural frame in terms of the manner in which the social and legal affairs of the first Islamic Community of Believers were to be governed.

The authenticity of the Constitution of Madina has been established by both Muslim and Western scholars as, for example, by Montgomery Watt, one of the leading Western scholars on the life of the Prophet Muhammad: "The document of this name preserved by Ibn Hisham is probably of a later date but appears to incorporate the essential provisions of the original agreement." [29] Another scholar, John Alden Williams, opines that: "One striking feature of this constitution is that the Jews of Medina are considered as a part of the Community, and there are detailed clauses regulating their relations with Muslims." He further observes that:

> One might suppose that this is because they were too powerful to ignore, but since there is no mention of the main groups of the Medinan Jews, there is good reason to assume that in the form which it survives, it comes from the time *after* Muhammad expelled and executed the main body of the Jews, when those who remained were only the weaker

> groups. If so, there was nothing to constrain him to consider them a part of his Community, as this unquestionably genuine text shows that he did. However, the date is not given.[30]

Reading through each and every of the forty-seven articles provided by the above English version of the Constitution, one gets the impression Muhammad had pledged to govern the affairs of the community based on a new concept of communal responsibility exemplified by Article 22 which states that: "No believer who accepts this document and believes in God and judgment is permitted to aid a criminal or give him shelter...."[31] Article 25 states that: "The Jews of the Banu Awf are community with the Believers; the Jews have their religion and the Muslims have their own...."[32] Article 47, one of the longest in the Constitution of Madina, relates to both the notions of justice and procedure under Muhammad:

> Whoever acquires any [guilt] does not acquire it for any but himself. God is the most just and loyal fulfiller of what is in this document. This writing will not protect a wrongdoer or a traitor. Whoever goes out is safe, and he who stays at home is safe in the town, unless he has done wrong or treachery. God is the protecting neighbor [jar] of whoever does good and fear Him, and Muhammad is the Messenger of God. Verily God is wrathful when His covenant is broken. Peace be upon you.[33]

This article prohibits guilt by association many centuries before modern theories of adjudication articulated the fact that one cannot be tried based on association alone.

Other primary sources Next to the "Constitution of Medina", the Islamic world also possesses a wealth of authentic primary documents such as the remains of a number of letters that the Prophet sent to contemporary rulers, asking them to submit to Islam. Other documents include "The Sermon of the Messenger of God at the First Friday Prayer,"[34] the text of the Prophet's sermon at his last pilgrimage to Macca, the *Hajj al-Wida*.

In sum, Muhammad, an ordinary (non-divine) and yet a man of the highest moral and religious integrity, could not but act in accordance with the Qur'anic principles of law. He was also instructed by the Qur'an to institutionalize the social and legal bases of Islam's Sacred Law first among bedouin Arabs and then spread its righteous model and messages to all humankind. Even some Western Orientalist scholars such as Schacht who cited what he characterizes as an "old definition of the shari`a" attributed to the historian al-Tabari's interpretation of (xlv, 18), argue that the Sharia already had embodied three aspects of the Sacred Law:

(1) The law of inheritance (faraid)
(2) The hadd Punishments
(3) The Commandments and Prohibitions. [35]

To conclude this chapter, it could be argued that the Sharia Law's genesis was shaped during Muhammad's tenure as he assumed the mantle of the Prophet of God, a period that began in 610 when Muhammad received his first divine revelation and came to its end with Muhammad's death in 632. The Maccan revelations formed the base of Muhammad's belief that he was receiving divine revelations that constituted the principal building blocks of the new faith, Islam, and of its divine Law, the Sharia. This Law, even though in its genesis, had to have moral, just and legalistic ingredients at its core. These principles, *mutatis mutandis*, had already been revealed by Allah to pre-Muhammad Prophets, but for various reasons, Allah's Divine Law and Commandments had been corrupted. Muhammad's mission was to resurrect them in the context of Islam and of its Sharia Law.

What makes Muhammad's claim to Prophecy legitimate is the representation of Allah in the Qur'an, even if the name of Allah appears among Maccan idols worshipped in the capacity of a lesser female idol. Muhammad's father's name, for instance, was Abd-Allah which means the slave to Allah. Naturally, from an historical perspective, it makes no sense to argue that Muhammad's father was a Muslim and therefore named Abd-Allah. The pre-Qur'anic concept of Allah was different from the concept of Allah presented by the Qur'an. There is also no credible evidence to argue that Muhammad, prior to receiving the revelations, worshipped idols in spite of some arguments put forward by Franz Buhl based on the statement of Ibn al-Kalbi – namely, that Muhammad, in his youth, had intended to sacrifice a lamb for one of the grand idols.[36] On the contrary, both the Qur'an and early sources give the distinct impression that Muhammad had no affinity with idolatry.

To replace idolatry and its laws, Muhammad had to change the *Jahiliyah* views of religiosity, law and social relations that included such concepts as Deity, Creation and divine law. The Maccan verses of the Qur'an, for instance, profoundly challenge the bedouin Arab's notion of the law, since the early Maccan revelations assert that: the True Deity was Allah; that Allah had created "Everything" in the cosmos including the very cosmos itself; and that the creation of human beings had been based on a divine plan. The logical implication of these beliefs was that, at that juncture, humankind needed a new set of laws that were just and equitable. The Maccan and Madinan revelations were to provide the bases for this tripartite aspect of the Sharia Law although in a rudimentary nature.

Muhammad's claim was that he was receiving revelations from a sublime source, the Qur'anic Allah, Who was the Absolute Creator (*Khaliq Mutlaq*), one Who had no rivals, was not born and did not give birth to offsprings, but one Who is Eternal. Because this Allah is portrayed in the Qur'an as the purveyor of "Everything", it stands to reason to argue that Muhammad's claim to prophecy had to include a concept of divine law that had to transcend idolatry and its laws. In other words, whereas for bedouin Arabs idolatry constituted a system of religious feelings and rituals that diffused the notion of power and law within the context of three grand idols' shared power, the Qur'an has centralized the Power (*Qadr*) and the Law (*Qanun*) in the Persona of Allah not as an Arab deity but one whose eschatological as well as real ranges of power are absolute, complete and universal. The concept of Law in the Qur'an, therefore, is of an all-encompassing nature with Allah as the eternal source of the Law in its totality. This totality, nonetheless, has to be gradually discovered by human beings and therefore the Sharia Law represents a certain road that has to be travelled by those who seek true salvation.

Notes

1. *The Glorious Qur'an*, text and translation by Mohammad M. Pickthall, (New York, Mostazafan Foundation of New York, 1984), p. 83.

2. *Ibid.*, p. 94.

3. *Ibid.*, p. 604.

4. Noel J. Coulson, *Conflicts and Tensions in Islamic Jurisprudence*, (Chicago and London, The University of Chicago Press, 1969), p.1.

5. *Ibid.*, p. 3.

6. Joseph Schacht, *An Introduction to Islamic Law*, (London, Oxford University Press, 1964), p. 21.

7. J.N.D Anderson, *Islamic Law in the Modern World*, (Westport, Connecticut, Green Wood Press Publishers, 1959), p. 2.

8. Fazlur Rahman, *Islam*, (Chicago and London, The University of Chicago Press, 1979), 2nd edn, pp. 37-38.

9. Parviz Saney, *Huquq-e Jaza-ye Umumi* (Criminal Law) (Tehran, Iran, Ganjedanesh Publications, 1995), vol. I, pp. 89-104.

10. Mohammad Mustafa Azmi, *Studies in Early Hadith Literature: With a Critical Edition of Some Early Texts*, (Indianapolis, Indiana, American Trust Publication, 1987).

11. Pickthall, *The Glorious Qur'an*, p. 7.

12. Anderson, *Islamic Law*, p. 11.

13. Fazlur Rahman, *Islam*, pp. 37- 38.

14. *Ibid.*, p. 38.

15. Imam Muhammad al-Bukhari, *Shaih Al-Bukhari*, (Beirut, Lebanon, Dar al-Arabiyah, 1985), vol.8, pp. 6-7.

16. *Ibid.*, vol. 6, Hadith no. 139, p. 110.

17. Qarib Muhammad, *Tabyin al-Luqat Lilbayan al-Ayaat*, (Tehran, Iran, Intesharat Bunyaad), vol. 1, p. 217.

18. *Ibid.*, pp. 317-318. Brackets are mine.

19. *Ibid.*, pp. 345-347.

20. Pickthall, *The Glorious Qur'an*, p. 162.

21. *Ibid.*, p. 65

22. *Ibid.*, p. 104.

23. *Ibid.*, p. 106.

24. *Ibid.*, p. 106.

25. Azami *Studies in Early Hadith Literature*, pp. 1-17.

26. "The Constitution of Medina" pp.11-15 cited in John Alden Williams (ed.), *Themes of Islamic Civilization*, (Berkeley, California, University of California Press, 1971), p. 11; for some details on this document see also al-Tabarai, Abu Jafar b, Jarir, *The History of al-Tabari, vol. Vii:: The Foundation of the Community*, (Albany, NY, SUNY Press, 1987), translated and annotated by W. Montgomery Watt and M.V. McDonald.

27. "The Constitution of Madina," *Ibid.*, p. 12.

28. *Ibid.*, pp. 12-13.

29. *The History of al-Tabari (Tarikh al-rusul wa'l-muluk), vol. Vii: The Foundation of the Community*, Foreword.

30. See the selection, "The Constitution of Medina," pp. 11-15 in John Alden Williams (ed.), *Themes of Islamic Civilization*, p. 12.

31. *Ibid.*, p. 13.

32. *Ibid.*, p. 14.

33. *Ibid.*, p. 15.

34. *The History of al-Tabari*, vol. Vii, pp. 2-3.

35. Schacht, "Sharia", in *Shorter Encyclopaedia of Islam*, H.A.R. Gibb and J.H. Kramers (eds), Ithaca, Cornell University Press, 1961, p. 524.

36. See Buhl, Franz, "Muhammad" p. 391 in *Ibid.*, pp. 390-405.

4 Women's Legal Status in the Sharia Law

Starting with this chapter, we turn our attention to the second purpose of this study: the formation of women's legal status under the Sharia Law as a prelude to exploring Iran's Sharia-based criminal justice system and its treatment of women in Iran, one of the most important Islamic countries. The primary purpose of this chapter is to give a synopsis of the formation of woman's legal status in the Sharia Law by concentrating on some of the factors that Muslim men of letters (*Ulama*) have utilized in their analysis of women's status in the Qur'an and in the Prophet Muhammad's Tradition.

Women's General Status in the Sharia Law

Historically speaking, the Sharia Law has contained a male-structured perspective as to what constitutes women's status at home and in society. At home, daughters are under the benevolent control of the father whereas married woman are under the benevolent control of the husband as reflected in the Sharia Law. This control covers the following: education, marriage, the use of financial resources, place of residence, child custody, travel and the mode of appearance in the public. The Law also provides for the punishment of women's crime. The penological philosophy is one of reciprocity between crime and punishment that ought to be consistent, swift and certain but not of a torturous or politically motivated nature. Punishment applies only after all mediation efforts for reconciliation have been exhausted.

This male-structured view formulated in both Sunni and Shii juristic texts, has been constructed through interpretation (*tafsir*) of the Qur'an and of the Hadith attributed to the Prophet Muhammad. In Shii creed, besides these two principal factors, the Shii Imam's Traditions contained in the corpus of *Akhbaar* (literally "the News") have been added to the process of interpretation. The central tenet of the Shii view of the Sharia Law is that the Imam's Traditions reflect Muhammad's Tradition, and therefore, the News (*Akhbaar*) pertaining to the Imam's Traditions ought to be considered as the third important source in the interpretation of women's legal status in the Sharia Law. The Sunni creed rejects most of the *Akhbaar* as concocted for political reasons and instead opts for other and secondary factors in the interpretation process. Deconstruction of this male-structured classical view as the basis of women's status in the Sharia Law (regardless of the Shii-Sunni dichotomy) is a profound challenge facing reform-minded intellectuals in modern Islamic societies.

The Notion of Social and Legal Status in the Sharia Law

The most important repository of women's traditional status in the Sharia Law is the Qur'an itself. By the term "status", I mean a socially constructed view towards women's place in society. Accordingly, a believing women has rights (*huquq*) as well as responsibilities (*masuliyat*) that are of a reciprocal nature as conceived in the Qur'an and, therefore, in the Sharia Law. For every right (*haq*) that the Qur'an has provided for women, there is a corresponding responsibility (*masuliyat*) that the Scripture has also recognized. The Sharia Law, therefore, has canonized the two aspects of women's status within the context of this reciprocity. For example, a believing woman has the right to her share of inheritance, education, child custody, marital and maternal love and respect. Belief here means belief in Islam, or in other Scriptures. The recognition of the reciprocity between the two is of paramount importance for any systematic attempt to improve women's traditional status in modern Islamic societies is bound to raise the question of whether such improvement, if unaccounted for in the Sharia Law, is "un-Islamic" and distracts women from their religiously legitimated social and legal responsibilities toward the family and society. This is a powerful argument advanced by traditionalist Islamic forces who argue that secular laws do not recognize the importance of this reciprocity. These forces are especially critical of what they perceive as lax moral values in modern post-industrialized societies, proposing that Western women have become cheap labourers and sex objects, dragged into an endless cycle of greed-based culture of consumption which has deprived Western women of their human and motherly instincts. That is one main reason as to why there is so much crime, juvenile delinquency, murder, rape and prostitution in Europe and North American societies, as well as divorce, suicide, illegitimate birth, and sexual promiscuity. By contrast, these traditionalist forces argue that in Islamic societies women have a cherished place at home and in public. Women and young girls are not stalked and raped in schools and college campuses, nor are they kidnapped, raped and mutilated by serial murderers because they are protected by their male relatives in public. Muslim women, by and large, do not commit crimes in the manner that women in Europe and in North American societies do. In addition, because Muslim women have a valued place at home as mothers and wives, and because they are good guardians, juvenile delinquency is not much of a problem in Islamic societies. In the face of these realities, how can one argue that secular laws are better than the Sharia Law?

On the other side of this debate, the proponents of modernity and secular laws argue that in Islamic societies women are treated as second-class citizens under the hegemonic control of a patriarchal system enhanced by the Sharia Law which deprives women of their capacity for self-actualization. It is true that women are not raped in public, but there are various forms of conjugal rape, domestic violence and battery that are not even acknowledged let alone criminalized in the manner that most democratic societies have done. Women in Islamic societies are not given freedom of choice with regard to marriage and divorce, place of residence, field of higher education, socialization with the opposite sex, travel or even their clothing. By and large, they are deprived of any meaningful participation in the field of justice. Two women's testimonies are equal to one man's testimony in terms of their worth. A husband can marry four wives and can divorce them any time he wishes.

As I shall establish in this chapter, the two sides have ample historical as well as epistemological arguments and evidences to substantiate their claims. The question is whether there is a middle ground between the two assertions. Put differently, does the Sharia Law allow for differences in the interpretation of its contents? This question focuses on the issue of interpretation of the sources from which women's social and legal status has been determined in the Sharia Law. Once it is posited in this context, one could show that there is much scope for reforming the Law.

The Dualistic Thrust of the Sharia Law Towards Women

As the primary source of the Sharia Law, the Qur'an maintains that women and men are equal in terms of their creation. It declares that both species are created from a "clot of blood" (*al-Alaq*). However, the Qur'an, in other verses, posits women one degree below men. In what follows below, I shall explain these positions of the Qur'an from the standpoint of these two perspectives. Naturally, the premises are expressed in the Sharia Law. Therefore, in what follows, the positions of the Qur'an and the Law are unanimous unless otherwise stated.

The Egalitarian Thrust of the Qur'an

Women and men comprise one unitarian spirit (*al-nfasi wahid*) in the eyes of the Qur'an as specified in the chapter *al-Nisa* (iv,1) which is also reflected in the Sharia Law. This egalitarian stance of the Qur'an, is repeated in different chapters (e.g., xvi,16; xlii,11). Muslim scholars[1] argue that the Qur'anic view debunks the notion that woman's creation was an afterthought, an alleged Biblical premise whereby it is stipulated that God created Eve from Adam's left rib.[2] There is a Hadith in which the Prophet Muhammad is purported as having said that women in the same manner of a rib are crooked. This Hadith implies that women ought to be put under a strict and harsh regime of treatment, a dubious premise that Muhammad Khazaeli argues has mistakenly been attributed to Muhammad, for it hardly befits Islam and its humanitarian approach to women.[3]

Unlike the medieval Biblical notion that Eve was the cause of Adam's fall from God's grace, and was therefore the main reason for Adam's expulsion from Paradise, the position of the Qur'an is that both Adam and Eve were tempted by Satan (ii, 36). They followed their human temptations and rebelled against Allah's injunctions and therefore were expelled from the Paradise (ii, 36). But once they repented, Allah forgave them and gave them bounty and happiness on this earth (ii, 37, 38, 39). Some of these themes are repeated in other chapters of the Qur'an (vii, 12; xv, 28, 33, 39) as the text establishes its general humanitarian-egalitarian thrust in regard to women's status.

Neither the Qur'an, nor the Sharia Law attribute to women any original sin; therefore women, in the Qur'an, have not been portrayed as the tempters of men, but as humans whose temptations follow the same rationale and causes as those of men. That is why the Qur'an and the Sharia Law have both made provision for a variety of social and legal factors that are believed to cause sin or law-infracting behaviour. The factors of temptation are different. Some are social such as greed, ambition, pride, or lack of faith. Other factors relate to the family and its dynamics, such as marital relations between the spouses be it love, respect or gratification (love and sex that is of a reciprocal nature applying to both sexes provided that such urges were to be satisfied within the institution of marriage). Naturally, the Qur'an has condemned any attempts to satisfy one's urges by illegal or immoral means (e.g., thievery is condemned in the same manner that premarital and extramarital sexual activities have been condemned and criminalized for both sexes as reflected in the Sharia Law).

It is common knowledge among the Muslim laity and intellectuals that in the Qur'an's valuation system, a believer's worth in the eyes of Allah depends on that believer's piety, righteous deeds and fear of Allah and not on extraneous factors such as sex, gender, race or class status. That is why the Qur'an reminds believers that on the Day of Judgment Allah will use a Scale (*al-Mizaan*), to weigh the believer's deeds. It is through this measure that Allah will determine believers' rewards or punishments, assigning believers to either Paradise or Hell. In this measurement, an absolute form of equality is maintained between believing men and women. The Qur'an, also called *al-Mizaan*, implores believers to do good and to refrain from evil, for it is an absolute certainty that humankind will taste death and will face Allah's Scale. The Sharia Law, as the temporal expression of this divine scale of justice, naturally has to follow the same criteria for the determination of guilt or innocence.

The Temporal Thrust

Next to these mostly theological concepts of equality between the sexes scattered throughout the text, there is one specific chapter of the Qur'an that is pertinent to our discussion. This chapter, entitled as *al-Nisa* (Women), is one of the longest chapters of the Qur'an, the bulk of which was revealed to the Prophet Muhammad in Madina. It consists of 176 verses (177 if the opening – i.e., the Benediction – was to be counted as a separate verse) [4] and covers a wide range of women's rights and responsibilities that have been inserted in the Sharia Law (both Sunni and Shii versions notwithstanding the procedural and substantive nuances). These rights and responsibilities enunciated in this and other chapters of the Qur'an pertain to property, inheritance, education, marriage and divorce, as well as to the general status of women in the family (e.g., women's parenting rights, conjugal relations, respect and love for mothers and wives).[5] A synopsis of each is provided below.

Property Rights and Responsibilities of Women

Prior to Islam, women owned property in Arab semi-settled and tribal societies. There were women traders (e.g., Khadijah, Muhammad's first wife) with financial capital in their possession. Financial capital, even then transformable into other forms of wealth including real estate and fixed property, gave these women a valued and powerful position in society. The

Qur'an not only institutionalized women's property rights, it also condemned many pre-Islamic practices that were deemed abusive in the utilization of property and financial capital as, for instance (ii:188), "And eat not up your property among yourselves in vanity, nor seek by it to gain the hearing of the judges that ye may knowingly devour a portion of the property of others wrongfully."[6] The term "property" in its plural form is *al-amwaal*, which ranges from private to fixed property (e.g., slaves, household items, arable lands, orchards, cattle, horses and camels, etc.). This term is also repeated in various verses of *al-Nisa* as for instance (iv:29), whereby a similar warning is given: "O ye who believe! Squander not your wealth among yourselves in vanity, except it be a trade of mutual consent, and kill not one another. Lo! Allah is ever Merciful unto you."[7]

Like their classical counterparts, modern commentators on the Qur'an have observed that these verses warned and/or enjoined Muslim women (and men) from abusing their properties, especially on practices such as bribery, usury and loan sharking, prostitution and gambling. These practices were prevalent in the *Jahiliyah* period representing what the Qur'an has characterized as the vile way of life among pre-Islamic tribal societies in the Hijaz region.

The Qur'an also provides for the redistribution of wealth, establishing a mechanism that requires a certain percentage of one's wealth to be given to charity. This mechanism is known as *al-Zakaat*. By encouraging these practices among the members of the Community of Believers in Madina, the Qur'an gave a powerful moral tone to the accumulation of financial capital based on hard work and honest conduct among Muslims. In effect, as many prominent classical and modern theologians and commentators on the Qur'an have argued, Islam (both Sunni and Shii) allows for private property but does not condone the concentration of unlimited wealth in the hands of few individuals. Thus, Islam lies somewhere between capitalism and socialism. What is certain is that the Qur'an has never been against women's participation in economic affairs, and has never argued that women have no economic responsibilities. These premises of the Qur'an are important for those reform-minded politicians and educators who advocate women's participatory roles in society, but are hard pressed by fundamentalist forces who argue that women's place is in the confines of the household. The challenge is to show that women's participation in economic affairs is beneficial both to general economic and household vitality.

Inheritance Rights and Responsibilities of Women

The Qur'an has regularized inheritance, the acquisition of which allows for further accumulation of different types of wealth. The text also allows for a wide range of persons to receive inheritance, regularizing the proportion to which each person is entitled. In the juristic texts, inheritance and its dynamics have been analysed under the heading of *Al-Faraid*.

The Qur'an allows orphans, freed slaves, married women, their offspring and their relatives to receive inheritance. The same applies to married men, as well as their offspring and their relatives. The relevant verses are scattered throughout the text.[8] This Qur'anic stance on the importance of the wide spread of the inheritance is, of course, reflected in the Sharia Law, to the effect that both Sunni and Shii jurists have elaborated complex scenarios and arithmetical formulas for dealing with the issue of the just apportionment of any amount of inheritance.

The Qur'an allows for both oral and written styles of bequeathing inheritance. Known as the *wasiya* – a term which stands for both written and oral last testaments – the Qur'anic stress, however, has been on the written format. For example (ii:180) advises leaving a written will by "him" who has property and feels the nearing of his death so that his inheritance (*tarakah*) can be bequeathed to his parents and known relatives. Verses (ii:181, 182) regularize the manner in which a will is to be administered and what is to be done in case a will is contested. The emphasis is on a negotiated settlement between the concerned parties.

Verse (ii:240) regularizes the bequeathing of provisions and of inheritance by a husband among his wives as he feels the approach of death. Of course, the use of the male personal pronoun does not negate the advisability of leaving a written will by women who own property, a practice that has centuries of history behind it. It is in the chapter of *al-Nisa,* however, that we find the more elaborate scenarios with regard to inheritance.

Verse 1 in *al-Nisa* can be looked upon as the text's aforementioned egalitarian approach with respect to the Qur'anic view of the Creation. The thrust of the verse is that Allah has created males (*al-rijal*) and females (*al-nisa*) as unitarian souls (*al-nafsi wahid*). It reads:

> O mankind! Be careful of your duty to your Lord who created you from a single soul and from it created its mate and from them twain hath spread abroad a multitude of men and women. Be careful of your duty toward Allah in whom

> ye claim [your rights] of one another, and toward the wombs [that bore you]. Lo! Allah hath been a Watcher over you.[9]

If man and woman are created from a single soul, then, in the eyes of Allah, they are spiritually equal. The problem is that this absolutist eschatological equality is not matched by a corresponding temporal equality in the Qur'an, as evinced by the verses that follow verse 1– a point to be dealt with shortly. Instead, the Qur'an stresses fairness and equity in dealing with orphans, women, slaves, and the sick and destitute who comprise the disenfranchised of society according to both Western and Muslim commentators of the Qur'an, a premise that is expressed in the Sharia Law. At the same time, there are verses that establish a power differential between males and females (e.g., verses that advise giving a larger portion of the inheritance to male offspring).

Verses 2, 3 and 6 in *al-Nisa*, for example, recommend a regime of fair treatment for orphans. Verse 2 reads: "Give unto orphans their wealth. Exchange not the good for the bad (in your management thereof) nor absorb their wealth into your own wealth. Lo! That would be a great sin."[10]

Verse 3 is one of the most controversial verses because although it legalizes polygamous relations, the verse also aims to put moral order and equity to these types of relationship that existed prior to Islam. The verse reads:

> And if ye fear that ye will not deal fairly by the orphans, marry of the women, who seem good to you, two or three or four; and if ye fear that ye cannot do justice [to so many] then one [only] or [the captives] that your right hands possess. Thus it is more likely that ye will not do injustice.[11]

Imam Bukahri narrates two Hadiths (nos 97 and 98) on the authority of Aishah that this verse was revealed in order to caution believers against marriages that bedouin Arabs used to enter and which were based upon material considerations but no affection. Hadith no. 97 gives the example of a man who married an orphan girl not for love, but because she had in her possession a date palm garden.[12] Hadith no. 98 not only repeats this caution but also reminds believers that "beauty" should not be one's prime consideration when contemplating marriage. The verse, in fact, regularizes polygamous relationships based upon fairness and justice towards orphans (if one were to marry them) rather than based upon property (*mal*) and beauty (*jamal*) that the Hadith specifies against. The Qur'an is not against beauty, but more important than outer beauty is the inner beauty of the believing women and men and, therefore, believers are advised to consider all relevant elements as they engage in marriage.

Commenting on this verse, Mirza Tahir Ahmad maintains that this verse can be explained in terms of five scenarios that then existed in relation to the guardianship of orphans:

(1) An unmarried man had orphans (both males and females) under his trust:
(2) A married man had orphans under his trust, but his spouse did not treat the female orphans justly;
(3) The same married man had to take care of his young orphan relatives (brothers, sisters, cousins), but his spouse did not treat the orphans justly;
(4) A man had strangers under his care and was unsure about how to treat them as orphans;
(5) A man had under his care a large number of orphans, and he felt that the only way to do justice to these was to marry some of the orphans (to the limit of four).

The verse, Mirza Tahir Ahmad argues, recommends marriage in these five situations.[13] In the third situation, the remedy is to marry a mature woman rather than a young girl so that adequate maternal care be provided for the man's young orphan relatives. One of the Prophet Muhammad's companions, Jabir, did precisely this.[14]

Verse 4 in *al-Nisa*, commands men to give to their spouse(s) whatever has been given to them as a marriage gift (*saduqaat*). If it is agreeable to the spouse, then the verse allows the husband to utilize such wealth. Again, the stress of the verse is on fairness and on equity and respect for the spouse's wishes (i.e., a kind of empowerment of women by the Qur'an).

Verses 5 and 6 regularize the practice of "guardianship" over orphans and mentally deranged or challenged persons. Verse 5 recommends guardians of mentally challenged persons not to give wealth to such persons who have been put under guardianship, but advises a regime of kindness and benevolence – a regime that includes feeding and clothing such persons in their care.

Verse 6, on the other hand, reads:

> Prove orphans till they reach the marriageable age; then, if ye find them of sound judgment, deliver over unto them their fortune; and devour it not by squandering and in haste lest they should grow up. Whoso [of the guardians] is rich, let him abstain generously [from taking the property of orphans]; and whoso is poor let him take thereof in reason [for his guardianship]. And when you deliver up their fortune unto orphans, have [the transaction] witnessed in their presence. Allah sufficeth as a Reckoner.[15]

There is unanimity among Muslim jurists (both Sunni and Shii) that a needy person to whose care an orphan's property has been entrusted is entitled to a reasonable amount of remuneration in respect of the management of such an estate. Imam Bukhari narrates a Hadith on the authority of Aishah that this verse was indeed revealed to regularize this aspect of guardianship in Islam.[16] The verse, however, warns that the estate has to be returned in its bulk to its rightful owners (e.g., the orphans) after they reach the age of maturity and of sound judgment. This is a moral responsibility that the Qur'an has placed on the shoulder of believers who, for whatever reason, have been charged with the trusteeship of orphans and of their properties.

Verses 7-9 in *al-Nisa* regularize the share of the male and female members of a family from their parental inheritance; fairness towards orphans is consistently emphasized. Verse 10 again reminds believers of the awful punishment that awaits them on the Day of Judgment if they stray from Allah's injunctions.

Gender-based inequalities in the apportioning of the inheritance Verse 11 in *al-Nisa* is a long one that regularizes the proportioning of the inheritance between male and female offspring in the family. With verse 11, gender-based temporal inequalities in the apportioning of the inheritance enter the picture, in spite of verse 1 mentioned above.

> Allah chargeth you concerning [the provision for] your children: to the male the equivalent of the portion of two females, and if there be women more than two, then theirs is two-thirds of the inheritance, and if there be one [only] then the half. And to his parents a sixth of the inheritance if he have [sic] a son; and if he have [sic] no son and his parents are his heirs, then to his mother appertaineth the third; and if

> he have [sic] brethren, then to his mother appertaineth the sixth, after any legacy he may have bequeathed, or debt [hath been paid]. Your parent or your children: You know not which of them is nearer unto you in usefulness. It is an injunction from Allah! Lo! Allah is Knower, Wise.[17]

In both Sunni and Shii jurisprudential schools, this verse has been utilized in the appertainment of inheritance among those who are entitled to receive it. The principal ones are children, parents, wives and husbands. Imam Bukhari narrates a Hadith on the authority of Jabir that this verse was revealed concerning Allah's command on the importance of parents' leaving inheritance for their offspring.[18] In modern Islamic societies, this and similar verses have been questioned in terms of justice and equity, a point to be elaborated upon later in this chapter.

Verse 12, on the other hand, regularizes the bequeathing of inheritance by a husband's wives (and explores various scenarios that may arise in the apportioning of the inheritance).

> And unto you belongeth a half of that which your wives leave, if they have no child; but if they have a child then unto you the fourth of that which they leave, after any legacy they may have bequeathed, or debt (they may have contracted, hath been paid). And unto them belongeth the fourth of that which ye leave if ye have no child, but if they have a child then the eighth of that which ye leave, after any legacy ye may have bequeathed, or debt (ye may have contracted, both hath been paid). And if a man or a woman have a distant heir (having left neither parent nor child) and he (or she) have a brother or a sister (only on the mother's side) then to each of them twain (the brother and sister) the sixth, and if they be more than two, then they shall be shared in the third, after any legacy that may have been bequeathed or debt (contracted) not injuring (the heirs by willing away more than a third of the heritage) hath been paid. A commandment from Allah. Allah is Knower, Indulgent.[19]

Again, in both Sunni and Shii jurisprudential schools, the premise has been that in the apportionment of a spouse's, or of spouses' inheritance, there are priorities that ought to be taken under consideration. The first priority has been the satisfaction of any debts or legacies (e.g., any financial obligations to charity, or endowment), that the deceased spouse(s) might have had incurred during their lifetime. Once this priority is satisfied, the rest of the bequest wealth ought to be apportioned in accordance with the provisions of the verse. Imam Bukhari narrates a Hadith (on the authority of Ibn Abbas, one of the most authoritative of Hadith narrators), to argue that the thrust of the verse is as follows:

> (In the Pre-Islamic Period) the children used to inherit all the property but the parents used to inherit only through a will. So Allah canceled that which He liked to cancel and decreed that the share of a son was to be twice the share of a daughter, and for the parents one-sixth for each one of them...or one-third...and for the wife one-eight...or one-fourth...and for the husband one-half...or one-fourth.[20]

The Hadith argues that these scenarios apply, based upon the deceased person's number of children. With the passage of time, Muslim jurists came up with various arithmetical formulae to calculate the proper inheritance, depending on the overall number of persons involved in the case. Imam Bukhari narrates a number of Hadiths that shed light on these scenarios. The following, narrated on the authority of Zaid bin Thabit, sheds some light on the subject.

> And Zaid bin Thabit said, `if a man or a woman leaves as an heir, a (single) daughter, then she inherits one half of the property; and if there are two daughters or more, they inherit two-thirds of the property; and if there is a son along with these daughters, then the other heirs (if there are any) are given their shares first, and what remains is to be distributed (among the daughters and the son) with the ratio of two shares for the male heir and one share each for the female heirs'.[21]

Imam Bukhari also narrates other Hadiths that reflect the Hanafi (a branch of the Sunni) school's view of what constitutes inheritance and how it should be apportioned.[22] The same complex picture of the classical view of inheritance is presented in Imam Muslim's *Sahih Muslim*[23] which again gives an idea about the Hanafi school's view of inheritance. For the Mailiki school,

Imam Malik bin Anas's *al-Muwatta* gives a complex picture of those who receive inheritance. [24] For the Shafii school, Imam Muhammad bin Idris's *Risala*[25] among others can give us an idea about this Sunni school's view of inheritance. For the main Shii school (the *Ithna Ashari*) view of inheritance, one could refer to a number of sources. [26]

There are similarities between the Sunni and Shii schools with regard to inheritance and its apportionment. There are also differences. To dwell upon these is beyond the scope of this study. It suffices to state that these differences found expression in the Sharia Law as Islam spread to various parts of the Near East, North Africa and Asia during Umar's reign.

Limits on inheritance Verses 13 and 14 of *al-Nisa* warn of those "limits" that Allah has imposed on believers. These verses also implore believers to obey Allah's messenger as a precondition for entering Paradise; the verses portray Paradise as composed of beautiful gardens designed for eternal residence.

Verses 15, 16, 17 and 18 in *al-Nisa,* on the other hand, advise the Community of Believers what is to be done with those women who have been accused of lewdness (*fahishah*) (verse 15), how to punish them (verse 16) and how to seek forgiveness and repentance (verses 17 and 18). These verses also represent the Qur'anic view that any set of rights is balanced by a corresponding set of responsibilities.

Verse 19 enjoins believers against reverting back to certain *Jahiliyah* practices with regard to women's inheritance. It reads:

> O ye who believe! It is not lawful for you forcibly to inherit the women [of your deceased kinsmen], nor [that] ye should put constraint upon them that ye may take away a part of that which ye have given them, unless they be guilty of flagrant lewdness. But consort with them in kindness, for if ye hate them it may happen that ye hate a thing wherein Allah hath placed much good. [27]

Concerning the importance of this verse, Imam Bukhari narrates a Hadith (on the authority of Ibn Abbas) that prior to Islam a widow was almost at the mercy of her husband's relatives. If one of them wished to marry her, she had to oblige such a wish. This obligation to her inner circle's wishes applied if she desired to marry an outsider. In order to do so, she had to receive her deceased husband's relatives'consent. The verse empowers widowed women in terms of their abilities for self-determination. The importance of this verse stems from the fact that widowed women comprised a vulnerable segment among the disenfranchised in the Arab *Jahiliyah* period. The verse, however, prohibits widowed women from lewdness. In the Prophetic Hadith, there has been much stress on marrying widowed women so that they may not fall into immoral practices with regard to sexual urges that the Qur'an treats as one of the most natural human wants. In the juristic texts, these issues have been discussed under *al-nikaah* and *al-talaaq,* two complementary concepts that respectively stand for marriage and divorce.

From the preceding discussion, the following general observations can be made with regard to the Qur'anic view of inheritance which have been inserted in both Sunni and Shii versions of the Sharia Law with regard to women. First, although Allah has created man and woman from the same soul, there is a gender-based asymmetry in the Qur'anic view of the apportioning of the inheritance. Male offspring receive more than female offspring. Two explanations can be cited for this: (a) Islam, like other great monotheistic religions of the world (Judaism and Christianity), is patriarchal and inheritance laws reflect patrimonial and patrilineal aspects of Islam as illustrated by the Qur'an, and the Sharia Law; (b) a gender-based asymmetry in the Qur'an reflects an historical reality of the class societies of the Old World into which Islam spread, rather than reflecting a God-ordained injunction. Depending on what explanation one is to adopt in modern Islamic societies, the resolution of the problem assumes strategic differences for women in terms of wealth generation and its redistribution.

Second, the existence of various scenarios in the Qur'an regarding inheritance and its passage from one generation to the next is indicative of the fact that Islam recognizes the validity of the private property, but does not condone the concentration of wealth in the hands of a few. Instead, the Qur'an aims to spread wealth among members of the family and, through them, facilitate its spread among members of society at large. This premise implies that the Sharia Law can be looked upon as a mediating instrument that tries to strike a balance between the interest of those segments of the population that the Qur'an has characterized as *al-Kaasib* (those who earn their living through trade and commerce) and as *al-Naas* (those who can be characterized as the common people). In other words, ideally speaking, the Sharia Law is not an instrument for one segment of society. Reflecting the Qur'anic stress on balance in social affairs, the Sharia Law aims to balance the common good of the society next to the interests of the *al-Kaasib* that the Qur'an maintains is dear to the eyes of Allah (*al-Kaasib Habib Allah*).

Third, those who acquire debt have to repay it during their lifetime or the repayment is incurred by the beneficiaries. The same applies to legacies that may include contractual obligations. In other words, one's death does not invalidate one's legitimate contractual obligations. This is a clear indication that the Qur'an's injunctions regarding inheritance were designed not to be disruptive to an emerging mercantile culture. These injunctions, however, aimed to improve these relations and put them onto a higher plane of righteousness and morality as well as deter some of the most abusive practices in the formation of wealth.

Fourth, the fact that husbands receive inheritance from their wives is, again, indicative of the fact that women did own property and that property did change hands within the family, passing to the next generation within the sides of both parents. As a result, these verses of the Qur'an give neither an exclusively patrilineal, nor a matrilineal, but a bilateral character to the Islamic view of inheritance. Notwithstanding the fact that a certain gender- based asymmetry in the distribution of inheritance has a Qur'anic base, in comparison with other prevailing systems as, for example, the Roman primogeniture laws of inheritance, the Qur'anic premise was a gigantic step towards elevating women's status in the Old World. Roman laws gave the first-born male the exclusive right to inheritance with the provision that, if he desired, he could give a portion of it to his siblings. The Qur'an, however, makes it mandatory that parental inheritance be distributed among all offspring and other deserving members of the family.

Fifth, asymmetry in inheritance has become a sensitive issue in modern times because these verses allow for the unequal distribution of inheritance between the male and female family members of the deceased. The traditional defence of this scheme has been that, because women receive the so-called *jahizah* (a certain form of wealth that the father bestows upon his marrying daughter) and women are promised *mahr* (a certain amount of wealth that the prospective husband promises to his wife) and because women receive *nafaqah* (daily household provisions), it is only fair that men should receive a higher proportion of the inheritance. Valid as it might have been in medieval agricultural societies, this argument is now partially defunct because, in many modern Islamic societies, the accumulation of wealth and the acquisition of property follow a different dynamic than that of medieval agricultural societies. For example, now women are not only educated, but they are also employed in the job market, earning wages and salaries that allow them to acquire property with all its empowering aspects: they divorce their espouses, and do utilize their property in the way they see it fit. It is no longer conceivable to argue that the traditional distribution of inheritance should necessarily be adhered to because it has a base in the Qur'an. In addition, because of the prevalence of family planning, coupled with the ongoing nuclearization of the family throughout the world and the prohibition of polygamous relations in most Islamic societies, the whole nature of family and its dynamics is changing.[28] In fact, the Qur'an itself has provided for a mechanism of interpretation of its contents. Known as the (abrogating and abrogated), this Qur'anic mechanism allows for the consideration of time and culture-bound factors of an allegorical nature (*mutishabihat*) and their insertion into some of its contents; these are to be dealt with and critiqued later in this study.

Educational Rights and Responsibilities of Women

Young girls and women have been entitled to education throughout Islam's fourteen centuries of existence. This allowance has much to do with some of the sex-neutral verses of the Qur'an that stress "the acquisition of knowledge" (*tahsil al-Ilm)*. The responsibility stems from the fact that women are enjoined not to put their acquired knowledge in ways unbecoming to a believer, and not to collude against their husbands. Married women are advised to safeguard the integrity of the household and of their husbands, and to pass their knowledge of the Qur'an and of the Hadith to their offspring as well as to whomever is desirous of such knowledge. Some of the Prophet Muhammad's wives (e.g., Aishah and Hafsah) were regularly consulted by those who sought the knowledge of the Prophet. In fact, in the *Tabaqat* texts, devoted to early Islam's personalities who possessed first-hand knowledge of the Qur'an and of the Hadith, we come across the so-called *Sahabiyat*, the Women Companions of the Prophet Muhammad. For example, citing information from Arabic sources, Mahmud Shahabi provides information on one hundred and thirty such women Companions, some of whom were in the position to give legal opinions on jurisprudential matters.[29]

From its inception, Sharia Law has followed the Qur'anic principle that believers are entitled to learn the contents of the Qur'an, since depriving any believer of the Qur'an is tantamount to committing a grave sin, if not an outright crime. In juristic texts, the importance of the acquisition of the knowledge of the Qur'an has been covered under the headings of *kitab al-`ilm* (book of knowledge, which means the knowledge of the Qur'an and Hadith) as, for instance, in *Shaih al-Bukhari*, *al-Muwatta*, *Muslim Sahih*, etc. Reading the juristic texts, one gets the distinct impression that parents are deemed responsible for their offspring receiving the proper knowledge of the Qur'an and of the Prophetic Hadith. Muhammad Azmi argues that the Prophet Muhammad in Madina set an "educational policy" to educate all the Madinans. He writes: "Sending teachers outside Madinah was one of the main features of the policy of the Prophet; at least forty of these teachers who were on their way to Bi'r Ma'unah were murdered."[30] This educational policy naturally covered young girls and women. Lamy al-Faruqi, citing Muhammad Fuad Abd al-Baqi's work, states: "The Prophet even commanded that the slave girls be educated, and he asked Shifa bint Abidallah to instruct his wife Hafsa bint Umar."[31] Similar views have been expressed in Aisha Lemu *e al.*,[32] and in Amina Wadud-Muhsin's work. [33]

The thrust of the Qur'an is that because Allah has revealed the Word to Muhammad for guidance and for salvation, believers should read the Qur'an and learn its contents so that they can apply them to their daily lives. There is a voluminous literature on the question of the compilation of the Qur'an that is beyond the scope of this study. The gist of the Muslim historiography on this issue is that the Qur'an was compiled during the Prophet Muhammad's tenure. Each revelation was committed to memory and was then recorded by the Prophet's scribes. The gist of Western scholarship is that the Qur'an was compiled during the reign of the third Caliph, Uthman ibn Affan (644-656). In any case, there is no doubt that, during the Prophet's time, the acquisition of knowledge of the Qur'an initiated a new era in the Muslim Arab's gigantic move towards enlightenment. This enlightenment, of course, is reflected in the Sharia Law's systematization. Those with first-hand knowledge of the Qur'an and of the Hadith were in a position now to apply their knowledge to the question of the law. In other words, the acquisition of Qur'anic knowledge not only enlightened the bedouin Arab's mind, it also redirected the Arab's view of the law from a tribal-ancestral-based view of the law (*sunna*) to a Qur'anic view of the law. This knowledge of the Qur'an was quite important. Whereas ancestral law could not be contested by reference to a corpus of law, the new one had this capacity. Every man and every woman was free to seek the knowledge of the Qur'an and of the Prophet's Tradition. Of course, this ability does not mean that anybody was free to challenge the authority of the Sharia Law based upon an arbitrary interpretation of the letter, or of the spirit, of the Law. The point is that a reference to the principal source of the Sharia Law was now available to those who sought justice. Justice could not be administered on an arbitrary basis. Not only did the judge have to explain the basis of his decision, he had to take into consideration the moral aspect of his decision.

The Qur'an does not allow for the formation of a privileged group of men with a monopoly on the acquisition of the knowledge of the Scripture. On the contrary, it encourages men and women believers, to read, to recite and to commit to memory its contents as well as to consult with one another over the contents of the Qur'an. At the same time, it advises believers not to stray from the path of the Scripture by dwelling on some parts that may seem strange to them. Those who dwelled upon the incomprehensible parts of their divine scriptures, strayed from the direct path of their scriptures and corrupted their religion, is the thrust of the Qur'an. In different verses as, for example, in (xx,114; lviii, 11), the text advises believers that Allah increases the "knowledge" of those who seek the Qur'an and especially those who seek it in earnest. The term *Ulama* indicates the common vernacular that Muslims call the Men of the Knowledge of Islam. But this recognition has never reached the status of a class of men whose sole profession has been to monopolize the exegesis of the Qur'an. There is one Hadith that says that the *Ulama* are inheritors (*wurrath*) of the Prophet(s) purporting that in Islam, it is the *Ulama* who are the official guardians of Islam. Believers, however, are duty bound to teach each other the matters of the religion and of the Qur'an and Hadith.

There are various Hadith and other historical documents that show that believers used to travel to various learning centres of the Islamic world (Rey, Qum, Harat, Marv, Bukhara, Macca, Madina, Kufah, Basra, Damascus, Cairo and Qirawan) to acquaint themselves with the knowledge of the Hadith.[34] Even during war, commentators observe, the Qur'an advises (ix:122) that some believers should stay behind and continue learning the affairs of the religion. The same learning principle applies to the Prophetic Hadith. That is why in all classical and post-classical Hadith manuscripts, we come across a section that is customarily called as "the Book of Knowledge" *(Kitab al-Ilm)* that contains various Qur'anic injunctions and Prophetic Tradition regarding the acquisition of knowledge.[35] In fact, knowledge is so important in the eyes of the Qur'an that one of the signs of "Hour" (the end of the this world) is when knowledge of religion is taken away to be replaced by ignorance – a Hadith that has been narrated on the authority of Anas Ibn Malik.[36]

Women have never been deprived of education in the Islamic world, and there were women educators of the Qur'an and of the Prophet's Tradition. Women and young girls, however, have historically been segregated in schools and in mosques, and therefore in modern times they have been deprived of the benefits of co-education on the grounds that such practices have a corruptive impact upon both sexes. But, from a purely legalistic perspective, it can be argued that the Sharia Law does have a positive disposition towards young girls' and women's education.

Witness Rights and Responsibilities of Women: An Argument

There is no doubt that the Qur'an, through a good number of its injunctions, some of which we have already discussed, elevated women's general standing in the Hijaz region, something on which most Muslim and Western scholars of the subject agree. There is, however, one enigmatic position of the Qur'an: the testimonial worth of women (educated or uneducated) in legal matters. This is enigmatic because, as I have already discussed, the Qur'an has regularized the propriety of various forms of property utilization through injunctions that apply to both sexes. Logically, the utilization of property in the form of selling, buying, renting, or bequeathing is capable of empowering the owner of the property. At the same time, this utilization of property is capable of improving one's educational opportunities, including those of women. Once men and women are equal in terms of their educational worth and abilities to utilize property, why not apply this empowerment to women's testimonial worth? In other words, what is the source of this gender-based inequality when it comes to women's testimonial worth in legal matters? If the Qur'an allows for education of women as well as allowing women to own property, why this inequality? Why is women's legal testimony considered to be unequal to men's? This needs some elaboration, and is discussed in the next sub-section.

The testimonial worth of women in legal matters Scholars have commonly observed that the Qur'an has equated the testimonial (*shahadah*) worth of two women to the value of one man's testimony as, for instance, in (ii:282) which is a very complex verse. The first part reads:

> O ye who believe! When ye contract a debt for a fixed term, record it in writing. Let a scribe record it in writing between you in [terms] of equity. No scribe should refuse to write as Allah hath taught him, so let him write, and let him who incurreth the debt dictate, and let him observe his duty to Allah his Lord, and diminish naught thereof....[37]

The above part of the verse is about the financing of debt and directed towards the general populace. It intends to regulate the abusive *Jahiliyah* practice in debt financing whereby the lender imposed inordinate interest on the principal of the loan. What is immediately apparent from the tone and thrust of the verse is that it was either directed towards men who, as a general rule, were more powerful than women, or those men who were more powerful than others. The next part of the verse concerns the incurring of debt by those who may be considered as the disenfranchised of the society in the Qur'an. It reads: "But if he who oweth the debt is of low understanding, or weak, or unable himself to dictate, then let the guardian of his interests dictate [in terms of equity]. And call to witness from among your men, two witnesses."[38] The third section of the verse is about the testimonial worth of men and women that following the thrust of the verse ought to have something to do with debt financing. This part reads: "And if two men be not [at hand] then a man and two women, of such as ye approve as witnesses, so that if the one erreth [through forgetfulness] the other will remember. And the witnesses must not refuse when they are summoned."[39] The fourth part of the verse advises that the debt contract be recorded in writing regardless of its amount. It reads:

> Be not averse to writing down [the contract] whether it be small or great, with [record of] the term thereof. That is more equitable in the sight of Allah and more sure for testimony, and the best way of avoiding doubt between you; save only when it is actual merchandise which ye transfer among yourselves from hand to hand. In that case it is no sin if ye write it not.[40]

The last part of the verse is about witness in the case of selling. It reads: "And have witnesses when ye sell one to another, and let not harm be done to scribe or witness, If ye do [harm to them] lo! It is a sin in you. Observe your duty to Allah. Allah is teaching you. And Allah is Knower of all things."[41]

The verse in its totality represents the Qur'anic view as to how transactions (selling and buying) are to be recorded, contracted and witnessed. Nonetheless, this verse and some others have been interpreted as taking two women's testimony equal to one man's testimony, provided that the man be not mentally deficient because women are supposedly more "emotional", "irrational", "whimsical" and "forgetful". However, the verse concerns itself with incurring debt, conducting trade and commercial activities that prevailed at that time.[42] In such a situation, equating two women's testimonies to one man's testimony was perhaps a cautionary practice. The verse, in my educated judgment, reflects a historical aspect rather than a biological "truth", as the verse has traditionally been interpreted. Because the verse reflects a historical aspect, it easily lends itself to time- and social condition-bound reinterpretation. In other words, the verse could and should be taken in its historical context and not as reflecting heaven's endorsement that women are less valued than men in the eyes of God.

This said, there is no doubt, however, that this verse has been interpreted to equate two women's testimonial worth (whether educated or not) to one' man's testimonial worth. It has become a fact that, in the Sharia Law, the testimony of two women carries the weight of one man's testimony (in all schools of Islamic jurisprudence). This interpretation of the verse is odd, considering that the general thrust of the Qur'an is that men and women are basically equal to one another notwithstanding some of the concrete physiological differences that separate them from each other. Although, as I shall explore later in this chapter, there are Qur'anic verses that put women a degree below men, there are verses that lend themselves to egalitarianism. The above interpretation is also odd because, if we lay out the dynamic relationship that has historically existed between the rise of private property and gender, we ought to reach a different conclusion about this verse, as is discussed below.

Property, education and the testimonial worth of women The owning of property allows for the development of certain capabilities in the realms of social action, such as entering the market, manipulating it, or withdrawing from it. Success in the market requires education and savvy; the market empowers the individual with its social, economic, and psychological dimensions. The question here is whether Islam, in its primordial format, restricted women by restricting their realms of social action. Most feminist scholars have argued that Islam, like Christianity and Judaism, represents the ideological blueprint of patriarchism, and of patriarchal social relations of production. Therefore, notwithstanding some of the advances that Islam might have brought, the general thrust of Islam has been restrictive towards women. Two of the most frequently cited examples to substantiate this argument are verses that advise modesty in appearance (*hijaab*), and verses that equate the testimonial worth of two women witnesses to one man (*shahdah*). However, as I have already established above, education is very much stressed in various chapters of the Qur'an. There are gender-neutral generic Qur'anic terms and verses on the importance of writing and learning as well as how to document transactions. These premises of the Qur'an applied to both men and women who conducted both local and long-distance trade, and therefore had to deal with various aspects of trade as, for instance, with incurring debt (ii:282) that we cited above. I have already dealt with the testimonial worth argument; the issue of veil (*hijaab*) I shall deal with in Chapter 8 of this study.

The Prophetic Tradition's Role in Shaping Women's Status in the Sharia Law

Another bastion of women's historical status in the Sharia Law has been the Prophet Muhammad's Tradition. In both Sunni and Shii juristic texts Muhammad's Tradition has been treated under the title of the Sunna of the Prophet which is also known by its more common term, the Hadith. Below, Hadith and Sunna are synonymous unless stated otherwise. Both Sunni and Shii juristic texts have unanimously stressed the importance of this source in shaping women's social and legal status notwithstanding the interpretive differences between the two versions.

The Prophetic Tradition covered a wide range of subjects that depict Muhammad's conduct at home and in the public. His conduct as a young man in Macca, and, later, as a judge and political leader in Madina, as well as his marriages and his campaigns against his adversaries constitute his Tradition that is preserved in a complex literature known as the *Sira*. The Prophetic Tradition (e.g., the Sunna, or Hadith), comprising the second source of the Sharia Law, is quite important for any basic understanding of women's status in the Law. In the rest of this chapter, I shall explain the meaning of the Hadith first, followed by the role that the Hadith has played in the canonization of women's status.

The Hadith

Hadith generally means something that has been said, has been communicated orally, or has been written down. It stems from the root word *ha-d-th* which means a new thing that has come about.[43] Its derivations appear in the Qur'an as, for instance, in (xii, 6), (xx, 113), (xxi, 2), (xxxiv, 19), (lxvi, 3) and (xcix, 4).[44] The importance of the Hadith stems from several factors. First, it can be attributed to the Prophet, and to the Shii Imams. Second, it is numerous, convoluted in very arcane language and terminology, and has historically been constructed by the Islamic male establishment reflecting a definite male-structured point of view towards the sacred and the mundane in Islam. Whether inadvertently or by design, the Hadith has been utilized by both

Sunni and Shii jurists in strengthening the base of power differentials between the sexes. As such, the Hadith helps to construct a male-centred view of women's status that has influenced the formation of the Sharia Law. This structured view does not lend itself to a Weberian value-free process of interpretation. It has to be challenged thoroughly by those reform-minded people in modern Islamic societies who want to improve women's social and legal status. This challenge has to be of an immanent nature – namely, it has to be based on the very source that gives legitimacy to the Sharia Law. In other words, to challenge the traditionalist Islamic forces, one should challenge them on their own game and not on a set of criteria that are alien to the Sharia Law. Naturally, this view does not apply to those Islamic countries which have abandoned the Sharia Law and have adopted secular laws.

Because of the sensitive nature of the Hadith (the fact that it could be used for unsavoury political ends), the Prophet allegedly enjoined Muslims from writing down the Hadith – a very contentious point among modern scholars.[45] Muslim theologians devised meticulous methods to check the authenticity of the Hadith, to the effect that it became an important branch in Islamic sciences in the first century of Islam.[46] These compilers, known as the *Muhaddithun* (literally men who compile the Hadith), were so concerned about preserving every memory of the Prophet, including his sayings and deeds, that they recorded every Hadith, even the most unlikely ones lest some valuable information about the Prophet be lost. At the same time, they tried their best to ensure that non-authentic ones would be weeded out through a re-evaluation process of the Hadith and of the chain of narrators. Thus, the classical methodology of the authentication *(Isnad)* of the Hadith emerged.

For any Hadith to be posited within the realms of authenticity, it has to have the following: (1) a written text known as the *matn* or an oral tradition known as the *riwayat*; (2) a document known as the *sanad*; (3) a chain of narrators of that Hadith known as the ***muhaddithun*** (for males), or ***muhaddithat*** (for females). The term *isnad* means authenticated documents pertaining to any Hadith.

Hadith can be authenticated based on the testimonies of men and women who surrounded the Prophet Muhammad during his life. These personalities not only committed to memory the verses that the Prophet received in the form of revelations, but also recorded and transmitted his sayings and deeds for future generations of Muslims. The primary purpose of this recording was, of course, to retain the memory of Muhammad in the most detailed form possible. There were other secondary purposes as well. One such secondary purpose of the Islamic *isnad* has to do with the fact that the compilers did not want to lose an iota of information that related to Muhammad's personality, life events or those who surrounded him, as previously stated. This concern had its inevitable outcomes: the authentic Hadiths, whose number barely reached a couple of thousand during the Prophet's and his Companions' tenures, reached such a multitude that Imam Bukhari (810-870 CE) when compiling his famous *Shahih al-Bukhari*, is reported to have had in his possession more than 600,000 Hadiths.

Different variations of the same Hadith, transmitted through multiple channels, had made the literature bulky and archaic. Phillip Hitti writes: "Bukhari, who was a Persian, selected out of 600,000 traditions he collected from 1000 sheikhs in the course of sixteen years of travel and labour in Persia, al-`Iraq, Syria, al-Hijaz and Egypt some 7397 traditions which he classified according to subject matter...." [47] Even that number is contested. Muhammad Muhsin Khan, a contemporary scholar, translating Imam Bukhari's compendium from Arabic to English, states that Bukhari, in sifting the forged Hadiths from the authentic, "...laboured day and night although he had memorized such a large number he only chose approximately 7275 of which there is no doubt about their authenticity." [48] He puts the larger number at "over 300,000 Hadiths..."[49] There is such a huge difference between these two figures that one wonders how the much smaller numbers (e.g., 7397 in Hitti and 7275 in Muhsin Khan's translation) could have been judged as authentic. This difference between the two numbers, of course, is a question of methodology. The posing of this question does not negate the fact that Bukhari and later compilers of the Sunni Hadith (e.g., Muslim, Abu-Dawud, Tirmizi, Ibn Majah, Hanbal, Nasai, Malik, Baihaqi, etc.), could sift authentic Prophetic Hadith from forged ones.[50]

Next to the *isnad*, Muslim men of letters (both Sunni and Shii) devised a methodology of tracing each Hadith to its sources. In this methodology not only every Hadith, but also every transmitter, had to be authenticated in accordance with a set of criteria. Was he/she[51] of sound mind, of appropriate requisite knowledge and judgment? Was he/she of good reputation? Was he/she trustworthy? Was it probable or possible for him/her to have had knowledge about the source and Hadith that was being cited? In other words, not every Hadith was acceptable, neither was every transmitter of such. The closer a transmitter was to the following: (1) the Prophet Muhammad, (2) Muhammad's Companions, (3) disciples of Muhammad's Companions, (4) the Prophet's immediate family, (5) the Madinan Helpers of the Prophet, (6) Maccan Emigrants, the more likely was a certain Hadith to be authentic. With the passage of time, the following classification emerged in the Sunni juristic texts regarding the degree of authenticity of any Hadith (for the Shii version a somewhat different classification.)[52] The following eight items (out of a total of fourteen categories) are taken from Ibn Majah, one of the so-called Six Authentic (*Sihah Sittah*) sources of Sunni Hadiths:[53]

(1) *Sahih*: Sound. The transmitter of the Hadith is known for his/her sound knowledge of the text, its history and its authentic sources. He/she is known for being a true believer, of high moral and sound character. There is no interruption in the chain of transmitters linking the original text to the Prophet Muhammad.

(2) *Hasan*: Good; The same as Sahih except for the transmitor's memory which is known to be weak. In principle, a Hasan Hadith ought not to contradict a Sahih one whose transmitter is known to possess an exceptionally strong memory.

(3) *Daif*: Weak. If a Hadith does not possess the qualities of Sahih-Hasan, then it falls within this category. Such a Hadith is defective in its chain of transmitters, and does not resonate harmoniously with the general beliefs concerning the Prophet Muhammad's Tradition.

(4) *Mutawatir*: Continuous. This Hadith is being reported by many authoritative sources of different times that make this category almost immune to any falsification.

(5) *Mashhur*: Well-known; A Hadith which is backed up by at least three authoritative sources.

(6) *Mauzu*: Spurious. It is a fabricated Hadith that is falsely attributed to the prophet Muhammad.

(7) *Mursal*: The authority for thus type of Hadith is traceable to a Tabii without the name of the Prophet Muhammad being mentioned. A Tabii is a disciple of the Prophet's Companions.

(8) *Munqati*: A Hadith whose chain of transmitters has been broken at a certain time in history, or does not lead all the way to the Prophet and other primary sources.

There are other Hadith classifications, some of which are of a less precise categorization. In both Sunni and Shii creeds, however, the Hadith occupies the most important source (next to the Qur'an), of the Sharia Law. In spite of this complex system of authentication, many forged Hadiths found their way into the juristic texts and therefore into the Sharia Law. In other words, one has to be extremely cautious about Hadith especially of those that aim to put women in a subservient and socially and legally marginalized position.

Subjects Covered in the Hadith

Many subjects were covered in the Hadith. For example, Bukhari's *Sahih al-Bukahri* covers subjects under 93 headings. The first volume is subsequently divided into 12 sub-heads, the so-called *baab* (pl. *abvaab*, literally means door) with 562 subjects covered in them. Other volumes are similar in detail, as, for instance, Muslim's *Sahih.* Other works on the Hadith and commentaries on the Qur'an (e.g., Muslim's *Sahih Muslim*, Ibn Sad's 8 volume *Tabaqat*, Tabari's *Jame al-Bayan*, Malik Ibn Anas's *Al-Muwatta*, Shafii's *Risalah*, etc.) are all of the same exhaustive nature. Hadith literature, Azmi opines, "is the richest source for the investigation of early Islamic history. It provides material for an understanding of the legal, cultural and religious ideas of those early centuries." [54]

Women in the Hadith

How are women treated in the Hadith? Both positively and negatively depending on the subject. Besides positive ones, especially those that pertain to a number of prominent women of Early Islam such as Khadijah bint Khuwaylad, Aishah bint Abu Bakr, Fatimah bint Muhammad, Hafsah bint Umar, Aminah bint Wahab and Zaynab bint Ali, there are quite a few Hadith that fit squarely within the "different spheres" context. The proponents of different spheres argue that women are men's spiritual equals, but they are not men's temporal equals. Women are created for different responsibilities than men because Allah has created the two sexes for "different spheres". They also argue that this difference has its concrete base in the Qur'an, as well as in the Hadith and therefore in the Sharia Law. They conclude that the Prophet Muhammad (and in the case of Shiism, the Shii Imams) not only supported this disposition towards women, but also practised the injunctions of "different spheres" that the Qur'an advises.

Those who propose the "different spheres" premise base their view on a number of Hadiths as, for example, one which maintains that: "Those who entrust their affairs to a woman will never know prosperity!" [55] This Hadith is cited in Bukhari's *Sahih al-Bukhari* as an authentic Prophetic Hadith giving much ammunition to the proponents of "different spheres" premise who are adamantly against any move in the direction of equality in gender relations, a move that has to be initiated through legal means and therefore constitutes a powerful challenge to the overall concept of the law in Islam. The "different spheres" premise has also been utilized by a good number of secular scholars who have proposed that Islam is inherently sexist and even misogynous, promoting inequity in gender relations.

Women's religious sincerity in the Hadith There are various Hadiths that cast doubt on women's religious sincerity, the so-called *ikhlaas* or *imaan* giving much ammunition to the misogynist view that women should not seek temporal equality with men because their religious sincerity is suspect. At the same time, this view is an important obstacle to women's much needed involvement in the field of Islamic jurisprudence one of whose primary requisites is sincerity in belief the cornerstone of piety, which is a quintessential of valid judgment within the context of the Sharia Law. Historically speaking, a number of verses and Hadiths have been utilized for this purpose. For example, Bukhari's very first narrations (on the subjects of "belief", "Muslims", "feeding", "love of apostle" and "sweetness (delight) of faith," covering about ten Prophetic Hadiths) give the impression that women believers were excluded.[56] Worse still, there is the following Hadith:

> Narrated by Ibn Abbas: The Prophet said: "I was shown the Hell-fire and that the majority of its dwellers were women who were ungrateful." I was asked, "Do they disbelieve in Allah?" (or are they ungrateful to Allah?) He replied, "They are ungrateful to their husbands and are ungrateful for the favours and the good (charitable deeds) done to them. If you have always been good (benevolent) to one of them and then she sees something in you (not of her liking), she will say, "I have never received any good from you".[57]

This Hadith has acquired a strange life of its own, having being transformed into a misogynist and absurd format in seeing women as basically ungrateful and therefore potential candidates for being sent to Hell. In fact, a dominant theme in Middle Eastern classical literature centres on the ungratefulness of women, a theme that has almost been elevated into a "genetic" characteristic of Middle Eastern women. What is completely ignored here is the symbolism of this Hadith: it centres on a regime of conduct based upon consistency in benevolence toward one's spouse. It was through this benevolence that the Prophet eradicated the many abusive practices that prevailed in *Jahiliyah* period, including those in family life.

The Hadith symbolically admonishes those women who, in spite of this improvement in their status, did not appreciate this Islamic benevolence.

Is it plausible to propose that the Prophet Muhammad could indeed cast doubt on the religious sincerity of women as a social category considering that it is the unequivocal position of the Qur'an that it is the piety (*taqwaa*) of believers that endear him/her to Allah and no other spurious factors (race, gender, creed, social class and its attributes)? Could the Prophet ignore this gender-neutral aspect of the Qur'an and utter such a misogynist Hadith in which the majority of Hell-dwellers are purported to be women? It should also be remembered that in Islam a believer's sincerity in faith requires reciprocity between words and deed. For example, the Prophet is reported to have said: "And belief is both saying and acting, and it increases and decreases".[58] The following verses of the Qur'an, among others, were revealed upon the Prophet concerning this aspect of belief: (iii:173), (ix:124), (xviii:13), (xix:76), (xxxiii:22), (xlvii:17), (xlviii:4) and (lxxiv:31).[59] Ironically, these are mostly gender-neutral, speaking about how one's faith may increase or decrease over time. Only (xviii:13) is about the faith of the allegorical men of *al-Kahaf*.[60] It is also important to briefly explore the content of belief in Islam. Believers are advised not to turn their faces to either East (the site of the mighty Sasanid Empire) or West (the site of the mighty Byzantine Empire) but towards Allah, to believe in the next world, in the Day of Judgment, in the Angels, in the Book, and in the Prophets, to set slaves free, to be compassionate towards the weaklings of society, to be patient in times of hardship, disease and ailments.[61] In the eyes of the Qur'an, men and women are equally responsible for good and evil. There are very powerful verses such as (xlviii:6) which addresses both males and females and calls upon them to ward against misdeeds, stating that Allah is aware of one's true intentions: "And may punish the hypocritical men and the hypocritical women, and the idolatrous men and the idolatrous women, who think an evil thought concerning Allah...." This strenuous warning is preceded by the promise "That He may bring the believing men and the believing women into gardens underneath which rivers flow, wherein they will abide, and may remit from them their evil deeds...." [62]

There are many verses, scattered in different chapters of the Qur'an that are gender-neutral, as well as verses that are directed towards one sex. The apparent use of the male personal pronouns in the Qur'an sounds a cautionary note about the text's language whereby a word may be used with differences in meaning, context and grammatical nuance. The language does not lend itself to a free and literal translation. Although male personal pronouns are being used more often to remind men who were then, and are now, in the position of power; women are not ignored. The lexicography of the Qur'an does not lend itself to literal translation. All word, term, verb, proposition, and even whole sentence structures argued over since the Qur'an's appearance, need to be put in their proper contexts.[63] This premise means that a free reading of the Qur'an without a proper knowledge of these contexts, can lead the reader to erroneous conclusions. However, it should not be construed that only an elite cadre of men have the God-given right to tell the rest of the world about the content of the Qur'an and the Hadith.

The issue of polygamy Among both Sunni and Shii classical commentators, the viability of polygamy is self-evident. Taking polygamy as a man's God-given right, in both Sunni and Shii versions of the Sharia Law, men are allowed to marry up to four permanent (*aqdi*) wives provided that they maintain "justice" and equity among their wives. This means a fair and just regime of conduct towards each and every wife. In modern times most Islamic societies have abolished *muta* in the same manner that they have abolished slavery, child labour and the application of the cruel and unusual punishments, because most modern Islamic societies have found these as misogynous practices and some others as impossible to carry out in this day and age. Are such abolitions anti-Qur'anic? We have already discussed the issue of crime and punishment in previous chapters. Let us now take the issue of polygamy.

The Qur'anic base of polygamy The fourth verse of the chapter *al-Nisa* first warns of the importance of being fair to orphans and then allows polygamy: "And if you fear that you will not be fair in dealing with the orphans then marry of the women as may be agreeable to you, two or three or four...."[64] This verse has historically been treated as an explicit Qur'anic justification for polygamy in spite of the fact that the second part of the verse is an important qualifier: "and if you fear you will not deal justly, then marry only one or what your right hand possess. That is the nearest way for you to avoid injustice." [65]

Mirza Tahir Ahmad, a modern commentator, argues that, although this verse allows a man to have more than one wife at a time, it should be understood in the context of his relations with the orphans under his care. He writes:

> As the permission concerning polygamy has been given in connection with the subject of orphans, it should be taken to be primarily based on the question of the care of that much-neglected class of society. There are cases when the interests of orphans can best be protected by marrying one or more

> wives from among the female wards or from other women as the exigencies of circumstances may require.[66]

To the above should be added the social and historical context of the verse. The verse was revealed in the aftermath of the Prophet Muhammad's Uhud campaign (625) against the Maccan idolaters, in which many Muslim men fell in the battlefield, leaving many young orphan girls and widows among the newly established Muslim community of Madina. This verse was interpreted as heaven's permission for Muslim men to marry as many as four permanent wives provided that they could establish a regime of just treatment among them even though verse 130 of *al-Nisa* maintains: "And you cannot keep perfect balance between wives, however much you may desire it...."[67]

The traditional defence of polygamy Those who defend polygamy have argued that man has "insatiable" desire for sexual gratification and see polygamy as a divinely sanctioned practice irrespective of time, conditions and the thrust of the very text itself which is modesty in all social affairs including sexual gratification. The logical implication of this stance is that this verse is of an everlastingly valid nature because men would always have insatiable desires. The Prophet Muhammad's marriages are also utilized to justify this stance. For example, in present-day Iran where polygamy has been legalized, the rationale has been given by the Ayatullah Murteza Mutahhari, who has formulated this stance, as follows: "man is slave to sexual gratification, woman is slave to kindness." [68] Let us explore this argument in detail below.

Does this verse make the Qur'an of a sexist nature because it finds a solution for man's supposedly insatiable sexual desires? Is it misogynous because it ignores the sexual desires of women? Those who argue that the verse is of an everlasting valid nature as a solution for man's "insatiable" sexual desires ignore the historical context of the verse. They also ignore the just treatment clause and the Qur'an's many warnings to maintain self-control. At the same time, those who consider this verse as misogynous ignore its context; nevertheless, one could easily read the verse in either direction if it were to be taken in isolation.

Traditionally, this verse has been taken as an explicit Qur'anic injunction and has been defended on the basis of "biologism". Simply put, men are looked upon as having biologically-induced insatiable sexual needs that, if unsatisfied, would lead to corruption. The rational solution is polygamy.[69] The alternative is corruption, prostitution, and all kinds of half-imaginary and half-true ills of non-Islamic societies. However, for these circles, the idea that women have sexual desires is only meaningful in so far as this desire is satisfied within the matrimonial context. The end result is overtly sexual men, who seek sexual gratification next to sexually marginalized women whose sexuality is passive and matrimonial. Ironically, the same defenders of biologism are offended rightfully of the charges that have been levelled against the Qur'an and the Prophet Muhammad. Accordingly, the Qur'an is concerned with the Prophet's conjugal relations because he is looked upon as the creator of the Qur'an (some argue that Muhammad was a womanizer, others argue that he was involved in self-indulgence).[70] However, once the verse is put in its historical context, a different picture emerges – one that in my judgment debunks charges of biologism and self-indulgence.

The Prophet Muhammad's marriages It is common knowledge that the Prophet Muhammad married nine permanent wives, five more than allowed by the verse. All the subsequent marriages took place after Muhammad's first wife, Khadijah, died in 619, a time that preceded the Prophet's emigration from Macca to Madina. It is a matter of historical record that Muhammad remained monogamous during his marriage to Khadijah which lasted for 28 years (or 25 years depending on whether one takes Muhammad's age at the time of marriage as 23 or25)[71] despite the fact that polygamy was practiced by men of wealth and prominence during the *Jahiliyah* period. By marrying Khaidjah, Muhammad was now in that position.

According to Muhammad Husayn Haykal, the Prophet's next wife (after Khadijah) was Sawda bint Zama, the widow of Sakran bin Amr bin Abd Sahams, a woman who had none of the worldly attributes (beauty, riches, political power, charm etc.) that could entice those who accuse the Prophet of being a "womanizer" to marry her. She was the widow of an early Muslim convert, having struggled for the spread of Islam.[72] Her plight was known to the Prophet after her husband had died, therefore he married her to elevate a deserving Muslim woman's position, pure and simple, Haykal argues. The charge of sensualism hardly makes any sense, considering whom he married and for what purpose. This charge also does not make any sense considering that, by the time of Khadijah's death, the Prophet was 49 years of age having had passed an important part of his mature adult life in a loving monogamous relationship. At the same time that the Prophet married Sawda, he also married Aishah. She was a juvenile (some sources cite her age as six, some as nine and, some as fourteen [73]) when she married the Prophet. All the sources maintain that the marriage was consummated only when Aishah had reached the age of puberty. [74] The sources maintain that Aishah possessed beauty and charm and, as narrated by Bukhari and Ibn Saad, the heavens had to intervene showing Aishah's image to the Prophet to lessen his grief over Khadijah's death.[75] This age difference is unusual for our time, but not necessarily for the time of the Prophet and given Arab customs of child marriage. In the Hijaz region's warm climate, young girls mature early. Even at that, the charge of sensualism makes no sense considering that both Muslim and Western scholars have argued that the Prophet's marriages to Aishah, and later, to Hafsa (the daughter of Umar), were politically motivated because both Abu Bakr and `Umar were among the prominent men of Mecca and their support was crucial to Islam's success.

Did they consent to marriage? The answer is a definite "yes" based on authentic Hadiths and the fact that the Prophet would have had hardly married them if he knew that consent was forced upon them. Not only is it a Qur'anic injunction that marriage should not be entered under duress as for instance in (4:19, 24, 25,), there are also authentic Hadiths on this aspect of marriage:

> Narrated by Abu Huraira: The Prophet said, "A matron should not be given in marriage except after consulting her; and a virgin should not be given in marriage except after her permission." The people asked, "O Allah's Apostle! How can we know her permission? He said, "Her silence (indicates her permission)."[76]

In the Hadith corpus, we come across marriages that were invalidated by the Prophet because consent was granted unwillingly, as for instance in the case of Khansa bint Khidam Al-Ansariya: "...her father gave her in marriage when she was a matron and she disliked the marriage. So she went to Allah's Apostle...and he declared that marriage invalid." [77]

Then, there is the Prophet's marriage to Zaynab bint Jahsh the wife of Zayd, his adopted son. This is one of the most glamorized stories about the Prophet's "sensualism", "lust" and a host of other such baseless charges. The "glamorized" version of the story, argues Hyakal, is that the Prophet went to see Zayd, but he was not home. The Prophet saw Zaynab in a provocative and charming dress in her bedroom and supposedly desired her.[78] Upon hearing the incident, Zayd supposedly proposed to divorce Zaynab so that the Prophet could marry her, but he refused whereupon the verse 37 of The Clans (*al-Azhab*) chapter was revealed. This verse makes it lawful for a believing man to marry his adopted son's wife, once all formal steps of divorce have been observed and the appropriate waiting period has elapsed. The real story of this incident is quite different, according to Haykal who utilizes primary sources in demystifying this marriage. Zaynab bint Jahsh was the daughter of Umayma bint Abd al-Muttalib, the parental aunt of the Prophet. She was Muhammad's cousin, brought up together with him from early childhood. Muhammad was quite aware of her charm and beauty as they grew up together. The fact that he arranged her marriage to Zayd easily debunks the idea of Muhammad's desire for her.[79] Zaynab was a proud woman from a well- to-do Qurayshite family. Her arranged marriage to Zayd was ill-suited because Zayd was a freedman from a lower class.

Following Haykakl's rationale, opines Pickthall, the arrangement by the Prophet was to destroy the *Jahiliyah* customs and pride in one's genealogy; therefore, Zaynab's feelings were not taken into consideration,[80] as an exception to the observation above that marriage was not to be allowed under duress. Both parties were unhappy, as evinced by their many complaints to the Prophet. Zaynab complained because she did not consider Zayd as her equal, Zayd complained because Zaynab would not submit to him in the manner expected from a believing wife.[81] The alternative was divorce. When Zayd asked the Prophet to allow him to divorce Zaynab, he was told to keep his wife and to fear God.

Because the marriage itself was ordained by the heavens (as evinced by the verse 36 in *al-Azhab*: "And a believing man and a believing woman, if God and his Apostle have decided a matter, may have no free choice in regard to their case....") it was only natural that its dissolution was ordered by the same source (verse 37). Haykal further argues that the Prophet's subsequent marriage to Zaynab should also be understood in the context of verse 4 in *al-Azhab* which reads: "And He has not made your adopted sons to be your actual sons...." This verse means that: "He allows the adopted son to marry one who had been the wife of him who adopted him, and also [He allows] the one who adopted to marry her who was the wife of him who was adopted." [82] By marrying Zaynab, the Prophet set a precedent for the above, for how else were this law to be realized, ponders Haykal?

Going through these and other marriages of the Prophet, one hardly finds a Prophetic allusion to biologism – the idea that polygamous relations are ordained by God because men have insatiable sexual desires. The overwhelming evidence is that the Prophet's marriages were initiated by a variety of social and political considerations, including his utmost concern for improving women's status.

It is true that we come across a number of Hadiths that give the impression that the Prophet was exceptionally endowed in sexual prowess, as, for example, in Bukhari's narration of Anas Ibn Malik: "The Prophet used to go around [have sexual relations with] with all his wives in one single night, and he had nine wives." [83] A similar Hadith is about the funeral procession of Maimuna, one of Prophet's wives. Narrated by Ata, on the authority of Ibn Abbas, the Hadith maintains that, during the procession, Ibn Abbas said: "This is the wife of the Prophet so when you lift her bier, do not jerk it or shake it much, but walk smoothly because the Prophet had nine wives and he used to observe the night turns with eight of them, and for one of them there was no night turn." [84] One has to take these and similar Hadiths with much caution, not that the Prophet did not try to maintain sexual justice among his wives, but that justice here implies more than perfect sexual relations. Justice also implies compassion, understanding, respect, sharing, taking one's spouse seriously by consulting with her, empathy, honesty and a host of other such attributes that make a relation long-lasting and fulfilling.

The Jahiliyah Marriages

It has often been observed that Islam is a misogynous religion because it reflects a patriarchal social and legal relations which by necessity treats women unequally. In contrast, pre-Islamic social and legal relations were based on matriarchy, a view that is supported by the sexual freedoms of women expressed in the *Jahiliyah* marriages. There is no doubt that Islam, like all other world religions has lent itself to various class-based interpretive nuances, some of which have been misogynous, a point that I have repeated and documented time and again in this study. However, the Qur'an has provided for the humanitarian treatment of women in general and married women in particular. Verse 5 in *al-Nisa* reads: "And give the women their dowries willingly. But if they, of their own pleasure, remit to you a part thereof, then enjoy it as something pleasant and wholesome."[85] The importance of this verse is to be understood in the context of two facts of the *Jahiliyah*. First, depending upon the type of marriage, the dowries were given to the family, or the clan of the bride, rather than to the bride herself. The practice was open to abuse because young daughters could in effect be sold to the highest bidder. This practice was especially abusive if the brides were orphans.

Second, the *Jahiliyah* practice of entering into marriage itself was quite varied and sometimes bordered on prostitution. For example, Aishah is narrated by Urwa bin al-Zubair concerning four types of marriage in the *Jahiliyah* period.[86] These were: *Sadiqa, Istibda, Muta*, and *Qaif*. A synopsis of each is provided below.

In the *Sadiqa* type of marriage, "...a man used to ask somebody else for the hand of a girl under his guardianship or for his daughter's hand, and give her Mahr and then marry her."[87]

In the *Istibda* type of marriage a man would ask her wife to have sexual relations with a man of higher social standing in order to be impregnated by him. The reason for this arrangement, we are informed by the above Hadith narrated by Aishah, was to get a child from the so-called noble breeds, the very notion the Prophet was fighting against.[88]

The *Muta* type of marriage is explained in the Hadith as follows: "...a group of less than ten men would assemble and enter upon a woman, and all of them would have sexual relations with her. If she became pregnant and delivered a child...she would send for all of them....naming who ever she liked...and he could not refuse." [89] Even if one argued that this was not prostitution *per se*, it could be of a very arbitrary and abusive nature in that the woman could name anyone as the child's father.

In the *Qaif* type "many people" would go to the same woman who would refuse none of the men sexual relations. If a child were born, the services of a *qaif* – one who had the expertise of resembling a child to his/her father – would be sought to identify the child's father.[90]

Only the *Sadiqa* type of marriage was retained in Islam because it was condsidered as an honourable marriage; other types were repudiated by the Qur'an for various reasons.

I would like to reiterate the fact that these *Jahiliyah* practices of sexual relations, whether or not one chooses to call them marriage, could indeed have initially been institutionalized within the Hijazi tribal settings and social relations for a variety of reasons other than prostitution. Some scholars have implied that these types of sexual relations were remnants of pre-Islamic matriarchy that granted women sexual freedoms. Islam, by contrast, is "patriarchal" with the Qur'an as its ideological chart restricting women's rights for the benefit of patriarchal relations.[91]

There is no doubt that there are verses in the Qur'an that allow for such interpretations and actual practices. One thing which is certain is the fact that Islam allows, enhances and regularizes sexuality within the family. This regularization of sexuality is important because Islam is a religion with distinct doctrines of morality, codes of conduct, world orientation, philosophy of creation and ideals of social bonds that ideally link believing men and women with one another and the community and God. In other words, if the family is the most basic unit of social organization, the Qur'an as the overall blueprint of an ideal type of Islamic community, has to address issues of sexuality, family, conjugal relations, and spouses' rights and responsibilities. It should also be remembered that the general thrust of the Qur'an is that it is a book for all seasons, containing all things for all people. This claim of the Qur'an by necessity gave, on the one hand, an evolutionary perspective to Islam's constructs (social, political, economic, civic and existential). On the other hand, it bestowed a unique role on the Prophet as an initiator, interpreter and reformer for his own time and the conditions that surrounded the Hijaz region.

Given the issue of sexuality and its restriction by Islam, the Prophet Muhammad's claim to prophecy would have hardly made any sense to Meccans if he had behaved in any other way but honourably before assuming the mantle of prophecy. He could not have frequented the places of ill-repute during his youth; he could not have been a man of dishonest conduct, a liar, a cheat, a womanizer, a drunk, an idolater, an aggressor, a psychopath, a sociopath, or a wishy-washy double talker as some Orientalist scholars intimate. Muhammad, like other Prophets of God, such as Abraham, Noah, Lot, Moses and Jesus, exemplified throughout his life what the Qur'an characterizes as the *uswah hasana* – those who heed righteousness and follow it.

The nascent Sharia Law incorporated Muhammad's Tradition and his view of women's status in society at a time when the Law could not remain indifferent to the complex post-Muhammad social and political realties as the faith of Islam was being transformed into a world-class civilizing force in the Near East. This brings us to what I call the Janus face of the Hadith, the subject of the next section

The Janus Face of the Hadith

Any authentic Prophetic Hadith is capable of a dual and contrary utilization: to marginalize, or to empower, women. This double utility constitutes the Janus face of the Hadith whose utilization for either of these purposes depends on: (1) who utilizes a particular Hadith, (2) for what purpose, and (3) under what conditions. For example, let us take the case of the Hadith that I cited from Fatima Mernissi's work and analyse it in the context of the three factors that I have proposed above. The Hadith purports that, according to the Prophet, "Those who entrust their affairs to a woman will never know prosperity!" This Hadith has given much ammunition to fundamentalist

Muslim circles who, as previously mentioned, are adamantly against any move in the direction of equality in gender relations.

The question of who Mernissi has dealt with this Hadith's historical background, showing that it was uttered by the Prophet when he was informed that in the then Sasanid Empire, a woman had ascended to the throne.[92] By the time of the Prophet Muhammad's appearance, the Sasanid Empire had long since entered its structural and ideological crises period. The ascension of a woman to the Sasanid throne was due to a wave of imperial fratricide that had decimated the male candidates for the Sasanid throne. Therefore the Prophet's utterance of this Hadith could be analysed in the context of the social and political conditions that surrounded the Sasanid Empire – a conclusion that Mernissi draws to caution that the Hadith should not be construed as meaning that the Prophet was against women's participation in political affairs. She then gives examples of the Prophet's life and the important role that women played in his social and political affairs. This interpretation results from the fact that Mernissi is of the opinion that the Prophet's conduct was positive towards women, and that there are therefore many authentic Hadiths that one can use to empower women. There are, however, negative sides to the Hadith especially those that relate to the power relations between the sexes, the subject of the next sub-section.

The question of purpose Aware of the devastating and historical impacts of such negative Hadiths, Mernissi tries to posit these Hadiths within the social and political climate of their utterance, arguing that the Prophet took a benevolent position with regard to women and, therefore, his utilization of this Hadith ought not be considered as his legitimation of its content. The problem, of course, resides with the fact that this Hadith has already opened Pandora's Box with regard to all kinds of misogynous use by generations of Muslim men who have considered women ill-equipped for involvement in the politics of power. One such historical example pertains to one of the destructive events in the history of Early Islam, an event that is known as the Camel Battle (*al-Jamal*) in 656. In this battle, one of the most controversial female figures of Early Islam, Aishah bint Abu Bakr confronted Ali Ibn Abi Talib, the Fourth Rightly Guided Caliph. It was during this event that a certain junior figure, by the name of Abu Bakra (not to be confused with the First Caliph, Abu Bakr), purportedly utilized this Hadith to side with Ali.

Mernissi's argument is that Abu Bakra was hardly in a moral position to be allowed to use such a Hadith, but he did it nonetheless in order to justify his choice. Thus, Abu Bakra can be classified among a multitude of Muslim men who have reverted to these types of misogynous Hadith to marginalize women. The gist of Mernissi's argument is that such misogynous Hadith ought to be read with much care and placed in their proper contexts – i.e., who is it that transmits a Hadith, under what circumstance, and for what purpose? Mernissi's argument is meritorious in my judgment.

Mernissi's methodology of tracing the root of the Hadith to its source is important because she shows that the modern feminist school of thought (on Islam and on women's status) suffers from a strategic neglect in its treatment of all those different schools of thought that have arisen since the mid-nineteenth century to present Islam in its new format; feminism does not positively engage the very sources by means of which women's subjugation and marginalization have been legitimated in Islamic societies. Simply put, the modern feminist school has created a powerful academic discourse that is, at best, alien to the concrete problems of women in modern Islamic societies. Because the discourse sounds antagonistic to Islam, it is very easily challenged by those who argue that Islam has provided a wide range of rights and responsibilities for women and, therefore, that Muslim women do not need "alien" Western concepts in order to attain their deserved status.

My argument, of course, is that the Qur'an is amenable to an egalitarian approach to its contents and therefore there is no dichotomy whereby on the one side we have Islam and on the opposite side we have feminist demands; these are not mutually exclusive of each other. Western feminist methodology can give a helping hand to the women's liberation movement in many modern Islamic societies. Conversely, by arguing that there is a monolithic Islam which is against women's liberation, feminist scholarship, by and large, enhances traditionalist forces and movements who use misogynous Hadiths to justify their argument that women should refrain from meddling in politics. However, both feminist and traditionalist forces ignore other authentic Prophetic Hadiths that give a totally different picture of Muhammad's conduct towards women. He never restricted women from involving themselves in politics during his life and tenure. In fact, it can be shown that, during his tenure and those of the Four Rightly Guided Caliphs, women did play an active and prominent role in political affairs.

In addition, there were other women in this period who played important roles in political events. These women are now being depicted as model Muslim women by all kinds of revivalist Islamic movements even though these movements do not want to acknowledge the fact that these model women gained stature and prominence because they actively participated in the affairs of the community, rather than being confined to the household as nonentities. Reading the Hadith literature, one gets the impression that these socially and politically active women advised men, quarrelled with them, shared their griefs and moments of joy and triumphs. The socially and politically active personalities of Early Islam's women hardly matches the ideal picture that revivalist movements present of this period. If women were active in Early Islam, how can we force them into the household, forcefully segregate them from the opposite sex, seclude them and force them under the veil, and then brag about Early Islam's humane treatment of women? It is a sad fact that in the first decade of the twenty-first century, fundamentalist revivalist movements following the cues of Islamic Iran want to present segregation, seclusion and forced veiling as ideals towards which the educated modern Muslim woman of the twenty-first century ought to strive.

Finally, there are those who argue that Islam is a total way of life, implying that one cannot pick and choose, but that one ought to adhere to all the edicts, rituals, laws, mores and norms of Islam, the Qur'an and the Hadith and Sunna. This is an impossible task for the simple reason that the world of Islam is an indispensable part of the modern world being impacted regularly by the profound changes that modern technology, urbanization and social and legal relations have brought about. Marvels of modern technology such as internet have added a new dimension to the human conscientiousness, making it a global collectivist product. Local cultures and traditions are no longer isolated in the manner of the past, immune to the kind of scrutiny that they are now in the age of the internet revolution.

A totalitarian view of Islam is especially problematic for improving women's status in many Muslim societies because its frame is that of pre-capitalist patriarchy with its agricultural social and legal relationships. Fundamentalist movements, due to the fact that they strive to revitalize a golden age that supposedly existed in the past march backwards and, therefore, they try to posit the issue of women's status within the structural and epistemological frame of the past. This repositing takes place without any consideration for women's input and perspectives. As such, all religious fundamentalist movements are reactionary, misogynous and criminogenic.

In the remaining chapters of this study, I will explore the treatment of women in the Islamic Republic of Iran's criminal justice system that replaced Iran's secular system built during the Pahlavi monarchy (1925-1979). The gist of my argument is that women in Iran have gone through a profound process of victimization at the hands of the newly established Islamic criminal justice system. This is because of the totalitarian approach that the new Islamic regime has adopted in the past two decades with regard to the strategic aim of the revolutionary movement that toppled the Pahalvi monarchy replacing it with an Islamic system of governance and social and legal organization in Iran. The aim has been to 'Islamize" every conceivable aspects of social, economic, political and legal relationships in Iran based on Islam's Sacred Law. In this Islamization endeavour, women are being treated as passive subjects whose views and wishes have totally been ignored. As I will show in the subsequent chapters, women have been deprived of occupying any viable position in the Islamic judiciary system, and of pursuing justice-related professions other than being allowed to become prison guards in female prisons whose number has steadily gone up. For the first time in Iran's long history we witness the feminization of violent crimes next to a deepening process of the feminization of poverty – both of which are the result of the forced and totalitarian Islamization process in Iran. At the same time, Iranian women have been involved in anti-state political activities with the result that a good number of women have also been arrested, tortured and executed at the hands of a large network of secret police and revolutionary courts from 1981 to the present.

Notes

1. Mirza Tahir Ahmad, *The Holy Qur'an*, vol. II, commentary on verse 2 of Al-Nisa, p. 491; Khazaili, *Iilam-e Qur'an*, pp. 18-20; Lamya al-Faruqi, *Women, Muslim Society and Islam*, (Indianapolis, IN, American Trust Publications, 1988), p. 36.

2. Khazaili, *Ilaam-e Qur'an*, p. 20.

3. *Ibid.*, p. 32.

4. This discrepancy in the number of verses is due to the fact that one gets the number 177 if one were to argue that the verse: "In the Name of Allah, the Gracious, the Merciful" is to be counted as a separate verse in spite of the fact that it appears as the first verse of every chapter except "*Baraat*, which, however, is not an independent chapter but a continuation of the chapter *Anfal*." See Mirza Bashir-ud-Din Mahmud Ahmad, *The Holy Qu'ran: With English Translation and Commentary*, vol. 1, (Islamabad, Islam International Publications Ltd., 1988), p. 6. Otherwise, one gets the number 176, as for instance in Mohammad Pickthall's *The Glorious Qur'an*, (New York, Mostazfan Foundation of New York, 1984).

5. For a modern general discussion see John Esposito, *Women in Muslim Family Law*, (Syracuse, NY, Syracuse University Press, 1982); see also Fatima Mernissi, *Beyond the Veil: Male-Female Dynamics in a Modern Muslim Society*, (Cambridge, Schenkman Publishing Co.

Inc., 1975), Chapter 3, which gives a detailed account of pre-Islamic marriage patterns; for a comparison between pre- and post-Islamic family relations and dynamics see B. Aisha Lemu and Fatima Heeren, *Women in Islam*, (London, The Islamic Foundation, 1978); see also Barbara Freyer Stowasser, *Women in the Qur'an, Traditions and Interpretation*, (New York, USA, Oxford University Press, 1994); see also Amina Wadud, *Qur'an and Woman: Reading the Sacred Text from a Woman's Perspective*, (New York, NY, Oxford University Press, 1999).

6. Pickthall, *The Glorious Qur'an*, p. 29.

7. *Ibid.*, p. 79.

8. For example, Pickthall, verses (ii: 180, 181, 182, 240) and in (iv: 1-9, 11-33, 176).

9. Pickthall, *The Glorious Qur'an*, p. 74.

10. *Ibid.*, p. 74.

11. *Ibid.*, p. 74.

12. Imam Muhammad al-Bukhari, *Sahih al-Bukhari*, vol. Vi, Hadiths nos 97 and 98 p. 79-80.

13. Mirza Tahir Ahmad, *The Holy Qur'an*, vol.II, p. 494.

14. *Ibid.*

15. Pickthall, *The Glorious Qur'an*, p. 75.

16. Imam Muhammad al-Bukhari, *Sahih al-Bukhari*, (Beirut, Lebanon, Dar al-Arabiyah) vol. Vi, Hadith no. 99, p. 81.

17. Pickthall, *The Glorious Qur'an.*, p. 75.

18. Imam Muhammad al-Bukhari, *Sahih al-Bukhari*, vol. Vi, Hadith no. 101, p. 82.

19. Pickthall, *The Glorious Qur'an*, p. 77.

20. Imam Bukhari, *Sahih al-Bukahri*, vol. vi, Hadith no. 102, p. 83. The parentheses are original.

21. *Ibid.*, vol. Viii, Hadith no. 723, p. 476.

22. *Ibid.*, vol. Viii, Hadiths nos 716 through 734, pp. 471-485.

23. Imam Muslim, *Sahih Muslim*, (Beirut, Lebanon, Dar al-Arabiyah), vol. iii, pp. 849-856.

24. Malik bin Anas, *Kitab al-Shuab al-Muwatta*, (np., nd.), pp. 312-323, corrected, prefaced by Muhammad Fuad Abad al-Baqi. For an abridged version see *Muwatta Imam Malik*, (Lahore, Pakistan, Sh. Muhammad Ashraf Publishers, 1991), pp. 333-336, translated from Arabic to English by Muhammad Rahimuddin.

25. For the English translation of this work see Majid Khadduri, *Islamic Jurisprudence: Shafii's Risala*, (Baltimore, MD, The John Hopkins Press, 1961).

26. See, for example, Muhammad Kulayni's *Kafi*, Muammad ibn Babuyah's *Min la-Yahzarah al-Faqih*, and Shaykh al-Taifa's *Al-Nihayah* as well as to Muahaqqaq Hilli's *Sharayi al-Islam*. For a general explanation of these works see Muhammad Taqi Daneshpadjuh, *Firhrestwareh Fiqh-e Hezar-o Chaharsad Saleh dar Zaban-e Farsi*, (Tehran, Iran, Shitkat-e Intesharat-e Ilmi wa Farhangi, 1367/1988); for other works on Shii schools see Ibn Nadim, *The Fihrist of al-Nadim*, vol. I, pp. 528-562; see also Shaykh al-Taifa Muhammad bin Hasan Tusi, *Tarjumeh Al-Nihayah fi Mujarrad al-Fiqh wa al-Fatawi*, vol. II, (Tehran, Iran, Intesharat-e Daneshgah-e Tehran, 1362/1983), pp. 424-468, translated from Arabic to Persian by A. Ahmad Yazdi; see also Muahaqqiq Hilli, *Tarjumh-e Farsi Sharayi al-Islam*, vol.II, (Tehran, Iran, Intesharat-e Daneshgah-e Tehran, 1364/1985), pp. 383-427, translated from Arabic to Persian by A. Ahmad Yazdi.

27. Pickthall, *The Glorious Qur'an*, p. 77

28. For some of these arguments see Lois Beck and Nikki Keddie (eds), *Women in the Muslim World*, (Cambridge, MA, Harvard University Press, 1978); see also Elizabeth Warnock Fernea (ed.), *Women and the Family in Middle East: New Voices of Change*, (Austin, TX, University of Texas Press, 1985); see also Leila Ahmad, *Women and Gender in Islam*, (New Haven, CT, Yale University Press, 1992); see also Valentine M. Mogahadam, *Modernizing Women: Gender and Social Change in the Middle East*, (Boulder, CO, Lynne Rienner Publishers, 1993); see also Hamid R. Kusha's entry, "Polygamy" in *The Oxford University Encyclopedia of the Modern Islamic World*, vol. 3, (Oxford, Oxford University Press, 1994), pp. 335-336.

29. Muhammad Shahabi, *Adwar-e Fiqh* (the Chronicles of the Jurisprudence), (Tehran, Iran, Intesharat-e Daneshgah-e Tehran, 1454/1975), p. 7.

30. Mohammad M. Azmi, *Studies in Early Hadith Literature*, pp. 4-5.

31. Faruqi, *Women, Muslim Society and Islam*, p. 37. She cites this information from Muhammad Fuad Abd al-Baqi's *al-Lulu wal Marjan fi ma ittifaqa fihi al-Shaykhani*, (Beirut: Dar al-Kitab al-Jadid, 1970), I, pp. 30-31.

32. Lemu and Heeren, *Women in Islam*, pp. 14-16.

33. Amina Wadud Muhsin, *Qur'an and Women*, (Kuala Lumpur, Malaysia,Penerbit Fajr Bakti Sdn. Bhd. 1993).

34. Azmi, *Studies in Early Hadith Literature*, pp. 198-199.

35. In Imam Bukhari's *Sahih al-Bukhari*, for example, this section covers fifty-four Hadiths, some of which interpret the Qur'anic stance on this important issue, and others of which interpret the Prophet's stance. See Imam Bukhar, *Sahih al-Bukhari*, vol. 1, pp. 50-99; In Imam Muslim's *Sahih Muslim*, this section contains twenty-three Hadiths. See *Sahih Muslim*, vol. 4, pp. 1402-1406.

36. Imam Bukhari, *Sahih al-Bukhari*, p. 68 (Hadith no. 80).

37. Pickthall, *The Glorious Qur'an*, p. 45.

38. *Ibid.*

39. *Ibid.*

40. *Ibid.*

41. *Ibid.*

42. For further detail see Hamid R. Kusha, "Minority Status of Women in Islam: A Debate Between Traditional and Modern Islam" in *Journal: Institute of Muslim Minority Affairs*, vol. XI., no. 1, January 1990, pp. 58-72.

43. Mohammad Qarib, *Tabyin al-Luqat Litibyan al-Ayat: Yaa Farhang-e Luqat-e Qur'an*, Vol. 1, (Tehran, Iran, Chap-e Marvi, 1987), p. 308.

44. *Ibid.*

45. See Azmi, *Studies in Early Hadith Literature*, Chapter 2.

46. A number of Western Orientalist scholars such as Ignaz Goldziher, and Joseph Schacht, writing on the subject of the Hadith, have opined that Hadith writing started in the second century of hijra – the Prophet's emigration to Medina in 622. Like most Muslim scholars, Azmi argues that this dating is wrong because both Guillaum and Schacht and Robson have followed Goldziher's misconception of the early writings and literatures of the Umayyad period in his much praised by Western scholars work, *Muhammedanische Studien*. The basis of the mistake is to be found in Goldziher's ignoring of a number of works that existed during the life of the Prophet, the Four Rightly Guided Caliphs and early Umayyad period maintains Azmi. He adds that "It seems as if in the period referred to works on the biography of the Prophet and other historical topics were in a very advanced stage. We find that work on the biography of the Prophet was begun by the Companions. Abdallah b. Amr b. al-Aas recorded many historical evens. It is possible still to trace his work in the Hadith narrated by Aamr b. Shuib (d. 118 AH) as he utilized his grandfather Abd Allah b. Amr's books." See Azmi, *Studies in Early Hadith Literature*, p. 5. Azmi also presents an excellent and extensive critique of Goldziher's premises and methodology (pp. 1-17).

47. Philip K. Hitti, *History of the Arabs: From the Earliest Times to the Present*, (New York, St. Martin's Press, 1970), 10th edn, p. 395.

48. Imam Muhammad al-Bukhari, *Sahih al-Bukhari*, Vol. 1, p. xv.

49. *Ibid*., p. xiv.

50. For a further detailed discussion of the problem of methodology see Azmi, *Studies in Early Hadith Literature*, pp. 28-33; Hitti, *History of the Arabs*, pp. 393-396. For a thorough critique of Goldziher's, Schacht's and Robson's treatment of the same subject see Azmi, *ibid*., pp. 18-27; for a Shii version of this methodology see Allameh Sayyid M.H. Tbatabai, *The Qur'an in Islam: Its Impacts and Influence on the Life of Muslims*, (London, Zahra Publications, 1987), pp. 47-63.

51. We know that there were woman transmitters of Hadith, such as Aisha, Hafsa, and Umm Salma, three of the Prophet's wives. See, for further detail, Kusha, "The Minority Status of Women in Islam" p. 64; for others see also Lemu and Heeren, *Women in Islam*, pp. 15-16; see also Azmi, *Studies in Early Hadith Literature*, p. 50.

52. For further detail see Hashim Maruf Hasani, *Akhbaar wa Athaar Saakhtegi: Seyri Enteqadi dar Hadith* (The False Khabar Documents: A Critical View in Hadith), (Mashahd, Iran, Intesharat-e Astan-e Qods-e Razavi, 1372/1994), translated from Arabic to Persian by Hosein Saberi (the Arabic title:*Al-mozuaat fi al-athar wa al-akhbar: arz wa daraseh*); see also Mostafa Hosseini Tabatabai, *Khiyanat dar Gozaresh-e Tarikh, Pasokhi be Ketab: Bist va Seh Sal*, (Dishonesty in Reporting History, A Response to the Book: Twenty Three Years), vol. 2, (np., 1986), pp. 13-23; see also Azmi, *Studies in Early Hadith Literature*, pp. 183-188.

53. This classification I have partially paraphrased and adopted from the "Introduction" section to the five volume English version of Imam Abu Abdullah Muhammad Ibn Yazid Ibn Majah al-Qazwini's *Sunan Ibn-I-Mjaha*, (Lahore, Pakistan, Kazi Publications, 1993). Translated from Arabic to English by Muhammad Tufail Ansari.

54. Azmi, *Studies in Early Hadith Literature*, p. xvii.; see also Fazlur Rahman, "Islam: An Overview", pp. 310-311, in *The Encyclopedia of Religion*, vol. 7, (New York, Macmillan Publishing Company, 1987), pp. 303-322.

55. Cited in Fatima Mernissi, *The Veil and the Male Elite: A Feminist Interpretation of Women's Rights in Islam*, (New York, Addison-Wesley Publishing Company, Inc., 1991), p. 1, trans. from French to English by Mary Jo Lakeland.

56. Imam Bukhari, *Shaih al-Bukhari*, vol. 1, pp. 18-21.

57. *Ibid.*, Hadith no. 28, p. 29.

58. *Ibid*, Hadith no. 1, p. 15.

59. *Ibid.*

60. The verse is taken from *Al-Kahaf.* It narrates the three questions that the Meccans had learned from Jewish Rabbis in Yathrib (Medina) and put upon the Prophet as a test of the authenticity of Muhammad's divine prophecy. Pickthall argues that verses 10-27 are about the first question: "the story of the youth who took refuge from persecution in a cave...and were preserved there as if asleep for a long period-a story which is generally identified by Western writers (e.g., Gibbon) with the legend of the Seven Sleepers of Ephesus." See, for further detail, Pickthall, *The Glorious Qur'an*, p. 290.

61. These are taken from *al-Baqara* (2:177) in the Qur'an.

62. Both verses are from the chapter *al-Fath* (Victory), Pickthall, *The Glorious Qur'an*, p. 558.

63. See on this subject, Hanna E. Kassis, *A Concordance of the Qur'an*, (Berkeley, CA, University of California Press, 1983); see also the late Ayatullah Mahmud Taliqani's *Partuwi az Qur'an, vol. 1, Surah-i Fateh al-Kitab, Ayah 1 to 144 Surah Baqarah*, (A Reflection from Qur'an, Chapter Al-Ftihah, Verses 1-144 of Chapter Al-Baqarah), (Tehran, Iran, Shirkat-e Sahami Intishar, nd.), pp. 1-22.

64. Ahmad, *The Holy Qur'an*, vol. 2, p. 493.

65. *Ibid.*

66. *Ibid.*

67. *Ibid.*, p. 568.

68. Murteza Mutahhari, *Nezam-e Huquq-e Zan dar Islam* (The Order of Woman's Rights in Islam), (Tehran, Iran, Intesharat-e Sadra, 1365/1986).

69. For a further analysis of this subject see my entry, "Polygamy" in *The Oxford Encyclopedia of the Modern Islamic World.* See also my paper "The *Mutaa* (Temporary Marriages) in the Islamic Republic of Iran: Choice, Consent and Legality" presented to the 1991 the Annual Meeting, American Society of Criminology, November 20-23, San Francisco, CA. For the analysis of the rationale of women who become mut'a (sighah) in Iran, see Shahla Haeri, "The Institution of Muta Marriage in Iran: A Formal and Historical Perspective" pp. 231-251, in Guity Neshat (ed.), *Women and Revolution in Iran*, (Boulder, CO, Westview Press).

70. For an extensive treatment of this theme and its critique see Norman Daniel, *Islam and the West: The Making of an Image*, (Edinburgh, Edinburgh University Press, 1962), reprint, pp. 135-161.

71. For example, Muhammad Husayn Haykal puts Muhammad's age at twenty-three despite the fact that "Most authorities put Muhammad's age at...twenty-five", argues Antonie Wessels

in his *A Modern Arabic Biography of Muhammad: A Critical Study of Muhammad Husayn Haykal's Hayat Muhammad*, (Leiden, E. J. Brill, 1972), fn. 14, p. 103; see also Muhammad Husayn Haykal, *The Life of Muhammad*, (Plainfield, IN, American Trust Publications, 1976), translated from Arabic to English by Ismail Ragi A. al Faruqi.

72. Haykal, *The Life of Muhammad*, pp. 290-292.

73. Haykal gives the age of eleven for Aishah at the time of he marriage to the Prophet, *ibid.*, p. 291; Rafiullah Sheahb, basing his argument on various early sources, gives a range of 9 to 20 years for Aishah's age at the time of marriage in his *Rights of Women in Islamic Shariah*, (Lahore, Pakistan, Indus Publishing House, 1986), pp. 50-56.

74. Imam Bukhari narrates two Hadiths about Aaisha's age at the time of her marriage to the Prophet, *Sahih al-Bukhari*, vol. 7, Hadith no. 64 and no. 65, p. 50.

75. Imam Bukhari narrates the following Hadith: "Narrated Aisha: Allah's Apostle said (to me), 'you were shown to me in a dream. An angel brought you to me, wrapped in a piece of silken cloth, and said to me, "This is your wife." I removed the piece of cloth from your face, and there you were. I said to myself, If it is from Allah, then it will surely be.'" *Sahih al-Bukhari*, vol. 7, Hadith no. 57, p. 42.Ibn Saad, *Tabaqat*, vol. 8, p. 54, cited in Stowasser, "The Status of Women in Early Islam," p. 29 in *Muslim Women*; see also the entry "Aisha" by Montgomery Watt, in *The Encyclopedia of Islam: New Edition*, vol. 1, (Leiden, E.J. Brill, 1960), pp. 307-308.

76. Imam Bukhari, *Sahih al-Bukhari*, vol. 7, Hadith no. 67, pp. 51-52.

77. Imam Bukhari, *Sahih al-Bukhari*, vol. 7, Hadith no. 69, p. 52.

78. Haykal, *The Life of Muhammad*, p. 295; Wessels citing Haykal in *A Modern Arabic Biography of Muhammad*, p. 101.

79. Haykal, *The Life of Muhammad*, p. 295.

80. Pickthall, *The Glorious Qur'an*, p. 439. Haykal, *The Life of Muhammad*, p. 110.

81. Haykal, *The Life of Muhammad*, pp. 296-297.

82. Wessels citing Haykal, *ibid.*, p. 111.

83. Imam Bukhari, *Sahih al-Bukhari*, vol. 7, Hadith no. 6, p. 5.

84. *Ibid.*, Hadith no. 5, p. 4.

85. Ahmad, *The Holy Qur'an*, vol. 2, p. 496.

86. Imam Bukhari, *Sahih al-Bukhari*, vol. 7, pp. 44-45.

87. *Ibid.*, p. 44.

88. *Ibid.*, pp. 44-45.

89. *Ibid.*, p. 45.

90. *Ibid.*

91. For this line of reasoning see "Islam's Appeal to Women in Iran: Illusions and Reality," p. 7, in Farah Azari (ed.), *Women of Iran: Conflict with Fundamentalist Islam*, (London, GB, Ithaca Press, 1983), pp. 1-71; see also Yvonne Yazbeck Haddad and John L. Esposito, (eds.), *Islam, Gender and Social Change*, (Oxford, Oxford University Press, 1998).

92. Mernissi, *The Veil and the Male Elite*, p. 50.

5 Iran's Criminal Justice System: From Secular to Sharia

In this chapter I shall explore Iran's experience with both the secular, and the Sharia Law-based criminal justice systems from 1925 to the present as a prelude to exploring women's crime and law-infracting behaviour under the two systems.

Iran's Secular Criminal Justice System under the Pahlavi Monarchy, 1925-1979

Iran's secular criminal justice system was formed under the Pahlavi Dynasty and its two monarchs, Reza shah (r.1925-1941) and Muhammad Reza shah (r.1941-1979). The Pahlavi Dynasty replaced the Qajar Dynasty (r.1779-1925) in 1925. An analysis of the reasons for this replacement is beyond the scope of this study. Suffice to state that from mid-nineteenth century, Iran's abject backwardness in social and economic spheres had become the main concern of a number of Qajar elite who had witnessed modern Europe's supremacy in every conceivable realms. Next to the Qajar elite, there were Iranian intellectuals who had reached the same conclusion. For these elite and intellectuals, the remedy for Iran's backwardness was the modernization of the state and economy and of the social relations, based on the European model. This modernization, of course, included a change in the legal norms based on secular laws. This simple proposal proved very difficult to implement because of internal and external factors that resisted such changes in Iran. Among these factors, Iran's traditional class and state structure, as well as the Shii religious establishment, played significant roles.

Behind their formation, these structures had centuries of evolution which had resulted in a very hierarchical concept of individual's place in the power structure. The person of the monarch was at the apex of the power pyramid followed by the elite who comprised a dual station of the men of the sword and the men of the cloth. The rest of the populace comprised the functionaries of the state and of the person of the monarch collectively characterized as the subjects (*ruaayaa*) of the sovereign. Law reflected the will of the sovereign in perpetuating the King's Peace in the realm, legitimated by the Twelve Imami Shii establishment who portrayed the sovereign as Allah's Shadow (*Zillullah*) on earth. The sovereign was looked upon as the purveyor of order in the realm and therefore as the protector of the Sharia and of its Law (*Sultan-e Shariat Panaah*).

Modernization was a direct challenge to Iran's traditional power structure and especially to the notion of law, its function, and its social and political thrust. Modern secular law challenges the Sharia Law's thrust that woman is not man's equal and that neither is a non-Muslim a Muslim's equal. Modern secular law conceives of persons as citizens of a country who have real and legal status equal in the proverbial eye of law regardless of sex, creed and religious affiliations. Monarchs, presidents and state functionaries are subjected to constitutional limitations. Since the French Revolution of 1789, there has arisen this profound idea that "men" are equal in the eyes of God (e.g., in the American Constitution) and in the eyes of humanity (e.g., in the French Declaration of Universal Rights). This, of course, is not new in Islam as we have already explained in some detail in previous chapters. What made the French notion of equality revolutionary in nature was the fact that this equality was being proposed within the confines of modern entrepreneurial capitalism which by and in itself was revolutionary.

Those who promoted these ideas in the late nineteenth-century Qajar Iran, gradually realized that their differences with the traditionalist forces were irreconcilable. This situation led to Iran's first modern revolution – the Constitutional Revolution that occurred between 1905 and 1911. Although many factors were responsible for this event, one factor of primary significance was the general perception that the Qajar shahs and their functionaries regularly abused the power of the state for their own benefit, an abuse that by the time of the Constitutional Revolution had already affected, quite negatively, the efficacy of Iran's traditional system of conflict resolution.

The Iranian constitutional revolutionaries, however, hoped that, through a parliamentarian form of governance, the cause of justice would be better served and a more rational and egalitarian system of conflict resolution would be institutionalized. It was the constitutional revolutionaries who also attempted to modernize Iran's criminal justice system so that it operated independently of regime politics.

Iran's First Modern Constitution

Iran's first modern Constitution was imposed by constitutionalist revolutionaries and popular will over and against the Qajar monarch, Muzaffar al-Din Shah, in 1906. He subsequently died and left the Qajar throne to his son Muhammad Ali Shah, a tyrannical despot who fought the constitutionalists fiercely and was finally deposed and sent into exile. The next and last Qajar, Ahamd Shah, was young, relatively enlightened and benevolent. He was deposed by the Iranian parliament on behest of Reza Khan, the ambitious and charismatic first Pahlavi (r.1925-1941). All these events took place between 1906 and 1925, a period during which attempts to institutionalize a constitutional form of governance comprised the social dynamics of the pre-Pahlavi era's social and political events. However, the constitutionalists were defeated at the hands of the First Pahlavi Shah, Reza Khan Sawaadkuhi, who established the Pahlavi Dynasty (1925-1979).

The Modern Judiciary and Courts in the Constitution of 1906

Consisting of 51 articles, the Constitution of 1906 established a parliament (called *Majlis*), and a senate defining the state organs' duties and responsibilities. A Supplementary Law was enacted in 1907 to clarify the rights of the people and of the members of the parliament, as well as the powers of the Shah, the ministers, the judiciary and the army.[1] Under the "Power of the Courts" there were 19 articles (Articles 71 through 89) and 5 Clauses in the Constitution of 1906 that defined the power, nature, and operational dynamics of the judiciary and courts. A synopsis of these articles gives the picture of a modern system of justice. The implementation of these articles, however, was a Herculean task for the state because of the Iranian powerful Shii establishment's resistance to modernity.

Iran adheres to Twelve Imami Shii Islam. However this brand of Shiism only became the country's official religion during the reign of the Safavid Dynasty (r.1501-1722). Prior to the Safavid reign, Iran adhered to Sunni Islam. There are commonalities between Shii and Sunni Islam, mainly in terms of principles such as the Unity of Allah, the Prophecy of Muhammad and the Day of Judgment. However, there are two principal beliefs that distinguish Shiism from Sunnism: justice as an eternal and intrinsic character of Allah and the necessity of perpetual leadership (*Imama*). Shiism, in turn, has several branches such as Zaydi, Ismaili, and Jafari. The last one is also known as Twelve Imami Shiism, which is prevalent in Iran. In this branch, adherents believe that, after the Prophet Muhammad, there were twelve perfect infallible beings (Imams) who followed Muhammad's footsteps in institutionalizing Shii Islam and its version of the Sharia Law. Because of their legacies of knowledge and pursuit of justice, the Imams have greatly affected

Iran's national psyche ever since Shiism became Iran's official religion during the reign of the Safavid Dynasty (r.1501-1722).

In the Shii version of Sharia Law, the struggle for temporal justice is quite important. The Shii clergy, as a loose corporate entity, has always maintained that temporal justice can be served only if the Shii Imams' heritage, and especially that of the First Imam, Ali Ibn Abi Talib, is emulated under the Shii clergy's hegemonic control. From the time of the Safavids, to the time of the Qajars, to the time of the Constitutional Revolution and the Phalavi monarchs, the Shii clergy has demanded that Iran's education and justice systems, as well as the institution of religious endowment (*awqaaf*), be left to its control. The Ayatullah Khumaini's battle cry against the Shah, Muhammad Reza Pahlavi, was that the shah had usurped the clergy's traditional rights in these areas. Like his predecessors, Khumaini was against the Phalavi shah's modernization of the education system and of law, crime, justice and penology based on secular norms and a modern system of conflict resolution. The Shii clergy's deep-rooted suspicion of secular law and system of conflict resolution can be explained in two ways. First, a secular-based system of law and conflict resolution renders the traditional Sharia system moot, weakening the clergy's hegemonic grip on the production and reproduction of Shii Islam's hermeneutics – that is, what Twelve Imami Shii Islam is and what constitutes its legitimacy insofar as the issues of the text, sub-text and their interpretive nuances about Shiism are concerned. Second, the Shii clergy has had, for several centuries, a privileged position in Iran's complex class structure. The clergy, as a loose corporate entity, has been part of Iran's intelligentsia. A select number of the Shii clergy have played a significant role in Iran's anti-establishment revolt movements (from the mid-nineteenth century to the time of the Islamic Revolution), at the same time that the majority of the Shii clerics have been in the camp of the traditionalist forces whose main function has been to enhance Iran's traditional power structure, including the Safavid, Qajar and Pahlavi monarchs.

This seemingly contradictory position of the clergy can be comprehended better if one were to consider that, prior to modernization efforts, the clergy occupied a very important position in Iran's traditional social and political structures of power. The clergy has historically maintained that it is the earthly representative of Allah and of the Prophet Muhammad on earth as the purveyor of law and justice. In addition, the clergy's power emanates from its loose, but nevertheless corporate, structure and knowledge of Shii Islam's complex and arcane corpuses. The clergy's expertise in the Shii version of Sharia Law, coupled with its loose corporate structure, has given the clergy a central position in Iran's traditional mechanism of conflict resolution.

Naturally, because of this historical legacy, any efforts to modernize Iran's justice system has always aroused suspicion in Iranian Shii religious circles. In fact, these and similar efforts in most Islamic societies, which started in earnest from the mid-nineteenth century to the present, have been looked upon as deviations from the ideals of true justice that can only be reached under the Sharia Law. The Islamic Revolution, for example, argued the regime's dignitaries, has made this idea possible. Accordingly, Iran is now under the one and only true version of an Islamic establishment that has tried to institutionalize the Twelve Imami Shii version of the Sharia Law and its style of conflict resolution. We have to go back to 1906 and explore the problem that the constitutionalist faced in resolving this secular-religious duality.

To resolve this problem, the drafters of the 1906 Constitution supplemented it with a number of clauses on 8 October 1907. Two of these are of especial importance for our purpose here. As observed by Abolghasem Sedihi, under the caption "General Principles," Article 1 reads: "The State religion of Iran is Islam, according to the true Jafariya doctrine, recognizing twelve Imams. The Shah of Iran must profess and propagate this faith."[2] Article 2 maintains that "...At no time may the enactments of the...National Consultative Assembly....be at variance with the sacred precepts of Islam...."[3] To safeguard this ideal, a body of clerics was charged with the duty of rendering judgment on this issue; this required giving the body veto power over bills that it believed to contravene Islamic precepts, edicts and injunctions. This mechanism in the Constitution of 1906 led to many parliamentary skirmishes in the newly established Iranian *Majlis*. The two main camps that comprised the Iranian political scene between 1906 and 1925 have been dubbed as the constitutionalists (*Mashrutih-khaahaan*) versus proponents of Shari Law (*Mashruih-khaahaan*). Both camps used this article as a focal point in their parliamentary manoeuvring as to what constituted Islamic and/or un-Islamic bills and legislation, including matters that pertained to the judiciary.

The mechanism proved to be inoperable because neither side was willing to compromise on this central issue. In the meantime, the would-be first Pahlavi shah (Reza Khan Sawaadkuhi), in his capacity as the Minister of War under the last Qajar Ahmad shah, was jockeying for power. He controlled Iran's only viable and disciplined Kasak Division, and was in league with the British-backed Iranian landed aristocracy and some prominent Shii clerics whose main concern was their share of the power in the volatile and yet dynamic Iranian political scene. The former sought to institutionalize post-Qajar Iran's social, economic and political institutions and progressions in the context of modern and secular laws; the latter sought this in the context of the Sacred Law. The position of the Minister of War, Reza Khan Swaadkhui, was not clear. He courted the two sides as he strove for power in post-Second World War Iran that had been occupied by the Allied Forces, an occupation that brought the country nothing but misery, hunger, and lawlessness.

The Rise of the Pahlavi Dynasty and its Modern Reforms

The first Pahlavi shah came to power in 1925 through a *coup d'état* against the last Qajar, Ahmad shah, who was subsequently arrested and sent into exile. Thus, the Pahlavi Dynasty was established with the blessing of the British and Russian Great Game diplomacy that had divided Iran into two distinct zones of influence. Reza Khan assumed the title of shah and ruled as a dictator until 1941, when he was forced into exile and replaced by his son Muhammad Reza Shah, an event that also took place through the interventionist policies of the Allied Forces who had invaded Iran during the Second World War.

Between 1928 and 1935, a number of reforms took place in the judiciary. More and more, Islamic precepts, such as marriage and divorce, were relegated to civil matters. The penal codes were regulated in accordance with the Western European (e.g., Belgian and French) concepts of crime and punishment, replacing those based on the Shii version of the Sharia Law. Some of these reforms took place in the Constitution itself. The Constitution of 1906 was amended in 1925, 1949, 1957 and 1967 in order to enhance the person of the monarch and his range of powers. As a result, under the two Pahlavis, three types of modern law were recognized in the judiciary – civil, criminal and administrative. A synopsis of each is provided. I would like to caution my reader that due to the paucity of English sources on the subject, I have relied on Georges Levasseur's and his co-author William Buttler's classical research on Pahlavi Iran's judicial system.[4]

Modern Civil Law

The conceptual and organizational inspiration for modern law came from the French system. Civil cases were put under the jurisdiction of the district court presided over by magistrates. Unless the competence of the court was questioned, the judgments of the civil courts could be appealed to the Civil Chamber of the Courts of Appeal sitting in each principal town of a department, according to Levasseur. Appeal in matters concerning error in law (i.e., in cassation) occurring in both courts were heard before a "Civil Chamber of the Court of Cassation, which is a single court for the whole country sitting in the capital at the Law Courts in Tehran."[5] In addition, small claims courts were institutionalized after 1965. Called the houses of equity, these tribunals were scattered all over the rural areas of the country in order to ameliorate the plight of those with small claims. In 1966, similar institutions, arbitration councils, were established in 300 towns throughout the country. The composition of the councils was similar to that of houses of equity: laymen were chosen from among leading citizens. These laymen dealt with a variety of minor cases.

Modern Criminal Law and Courts

Levasseur argues that the inspiration for Iran's modern courts came from the French model in which offences were recognized and categorized based on secular norms which, in turn, required their insertion in a modern criminal code. These offences (I have paraphrased from Levasseur) had a definite hierarchy in terms of their importance in the new criminal code:

(1) Offences against the state, the person of the sovereign, the constitution and government.
(2) Offences against the public order and security.
(3) Offences against public property and/or state officials.
(4) Offences against a person's physical well-being, followed by those committed against a person's freedom.
(5) Offences against children and the deceased.
(6) Offences against family and public norms of morality.
(7) Offences that injure the public's sense of fiduciary trust and responsibility, such as lies and perjury.
(8) Offences against private goods, or the individual's right to private ownership.
(9) Alcohol-and drug-related offences.
(10) Rural offences.

As the above list clearly indicates, the pre-Islamic Revolution criminal code followed offence conception based on modern capitalist notions of crime and misdemeanours, at the same time that the state's security took precedence over individual liberty. With the passage of time, this stress on the security of the state against both external and internal threats turned into a bizarre notion that any threat to the state was a direct threat to the person of the sovereign and vice versa. This official mentality was expressed within the context of a slogan "God, King and Country" that in the eyes of the Pahlavi political establishment became a litmus test of the average Iranian's sense of loyalty to everything that the Pahlavi monarchy stood for, including, ironically, its view of Islam and its rather long list of Shii cleric supporters from the 1920s to the 1970s.

Besides having a modern criminal code, Iran's secular criminal justice system followed a modern view of conflict resolution in the context of duly appointed courts of law. Criminal cases were referred to ordinary and/or special courts, depending on the nature of the case under consideration.

The ordinary courts were composed of the following:

(1) The police courts
(2) The houses of equity
(3) The arbitration councils
(4) The criminal courts
(5) The assize courts.
(6) The special courts were composed of the following:
(7) The military tribunals
(8) The juvenile courts
(9) The criminal court of governmental officials
(10) The financial court.

It is beyond the scope of this study to go into the details of these courts and their operational dynamics other than giving a synopsis of each below. What is certain is that Iran, under the Pahlavi monarchy as I will show in Chapter 7, was among "nations not obsessed with crime" to use Freda Adler's famous title of a comparative study, in which she discusses the issue of crime in modern Third World and Islamic, as well as ex-Iron Curtain, societies.[6] Although Iran was not included in that study, Adler's rationale applies to Iran under the Pahlavi regime. For example, following Iran's tradition of resorting to informal means of conflict resolution, the family played a very important role in settling disputes between members of the family and among residents of the neighbourhoods. Resorting to the police was frowned upon, especially when the parties to a conflict had not exhausted their informal options. That is why the police court was a last resort as far as the general public was concerned. It was looked upon as a formal mechanism for those who lacked the more respected informal means of conflict resolution.

The criminal courts had jurisdiction over more serious crimes. Sitting in the principal town of the district and presided by several justices, the criminal courts had jurisdiction over cases that could not be heard in the above mentioned courts. Their decisions could be appealed "to a criminal chamber of the court of appeal. This sits in the principal town of the department (Art. 340 et seq. C.C.P.)."[7]

Finally, there were the assize courts which presided over criminal cases, for which a minimum of two years' imprisonment were prescribed. Functioning without a jury, these cases could be referred to military tribunals, especially when the offences were political in nature. The decisions were delivered by three to five professional judges, depending on the severity of punishment, ranging from life imprisonment to capital punishment. "Appeal by way of 'cassation' is available against the decisions of courts of final jurisdiction. The appeal lies with the criminal chamber of the Court of Cassation (Art. 430 C.P.P.)."[8]

The special courts were those that had original jurisdiction over cases that could not be referred to the above mentioned courts. These were: (1) the military tribunals, (2) the juvenile courts, (3) the criminal court of government officials, and (4) the financial court. A synopsis of each is given below.

The military tribunals, states Levasseur, were composed of three superior officers in the first instance cases and five in the appeal process; these tribunals presided over cases that concerned purely military offences, common law offences committed by members of the armed forces, and the cases that involved the internal or external security of the state. In the prosecution and defence of the cases, only military judges, prosecutors and defence counsels participated. A civil defence was not allowed. The death penalty could be imposed, with the shah having the power to commute death sentences to a lesser type of penalty. On the question of the death penalty, Levasseur observed that:

> One example is drug offenses, in respect to which the law is particularly severe....Other examples are offenses against the external or internal security of the state, sabotage of public services, particularly water, gas and electricity. Military Tribunals had already been entrusted with cases of armed robbery by about 1960. Subsequently they were entrusted

> with cases of arms smuggling and more recently still consideration has been given to making them responsible for trying offenses against economic laws (partly failure to reduce prices in accordance with price control) following the promulgation in August 1975 of principles 13 and 14 o the White Revolution.[9]

The end result was the clogging of the military tribunals, especially considering that these tribunals did not have specialized sections to deal with the variety of cases brought before them. Insofar as appeal was concerned, Levasseur observed:

> It may be noted that the decisions of military tribunals are always taken by a simple majority, whatever may be the gravity of the sentence. The only means of recourse against decisions of the appeal tribunals is the appeal by way of cassation, but this will only lie if the Shah gives leave for the exercise of this recourse.[10]

The establishment of the juvenile courts, observed Levasseur, goes back to the year 1959. Delinquent acts relating to two types of minors were heard before these special courts: minors between the ages of 6 to 12, and minors between the ages of 12 to 18 years. Detention in penal institutions applied to minors over the age of 12. The time of detention could vary between six months to five years. Serious criminal acts of minors over the age of 15, could earn them between a minimum of two and a maximum of eight years' imprisonment. Upon completing one-third of the sentence term, the adjudicated juveniles could be reconsidered for parole.[11]

The criminal court of governmental officials presided over offences committed by governmental officials. Established in June 1928, and presided by administrative officials, this court went through a number of changes in 1931, 1936, 1949 and 1954. It consisted of a public prosecutor, advocates general and deputies, as well as specialized examining magistrates. Whereas the prosecution could detain the accused pending trial, the examining magistrates were authorized to gather information from various sources. The magistrates could order the seizure of property, its release, bail and warrants. Before holding a public hearing, the court established *in camera* its *prima facie* case against the defendant(s). Insofar as appeal was concerned, Levasseur says: "Since the Criminal Court for Government Officials has the rank of a court of appeal, its decisions cannot be appealed except by recourse to the Court of Cassation. This recourse is open to the prosecution even in cases of acquittal."[12]

The financial court presided over fiscal fraud. It seldom brought charges of financial fraud against powerful personalities who were connected with the Pahlavi Imperial Court. Close relatives of the shah were known for their financial corruption and nepotism. Following the 1973 boom in crude oil prices initiated by the OPEC, Iranian oil revenues skyrocketed leading to grandiose development and modernization plans. Iran spent a vast amount on all kinds of sophisticated weapon procured from such Western powers as the United Kingdom, Germany, France, Italy and the United States of America. The waste, bribery, corruption and misuse of oil revenues reached unprecedented levels. The ineffectiveness of the Iranian modern judiciary was nowhere more pronounced than in its total neglect of this type of white-collar crime.

Modern Administrative Law

Inspired by the French model, the Council of State was the court authorized to preside over administrative acts. "Created by a law of 1960, duly promulgated and published, this court has unfortunately never been constituted, so that its role is non existent and the law passed on this subject has received no practical application," observes Levasseur.[13]

The Partisan Nature of the Modern Secular Justice System, 1925-1979

Iran's modern justice system was inspired by the French system without the rationale that permeated the more neutral and non-partisan operational dynamics of the French courts, police and corrections. For example, the modern Iranian criminal law, codified as a penal code, was adopted from the Napoleonic codes at the beginning of the twentieth century. However, whereas the Napoleonic codes followed the rule of law philosophy within French democracy and institutions, reflecting the operational dynamics of the French judiciary, the Iranian criminal law could hardly reflect this philosophy. One important reason was that the two Pahlavi shahs did not show any respect for the impartial operations of the Iranian justice system. Both shahs had assumed power through foreign interventions and therefore regarded the judiciary as a political instrument at the service of the monarch's powers. The thrust of the

1906 Constitution was that the monarchy was not a reigning, but rather a symbolic, institution.

Second, the Pahlavi modernization efforts, important as they were in improving the organs of the state and bureaucracy, did not promote independent decision-making, democracy and democratic institutions. This inability to progress towards democracy became the battle cry of the Iranian intelligentsia who argued that, following the *coup d'état* that had overthrown the democratic regime of Muhammad Musaddiq in 1953, Iranian modernization and development schemes were of an externally imposed and superficial nature designed to promote Iran's dependent nature as a rich source of raw material (oil, natural gas and other minerals). Iran was to be incorporated into the world capitalist division of labour not based on democratic institutions but as a client state of the world hegemonic capitalist core power, the United States of America. The Iranian intelligentsia was especially critical of the partisan nature of the judiciary, arguing that it had lost its integrity and independence by being transformed into an instrument of oppression in the hands of the shah. This position, of course, is not completely true and there is this rethinking that the judiciary did try to maintain its integrity and there were judges and prosecutors who resisted the Pahlavi courts' attempts to undermine the judiciary's independence and integrity.

Third, following the shah's reform measures in the 1960s (known as the White Revolution), Iran's judiciary, many believed, had become thoroughly politicized. Any criticism directed against the shah's reform measures was treated as "subversion," inspired by what the shah characterized as the "forces of Black and Red Reactions". Black symbolized religious fanaticism and red stood for international communism. Based on this conspiratorial rationale, the security of the state became synonymous with the intactness of the shah's dictatorial powers, requiring brutal suppression of every form of dissent, whether civil, social or political. This state of affairs towards dissent was the Pahlavi shah's notion of the rule of law, a premise discernible from the Establishment of the Security Organization Act of 1336 (1957). Although composed of five articles, the Act has relevance for our discussion in the first two articles:

> Article 1. For the purpose of security of the country and prevention of any kind of conspiracy detrimental to the public interests, an organization under the name and style of "the National Information and Security Organization," affiliated to the Premier's Office shall be established. The

Chief of the Organization shall hold the rank of the Assistant to the Prime Minister and shall be appointed by a Decree of His Imperial Majesty the Shahanshah.

Article 2. The functions of the National Information and Security Organization are as follows:

a) Obtaining and collecting items of information required for the maintenance of national security.

b) Pursuing the activities which constitute a portion of espionage and the acts of such elements conducted against the independence and integrity of the country or those who act in the favour of an alien.

c) Repressing the activities of those groups whose establishment or management has been or will be declared as illegal; likewise preventing the formation of the groups whose aim or policy is against the Constitution.

d) Foiling conspiracies and plots against the national security.

e) Inspecting, discovering and investigating the following crimes:

1. The crimes which are provided for in the Treason Act, approved on 22nd Khordad 1310 (1931).

2. Misdemeanours and/or felonies provided or in Chapter One, Part Two of the Penal Code approved on 23rd Dey 1304 (1925).

3. The crimes mentioned in Articles 310, 311, 312, 313, 314, 316 and 317 o the Court-Martial Act 1318 (1939).[14]

The other articles, 3, 4, and 5, describe the operational dynamics of the National Information and Security Organization that came to be known by its acronym SAVAK. With the passage of this Act, Iran under the shah, Muhammad Reza Pahlavi, was transformed, step-by-step, into a police state with SAVAK, the armed forces, police and gendarmerie as its main organs for oppressing any form of dissent. Concurrently, the judiciary was forced into a partisan and mostly oppressive instrument of coercion at the service of monarchy and its parasitic comprador bourgeoisie and international allies.

The Pahlavis' modernization efforts propped up a justice system that reduced, quite mechanically, some types of predatory crime (e.g., homicide, burglary, robbery) in Iran at the expense of democratic rights of the people; at the same time, it ignored financial corruption. The Islamic Revolution hoped to rid the judiciary of such partisanship. The next section gives a synopsis of the Sharia Law-based criminal justice system.

Iran's Sharia-based Criminal Justice System, 1979-1999

The present criminal justice system in Iran, based on the Twelve Imami Shii version of the Sharia Law, is a product of the Islamic Revolution in 1979. This system of law and conflict resolution, formed in the early 1980s during the tenure of the Ayatullah Ruhullah Musavi Khumaini, replaced the secular system that the two Pahlavi monarchs had established in Iran during their consecutive reigns.

The Constitution of the Islamic Republic

The Constitution of the Islamic Republic, replacing the Constitution of 1906, is composed of 175 articles and a Preamble (amended in 1988) and provides for a republican form of government structured upon the Ayatullah Khumaini's notion of Islam. As I shall explore in some detail, this Islam of Khumaini is premised on the doctrine of the Jurist Council (*Wilayat-e Faqih*) with a set of criteria pertaining to the following:

(1) Leadership
(2) The theory of the state
(3) The nature of authority
(4) The administration of justice within an Islamic constitutional system of checks and balances.

It is within this structure that Iranian women's social and legal status, proposes the Islamic Constitution, ought to be structured so that women can attain a highly deserved puritanical status in an ideal Islamic society. The implication of the Constitution's thrust is that once this status is achieved, women will lead an ideal, puritanical, and crime-free way of life.

Women's Status in the Islamic Constitution

The Preamble to the Constitution praises the positive role of Iranian women in the success of the Islamic Revolution. The Preamble states that woman is central to the viability of the family in which woman's main duty has been defined as motherhood. This "centrality" of motherhood is not a matter of choice, it is an absolutely God-ordained and self-evident reality in the eyes of the drafters of the Constitution. This status, therefore, has to be institutionalized within "Islamic criteria" (*mawazin-e Islami*), a very important concept to be explored in Chapter 8. The Preamble also states that Iranian women had suffered more than men under the Pahlavi monarchy because the Pahlavi regime was, accordingly, at the service of colonialism and therefore Iranian women now need more compensation in terms of their rights.[15]

The Preamble states further that "the family" constitutes the essential social institution that facilitates human development and progress. It also rejects the subjugation of woman as an object of sexual pleasure, rejecting the transformation of women as instrument of work by lauding "motherhood" as a critical responsibility for Iranian women.

The Preamble charges the Islamic government with the responsibility for facilitating the reproduction and training of *avant garde* and ideological human beings. Iranian women are to become such citizens within the embrace of an ideal Islamic structure that the government has to establish (according to the Preamble). Because of the central role of an Islamic government in carrying out these charges, it is constructive to give a synopsis of the theocratic government structure that the Ayatullah Khumaini has built in Iran.

A Theocracy Based on the Shii Version of the Sharia Law

The Islamic Republic of Iran is a theocracy which has been built on the Shii version of the Sharia Law. A synopsis of the Constitution of 1979 affirms this view.

Article 1 of the Constitution recognizes the government as an Islamic Republic to which the Iranian nation has given its overwhelming assent to be created under the auspices of the "Imam Khumaini."[16]

Article 2 maintains that the Islamic Republic of Iran is an order based on:

(1) Belief in God
(2) Belief in heavenly revelations

(3) Belief in life after death
(4) Belief in justice
(5) Belief in perpetual leadership (*Imamat*)
(6) Belief in freedom, human responsibility toward God, a responsibility made possible through "perpetual Ijtihad of jurors of highest competency based on the Book [the Qur'an] and the Tradition of the Sinless [Imams]....[17]

Article 2 also implores the use of modern technology in eradicating those criminogenic social conditions that facilitate "...inflicting injustice, exploitation, domineering, and acceptance of being domineered."[18] The rest of this article is devoted to national unity that is deemed achievable through the establishment of the Islamic constructs of equity, justice, and political, economic, social and cultural independence.

Article 3 foresees the ideals expressed in Article 2 as achievable through the establishment of various "modern" institutions and government programmes. For example, item 1 aims at the construction of a suitable medium for the propagation of moral virtues; item 2 aims at the elevation of public awareness through free expression of thought in print media and public communication networks; item 3 aims to create "free education" for the populace; item 4 aims at the propagation of research, science and technology; item 5 aims at the expulsion of colonialism and foreign influence; item 6 aims at the destruction of any form of dictatorship and monopolization of power in the hands of a few; item 7 aims at providing all kinds of political freedom that could be exercised through various political parties; item 8 aims at facilitating people's political participation in social affairs; item 9 aims at the eradication of all forms of discriminatory practices; items 10 through 13 aim at the establishment of national defence, economy, employment and social security; item 14 (of especial significance for our purpose here) aims at the establishment of "...judicial security for all, and equality of all before the law."[19]

Article 4 frames these constitutional rights and responsibilities within an all-encompassing Islamic perspective, stipulating that: "All civil, criminal, financial, economic, administrative, cultural, military, political, etc., laws and regulations ought to be based on Islamic criteria." This article further implores that this principle has to be safeguarded by a body of religious jurists in the Guardian Council (*Shaura-ye Negahban*) of the Constitution.[20] The main responsibility of this body is to guarantee that the legislative bills presented to the parliament do not contravene Islam's Sacred Law. Any such bills would be vetoed and returned to the parliament for reconsideration. This Council is elected from among those Twelve Imami male jurists whose credentials have been accepted by the Glorious Leader of the Islamic Revolution. This body, in turn, determines if the Leader is fit to stay in office.

Article 5 concerns the concept of the Jurist Council (*Wilayat-e Faqih)*:

> During the absence of Hazrat-e Wali-ye Asr...in the Islamic Republic of Iran Leadership [*Imamat*] and Governance of Affairs [*Wilayat-e Amr*] falls upon the shoulders of just [*aadil*] juror [who is] pious, aware of time's realities, courageous..., and that the majority of people have recognized and accepted him for leadership....[21]

It should be noted that the term *Hazrat-e Wali-ye Asr* in the above article of the Constitution means the Twelfth Shii Imam, Mahdi, whose return, Shii Muslims believe, would precede the end of the world and the coming of the Day of Judgment. The thrust of Article 5 is that, until the return of the Twelfth Imam, leadership in governing the affairs of the Iranian nation ought to be relegated to the Iranian Shii men of the cloth. The rationale for this is that it is only the men of the cloth who are fit to run the affairs of an Islamic society because of their knowledge of Islam and of the Sharia Law. The implication of this article is that, until the time of Mahdi's return, it is the clergy that has a God-given right to govern the affairs of Iranian society, including government. This is the hallmark of a theocracy and the crux of all the problems that Iranian society has faced from 1980 to the present: political power has been monopolized in the hands of the clergy without any prospect of sharing power with non-religious forces.

Article 6 stipulates that any public office can only be assumed through popular elections. This article is contradictory to both the letter and spirit of Article 5. In a theocracy, election to office based on popular will is quite meaningless especially when it is stipulated in the Constitution that only the members of the Shii clergy are entitled to high governmental offices and positions.

Article 7 follows the two famous Qur'anic pieces of advice (*wa amrihum shura biynahum* and *shawirhum fi al-amr*): Muslims ought to consult with one another with regard to issues that concern everyone. Based on this article, consultative bodies ranging from the national parliament to lower-level ones ought to be assembled at state, county and district levels in running the society's affairs.

Article 8 is premised upon the famous Qur'anic advice. It reads:

> In the Islamic Republic of Iran, *al-amr bil-maruf wa al-nahy an al-munkar* is a universal and reciprocal duty that must be fulfilled by the people with respect to one another, by the government with respect to the people, and by the people with respect to the government. The conditions, limits, and nature of this duty will be specified by law. This is in accordance with the Qur'anic verse: "The believers, men and women, are guardians of one another; they enjoin the good and forbid the evil [9:71]...."[22]

The application of this article has had a deep criminogenic impact upon Iranian society, and especially on women's law-infracting behaviour – an issue which be explored in some detail later in Chapter 7. Based on this article, the state has taken a very intrusive role in the daily lives of Iranian citizens, and especially those of women, arguing that the citizens have to conduct their lives according to the state's puritanical values that are of a totalitarian nature.

Article 9 safeguards the freedom, independence and territorial integrity of the country and stipulates that the responsibility for safeguarding these falls on the state and citizens. No person, social group or official is allowed to infringe upon these rights in the name of state security.

Article 10 gives primacy to the family as the main social institution in Islamic society, stipulating that every conceivable step ought to be taken in order to strengthen family and its social relations, based on Islamic laws and morality.

Article 11 follows another Qur'anic piece of advice in seeing the Islamic world as a unified community of believers (*ummah*), stipulating that the Islamic Republic ought to follow a policy to unify Islamic societies.

Articles 12 stipulates that Iran's official religion is Islam and is based on the Twelve Imami denomination. This is of an "eternal and unchangeable" nature, according to this article. Adherents of other denominations (such as Hanafi, Shafii, Maliki, Hanbali and Zaydi) are given constitutional recognition in this article.

Article 13 gives a religiously protected status to Iranian citizens who adhere to Zoroastrianism, Judaism or Christianity. These are the only religious minorities protected by the Constitution. No mention is made of the Bahia and Saabein.

Article 14 follows another Qur'anic piece of advice stipulating that an Islamic state and Muslims are duty-bound to treat non-Muslims with the Islamic sublime ideals of equity and justice. The article further stipulates that a regime of fair and just conduct applies only to those who have not conspired to act against Islam and the Islamic Republic of Iran.

The second part of the Constitution is about Iran's official language, script, calender and national flag.

Citizens' Rights in the Constitution

The third part of the Constitution provides for the nation's rights (*huquq-e mellat*) in spite of the fact that the thrust of the Constitution is to transform the Iranian nation into a religious entity, (*ummah*), as previously observed.

The nation's rights are enunciated in 24 articles (Articles 19 through 42). These pertain to the rights of nationalities (Article 19), gender-related rights (Article 20), women's rights (Article 21), individual rights (Article 22), freedom of expression and belief (Article 23), freedom of print (Article 24), inviolability of communication rights through post, telephone and telegraph services (Article 25), freedom of assembly and formation of political parties, gathering and demonstrations (Articles 26 and 27), freedom of choice in career (Article 28), and the right to social security, retirement and unemployment benefits (Article 29). The exercise of some of these articles (e.g., 20, 21, 24, 26, 27 and 28) are contingent upon a vague and unspecified premise, the non-violation of Islamic criteria.

Articles 32, 34, 35, 36, 37, 38 and 39 pertain to the operational dynamics of the Islamic criminal justice system that cover the criteria for arrest; arraignment; appearance before the judge; right to counsel; right to cross-examination of the witness; and right to appeal. Ironically, although none of these later articles is contingent upon any Islamic criterion, all have egregiously and continuously been violated, a point I have dealt with elsewhere.[23] These articles have been ignored in the judicial treatment of tens of thousands of Iranian women who have been arrested for acts such as deliberate mal-veiling (*bad-hejaabi*), and defiance of the veil (*bi-hejaabi*). The next section is devoted to a description of the Islamic criminal justice system (1982-present).

The Islamic Judiciary

Through Articles 156-174, the Islamic Constitution has provided for an

Islamic system of judiciary.[24] Article 156 provides for an independent judiciary in disseminating justice and safeguarding individual and social rights and freedoms. The judiciary has theoretically been entrusted with five main responsibilities: (1) presiding over grievances; (2) dissemination of justice; (3) detection of crimes and criminals based on the due process of the law; (4) providing a suitable medium for crime prevention and rehabilitation of `criminals; and (5) observance of the Islamic criteria in these efforts.[25]

Article 157 provides for the formation of a Supreme Judiciary Council (*Shaura-ye Aali-ye Qazaii*) entrusted with three responsibilities: (1) the administration of justice; (2) the preparation of appropriate judicial bills; and (3) management responsibilities pertaining to judges and judiciary personnel.[26] This Council is empowered to act in the capacity of Iran's Supreme Court.

Article 158 provides for the formation of this Council with five members composed of: the Chief of the Council (*Rais-e Diwan-e Aali-ye Keshvar*), the Prosecutor General (*Dadsetan-e Kull-e Keshavar*), and three just religious judges (*Qazi-ye mujtahid wa aadil*) capable of producing religious edicts. The members are elected for a period of five years with possible re-election. The conditions for election are prescribed by the law.[27]

Article 159 empowers the judiciary as the sole official venue for initiation of all grievances based on law. The Article maintains that the courts shall be constituted through law.[28]

Article 160 provides for a Minister of Justice to be elected from among the candidates that the Supreme Judiciary Council finds suitable to present to the Prime Minister. With the abolition of the Office of the Prime Minister in 1988, this article has been amended.

Articles 161, 162, 163 and 164 elaborate the responsibilities of the Supreme Judiciary Council, the moral character of its members, and some other aspects of its operational dynamics (e.g., the independence of the judges and under what conditions they can be removed from the bench. The stress is on the acceptability of these members from the standpoint of Islamic jurisprudence.

Articles 166, 167 and 168 describe how the courts are to be instituted and under what conditions the courts, normally "open" to the public, may be held *in camera*.[29] With the passage of the 1982 Islamization of the Judiciary Act, all codified laws of the Pahlavi era were declared null and void for having had no basis in Islam's Sacred Law.

Article 168 provides the mechanism for the adjudication of political and press-related crimes. These offences must be heard in public before a jury and instituted by law, a principle that to this date has been adhered to only in some highly charged prosecutions, as for instance in the case of Sadeq Qutbzadeh (an ex-official of the Islamic government in the early 1980s), the eight members of the Central Command of the Tudeh Party of Iran in the mid-1980s, and the trial of Tehran's ex-mayor, Gholamhossein Karbaschi, in 1997-1998.

Articles 169 through 174 detail the various aspects of public-initiated grievances against the judiciary and other branches of the government, procedures that remain largely theoretical.

Article 173 provides for the formation of a Commission of Justice under the jurisdiction of the Supreme Judiciary Council, while Article 174 provides for a General Investigative Commission under the jurisdiction of the judiciary. The purpose of this Commission is to investigate, throughout the country, public-initiated grievances.[30] This article, again, has remained a paper tiger to this date. The way in which the judiciary has been structured in the Constitution has made adjudication a monopoly of the Shii clergy and has excluded women from a meaningful participation in it.

The Court System

The present Islamic court system came into being following the Ayatullah Khumaini's Islamization decree. In August 1982, the Supreme Judicial Council abolished Iran's secular civil and criminal codes as the basis of both civil and criminal prosecutions that had been institutionalized under the Pahlavi regime. The Council believed that the codes did not conform to Islam's notion of law, crime, justice or penology. In October of the same year, the modern civil and criminal courts were abolished. Also, in June 1987 a tribunal named the Special Court of the Clergy (*Dadgah-e Widheh-e Ruhaniyat*) was established with the sole duty of presiding over cases that involve offences of the Shii clergy. This special court, of course, contravenes the Constitution in both its letter and spirit because it treats the clergy as a privileged group whose offences are treated differently from those of other citizens.

The structure of the courts I would like to caution the reader that, since the 1980s, the Islamic criminal justice system has gone through a tumultuous change without really being unified in terms of structure, function or operational dynamics. According to the Iran Almanac, the following court structure applied in the 1980s.

First, the Supreme Court functions as the highest court in the land. Then there are two types of courts – public and special. Public courts include:

(1) The high penal court which adjudicates three categories of crime: those that are punishable by capital punishments such as hanging, beheading by a sword, stoning to death, crucifying, dismembering, and banishment; those crimes that are punishable by prison terms of ten or more years; and those crimes that are punishable by fines equal or exceeding two million rials (1 US $=3000 rials) or fines equal to or exceeding two-fifths of the defendant's assets. The enforcement of the high penal court's verdicts is contingent upon confirmation by the Supreme Court.[31]

(2) The low penal court which adjudicates petty crimes and misdemeanours. The verdicts of this court cannot be appealed unless: the verdict contravenes legal or religious criteria (by a judge other than the adjudicating judge); it is a mistaken verdict; the judge is found to be unqualified in rendering a judgment.[32]

(3) The high civil court adjudicates civil claims whose monetary value exceeds two million rials. The enforcement of the high civil court's verdicts is contingent upon confirmation by the Supreme Court.[33]

(4) The low civil court which adjudicates civil claims whose monetary value does not exceed two million rials. The verdicts of this court cannot be appealed unless conditions explained in no. 2 above apply.[34]

(5) The special civil court. As a public court, it adjudicates disputes concerning marital relations, divorce, custody of children, inheritance, etc. Established in provincial centres, the verdicts of this court are final.[35]

As I shall explore in Chapters 6 and 7 on Iranian pre- and post-Islamic Revolution crime, in the 1980s this court structure proved to be quite criminogenic due to its arbitrary manner of conflict resolution with the result that the whole system had to be reformed in April1994. Although it has been argued that these reforms have made the courts more efficient in terms of their ability to expedite cases, the available data used in this study shows a different picture of inefficiency and miscarriage of justice.

Next to theses courts, the Islamic revolutionary tribunals are scattered all over the country under the direct jurisdiction of the Supreme Judicial Council. Initially formed on an ad hoc basis to safeguard the Revolution and to combat the remnants of the *ancien regime*, these tribunals became a political arm of the state, neutralizing social and political dissent. In May 1983, "The Law on Jurisdiction of Islamic Revolution Courts and Prosecutor's Office" was passed by the clergy-dominated parliament in order to give some shape to these primitive and unruly tribunals that had been responsible for tens of thousands of illegal arrests, misappropriation of funds, confiscation of lands and houses, and outright illegal and criminal executions. The Law puts these tribunals under the supervision of the Supreme Judicial Council.[36] However, to date, these primitive tribunals continue to operate in the most arbitrary style. The jurisdiction of these tribunals covers three types of offence: drug pushing and smuggling, political and anti-state activities, and economic offences (hoarding, black-marketing, price fixing, etc.).

The Police

Iran's modern police force was created in 1930s during the reign of Reza Shah Pahlavi (r.1925-1941). It was charged with urban policing and a municipality-based law enforcement mandate. Named as the National Police and Municipality Police *(Polis wa Sharban-ye Kull-e Keshavar*), and head-quartered in Tehran, it was put directly under the Ministry of Interior. On paper, its main function was to serve and protect citizens against crime, regulate traffic, investigate crime scenes, and enforce laws in the urban areas. In rural areas, it was the National Gendarmerie (*Janadami-ye Kull-e Keshavar*) that was charged with law enforcement functions and responsibilities. In the case of large operations against drug smugglers, the National Police and Gendarmerie collaborated with the army units.

The police and power politics Despite its mandate to serve and to protect, the police were a very important instrument of Reza Shah's dictatorial power. Under the Directorate General Mukhtari, the police gained a notorious reputation for its internal intelligence-gathering against average Iranian citizens, particularly for its manhandling of political dissidents. Under the Shah, Muhammad Reza Pahlavi (r.1941-1979) the police were also responsible for internal security throughout the country. They carried their internal security responsibilities in direct collaboration with a number of intelligence gathering organizations that the shah's regime had created in consultation with the American Federal Bureau of Investigation and American military advisers in Iran. The most prominent among these was the Army Intelligence Unit and the National Information and Security Organization (*Sazman-e Ettelaat wa Amniyat-e Keshvar*).

Known by its acronym as the SAVAK, this infamous policing organization was created through "The Establishment of Security Organization Act,"[37] which was approved by the Iranian Parliament in 1957. Composed of five articles, this act gave a wide range of intelligence gathering and arrest and investigation powers to the organization. To enhance the power of its directorate, it was given the administrative rank of the Assistant to the Prime Minister to be appointed directly by a decree of the Shah. With the passage of the time, the SAVAK became notorious for the illegal arrest, imprisonment, torture and execution of hundreds of Iranian political dissidents.

Under the Islamic Republic, the SAVAK has been upgraded to a higher status as the National Ministry of Information and Security, known by its acronym as VEVAK. Next to the National Police and Gendarmerie which the Islamic regime inherited almost intact from the monarchy, the regime has created a large network of intelligence gathering units in a number of parallel post-revolutionary organizations such as the Revolutionary Guards of the Islamic Revolution and the Patrol of the Oppressed, which act in the context of semi-official vigilante groups with arrest and detention powers. In addition to these, the Islamic regime has also empowered various paramilitary and vigilante groups in the form of patrol units with detention and arrest powers. These are named as the *Gasht* which stands for patrol. Alongside these, there are organizations that aim to export the Islamic Revolution to other Middle Eastern countries. These organizations are secretive. Some have been implicated in state-sponsored "revolutionary" activities in Middle Eastern countries (e.g., the *Sepaah-e Quds*); others have been implicated in the extra-legal assassination of Iranian political dissidents abroad, the deadly results of which I have explored in Chapter 7 of this study. In spite of all these intelligence-gathering and patrolling activities, Iranian cities have been infested with various types of crime, an issue further explored in Chapter 7.

The Corrections

Like other components of its criminal justice system, Iran's modern correctional philosophy and institutions go back to the time of Reza Shah. Modern penological philosophy rested on the idea that punishment ought to be both punitive (*mujazaat*) and penitential (*nedaamat*) effects on criminals.

Modern prisons and correctional facilities were built throughout the country during the two shahs' reigns. Adult facilities were known as *zendan*, which stands for prison, sometimes as *nedaamatgaah,* which stands for penitentiary. Juvenile facilities were known as *daar al-tadib* standing for the houses of correction. Next to relatively modern prisons and houses of correction, provisions were made for bail and surety in cases involving pre-trial release. Prisons were managed by a central authority named the National Prison Authority.

Although seemingly modern, in both organizational and penological philosophy, Iranian prisons were notorious in terms of their treatment of their clients. Prisons like Qasr, Qezel Qaleh, Evin, Gohar Dasht (in Tehran and its vicinity) had a notorious reputation for manhandling both political and apolitical prisoners. Evin and Gohar Dasht prisons were built in the late 1960s and 1970s to house Iran's rising number of political prisoners. These were highly educated and came from various lower-middle, and middle-class, families as well as from the bazaar (Iran's traditional market) and from Shii seminary students. These Iranian prisons played a role similar to the street-based colleges that politicized Maxim Gorki; in effect, prisons further radicalized Iran's dissident intelligentsia.

Under the Islamic Republic, all previous correctional facilities have been used to their maximum capacities alongside many non-correctional facilities that have been turned into temporary detention facilities. From 1981 to the present, a large number of political dissidents have been housed with common criminals; the United Nations Human Rights Committee has voiced much concern over this practice – a point to be dealt with later. The Islamic Republic's penological philosophy has followed a kind of eighteenth-century Cesare Beccarian rationale in its official declarations, namely, that punishment ought to be swift, certain and equitable in its application. In practice, however, punishment has been arbitrary, going to the very pre-Beccarian rationale of applying punishment on the basis of who is being punished and not on the nature of the criminal act committed.

The Issue of Dissent

When in exile and in opposition to the Pahlavi monarchy (1964-1979), the Ayatullah Khumaini in his speeches and sermons argued that Iran's modern and secular system of justice under the two shahs was illegitimate because the system was not only based on Western secular law and penology, but dissent had been criminalized. He was especially critical of the manner in which the system dealt with political dissidents, arguing that justice had become a rare commodity under a brutal system whose mandate was to perpetuate the interests of a corrupt monarchy. Khumaini was also concerned about women's status, arguing that Iranian women had been deprived of their deserved social and legal status because of corrupt Western laws that the monarchy had imposed to regulate women's social and legal affairs in Iran. In the eyes of Khumaini, one such corrupt law was the "Family Protection Law," which aimed at controlling procreative processes in family, at the same time that it sought to improve lower-middle and middle-class women's education and employment opportunities.

The Family Protection Law, passed by the Iranian parliament in 1961, was part of a reform movement that the Shah, Muhammad Reza Pahlavi, had initiated in 1963, later called the White Revolution of the Shah and People. These reform measures, as I have explained elsewhere,[38] came under immediate criticism from Iran's powerful and yet tradition-bound Shii clergy, which Khumaini spearheaded. Responding to the clergy's call to action, several thousands of bazaar shopkeepers, street peddlers and seminary students held public protests in a number of large cities and especially in the holy city of Qom, one of the most important Shii centres of learning. The state's response was severe and bloody, resulting in the massacre of several thousand unarmed civilian protesters on 10 June 1963. Khumaini was subsequently put under house arrest and was later sent into exile, first in Turkey and subsequently in Iraq. Khumaini chose to reside in the holy city of Najaf until 1979.

This anti-state position gave prominence to the Ayatullah Khumaini and to his anti-Pahlavi political views among a faction of the Iranian bazaar, as well as factions of the Shii clergy and seminary students in Qom and other holy cities in Iran (e.g., Mashad). Khumaini was now in a position to call attention, among other things, to Iran's criminal justice system as corrupt and oppressive, and at the service of the Pahlavi court and its foreign (e.g., American and British, and later Israeli) interests in Iran. He implied that a judiciary based on the Islamic Sharia Law would be impeded by no such malaise and would act in accordance with the ideal qualities of Islamic jurisprudence: equity, impartiality, fairness, compassion and knowledge. Through the application of this system, Iranian women would gain their humane and Islamic status.

The Islamization of the Judiciary

Naturally, once in power with an overwhelmingly popular mandate, Khumaini tried to replace Iran's secular laws with Islamic ones, an endeavour that logically should have required the participation of Iran's trained lawyers, prosecutors, judges and reform-minded social workers. Instead, most of the highly educated and trained judges and prosecutors were purged, replaced by a cadre of Khumaini's partisan Shii men of the cloth.

The Islamization of the law As a jurist, Khumaini had proposed in his writings that only under a purely Islamic government could "true" justice be administered.[39] He wrote: "The body of Islamic laws that exist in the Qur'an and the Sunna has been accepted by the Muslims and recognized by them as worthy of obedience."[40] This premise of Khumaini the jurist is, of course, only partially true. For example, in the body of Islamic laws, slavery-related laws occupy a significant place. All modern Islamic societies have abolished slavery, including Iran. No sane Muslim jurist, politician or academician would argue that, because slavery was once part of the body of Islamic laws, it should be so today. The same rationale applies to adjudication and punishment regimes.

Theoretically speaking, in most Islamic societies the ideal of crime detection and punishment regimes follow internationally recognized principles of due process of law. Many Islamic states are signatories to modern and humanitarian covenants such as the "International Covenant on Civil and Political Rights"; the "International Covenant on Economic, Social and Cultural Rights", the "Convention on the Prevention and Punishment of the Crime of Genocide and the Geneva Convention of 12 August 1949, Relating to the Protection of Victims of International Armed Conflicts."[41] Likewise, the Islamic Republic of Iran is a signatory to these covenants and has not officially withdrawn its signature from them. At the same time, the ideal of the Islamic Revolution was not a return to the past, but to a modern Iran that was to be built upon technological advances in many fields and in social relations. Therefore, when Khumaini in power attempted to institutionalize the totality of the "body of Islamic laws," three strategic questions were raised. What constituted this totality? Who should determine the range of this totality? How was this totality to be implemented? Khumaini's position was that Shii men of the cloth (the so-called *ulama*) were the natural candidates for this determination because they possessed the requisite expert knowledge about Islam. From among the men of the cloth, it was the jurists (the so-called *fuqaha*) who were the "expert" legitimate echelon for this undertaking because they possessed expert knowledge of Islam's elaborate "science of jurisprudence." Khumaini devised yet another prerequisite – namely, that only those jurists who believed in the mandate of the Islamic Revolution (which meant, in essence, the *Wilayat-e Faqih)* were to be empowered for this determination. Khumaini's uncompromising stance created a huge public uproar, especially among Iran's Lawyer's Guild which had played a prominent role in defending Iran's political dissidents and prisoners in the 1960s and 1970s. After three years of skirmishes with opponents of this endeavour that entailed several thousand illegal arrests and indiscriminate and summary executions of the opponents by the state, on 23 August 1982, the Supreme Judiciary Council, under the Ayatullah Musavi Ardabili declared that based upon "Imam" Khumaini's directive:

> All previous laws that are against Islam are void and null. It is incumbent upon the county and district court judges, throughout the country to refrain from rendering judgment based on these laws and the State Regulatory Court would punish, based on Islamic Sharia, any judge operating on the basis of such laws. Prior to the announcement of laws ratified by the Majles in situations whereby judges recognize that present laws contravene the Islamic Sharia, judgment should be rendered on reputable jurisprudential sources/or reputable sermons. In cases where judges suspect that present laws contravene Islamic edicts they should get in touch with the jurors of the Guardian Council who are the legitimate sources in discerning the contravention of laws with the Sharia. In cases where the laws contravene Islam and judges are uninformed about the corresponding Islamic edicts, they should get in touch with the Supreme Judiciary Council or Imam's Office and familiarize themselves with the appropriate Islamic edict, and apply such in their actions.[42]

This attempt to abolish Iran's modern criminal code and secular judiciary and replace the two with a set of Islamic codes by decree under a cadre of religious judges has proven to be discriminatory, disruptive and a criminogenic endeavour, points that I have documented elsewhere, including the structure of the present Islamic judiciary.[43]

Islamization of crime and punishment categories In the present Islamic criminal justice system, notions of crime and punishment follow a strictly Sharia basis to their conceptualization and implementation in accordance with "The Islamic Penal Code" (*Qaanun-e Mujazat-e Islami*) that was ratified in 1982 by the clergy dominated parliament. This Code has indexed four types of law-infracting behaviour as follows: (1) *Hudud*, (2) *Qisaas*, (3) *Diyaat*, and (4) *Taazirat*. I shall explore these in more detail in subsequent chapters.

The Operational Dynamics of the Islamic Criminal Justice System

The formation of Iran's Islamic criminal justice system and its operational dynamics have yet to be thoroughly researched. From available data, however, it can be shown (see Chapters 6 and 7) that the system has gone through a tumultuous process of upheaval and reorganization from 1982 to the present. Out of these processes, the present system has emerged with three main components: the courts, the police and corrections. Besides these official organs of the system which have been superimposed on the structural remnants of the past, there are a number of extra-legal organizations that work clandestinely to enforce a set of arbitrary rules and regulation throughout the land. In the previous section, a synopsis of the official components of the system was provided. Next, I will give a synopsis of the Sharia base of the system. Once the general features of the system is laid out, women's treatment in the system will be further explored.

To begin with, because the system is theoretically based on the Shii version of the Sharia Law, we have to analyse its operational dynamics from the standpoint of its adherence to what it claims gives it legitimacy, the Qur'an, and the Prophetic and Shii Imam's Traditions. However, theoretically speaking, this Islamic system has also a constitutional basis to its operational dynamics that include a set of modern checks and balances that ought to be observed in each constituent of the system. The contradictory nature of the system has led to discriminatory and criminogenic outcomes which particularly victimize women as a social category.

The Sharia Base of the System

As previously mentioned, adjudication (*qazaa*) in Islam has almost fourteen centuries of tradition behind it. Following the Prophet Muhammad's Tradition, in all Shii and Sunni schools the following principles have to be adhered to in the adjudicative process: (1) the fairness and impartiality of the judge in the search for truth; (2) the judge's appropriate knowledge of the case, of the sources of law, and of the precedent; (3) a presumption of innocence; (4) a proportionality between crime and punishment; (5) the circumstances surrounding the crime; and (6) action, not thought, constitutes crime. A synopsis of each is presented below.

The fairness and impartiality principle An ideal Islamic judge has to be fair and impartial in the adjudicative process. This principle necessitates that a judge cannot sit in judgment with a preconceived notion as to the guilt or innocence of the accused. The judge has to allow the accused to present his/her evidence, carefully listen to the evidence, analyse it, and take into consideration all mitigating and aggravating circumstances. A judge should not allow his/her personal feelings to intervene; neither should a judge allow non-adjudicative factors (e.g., bribes, favouritism, kin and blood considerations) to influence his/her judgment. The Qur'an states categorically that Allah watches over those who sit in adjudication and that those who corrupt Allah's laws will be punished severely. For example, (iv: 136) maintains:

> O ye who believe! be strict in observing justice, *and be* witnesses for Allah, even though it is against yourselves or *against* parents and kindred. Whether he be rich or poor, Allah is more regardful of them both *than you are*. Therefore follow not low desires so that you may be able to act equitably. And if you conceal *the truth* or evade it, then *remember that* Allah is well aware of what you do.[44]

This verse is self-explanatory. Judgment of the guilt or innocence of an accused person is of paramount importance in the Sharia Law. No extra-legal consideration should enter the justice process. Rendering a just verdict is like witnessing on behalf of Allah, maintains the verse, implying that Allah takes the business of justice very seriously.

The knowledge principle Given the stern warnings of the Qur'an, an adjudicating judge ought to acquaint himself/herself properly with the case, so that appropriate laws can be applied. At the same time, the judge has to have a thorough and exhaustive knowledge about the sources of the Sharia Law, which means in essence the Qur'an, the Prophet Muhammad's Traditions, and the precedents of the case law.

The presumption of innocence principle It is a Qur'anic principle that if an innocent person is killed, it is as if humanity has been killed. The logical implication of this Qur'anic stance has been that taking a life without a just cause constitutes a grave sin in the eyes of Allah. This premise of the Qur'an has led to the rise of the presumption of innocence (*Baraat)* doctrine that also has its precedents in the Prophet Muhammad's and "the four Rightly Guided Caliphs'" adjudication styles. A judge has to assume that the accused is innocent until proven otherwise. In fact, in the inquisitive traditional style of Islamic adjudication, the inquisition process is not initiated by the judge or by any other official organs of the state, but by the claimer (*muddai*) to whom an injustice, a wrong or a harm has been inflicted. This process has historically been known as the process of eradicating injustices (*raf'i madaalim)* that has a long history in the Islamic world. Muhammad Hussain Saket cites the following Hadith as an example of Caliph Umar's style of adjudication (corrected by the First Shii Imam's style of search for truth):

> A woman fell in love with an Ansari lad but could not get her way with him. She thought of a scheme. One day she took an egg, threw out its yolk and spread the white part on her clothes and legs and then went to Umar Ibn Khattab and said: this lad has ambushed me in such and such place and has raped me, and that which you see on my clothes and legs is his ejaculation. Umar accepted her complaint and attempted to punish the lad. Imam Ali who was present in the adjudication session addressed the Second Caliph [Umar] and said: haste not! Maybe this woman has concocted this scheme. Then Ali commended for hot boiling water to be brought. Upon presentation of the water, Imam Ali commended that part of the dress be soaked in the hot water to be tasted. Once it was found[,] through this method[,] that the stain tasted like the whites of an egg the woman confessed to her scheme. [45]

Saket reaches the conclusion that it was this type of inquisition that helped `Ali spearhead the establishment the new style of justice, whose genesis the Prophet Muhammad had delineated. There are similar Hadiths (both Sunni and Shii) that depict a meticulous system of truth seeking that Muslim judges and jurists established, at least theoretically, throughout Islam's long history of adjudication. The Qur'an is quite specific about the proportionality between crime and punishment. Table 5.1 shows the categories of crimes for which punishment (*hadd*) has been specified.

Table 5.1 Crime and punishment in the Qur'an

Crime Categories in the Qur'an	Prescribed Punishments	In the Prophet's Sunna
Murder (*qatl*)	Retribution or blood money	Retribution or blood money
Maiming (*zarb wa jarh*)	Retribution in kind or monetary restitution	Monetary retribution based on authentic Hadiths
Thievery (*sirqat*)	Amputation of four fingers	Amputation of four fingers for theft of weapons based on authentic Hadith
Adultery (*zina*)	Public flogging of the two parties involved in adultery	Different Hadiths
Male homosexuality (*lawat*)	Public flogging	Different Hadiths
Female homosexuality (*musahiqah*)	Public flogging	Different Hadiths
False witness (*kazib shadah*)	Public flogging	Different Hadiths
Drinking alcoholic beverages (*al-khamr*)	Public flogging	Different Hadiths
Use of mind-altering substances (*al-maysar*)	Public flogging	Different Hadiths

The punishment applies only after proof has been established. The proof involves eyewitnesses (*shaid eyni*), voluntary confession (*iqrar*), oath (*qasma*) weapon(s) by means of which murder has been committed (*alat-e jurm*). These constitute elements of a habeas corpus. The Qur'an is absolutely against surveillance for the detection of unlawful activities in which one may engage in one's private residence (e.g., drinking, illicit sex or use of drugs). In fact, the Qur'an advises believers, including spouses, to safeguard each other's secrets. The same goes for confessions that are extracted under duress (*ikraah*) or torture (*mutlah, shekanjeh, tqtial*). In fact, when it comes to illicit sex, the Qur'anic mechanism of proof is one of the most stringent among all systems. It requires four just eyewitnesses (*shaid aadil*) who ought to testify that they have seen the actual act of penetration. Those who accuse others (married or unmarried women and men) unjustly of such crimes receive the punishment of a public lashing (*jild*).

There is also a category of crime that is known as the *Ifsad fi al-Ard* standing for "Corruption on Earth" crimes. In the past these crimes had vague definitions that covered those which were of a grand scale or of a horrendous nature, such as setting ablaze a mosque, a bazaar or a whole village, or destroying a city block during internal rebellions. In the Islamic Republic, this category has taken on a new meaning to be dealt with later in this chapter. The same goes for the so-called *Harb* category, that includes waging war against the Prophet Muhammad and against Allah. In the Islamic Republic, this theologically-based crime category has gone through a bizarre transformation, to the effect that any criticism of the state, of Khumaini as an "Imam," and of the Leader of the Glorious Islamic Revolution, puts the detractor in grave dangers in terms of life, limb and liberty.

In cases of capital crimes, the Qur'an emphasizes restitution, provided that the wronged party can be persuaded to such compensatory measures; if this fails then punishment in kind applies. Following the Mosaic principle of an eye for an eye, a tooth for a tooth, the Qur'an also stipulates that the weaker members of the society cannot be used as substitutes for the punishment of the stronger social members. That is why the text advises the proportionality principle in the formula of: a free man for a free man, a woman for a woman, and a slave for a slave.

The Qur'an is also adamant that on the Day of Judgment, each person is responsible for his/her deeds. Allah will not accept one's intercession on behalf of others, except the intercession of a few select souls. At the same time, the Qur'an maintains that, on the Day of Judgment, every person's good and evil deeds will be measured. In (xcix) verse 6 reads: "That day mankind will issue forth in scattered groups to be shown their deeds"[46]; verse 7 reads "And whoso doth good an atom's weight will see it then," followed by verse 8 "And whoso doth ill an atom's weight will see it then."[47] This means that Allah will not only judge our deeds, but also render a valid and appropriate judgment, a serious balancing act as to what kind of wrong/crime has been perpetrated, as well as under what conditions and for what discernible reasons. This premise of the Qur'an reflected in the Sharia Law means that if someone is charged with a crime, he/she ought to be subjected to a proper punishment only after a thorough investigation has been conducted to the satisfaction of the judge. The punishment ought to fit the crime. Both Sunni and Shii jurists have argued that the Prophet Muhammad meticulously adhered to this principle in his adjudication of cases.

The circumstance principle As a matter of the Prophet's style of adjudication, the judge ought to take into consideration the circumstance of the case. If the wronged party were to reject all efforts towards conciliation and compensatory measures, the punishment ought to fit the crime, be not revengeful and carry proportionality. As a matter of procedure, the judge ought to take oath on the Qur'an affirming his/her (there is no Qur'anic injunction against women's assuming the role of a judge to adjudicate cases) obedience to law and the criteria of justice. Adherence to these has been of paramount importance in all Sunni and Shi`i schools of jurisprudence, both in theory and in practice.

The action principle The Qur'an maintains that it is the believers' actions (*al-amaal*), rather than their intentions (*al-niyya*), that Allah will take into consideration on the Day of Judgment. The implication of this Qur'anic premise has been that no one can be punished for ill thoughts that have not been acted upon. Guilt by association is categorically rejected in the Qur'an and in the Prophetic style of adjudication.

In sum, by Islamizing Iran's law, crime, justice and penology based on the Sharia Law, the state has assumed a Herculean task of restructuring Iran's criminal justice system based on Khumaini's ideals of Islam. This Islamization process, as a matter of the Constitution of the Islamic Republic, is theoretically subjected to various modern checks and balances.

The Constitutional Checks and Balances of the System

As I have already explored above, the Constitution has provided for a number of checks and balances that ought to be adhered in the application of the justice process. All arrests, and search and seizures of the police or other law enforcement officials, are subject to the presentation of valid warrants. The presumption of innocence, the right to a speedy trial, the right to a jury, the right to pre-trial release based on bail and/or own recognizance, as well as the right to be presented by competent lawyers, are among the modern amenities that the Constitution of the Islamic Republic has recognized. In its procedural reality, however, we have a very different process at work that can only be characterized as anomic at best. The best example is the adjudication style of the Ayatullah Sadiq Khalkhali, the first judge that Khumaini appointed after the success of the Revolution in 1979. Below are two examples of procedures that were carried out by the Islamic Republic's revolutionary judiciary in the early 1980s.

First, the daily *Etellaat* on 24 June 1981 (Tir 3, 1360) under the heading "The Invitation of the Revolutionary Prosecutor of the Parents of Arrested" reported the following:

> This morning a communiqué was issued by the Public Relations Office of the Revolutionary Prosecutor concerning convicts who have been arrested in recent anti-revolutionary activities and for whom the verdict of the court has been carried out, [this communiqué is] as follows: It is brought to the attention of the families whose offspring (farzandan) have been arrested in recent anti-revolutionary events and against whom the verdict of the court has been carried out: please contact the Central Office of the Evin Prison with appropriate pictured birth certificates to identify your offspring whose pictures have been published herewith in order to receive them.[48]

Obviously the implementation of the court's above verdict, which turned out to be execution, had preceded the identification process. In other words, those arrested had already been executed; it also turned out that the so-called anti-revolutionaries were mostly juveniles some of whom were in their teens. Now, those responsible for the above executions either have to claim that in Shii Islam's procedural laws (as they apply to tenets of adjudication) a defendant is allowed to be executed for an alleged crime without being identified first, or they have to concede that these executions ought to be considered as premeditated murder (*qatl-e amd*) resulting in the removal and prosecution of the judge as a criminal defendant in accordance with the very Shii juristic corpus and sources that give legitimacy to an Islamic form of adjudication in present-day Iran.

Worse yet, those who carried out these arbitrary executions either have to claim that, in Shii Islam's tenets of adjudication, a juvenile (*saghir*) defendant is allowed to be executed for an alleged crime without even having been identified, or they have to concede that these executions ought to be considered as the premeditated murder of juveniles resulting in the removal of the judge as a criminal defendant. To the best of my knowledge, and to this day, none of those involved in such executions has been reprimanded, let alone been removed from office and charged with the premeditated murder of innocent juveniles. In fact the people involved have been promoted to various offices in the government, exemplified by the Khalkhali's election to a seat in the parliament.

Finally, those who carried out these executions have to show a viable precedent whereby either the Prophet Muhammad, or Ali ibn Abi Talib, have executed unidentified defendants, let alone juveniles. This of course is a futile attempt because both authentic Sunni and Shii sources have depicted an impeccable fairness applied by the Prophet Muhammad and Ali ibn Abi Talib in judging cases. I provide one example below:

> Narrated Sahl bin Abi Hashim...that a number of people from his tribe went to Khaibar and dispersed, and then they found one of them murdered. They said to the people with whom the corpse had been found, "You have killed our companion!" Those people said, "Neither have we killed him, nor do we know his killer." The bereaved group went to the Prophet...and said, "O Allah's Apostle! We went to Khaibar and found one of us murdered." The Prophet...said, "Let the older among you come forward and speak." Then the Prophet...said, to them, "Bring your proof against the killer." They said, "We have no proof." The Prophet...said, "Then they [the defendants] will take an oath." They said, "We do not accept the oaths of the Jews." Allah's Apostle...did not like that the Blood-money of the killed one be lost without compensation, so he paid one hundred of the camels of Zakat [to the relatives of the deceased] as Diya [Blood-money].[49]

This Hadith signifies the paramount importance of positive proof in Prophetic model of adjudication and punishment. Lacking proof, no judgment was rendered against the Jewish defendants. The compensatory blood money of the murdered victim was paid from the *Zakat* which is a property-based tax given to the state treasury. Likewise, in Shii primary sources the authenticity of the above Hadith has been acknowledged. These sources depict an impeccable sense of justice, impartiality, fairness and compassion in both the Prophet Muhammad's and Ali ibn Abi Talib's style of adjudication. These sources (some of which we have already consulted above) do not allow a judge to execute an offender without proper identification, let alone if such defendants were to be juveniles. On the contrary, these sources have provided elaborate scenarios through which provisions for proof have to be examined one by one – a point to be explored shortly and in detail below.

It is constructive to remind the reader that, as a general rule, the Shii sources agree with the Sunni sources with regard to the Prophet Muhammad's legendary sense of justice. Therefore, throughout this study, I have utilized Hadiths from both Sunni and Shii sources in this regard. This methodology is absolutely sound and has centuries-old precedents behind its utilization. Nor can it be faulted from a Sunni-Shii perspective in terms of Prophet Muhammad's sense of justice and equity in the application of Islam's Sacred Law. In other words, both Sunni and Shii Muslims believe in the paramount importance of justice in Prophet Muhammad's conduct towards his foes and friends alike. Therefore, my usage of the Sunni Hadith in support of my argument here cannot be faulted by those who may argue that Shii jurisprudence is not bound by the Sunni Hadith as it relates to the depiction of the Prophet's and/or Ali's sense of justice and impartiality in adjudication.

The second example pertains to the summer of 1980, a time that corresponded to the ongoing arbitrary and indiscriminate waves of executions that were being carried out in various parts of Iran in the name of fighting the anti-revolutionaries. The champion of these executions was the same Khalkhali, one who had already won for himself the epithet of "hanging judge" by the world media which was closely following the events in Iran. Khalkhali was interviewed by one Iranian journalist concerning his activities as an Islamic judge. The questions and answers are of interest to this subject.

> [Question:] As I understand it, according to Islam, an Islamic judge can exercise his power only in the area he is in charge of, which covers a certain number of people. Above this number, more than one judge is needed. So how is it that you were in charge of justice for the whole of Iran?
> [Answer:] Nonsense. How is it that there can be the Imam or a president for the whole country, but not a judge? Even if there is such a law in Islam my case is an exception. On Imam Khomeini's orders, I became the Islamic judge of Iran. The Imam is the only person I take orders from and report back to. I went to every part of this country. I executed, imprisoned, and confiscated. I have done the job of eight judges. All the others have one jurisdiction, while I covered eight regions.[50]

Now, the Ayatullah Khumaini, as the so-called Jurist Council in the Constitution, was empowered to appoint judges, but the same Constitution did not empower him to appoint one judge to cover entire Iran, a country with a population of around 35 million then, and with an area that covers 1, 648,000 square kilometers, making Iran the sixteenth largest country in the world. This is not to mention the heterogeneity of Iranian culture – a culture that comprises different languages (Persian, Kurdish, Azari Turkish, Arabic, etc.), elaborate cultural norms, traditions, mores, folk customs, and a modern court structure that existed then. Putting aside the issue of cultural heterogeneity and legality, Khalkhali's impartiality, fairness, sanity and state of mind could be checked, based on his own testimony:

> [Question:] Then why were you called back to Tehran while you were still in the middle of your executions in Kurdistan?
> [Answer:] At the time the government thought they could solve the problem through negotiations, but they have now reached the conclusion that I was right. All the people that are opposed to our revolution must die.[51]

The above answer – quite indicative of Khalkhali's arbitrary mindset, to say the least – is absolutely contrary to the impartiality, and justice clauses in Shii Islam's criteria for adjudication. All those opposed to the ideals of the Islamic Revolution had to be killed according to Khalkhali, a judge who was to conduct investigations to determine the guilt or innocence of the accused and disseminate justice based on the Prophetic model among a people (e.g., the Iranian Kurds) whose language he could not even speak. This cavalier attitude was quite evident from Khalkhali's following answer to the same journalist's question:

> [Question:] During your one week in Kurdistan, how many people did you execute? Where they all, including a Tehrani doctor, counter-revolutionaries?
> [Answer:] How do you expect me to remember how many they were? Forty or 50, or maybe more. Most of them were counter-revolutionaries like the Kurds or Fedayi. The doctor you mentioned, Bolghasam [Abulghasim?] Rashmand Sardarri, was also a traitor, by treating the Kurds. There were others too – the rapists, addicts...[52]

In other words, Khalkhali, an Islamic judge who was to follow the Qur'anic injunctions and Prophet Muhammad's model of application of the law had investigated, within one week, forty persons (the least number of people that he himself found plausible), finding all those guilty for being counter-revolutionaries, rapists and addicts, including one "traitor," whose name he could not even pronounce correctly. In the meantime, Khalkhali was also involved in other activities:

> [Question:] How do you justify the executions of 300 alleged drug dealers during your three months as head of the drug squad?
> [Answer:] The drug dealers' activities brought two million young people to nothingness, thousands of couples to separation, thousands of children to a miserable life....So far, I have seized 500 kilos of heroin and saved many young people from falling into this trap. A month ago hundreds of drug addicts lined the streets of Jamshid Quarter. After three public executions of dealers, almost all of them have disappeared now. Killing makes people think. And I kill only those who are harmful to our society – the top international smugglers. The rest, the very sick addicts, are sent to hospitals.[53]

The answers do not make any sense. Khalkhali claimed to have seized 500 kilos of heroin in Tehran's Jamshid quarter (a place that has traditionally been a hotbed for drug pushing), but how this justified the execution of 300 persons in Kurdistan Province without any linkage between the two is beyond any standards of adjudication. In addition, these executions were of a summary nature, all taking place within the span of three months, so it is therefore very likely that many innocent persons perished. In such an atmosphere of terror, any opponents of the new regime could be labelled, and have been labelled, time and again, as drug dealers to be executed, a practice that very early on came to the attention of the world human rights organizations. Ironically, the Ayatullah Khumaini, in opposition, had condemned the shah's regime for executing petty drug users arguing that: "They kill people for possessing ten grams of heroin and say, 'That is the law'...."[54] During the Shah, Muhammd Reza Pahlavi's tenure, it was rumoured that the regime executed its political opponents as drug dealers.

It may be argued that Khalkhali's style applies to the beginning of the Revolution, a tumultuous time when the Islamic state was in its infancy and such miscarriages of justice were only natural. The problem is that, after two decades, the same arbitrary and discriminatory style prevails as I shall explore in the rest of this study. This is due to a strategic incongruity between form and content. The Islamic Republic is a theocracy with its ideological base in Khumaini's doctrine of the Jurist Council (*Wilayat-e Faqih*). The political regime strives to institutionalize this theocratic structure within the confines of a modern republican form of governance based on popular will whereby all executive decisions are incumbent upon the will of one unelected official, the Jurist Council. The Constitution grants him almost unlimited powers, to be explored shortly. For example, if the Jurist Council wishes, he can dismiss "elected" officials, shut down the parliament, declare war and peace on others, and let free the most horrendous criminal who has been convicted and is due to be executed. Therefore, notwithstanding the republican rhetoric of the regime, it cannot be institutionalized. This strategic incongruency between form and content has led to chaotic results in every realm including the sphere of the justice. But what is the doctrine of the Jurist Council?

The doctrine of the Jurist Council This doctrine maintains that, in the absence of the Prophet Muhammad and of the Twelve Shii Imams, Shii men of the cloth and jurists are duty-bound to guarantee that the affairs of an Islamic society are conducted by those most competent in Islam and in its Sacred Law, the Sharia. Article 5 of the Constitution, recognizing this doctrine, gives a wide range of powers to one central figure, the so-called Jurist Council *(Wali-ye Amr)*, and empowers this figure as the final authority in all affairs of the society. Without the Jurist Council's seal of approval, no executive, legislative and judiciary decisions can be enforced. The Office of the Jurist Council, based on the strict word of the Constitution, can only be filled by a male, who is a believer in Twelve Imami Shiism, and is a total believer in the primacy of this doctrine. At the time of this article's enactment, it was the Ayatullah Khumaini who satisfied these conditions in the eyes of the drafters of the Constitution. Now, it is Ali Khamenehi, a junior cleric who has gradually been elevated to the stature of the "The Global Guardian of the Affairs of Muslims" *(Waliy-e Muslimin-e Jahan)*. Among his hard-core followers, Khamenehi has the absolute mandate over life, limb and property of close to a billion Muslims throughout the world, whether Sunni or Shii Muslims. This view of Khamenehi's range of powers, of course, is not a rational position that any

Muslim can take seriously. It is a hyperbole that, nonetheless, has created many problems for the regime in terms of internal and foreign policies.

Powers of the Jurist Council Under the subsection of the "Powers of the Leader," Article 110 of the Constitution gives the following powers to this central figure:

(1) Appointment of the fuqaha [jurists] on the Guardian Council;
(2) Appointment of the supreme judicial authority of the country;
(3) Supreme command of the armed forces, exercised in the following manner:
   a. appointment and dismissal of the joint chief staff;
   b. appointment and dismissal of the chief commander of the Islamic Revolution Guard's Corps;
   c. formation of the Supreme National Defence Council, composed of the following seven members:
   - the president,
   - the prime minister,
   - the minister of defence,
   - the chief of the joint staff,
   - the chief commander of the Islamic Revolution Guard corps, and
   - two advisers appointed by the leader;
   d. appointment of the supreme commanders of the three wings of the armed forces, on the recommendation of the Supreme National Defence Council; and
   e. the declaration of war and peace, and the mobilization of the armed forces, on the recommendation of the Supreme National Defence Council....[55]

Other sections in Article 110 further empower the Jurist Council; he can also approve the election of the President of the Republic, dismiss the President, and pardon or commute the sentences of convicted criminals.[56]

This is an unprecedented range of power entrusted to an unelected figurehead in Iran's modern history (from the time of the Constitutional Revolution to 1979) that neither the Qajar, nor the Pahlavi shahs could even dream of, let alone possess. The end result has been a long cycle of internal conflicts, war, population dislocation, deep-rooted corruption and the over-criminalization and victimization of women. The subsequent chapters explore these outcomes.

Notes

1. For further information on Iran's 1906 Constitution see, Abolghasem Seidhi's entry, "Iran" in A.P. Blaustein and G.H Falnz (eds.), *Constitutions of the Countries of the World*, (Dobbs Ferry, NY, Oceana Publications Inc.), pp. 2-27.

2. *Ibid.*, p. 13.

3. *Ibid.*

4. See Georges Levasseur, "On the Legal System in Iran," pp. 43-72 in William J. Butler and Georges Levasseur, *Human Rights and the Legal System in Iran*, (Geneva, Switzerland, International Commission of Jurists, 1976).

5. *Ibid.*, p. 45.

6. See Freda Adler, *Nations Not Obsessed with Crime*, (Littleton, CO, Fred B. Rothman & Co., 1983).

7. Levasseur, "On the Legal System in Iran," p. 47.

8. *Ibid.*, p. 47.

9. *Ibid.*, p. 48.

10. *Ibid.*

11. *Ibid.*, pp. 48-49.

12. *Ibid.*, p. 49.

13. *Ibid.*, p. 49-50.

14. William Butler, "Report on Human Rights in Iran," pp. 1-42, in Butler and Levasseur, *Human Rights and the Legal System in Iran*, p. 32.

15. See the *Qaanun-e Asaasi-ye Jumhuri-ye Islami-ye Iran: Musawwab-e Majles-e Khebregan Saal-e 1358* (The Constitution of the Islamic Republic of Iran: Ratified by the Assembly of Experts Year 1358), (np, nd, Introduction); see also Seyyed Jalal Madani's four-volume, *Huquq-e Asasi dar Jumhri-ye Islami-ye Iran, jeld-e 2, Hakemiyyat, Wilayat-e Faqih*

(Rahbari), Quway-e Hakem, (The Constitutional Rights in the Islamic Republic of Iran, volume 2, Governance, Wilayat-e Faqih (Leadership), the Executive Branch), (Tehran, Iran: Surush, 1364/1985); for the English translation of the Constitution see *Al-Tawhid*, vol. 3, no. 1 (1406/1985), pp. 130-92, cited partially in Said Amir Arjomand (ed.), *Authority and Political Culture in Shiism*, (Albany, NY, SUNY Press, 1988), pp. 371-382; see also Yahya Noori, *Islamic Government and the Revolution in Iran*, (London, Royston Limited, 1985), 2nd. edn.

16. Madani, *Huquq-e Asaasi dar Jumhuri-ye Islami-ye Iran*, vol. 2, p. 211.

17. *Ibid.*, pp. 211-212.

18. *Ibid.*, p. 212.

19. *Ibid.*, p. 213.

20. *Ibid.*

21. *Ibid.*

22. Arjomand, *Authority and Political Culture in Shiism*, p. 376.

23. See Hamid R. Kusha, "Punishment or Political Intimidation: The Case of the Sharia Courts in the Islamic Republic of Iran," presented to the 1991 Annual Meeting, Academy of Criminal Justice Sciences, Nashville, TN.

24. See the *Qanun-e Asasi-ye Jumhuri-ye Islami-ye Iran: Musawwab-e Majles-e Khebregan Sal-e 1358* (the Constitution of the Islamic Republic of Iran: Ratified by the Assembly of Experts Year 1358), (np, nd, Introduction); for a more elaborate and annotated version see also Madani's four-volume *Huquq-e Asasi dar Jumhuri-ye-Islami-ye Iran*.

25. Madani, *Huquq-e Asasi dar Jumhuri-ye Islami-ye Iran*, vol. 2, p. 252.

26. *Ibid.*

27. *Ibid.*, p. 253.

28. *Ibid.*

29. *Ibid.*, pp. 254-255.

30. *Ibid.*, p. 256.

31. See the section "Law and Order" pp. 92-109 in *Iran: Year Book 88*, (Bonn, Bonner Universität-Buchdruckerei, 1988), p. 96; for further information see the section "The

Judiciary" pp. 201-2 in I. Mertz and Helen Chapin (eds.), *Iran: A Country Study*, (Washington, DC, Federal Research Division Library of Congress, 1989), fourth ed.

32. "Law and Order" *Ibid.*, pp. 96-97.

33. *Ibid.*

34. *Ibid.*, p. 97.

35. *Ibid.*, p. 98.

36. *Ibid.*

37. William J. Butler, "Report on Human Rights in Iran" pp. 3-42, in William J. Butler and Georges Levasseur (eds.), *Human Rights and the Legal System in Iran*, p. 32.

38. Hamid R. Kusha, "Iran: The Problematic of Women's Participation in a Male-dominated Society", *Working Papers*, no. 136, (Office of Women in International Development, 1987), pp. 9-10.

39. See Ayatullah Khumaini, "Islamic Government," pp. 27-166 in Hamid Algar *Islam and Revolution: Writings and Declarations of Imama Khomeini*, (Mizan Press, Berkeley, CA, 1981), translated and annotated by Hamid Algar.

40. *Ibid.*, p. 56.

41. For more detail on the text of some of these covenants and various signatories including the Islamic Republic of Iran, see Edward Lawson (ed.), *Encyclopedia of Human Rights*, (New York, Taylor & Francis Inc., 1991); for various violations of these covenants in Iran, see Amnesty International, *Iran: Violations of Human Rights, Documents Sent by Amnesty International to the Government of the Islamic Republic of Iran*, (London, Amnesty International Publications, 1987); see also Winston E. Langley, (ed.), *Human Rights: Sixty Major Global Instruments*, (Jefferson, North Carolina, McFarland & Company, Inc., Publishers, 1992).

42. Cited in *Iranshahr*, vol. iv, no. 23, August 27, 1982. I have dropped the numbering of items in the original text for the sake of clarity.

43. See my paper, "The General Picture of Crime in the Islamic Republic of Iran: Has Islamization Been Able to Stamp-out Crime?" presented to the 1994 Annual Meeting, Academy of Criminal Justice Sciences, Chicago, IL.

44. Ahmad, *The Holy Qur'an*, vol. 2, p. 571. Italics are in the original.

45. Muhammad Hussain Saket, *Nahad-e Daadrasi Dar Islam: Padhuheshi dar Rewand wa Ravesh-e Daadresi wa Sazmaanhaa-ye Wabasteh az Aaghaaz taa Sadeh-e Sizdah-e Hejri* (The

Institution of Jurisprudence in Islam: A Study in the Jurisprudential Process and Relevant Institutions from the Beginning until the Thirteen Hijri Century), 83. Saket cites this Hadith from Muhammad Albaji, *Mathal `Aliya Min Qaza al-Islam,* (Tunisia, Al-Maktab al-Sharqiyah, 1376 Hijri), al-Tab al-Awal, pp. 74-79. fn. 82.

46. Mohammad M. Pickthall, *The Glorious Qur'an*, (New York, NY, Mostazafan Foundation of New York, 1984), p. 727.

47. *Ibid.*

48. *Ettelaat*, (Tir 3, 1360), 24 June, 1981.

49. Imam Bukhari, *Sahih al-Bukhari*, (Beirut, Lebanon, Dar al-Arabiyah, 1985), vol. 9, p. 25.

50. See this interview under the caption: "Sadegh Khalkhali: 'All the people who are opposed to our revolution must die.'" pp. 30-31, in *MERIP Reports*, no. 104, March-April 1982, p. 30.

51. *Ibid.*

52. *Ibid.*, pp. 30-31.

53. *Ibid.*, p. 31.

54. Khumaini, "Islamic Government" cited in Algar, *Islam and Revolution*, p. 33.

55. Cited in Arjomand, "Clerical Authority in the Constitution of the Islamic Republic of Iran," pp. 371-382 in Arjomand (ed.), *Authority and Political Culture in Shiism*, pp. 379-380.

56. *Ibid.*, p. 380.

6 The Criminogenic Impacts of the Sharia-Based Criminal Justice System in Iran, 1979-1999

With the establishment of a criminal justice system based on the Sharia Law, and with its almost two decades of operation, the following serious crimes and misdemeanours have risen sharply in Iran:

(1) Homicide (both intentional and unintentional)
(2) Inflicted battery and injury
(3) Vandalism
(4) Theft
(5) Use of alcoholic beverages (a crime in Iran)
(6) Use of illicit drugs (e.g., hashish, heroin and opium) a capital offence in Iran
(7) Cheques drawn on insufficient funds
(8) Fraud, embezzlement and other financial crimes
(9) Moral crimes
(10) Traffic crimes
(11) Narcotic crimes
(12) Political crimes.

As I will show in this chapter, for the first time in Iran's long history, women and even young girls have been involved in many of these types of crime that historically had remained, until the 1979 Revolution, the province of male criminals. At the same time, the suicide rate of women and young girls has risen dramatically despite the fact that, in Islam as a faith and in Iranian popular culture, suicide is denounced as a grave sin and anti-social act. Through various tables constructed from official crime data disseminated by the Ministry of Justice I will explain the reasons for the surge in the general and feminine crimes in the post-Islamic Revolution period.

Crime Data, Sources and Interpretation

In the past, official data could be gathered from various sources such as the Organization of Planning and Budget's Centre for Statistics on Iran, and various university-affiliated research centres. For example, one could gather data from official sources such as court dockets, as well as by conducting interviews with judges, prosecutors and even police chiefs. At the same time, one could get valuable data from dissident lawyers, various human rights groups such as Amnesty International (AI), and United Nation (UN)-affiliated organizations that monitored the situation of human rights in Iran under the Shah, Muhammad Reza Pahlavi (1941-1979). After the Islamic Revolution, and the rise of an ideological political establishment bent on exporting its brand of "revolutionary" Islam to the rest of the world, independent research has been impeded by the state's restrictions on the dissemination of crime and justice data. The leaders of the present regime have regarded Iran's post-Revolution social and political structures as the culmination of a pure Islamic and revolutionary entity, capable of providing a model for other Islamic societies to emulate. Because of these presumed characteristics of the state and of its revolutionary organs (e.g., the Islamic criminal justice system), these dignitaries argue that Islamic Iran presents a tangible threat to Western "moral decay" in terms of crime, justice and law, as well as undermining the Western powers' interests in the Middle East. Because of its presumed revolutionary character, the political establishment has been besieged by "enemies" who want to portray Islamic Iran as backward and reactionary, and filled with crime and violence.

Naturally, in an atmosphere of official suspicion towards research, it is very difficult to get an accurate estimate of actual crime rates, or of the current etiology of crime. For example, the only criminal justice statistics available to the non-Iranian scholarly community pertains to arrest statistics for the first half of the 1970s. All other "official" indices of crime and criminal justice system are in the category of "not available," as shown by Table 6.1.

Table 6.1 United Nations' profile on Iran's criminal justice system

CJS Statistics (1970-1980)	Offenders convicted	Sanctions-Background	Prisoners	CJS Personnel and resources
Not available	Not available	Not available	Not available	Not available
CJS Statistics (1980-1985)	Offenses Reported to the Police	Offenders apprehended or arrested	Offenders convicted	CJS Resources Stat
Not available	Not available	Not available	Not available	Not available

Source: http://www.ifs.univie.ac.at/~uncjin/profiles/iran.html
CJS: Stands for criminal justice system.

To get an idea about crime and its commission, I have relied on two types of source of crime statistics available: (a) the official data whose accuracy cannot be taken for granted, given the "ideological" considerations of the state or (b) semi-official crime data whose source can be enumerated as:

(1) News about various crimes disseminated by the press and print media
(2) News about punishment disseminated by press and print media
(3) Interviews of the Islamic judiciary
(4) Information on crime and punishment gathered by Amnesty International (AI) and United Nations' Human Rights Committee (UNHRC) and foreign governments (e.g., US State Department)
(5) Information on political dissent leading to the arrest and execution of dissenters disseminated by the political parties and groups in exile.

Based on a combined utilization of the official, and of the semi-official sources in this study, it can be shown that since the 1979 Revolution, Iran has gone through a tangible process of over criminalization evinced by the commission of serious crime (both property and violent crime categories), accompanied by consistent high rates of arrest and executions; this over-criminalization is further evinced by the construction of many new prisons and detention facilities. Various tables constructed for this purpose covering the post-Islamic Revolution period from 1985 to 1993 give an idea about the first ten crime categories that we enumerated above. The next section, however, gives some preliminary information about crime in the pre-Islamic Revolution period (1970-1975).

A General Picture of Crime in the Pre-Islamic Revolution Period, 1970-1979

During the 1960s and 1970s Iranian society entered into a period of modernization and industrialization that led to a general cycle of prosperity which, in turn, led to a relatively anti-criminogenic social and legal process in the 1970s.

As a general rule, serious crime and misdemeanours were of an urban nature and were concentrated in a number of large cities that comprised the provincial capitals. Historically speaking, the provincial capitals were the most populous cities functioning as the seat of the governors who were appointed by the person of the king responsible for disseminating King's Peace. Under the two Pahlavi monarchs, the governors were responsible for carrying out the monarch's reform measures which included, among others, those in Iran's modern criminal justice system. Table 6.2 sheds light on 36 types of crime and misdemeanour committed in Iran's Central Province in 1972.

Table 6.2 Thirty-six types of crime and misdemeanour committed in the Central Province of Iran in 1972 as reported by the municipal police

Crimes and misdemeanours	Total	Tehran	Other
Slander	2,380	2,339	41
Family disputes	4,579	3,481	1,098
Embezzlement	30	28	2
Real estate disputes	611	106	505
Industrial and commercial copyright violations	64	60	4
Illegal sale of alcoholic beverages	125	122	3
Illegal confiscation of property and public nuisance	419	216	203
State employees' violations of citizens' rights	10	5	5

Table 6.2 Continued

Disrespect and insult to state agents during their performance of their duties	588	536	52
Threat and compulsion	59	42	17
Cheating in commerce-related activities	56	13	43
Counterfeiting of, and tampering with, documents	325	308	17
Crimes against children	100	74	26
Crimes against the dead	2	1	1
Knife slinging	585	417	168
Drawing cheques on insufficient funds	6,268	5,659	609
Violation of trust	620	569	51
Fencing of stolen goods	12	4	8
Opening of places of ill-repute and forced prostitution	88	86	2
Kidnapping of persons, women and children	17	14	3
Bribery	9	9	0
Driving without a licence	6,586	4,849	1,737
Armed robbery	22	4	18
Counterfeiting coins	14	14	0
Falsifying titles and professions	14	14	0
Abetting the escape of convicts and giving them safe refuge	122	121	1
Smuggling activities	1,420	1,290	130
Gambling and opening of gambling houses	589	519	70
Fraud	790	739	51

Table 6.2 Continued

Intentional and unintentional poisoning	103	46	57
Male disturbance of adult and young women	1,222	1,045	177
Disrespect towards state employees and representatives	22	19	3
Fist fights	239	230	9
Child abandonment	313	297	16
Miscellaneous crimes	14,625	10,258	4,367
Total	**43,001**	**33,525**	**9,476**
Percentage	**100%**	**78%**	**22%**

Source: Adapted from *Aamaar Naameh Ostan-e Markazi Tir 1352* (The Statistical Compendium of the Central Province, April 1972), Table 88, pp. 124-125.

As Table 6.2 clearly indicates, of the 36 types of crime and misdemeanour committed in Iran's Central Province in 1972, 78 per cent took place in the Province's largest urban centre, Tehran. Insofar as the arrest statistics for these 36 crimes and misdemeanours are concerned, Table 6.3 shows for the Central Province in 1972.

Table 6.3 Municipal police arrest statistics in thirteen cities in the Central Province in 1972, categorized by gender and age

36 crimes/ misdemean-ours	Sex/age		Up to 18 yrs		19-30 yrs		31–60 yrs	
	M	F	M	F	M	F	M	F
Total arrested	**35,857**	**6,763**	**2,738**	**752**	**16,723**	**3,906**	**15,384**	**1,935**
Tehran	25,910	5,669	1,706	516	12,803	3,349	10,746	1,667
Damawand	245	19	14	0	87	10	137	9
Firuzkuh	245	23	21	4	91	7	129	12

Table 6.3 Continued

Khumain	652	7	51	3	212	2	377	2
Arak	2,118	142	96	10	846	80	1,071	46
Saweh	705	105	70	27	259	73	372	5
Qazwin	1,404	331	192	65	538	181	597	84
Qom	869	224	153	53	361	88	293	58
Kashan	1,294	109	165	42	620	49	468	18
Karaj	1,132	91	134	28	408	44	572	18
Garmsar	398	24	40	4	109	12	240	8
Mahallat	397	6	54	0	151	2	182	4
Varamin	488	13	42	0	238	9	200	4

Source: Adapted from *Aamaarnaameh Ostan-e Markazi, Tir 1352* (Statistical Compendium of the Central Province, April 1974), Table 86, pp. 122-123.

Comparing Table 6.2 with Table 6.3, it is apparent that there was a close correspondence between the total number of crimes and misdemeanours committed as reported by the municipal police (43,001) and the number of arrests reported (42,620) by the same agency of law enforcement in the Central Province in 1972. We also possess disclosed and narcotics-related, arrest statistics as reported by the municipal police for the same province and year. The data presented in Tables 6.4 and 6.5 indicate these statistics with the proviso that the data pertain to eight cities and towns in the Central Province in 1972.

Table 6.4 Narcotics disclosed by the municipal police in eight cities of the Central Province in 1972

City name	Morphine		Heroin			Opium		Shireh	
	cm	gr	cm	gr	kg	gr	kg	gr	kg
Tehran	80	100	48	494	41	364	196	654	6
Karaj	0	0	0	0	0	241	0	0	0

Qazwin	0	0	94	53	0	336	1	81	0
Qom	0	0	14	809	0	296	18	35	0
Garmsar	0	0	0	0	0	573	3	0	0
Arak	0	0	73	723	0	372	1	116	0
Kashan	0	0	50	0	0	15	0	26	0
Saweh	0	0	59	533	4	53	0	6	0
Total	**80 cm**	**100 gr**	**338 cm**	**2,612 gr**	**45 kg**	**2,250 gr**	**218 kg**	**918 gr**	**6 kg**

Source: Adopted from *Aamaarnaameh Ostan-e markazi, Tir 1352* (Statistical Compendium of Central Province, April 1974), Table 87, pp. 122-123. Others*: This category omitted from the above table contains two traditional narcotics known as *Taryak-e sukhteh* (residuals of the smoked opium), *Mayeh shireh* (a condensed form of opiate), and unidentified illicit drugs categorized as others.

Table 6.5, on the other hand, presents narcotics-related arrest statistics in the eight cities of the Central Province in 1972.

Table 6.5 Narcotics-related arrests by the municipal police in eight cities of the Central Province in 1972, categorized by gender and age

Narcotics-related arrests	**Total**		**Up to 18 yrs**		**19-30 yrs**		**31–60 yrs**	
City name	M	F	M	F	M	F	M	F
Tehran*	2,903	372	36	5	765	112	1,788	241
Karaj	11	1	0	0	0	0	10	1
Qazwin	131	6	3	0	38	3	80	3
Qom	90	3	2	0	28	1	54	2
Garmsar	3	0	0	0	0	0	3	0
Arak*	64	3	4	1	15	0	42	0
Kashan	5	0	0	0	0	0	5	0

Table 6.5 continued

Saweh	7	2	0	0	4	1	3	1
Total	3,214	387	45	6	850	117	1,98 5	248

Source: Adapted from *Aamaarnameh Ostane Markazi, Tir 1352* (Statistical Compendium of Central Province, April 1974), Table 87, pp. 122-123. * In the original Table 8727 numerical discrepancies have been recorded by this author.

Tables 6.2, 6.3, 6. 4 and 6.5 show the following about serious crimes and misdemeanours committed in Iran's most important and populous province in 1972: Tehran, as the most important urban centre in the Central Province, as well as the whole country, occupied a very important place in the commission of serious crime and misdemeanours (78 per cent). The city also occupied an important place in the use of illicit drugs among eight provincial towns of the Central Province in 1972 (100 per cent in morphine, 90 per cent in opium, 100 per cent in shireh, 79 per cent in hashish and 92.5 per cent in Other categories). The bulk of the arrests pertaining to the 36 types of serious crime and misdemeanour belonged to Tehran (74 per cent). The bulk of the arrests pertaining to narcotics use took place in Tehran (90.32 per cent of the total male arrests and 96.12 per cent of the total female arrests in the Central Province).

In 1972, there were seventeen urban centres in which, it is logical to presume, similar types of urban crimes and misdemeanours, including narcotics-related ones, were committed. This data, juxtaposed next to the available United Nations data on total arrests for the year 1972 in Iran, can give an approximate view of the aggregate crimes and misdemeanours committed in 1972. This, in turn, can be used as a basis of comparison between the pre-and post-Islamic Revolution rate of the commission of serious crime and misdemeanours. Tables 6.6 and 6.7 serve this purpose.

Table 6.6 General arrest statistics for Iran during 1970-1975

Year	1970	1971	1972	1973	1974	1975
Population in million	28. 6	29.9	30.7	31.6	32.5	33.4
Adult arrests	158,787	155,169	173,219	187,162	220,152	203,387
Juvenile arrests	1146	893	917	1252	Not available	Not available
Number of adult arrests per 100,000	544	518	563	592	677	609
Number of juvenile arrests per 100,000	4	3	3	4	Not available	Not available

Source: United Nations Criminal Justice Information Office's Profile on Iran.

Considering the fact that one has access to the actual number of thirty-six crimes and misdemeanours committed in the Central Province in 1972 next to narcotic arrest statistics (see Table 6.2), one can reasonably argue that it was the commission of these in Tehran, and in sixteen other urban centres, that led to the bulk of 173,219 arrests in the same year. Based on the population distribution of these urban centres, a crime-arrest distribution estimate can be made for the whole country in 1972. Table 6.7 is constructed for that purpose, taking Tehran as a representative base for violent, property-, and narcotics-related crime and arrests in 1972.

Table 6.7 shows a relatively low rate of crime commission for seventeen populous urban centres in Iran in 1972. The rates are 1,097 crimes per 100,000 general urban population, and 780 arrests per 100,000 general urban population. The remaining arrest statistics (174,316-59450=114,866) pertains to the rest of the population in Iran in 1972. This gives an arrest rate of 493 per 100,000 non-urban general population. This rate holds true if one were to assume a one-to-one correspondence between crime and arrest which is not the case in most countries. In other words, the aggregate arrest (e.g., 174,316 in this case) does not correspond to the same number of would-be criminals but more likely for lesser numbers of criminals, composed of

Table 6.7 Approximate crime-arrest distribution for seventeen urban centres in Iran in 1972

City	Population	ENCM	ECPR	ENA
Isfahan	605,000	6,758	1.11%	3,424
Mashad	592,000	6,484	1.11%	3,387
Tabriz	510,000	5,586	1.11%	2,890
Shiraz	373,000	4,085	1.11%	2,113
Abadan	312,000	3,417	1.11%	1,768
Ahwaz	302,000	3,307	1.11%	1,711
Kermanshah	249,000	2,727	1.11%	1,411
Rasht	175,000	1,917	1.11%	992
Qom	170,000	1,862	1.11%	963
Rezaiyah	155,000	1,698	1.11%	878
Hamdan	144,000	1,577	1.11%	816
Yazd	122,000	1,336	1.11%	691
Dezful	119,000	1,303	1.11%	674
Khorramshahr	109,000	1,194	1.11%	618
Qazwin	107,000	1,172	1.11%	606
Kerman	106,000	1,161	1.11%	601
Kerman	106,000	1,161	1.11%	601
Total (including Tehran)	7,445,000	81,673	1.11%	59,450

Source: Population data adopted from *The Middle East and North Africa 1974-75*. Arrest data adapted from United Nations Criminal Justice Information Office's Profile on Iran. Population (1973 estimates): 3,295,000 for Greater Tehran. Total number of arrests: 174,136 for the year 1972. Crime base: (33,534+3,275=36,089) actual number of serious crime and misdemeanours including narcotics committed in Tehran in 1972. ENCM=estimated number of crime and misdemeanours; ECPR=estimated crime-population rate; ENA=estimated number of arrests.

recidivists, as well as occasional and professional criminals. Following this rationale for the 1970s, one can reach the conclusion that the pre-Islamic Revolution was a period of relative prosperity, coupled with a relatively effective crime control strategy, making Iran one of those societies not obsessed with violent or property crimes. Although Table 6.7 shows a fluctuating aggregate arrest trend, which most likely signifies a corresponding crime trend, Iranian urban centres were relatively safe places in which to live and to raise a family in the pre-Islamic Revolution period. Juvenile crime was also negligible thanks to a thriving educational system that taught respect for authority, and prepared youths for a very competitive vocational job market as well as for the higher education system.

Crime in the Post-Islamic Revolution Period

Crime data for the post-Revolution period are presented in Tables 6.8 and 6.9. These tables represent 13 types of crime and misdemeanour prosecuted in four types of courts (the court of general jurisdiction, the high penal court, the law penal court, and the county courts of general jurisdiction) throughout the country, for which official data are available.

Table 6.8 Thirteen types of serious crime and misdemeanour committed and prosecuted in four types of court during 1985-1990

Year	1985	1986	1987	1988	1989	1990
Population (in millions)	47.82	49.44	50.67	51.92	53.14	54.47
Total, Ih*	3,098	3,456	3,740	4,501	5,295	4,996
Ih rate per 100,000 general population	6	7	7	9	10	9
Total, Uh*	22,473	23,249	23,812	23,087	24,853	24,101
Uh rate per 100,000 general population	47	47	47	44	47	44
Total, Ib* and In*	213,134	214, 796	218,310	223,299	243,599	242,706

Table 6.8 continued

Ib and In rate per 100,000 general population	446	434	431	430	458	446
Total Va*	35,643	38, 992	41,570	41,353	43,291	46,518
Va rate per 100,000 general population	75	79	85	80	81	85
Total, Ia*	37,450	48,542	40,299	43,634	50,634	50,099
Ia rate per 100,000 general population	78	98	80	84	95	92
Total, Em*	47,231	42,280	48,042	53,413	61,029	66,087
Em rate per 100,000 general population	99	86	95	103	115	121
Total, Th*	77,888	93,033	94,914	96,866	110,356	113,844
Th per 100,000 general population	163	188	187	187	208	209
Total, Fc* and Pn*	71,607	75,470	80,715	79,976	82,888	86,762
Fc and Pn rate per 100,000 general population	150	153	159	154	156	159
Total, cheques drawn on insufficient funds	73,451	85,578	85,886	104,794	139,279	166,080
Cheques drawn on insufficient funds rate per 100,000 general population	154	173	170	202	262	305
Total, alcohol consumption	16,283	15,818	15,015	14,774	22,752	24,790
Alcohol consumption rate per 100,000 general population	34	32	30	28	43	46
Total, driving w/o a licence	93,131	100,204	113,891	119,118	116,656	106,554

Table 6.8 continued						
Driving w/o a licence rate per 100,000 general population	195	203	225	229	220	196
Total, traffic and driving violations	358,928	614,143	515,824	356,842	462,377	502,484
Traffic and driving violations rate per 100,000 general population	751	1,242	1,018	687	870	922
Total, misdemeanours	109,456	112,645	100,017	106,324	96,498	97,976
Misdemeanours rate per 100,000 general population	229	227	197	205	182	180
Total, honour-based inappropriate use of language	3,242	2,897	2,680	3,432	3,322	3,543
Honour-based inappropriate use of language rate per 100,000 general population	7	6	5	7	6	7
Grand Total	1,163,015	1,471,103	1,384,715	1,271,413	1,462,829	1,536,540
Aggregate crime rate per 100,000 general population	**2,431**	**2,976**	**2,733**	**2,449**	**2,753**	**2,821**

Source: Adapted from *Saalnaameh Aamari-ye Keshvar 1370* (Iran Statistical Yearbook, March 1991-March 1992), pp. 229-231

Ih*= intentional homicide; Uh* = unintentional homicide; Va*= vandalism; Ib*= inflicted battery; In* = injury; Em* = embezzlement; Ia* = immoral acts; Th*= thievery; Fc*= forced confiscation; Pn*= public nuisance.

Table 6.9, on the other hand, gives a picture of crimes and misdemeanours pertaining to the first half of the 1990s. The reason for separating the two tables has a lot to do with the fact that Table 6.8 data pertain to the first decade of the post-Islamic Revolution, a decade whose social and political characteristics were shaped by a devastating eight years of war with neighbouring Iraq (1980-1988), coupled with internal conflicts, Iran's isolation from regional and international politics and many attempts by the new Islamic political establishment to reorganize the Iranian economy and society based on the Ayatullah Khumaini's ideals of Shii Islam and its version of the Sharia Law. The second decade was supposed to be a period of post-war reconstruction and reintegration of the Islamic Republic into a more moderate and rational system of governance and polity. By separating the two tables, I aim to give the reader a tangible measure for comparison between the two decades; this yardstick can also be used to compare the pre- and post-Islamic Revolution period's data on crimes and misdemeanours.

Table 6.9 Thirteen types of serious crime and misdemeanour committed and prosecuted in four types of court during 1990-1993

Year	**1991**	**1992**	**1993**
Population (in millions)	**55.80**	**57.20**	**58.49**
Total, Ih*	1,863	2,031	2,099
Adjusted (60%) total	2,981	3,250	3,358
Adjusted rate of Ih per 100,000 population	5	6	6
Total, Uh*	9,905	9,768	8,880
Adjusted (60%) total	15,848	15,629	14,028
Adjusted rate of Uh per 100,000 population	28	27	24
Total, In*	75,717	74,981	78,741
Adjusted (60%) total In	121,147	119,970	125,986
Adjusted rate of In per 100,000 population	217	210	215
Total, Va*	14,386	16,417	16,498
Adjusted (60%) total Va	23,018	26,267	26,397

Table 6.9 continued

Adjusted rate of Va per 100,000 population	41	46	45
Total, Ia*	25,802	28,282	29,588
Adjusted (60%) Ia	41,283	45,251	47,341
Adjusted rate of Ia per 100,000 population	74	79	81
Total, Em*	21,724	24,770	28,527
Adjusted (60%) total Em	34,758	39,632	45,643
Adjusted (60%) total Em	34,758	39,632	45,643
Adjusted rate of Em per 100,000 population	62	69	78
Adjusted (60%) total Th	66,347	64,336	62,494
Adjusted rate of Th per 100,000 population	119	112	107
Total, Fc* and Pn*	25,603	29,753	31,016
Adjusted (60%) total of Fc and Pn	40,965	47,605	49,626
Adjusted rate of total Fc and Pn per 100,000 population	73	83	85
Total, cheques drawn on insufficient funds	56,009	85,695	118,298
Adjusted (60%) total of cheques drawn on insufficient funds	92,614	137,112	189,277
Adjusted rate of cheques drawn on insufficient funds per 100,000 population	166	239	324
Total, consumption of alcoholic beverages	17,963	17,917	17,793
Adjusted (60%) total of consumption of alcoholic beverages	28,741	28,667	28,469
Adjusted rate of consumption of alcoholic beverages per 100,000 population	51	50	49

Table 6.9 continued

Total, driving w/o a licence	89,118	180,349	94,491
Adjusted (60%) total driving w/o licence	142,589	288,558	151,186
Adjusted rate of driving w/o licence per 100,000 population	256	504	258
Total, traffic and driving violations	202,373	221,605	196,024
Adjusted (60%) total of traffic and driving violations	323,797	354,570	313,638
Adjusted rate of traffic and driving violations per 100,000 population	580	619	536
Total, misdemeanours	63,050	65,614	50,912
Adjusted (60%) total misdemeanours	100,880	104,982	81,459
Adjusted rate of misdemeanours per 100,000 population	181	184	139
Total, honour-based inappropriate use of language	5,540	3,412	5,141
Adjusted (60%) total honour-based inappropriate use of language	8,864	5,459	8,226
Adjusted rate of honour-based inappropriate use of language per 100,000 population	16	10	14
Adjusted (60%) Grand Total	1,040,832	1,326,086	1,220,907
Adjusted (60%) aggregate crime rate per 100,000 population	1,866	2,318	2,085

Source: Constructed with data adopted from *Iran Statistical Yearbook 1375* (March 1996-March 1997), pp. 447-448.

Ih*= intentional homicide; Uh*=unintentional homicide; Va*=vandalism; Ib*= inflicted battery; In* = injury; Em*=embezzlement; Ia*=immoral acts; Th*=thievery; Fc*= forced confiscation; Pn*=public nuisance.

The available crime data on the early 1990s hardly gives a picture of a political establishment which has been able to establish a rational and anti-criminogenic criminal justice system based on an ideal Sharia Law that the regime claims in its official declarations defending the system. In fact, when approached from a multi-dimensional perspective based on: (1) a combined analysis of serious crime and misdemeanours, (2) of general poverty, (3) of consistent rates of high arrest and executions, and (4) of a deepening disorganization in social and political spheres, the picture that emerges is one of a total failure in the Islamic Republic's efforts to control crime through the Sharia Law.

To make Tables 6.8 and 6.9 meaningful, one has to compare and contrast the rate of commission of these crimes and misdemeanours with the similar ones already established in Table 6.3. However, in doing so one comes across a problem: Table 6.3 represents thirty-six crimes and misdemeanours for Iran's seventeen urban centres in 1972, whereas the post-Islamic revolution data do not reflect these crimes and misdemeanours. This lack of crime data is not due to lack of commission, but the fact that, under the Islamic criminal justice system, one encounters crimes that are no longer considered crimes in many other societies. For example, moral crimes in Iran occupy a significant place in the Islamic Criminal Code and their commission has led to a large number of arrests and detentions, whose statistics have to be gathered from semi-official data as I have done in this study and analysed in Chapter 7. Most of these crimes relate to female sexuality that, based on the Islamic regime's official ideology, can be characterized as feminine crimes (e.g., female style of walking, female gaze, female attire) to be explored in some detail in Chapter 7. Because of these limitations in the available official data, I have chosen only those which are similar to the ones reported in the pre-Islamic period data set above. Table 6.10 serves this purpose.

Table 6.10 A comparison between thirteen comparable pre- and post-Islamic Revolution crimes and misdemeanours

Crime type per 100,000 of general population	1972	1987	1988	1989	1990	1991	1992
Intentional homicide	NA	7	9	10	9	5	6
Percentage change between pre-and post-Islamic Revolution	NA	------	------	------	------	------	------
Unintentional homicide	NA	47	44	47	44	28	27
Percentage change	NA	------	------	------	------	------	------

Table 6.10 continued

between pre-and post-Islamic Revolution							
Inflicted battery, injury	25	431	430	458	446	217	210
Percentage change between pre-and post-Islamic Revolution		**1724**	**1720**	**1832**	**1784**	**868**	**840**
Inflicted battery, injury	25	431	430	458	446	217	210
Percentage change between pre-and post-Islamic Revolution		**1724**	**1720**	**1832**	**1784**	**868**	**840**
Crime type per 100,000 of general population	1972	1987	1988	1989	1990	1991	1992
Vandalism	NA	85	80	81	85	41	46
Percentage change between pre-and post-Islamic Revolution							
Immoral acts	25	80	84	95	92	74	79
Percentage change between pre-and post-Islamic Revolution		**320**	**336**	**380**	**368**	**296**	**316**
Embezzlement, fraud and counterfeiting	7	95	103	115	121	62	69
Percentage change between pre-and post-Islamic Revolution		**1,357**	**1,471**	**1,643**	**1,729**	**886**	**986**

Table 6.10 continued

Thievery	0.42	187	187	208	209	119	112
Percent change between pre-and post-Islamic Revolution		**44,524**	**44,524**	**49,524**	**49,762**	**28,333**	**26,666**
Forced confiscation and public nuisance	8	159	154	156	159	73	83
Percent change between pre-and post-Islamic Revolution		**1,987**	**1,925**	**1,950**	**1,987**	**912**	**1,037**
Cheques drawn on insufficient funds	121	170	202	262	305	166	239
Percent change between pre-and post-Islamic Revolution		**141**	**167**	**217**	**252**	**137**	**198**
Alcohol-related crimes	2.4	30	28	43	46	51	50
Percent change between pre-and post-Islamic Revolution		**1,250**	**1,166**	**1,792**	**1,917**	**2,125**	**2,083**
Driving without a licence	127	225	229	220	196	256	504
Percentage change between pre-and post-Islamic Revolution		**177**	**180**	**173**	**154**	**202**	**397**
Traffic and driving violations	145*	1,018	687	870	922	580	619
Percentage change between pre-and post-Islamic Revolution		**702**	**474**	**600**	**636**	**400**	**427**
Misdemeanours	281	197	205	182	180	181	184
Percentage change between pre-and		**-143**	**-137**	**-154**	**-156**	**-155**	**-153**

Table 6.10 continued

post-Islamic Revolution							
Honour-based inappropriate use of language	46	5	7	6	7	16	10
Percentage change between pre-and post-Islamic Revolution		**-920**	**-657**	**-767**	**-657**	**-287**	**-460**
Total of comparable crimes and misdemeanours per 100,000 population	774	2,736	2,249	2,753	2,641	1,869	2,238
Total, percentage change between pre-and post-Islamic Revolution		**353**	**291**	**356**	**341**	**241**	**289**

Source: 1972 data are adopted from Table 88 in the *Amaar nameh Ostan Matkazi,Tir 1352* (Statistical Compendium of the Central Province, July, 1974), pp. 124-125. Data on the 1972 traffic and driving violations have been adapted from Table 91, p. 129 of the same source.
NA: not available.

Total population for the Central Province is estimated at 5,200,000.

As Table 6.10's pre-Islamic Revolution data pertaining to the year 1972 clearly shows, except for two categories of intentional and unintentional homicide for which no data was available, and two other categories which show a lower rate of commission, all other comparable pre-Islamic Revolution crimes and misdemeanours have risen sharply in comparison with the post-Islamic Revolution period. Although in the early 1990s, a decline seems to have taken place in some of the serious crimes in comparison with the 1980s, the sharp contrast with the pre-Islamic Revolution period is, nonetheless, glaring. The main reason has to be located in the Islamic regime's mismanagement of Iranian economy which, as previously documented, has led to a criminogenic process of social disorganization. This process was further enhanced by the general disrupting impacts of the eight-year devastating, costly and futile war with Iraq (1980-1988).

Table 6.10's 1972 data are important because they pertain to Iran's Central Province whereby Iran's most important and populated city, Tehran, is located. Tehran has functioned as the nerve centre of the country for at least two centuries. In fact, as indicated by Table 6.11, during the monarchy and under a rather effective crime control mechanism (both formal and informal), Tehran's crime rates were not comparable with any other large cities, whether in the Central, or in any other provinces of the country. To give an example, of the available crimes and misdemeanours committed in the thirteen towns of the Central Province in 1972, the overwhelming majority was committed in the city of Tehran.

From the above tables and other sources pertaining to the 1970s, it can be shown that, whereas a large number of urban crimes and misdemeanours were committed in large cities such as Tehran and the sixteen others discussed above, other provincial towns remained relatively free of serious crime. In the post-Islamic Revolution, this picture has changed dramatically; serious crimes and misdemeanours have spread from large cities to provincial towns. The spread of serious crimes and misdemeanours is evidenced by the available official and semi-official data on arrest rates, as well as by the boom in the construction of prisons and penitentiaries throughout the country. Table 6.11 documents this phenomenon.

Table 6.11 Prisons and detention centres created since the Islamic Revolution, 1979-1998

Province	1976* pop	1998 pop	Pre-1979 CF**	Post-1979 CF	% Rise in CF	% Rise in pop	% DATC **
Tehran*	5565303	11176139	8	35	437	201	236
Khorasan	1,245,255	6,047,661	1	8	800	486	314
Mazandaran	502,803	4,028,296	2	22	1100	801	299
Esfahan	1,241,904	3,923,355	4	14	3500	316	3184
Fars	827,769	3,817,036	10	17	170	461	-291
Khuzestan	1,275,109	3,746,772	1	21	2100	294	1806
East Azarbaijan	1,188,286	3,325,540	8	34	425	280	145
West Azarbaijan	446,714	2,496,320	8	23	287	559	-272

Table 6.11 continued

Gilan	722,571	2,241,896	4	45	1125	310	815
Kerman	350,806	2,004,328	3	14	470	571	-101
Gilan	722,571	2,241,896	4	45	1125	310	815
Kerman	350,806	2,004,328	3	14	470	571	-101
Bakhtaran	441,885	1,778,596	2	17	850	402	448
Baluchestan Sistan	371,838	1,722,579	3	12	400	563	-63
Hamedan	325,176	1,677,957	3	8	267	516	-249
Province	1976* pop	1998 pop	Pre-1979 CF**	Post-1979 CF	% Rise in CF	% Rise in pop	% DATC **
Lorestan	294,618	1,584,434	1	3	300	538	-238
Kordestan	227,521	1,346,383	1	10	1000	591	409
Markazi	476,127	1,228,812	1	8	800	258	542
Ardebil	147,865	1,168,011	1	10	1000	800	200
Hormozgan	123,462	1,062,155	1	4	400	860	-460
Zanjan	144,612	1,036,873	2	3	150	717	-567
Qom*	247,219	853,044	1	5	500	345	155
Charmahal - Bakhtiari	187,204	761,168	------	------	------	------	------
Yazd	218,233	750,769	1	1	0	344	0
Bushehr	119,144	743,675	1	6	600	624	-24
Semnan	190,254	501,447	1	4	400	264	136
Kohgiluyeh-Boir ahmadi	30,867	544,355	------	------	------	------	------

Table 6.11 continued

Ilam	48,595	487,886	1	3	300	1004	-704
	16,971,273	60,055,488					
Total	*	*	68	317	16,381	11,514	4,867

Source: Designed from data on Iran's prisons and houses of detention disseminated by the National Council of Resistance of Iran's Official Publication, *SHOWRA*, no. 51, January-February 1990, pp.231-276. The 1976 population data is taken from *Rahnama-ye Jamiyat-e Shahrha-ye Iran 1335-1370* (Demographic Statistics on Iranian Cities 1956-1991), Table 1-3, pp. 49-72 excluding village population; population data on Iranian provinces have been obtained from *The Middle East and North Africa*, 1999 based on the 1996 census in Iran which includes the village population*, 1976 has been adjusted to include the village population giving a total of 33,591,875.
**CF= correctional facilities; DATC= difference attributable to the rise in crime.

In reading Table 6.11, it should be noted that the data on prisons and houses of detention are gathered from both semi-official sources as well as form opposition sources. Although the data is of an estimated nature, it is nonetheless substantiated by the semi-official data on arrest and executions statistics to be analysed in Chapter 7.

7 Feminine Crime under the Sharia-Based System in Iran

This chapter explores the reasons behind the surge in serious crimes and misdemeanours committed by women, as well as feminine involvement in anti-state activities (e.g., political crimes) in the post-Islamic Revolution period. The central argument of the chapter is that, until the 1979 Revolution, Iran's general prosperity, coupled with the monarchy's formal crime control strategies, were effective in the control of serious crimes and misdemeanours in Iran which, like most other Islamic countries, had a heritage of equating crime with masculine endeavour. Under the Islamic Republic, however, this trend has changed drastically. This change can be explained through the mismanagement of Iranian economy, which has led to general poverty. In turn, poverty has led to a general surge in both masculine and feminine crimes. In addition, the surge in feminine crime can also be explained by women's social and political reactions to the operational dynamics of Iran's Sharia Law-based criminal justice system, a system which has tried to revitalize a pre-capitalist and agriculturalist notion of law, justice and penology and which has resulted in the feminine reactions against the system.

The Mismanagement of the Iranian Economy

Since the 1979 Islamic Revolution, Iran has gone through a tumultuous process of social change, population surge and dislocation – a retrogressive economic differentiation, mostly at the expense of the general prosperity that was the hallmark of the 1960s and 1970s. Whereas most of the primary social and economic indicators of the 1960s and 1970s showed a gradual improvement in the social and economic status of Iranians, including that of women, the same cannot be said about the following two decades. In fact, these indicators show a general decline in women's social and economic status, and are briefly analysed below. From a critical criminological school perspective, this study holds that the present feminization of poverty, coupled with the criminogenic impacts of the Sharia-based oppressive laws, can explain the present surge in crimes committed by women. The most important

social and economic factors for the feminization of poverty include the following:
(1) Population and its dynamics
(2) Economic activity by sex
(3) Literacy by sex
(4) Positions of power occupied by women.

Indicators on Population and Its Dynamics

We start with the general picture of population dynamics in the 1960s and 1970s.

Table 7.1 Area and population dynamics in Iran

Area and Population			
Area	1,648,000sq. Km, or 636,296 sq miles		
Population (census results)	November 1966	November 1976	
	25,758,210	33,591,875	
Average annual birth rate	45.3 per 1000 in 1965-70 and 1970-75		
Death rate	17.4 per 1000 in 1965-70, 15.6 per 1000 in 19750-75		
Economically active population	M: 6,957,529	F:767,120	T: 7,724,649

Source: Adapted from the entry "Iran," *The Middle East and North Africa, 1979-80*, London, UK, Europa Publications Ltd., p. 365.

Table 7.2 Demographic change in Iran, 1956-1996

Year	Population	Average Rate of Annual Increase (%)
November 1956	18,954,704	3.1
November 1966	25,788,722	3.1
November 1976	33,708,744	2.7
October 1986	49,445,010	3.9
November 1996	60,055,488	1.5

Source: Adapted from *Iran Statistical Year Book 1375* (March 1996-March 1997), p. 33.

As Table 7.1 indicates, the Iranian population, with a very high birth rate of 45 per 1000, increased dramatically during the 1976-1986 decade and then declined to its present rate of 1.5 per cent. The United Nations Statistical Division has given a higher rate of 1.66 per cent projected for 1995-2000.

Based on Table 7.2, Iran's population went through a dramatic increase starting with the year of 1956 (1335 in the Iranian calendar). The pre-Islamic Revolution population surge was due to the combined impacts of two sets of policies. First, under the monarchy, there occurred a systematic and gradual improvement in Iran's health, education, as well as environment and economic systems, all of which allowed for an increase in the population coupled with a general decrease in the death rate due to improvement in the health and nourishment of the general population. Second, Iran, under the monarchy had gone through social and economic modernization and, therefore, was an important dependent constituent of the world capitalist system. As a dependent structure, Iran's social relations of production necessitated the monarchy to adhere to modern theories of economy which, in turn, required population control and family planning. The surge in the population was absorbed positively, if unevenly, in various developing sectors, as indicated by Table 7.5 which depicts Iran's economically active population by gender.

Under the Islamic Republic, Iranian society has gone through a tumultuous re-Islamization process despite the fact that Iran is one of the earliest societies in the Middle East to convert to Islam and has, in fact, contributed tremendously to the internationalization of Islam as a faith and civilizing force. This effort to re-Islamize Iran a second time has forced the Islamic political establishment to try to restructure Iran's economy, laws and social relations of production into an ideal Islamic system whose super-structure is supposed to be a Twelve Imami Shii version of the Sharia. As may be recalled from Chapter 6, Article 4 of the Constitution has decreed that this conversion has to be all-inclusive, covering every aspect of Iranian culture, laws, and social and economic relations under the supervision of the Guardian Council, a body of very traditional-minded religious legislatures composed of a select number of Shii jurists. The main function of this body is to make sure that bills passed by the Iranian parliament do not contravene the criteria of the Islamic Sacred Law (*Mawazin-e Shar-e Islam*).

In Chapter 6 we explored some of these criteria with regard to the social and political status of women, as well as their impact on the Islamic Republic's treatment of women and their criminality. Because the forced re-Islamization of Iranian society and economy has constituted the *raison d'être* of the Islamic Revolution, the new political establishment, under the tenure of the Ayatullah Khumaini, took it upon itself to create a model and revolutionary view of Islam that could rival both the East (the ex-Soviet bloc) and the West (the capitalist Western Europe and North American societies). This revolutionary Islam, in the eyes of its architects, required dedicated young Muslim revolutionaries, both men and women, to carry the banner of Islam. Thus, Iran's post-Revolution policies with regard to population dynamics were geared towards this end, leading to a dramatic surge in the population. These policies were facilitated by the official encouragement of procreation through the legalization of the traditional Islamic polygamous relations, the lowering of the legal age of female marriage, and a total disregard for the family control plans of the monarchy. The end result was catastrophic in terms of population explosion as indicated by Tables 7.1 and 7.2 above.

It is common knowledge that population is a double-edged sword. If a country's population and its dynamics (birth rate, death rate, infant mortality rate, the male-female ratio) were studied in the context of a human capital model, requiring both the state and the private sector to facilitate the positive utilization of the workforce, a surge in the population can enhance a country's economic growth. On the other hand, a population left to politically and ideologically reactive and medievalist charged measures is bound to set a retrogressive and even criminogenic process in motion. This latter policy, of course, would have negative consequences on the social and economic factors by means of which a country's general progress is managed.

As previously mentioned, the new Islamic political establishment's population policy was shaped by the belief that revolutionary Iran needed dedicated foot soldiers, not only to fight Iran's internal and external enemies, but also to export Khumaini's brand of Islam to the rest of the world, a view that was prevalent during 1979-1989 and especially during the war years with Iraq. As shown by Table 7.2, the policy implications of this view led to Iran's having one of the highest birth rates in the world during the 1980s – a trend which persisted into the mid-1990s. Despite the lowering of both the birth and death rates that occurred in the 1990s, Iran still suffers from one of the fastest population growth rates in the world.

Traditionally speaking, in Islamic societies, including Iran, a child-bearing mother is protected and cherished. The very fact of the pregnancy gives her a subtle position of power in the family. Where in post-industrialized societies, career-oriented women have to be very careful about an untimely pregnancy that may impede their career ambitions in a male-dominated corporate world, in Islamic societies pregnancy has its tangible social and psychological rewards. Unlike post-industrialized and democratic societies, where the decision to postpone marriage for the sake of a career is not uncommon, in Islamic societies, educated women don't necessarily have that choice. Pregnancy in Iran's presently highly skewed and depressed job market is an immediate cause for termination of the employment despite a number of progressive-sounding laws that have remained, like others, paper tigers.

Table 7.3 Birth and death rates, 1980-1995

Birth and Death Rates (UN estimates, annual averages)			
Rate	1980-85	1985-90	1990-95
Birth rate (per 1000)	46.1	41.4	35.5
Death rate (per 1000)	10.4	8.1	6.7

Source: Adapted from the entry "Iran" in *The Middle East and North Africa 1998*, p. 494.

Indicators on Economic Activity by Gender

Again, we have to make a comparison between the monarchy and the Islamic Republic's economically active population by gender. Based on the 1971 sample survey, Table 7.4 gives an idea about this important indicator.

Table 7.4 The economically active population under the monarchy, based on the 1971 sample survey (population 33,591,875)

Economic Sector	Number of Males	Number of Females	Total
	17,277,656 in GP*	16,314,219 in GP	33,591,875
Agriculture, forestry, hunting and fishing	3,616,537	83,850	3,700,387
Rate of employment	20,932 males per 100,000 males in GP	514 females per 100,000 females in GP	21,446
Mining and quarrying	14,290	107	14,397
Rate of employment	82 males per 100,000 males in GP	0.65 females per 100,000 females in GP	82.65
Manufacturing	931,657	487,835	1,419,942
Rate of employment	5,392 males per 100,000 males in GP	2,990 females per 100,000 females in GP	8,382
Construction	532,777	2,822	535,599
Rate of employment	3,084 males per 100,000 males in GP	17 females per 100,000 females in GP	3,101
Electricity, gas, water supply	45,404	1,615	47,019
Rate of employment	263 males per 100,000 males in GP	10 females per 100,000 females in GP	273
Commerce	706,473	10,385	716,858
Rate of employment	4,089 males per 100,000 males in GP	64 females per 100,000 females in GP	4153
Transportation, storage and communication	293,028	2,547	292,596

Table 7.4 continued

Rate of employment	1,696 males per 100,000 males in GP	16 females per 100,000 females in GP	1,712
	17,277,656 in GP*	16,314,219 in GP	33,591,875
Services	720,000	165,058	292,569
Rate of employment	4,167 males per 100,000 males in GP	1,012 females per 100,000 females in GP	5,179
Others (not adequately described)	20,363	907	885,058
Rate of employment	118 males per 100,000 males in GP	6 females per 100,000 females in GP	124
Total in employment	39,823 males per 100,000 males in all sectors	4,064 females per 100,000 females in all sectors	7,635,649
Unemployed	77,000	12,000	89,000
Total labour force	6,957,529	767,120	7,724,649
Rate of employment	90%	10%	100%

Source: Adapted from the entry "Iran" in *The Middle East and North Africa 1979-80*, p. 365.
GP*= general population.

As Table 7.4 indicates, the biggest sector for female employment was manufacturing, with a total of 487,835 female labourers. This figure has diminished drastically under the Islamic Republic in terms of both number and percentage, as indicated by Table 7.5. Tables 7.5 and 7.6, on the other hand, illustrate the drastic changes that have taken place in Iran's economically active population to the detriment of women's participatory roles in the economy, thus leading to the feminization of poverty.

Table 7.5 The economically active population under the Islamic Republic, based on the 1991 census (population 55,837,163)

Economic Sector	Number of Males	Number of Females	Total
	28,768,450 in GP*	27,068,713 in GP	55,837,163

Table 7.5 continued

Agriculture, hunting, forestry and fishing	3,046,283	159,147	3,205,430
Rate of employment	10,589 males per 100,000 in GP	588 females per 100,000 in GP	11,177
Mining and quarrying	97,664	2,881	3,205,430
Rate of employment	339 males per 100,000 in GP	11 females per 100,000 in GP	350
Manufacturing	1,710,857	302,867	2,013,724
Rate of employment	5,946 males per 100,000 in GP	1,119 females per 100,000 in GP	7,065
Electricity, gas and water	125,757	3,243	129,000
Rate of employment	437 males per 100,000 in GP	12 females per 100,000 in GP	449
Construction	1,364,117	8,320	1,372,437
Rate of employment	4,742 males per 100,000 in GP	34 females per 100,000 in GP	4,776
Trade, restaurants and hotels	1,221,712	16,593	1,238,305
Rate of employment	4,247 males per 100,000 in GP	61females per 100,000 in GP	4,308
	28,768,450 in GP*	27,068,713 in GP	55,837,163
Transport, storage and communications	750,984 in this sector	11,194 in this sector	762,178
Rate of employment	2,610 males per 100,000 in GP	41females per 100,000 in GP	2,651

Table 7.5 continued

Financing, insurance, real estate and business services	179,016	15,670	194,686
Rate of employment	622 males per 100,000 in GP	58 females per 100,000 in GP	680
Community, social and personal services	2,908,674	609,223	3,517,897
Rate of employment	10,111 males per 100,000 in GP	2,251 females per 100,000 in GP	12,362
Activities not adequately defined	460,325	102,088	562,413
Rate of employment	1,600 males per 100,000 in GP	377 females per 100,000 in GP	1,977
Total labour force	11,865,389	1,231,226	13,096,615
Rate of employment	90.59%	9.41%	100%

Source: Adapted from the entry "Iran" in *The Middle East and North Africa 1998*, p. 494. The calculations belong to this author.
GP= general population.

To make the two tables more meaningful, I have constructed Table 7.6 to compare and contrast these changes in terms of the pre- and post-Islamic Revolution rates of an active male-female population.

Table 7.6 A comparison between pre- and post-Islamic Revolution share of economically active population by gender

Change in the Economically Active Population 1976-1998 (per 100,000)								
Economic Sector	1976	1998	Change		1976	1998	Change	
	M	M	P	N	F	F	P	N

Table 7.6 continued

Agriculture, forestry, hunting and fishing	20,932	10,589		10,343	514	588	74	
Mining and quarrying	82	339	257		0.65	11	10.35	
Manufacturing	5,392	5,946	554		2,990	1,119		1,871
Construction	3,084	4,742	1,658		17	34	17	
Electricity, gas, water supply	263	437	174		10	12	2	
Commerce	4,089	4,247	758		64	61		3
Transport, Storage and Communication	1,696	2,610	914		41	16		25
Services	4,167	10,111	5944		1,012	2,251	1239	
Others (not adequately specified)	118	1,600	1,482		6	377	371	

M= male
F= female
P= positive change
N= negative change

As Table 7.6 indicates, despite some positive changes in the post-Islamic Revolution rates of female participation in some sectors of the economy, a drastic decline has taken place in the female rate of participation in manufacturing that, next to the oil and gas industry, constitutes one of the most important branches of activity in Iran's economy. In 1998, for example, the total number of females employed in the manufacturing sector was 302,867 out of 2,013,724 (male and female) labourers employed. This number (302,867), gave a female participation rate of 15.04 per cent whereas the male rate was about 84.95 per cent. This increase in the male rate compared to a drastic decrease in the female rate can be explained by the combined effects of two related policies. First, the overall deterioration of Iran's manufacturing industries in the 1980s and 1990s has led to periodic massive lay-offs in which women have been the first to be fired. As a result, the International Labour Office put Iran's "women's share of the adult labour force" at 24 per cent in

1995. Thus, Iran ranks 61among 68 Asian countries in terms of this important social and economic indicator for women's participatory role.[1]

More important is the second factor relating to the Islamic regime's strategic view that a strict sexual division of labour is God-ordained and sanctified by the Sharia Law that has to be adhered to for the sake of society's moral and functional progress. This view, as we have already explored in Chapter 6, maintains that women's most important duty is motherhood, and this duty has been inserted in the Constitution of the Islamic Republic. The policy implications have been drastic for educated women. Not only have the state's major policies and laws been drafted to perpetuate a strict gender-based division of labour, but the private sector has also been affected by this official view, deepening women's social and economic dependency on an already existing but receding patriarchal system under the monarchy that has now been resuscitated and relegitimated by the present Islamic political establishment. Ironically, although the dignitaries of the political establishment argue that in an ideal Islamic society, a woman's place is in the home, during the eight years of war with Iraq (1980-1988), out of necessity, women were employed at a much higher rate. This increased rate continued until 1991, a year which corresponded to the start of Iran's post-war reconstruction plans under the presidency of the Hujjat al-Islam Ali Akbar Hashemi Rafsanajani (1989-1997). In spite of this reconstruction effort, the total number of women employed was 210,787, many fewer than the last years of the pre-Revolution period (487,835) and fewer still than the war years (639,099). In other words, with one of the fastest growing population rates in the world, and after almost a decade of reconstruction efforts, women's rate of employment in Iran's manufacturing sector has hardly reached the pre-Islamic Revolution level.

Insofar as other economic indicators are concerned, the only noticeable factors besides manufacturing was the service industry. For example, a comparison between the two tables shows that during the pre-Revolution period, the rate of female employment in the service sector was about 18.64 per cent; in 1991 this rate was 17.31 per cent, despite the huge increase in Iran's population during the 1980s and 1990s. In the 1998 statistics, this rate was the same. In 1999 the service sector was divided between "education," "health and social work," and "other community, social and personal services activities". The only significant rates among these are the rates of female employment in education, health and social work that have historically been female professions.

Indicators on Literacy by Gender

Again, we have to make a comparison between the pre-Islamic and post-Islamic Revolution periods with regard to literacy. Table 7.7 illustrates Iran's literacy situation from 1956 to 1996.

Table 7.7 Literacy rates, 1956-1996, categorized by gender

Decades and population	**Number** Male and Female	Male	Female
November 1956	1,911	1,454	457
Population: 18,954	ALR* 10%	MLR* 7.67%	FLR* 2.4%
November 1966	5,556	3,928	1,628
Population: 25,788	ALR 21.54%	MLR 15.23%	FLR 6.31%
November 1976	12,877	8,198	4,679
Population: 33,708	ALR 38.20%	MLR 24.32%	FLR 13.88%
October 1986	23,913	14,078	9,835
Population: 49,445	ALR 48.36%	MLR 28.47%	FLR 19.89%
November 1996	41,582	22,465	19,118
Population: 60,055	ALR 69.23%	MLR 37.40%	FLR 31.83%

Source: Adapted from *Saalnaameh Aamaari-ye Keshvar 1375*, (Iran Statistical Yearbook March 1996-March 1997), Table 16.1, p. 514.
ALR*=aggregate literacy rate.
MLR*=male literacy rate.
FLR* =female literacy rate.

As Table 7.7 indicates, there was a steady raise of aggregate literacy in Iran from 1956 to 1996. This gradual rise indicates that, in 1996, Iran's total literate population was 41,582,000 out of a total population of 60,055,488 giving a general literacy rate of 69.2 per cent. The table also gives a gender-based literacy rate that shows a steady rise in the literacy rate of the two sexes. This apparent rise in female literacy, positive as it is, has not led to the desired results because Iran's post-Islamic Revolution retrogressing economic base has negatively impacted female employment opportunities (see

Table 7.5). In 1996, for example, the total female labour force was 1,765,402 out of a total labour force of 14,571,572. Considering that, in the same base year, the number of educated females of employment age (from 18 to retirement age) was 14,470,000 (see Table 7.6), it means that female employment was 12.2 per cent. This percentage, in turn, implies that out of every one hundred educated and employable women, only twelve enjoyed employment and its privileges. The rest had to settle for seasonal jobs and underemployment practices (e.g., part-time job and seasonal jobs) leading to the deepening of economic dependency and feminization of poverty. A percentage of the unemployed or underemployed female population may revert to unsavoury and outright criminal acts.

Positions of Power Occupied by Women

The number of important positions that women occupy in a society's social, economic, political and legal sectors is one of the most important indicators of that society's view of the role and importance of women. The 1996 data provided by the United Nations' Statistics Division on this indicator puts Iran among the least developed Asian societies with 0 per cent of women in "ministerial level" posts and 0.5 per cent at "sub-ministerial level."[2] The same data gives a percentage of 13.0 percent to both Israel and Sri Lanka, 12.5 per cent to Bhutan, 10.5 per cent to Kyrgyzastan, 7.7 per cent to Bangladesh, 6.1 per cent to China and 6.8 per cent to the Syrian Arab Republic with similar percentages in the sub-ministerial levels. These percentages are even more dramatic when compared to women's positions of power in advanced regions of the world, with 40 per cent of these positions occupied by women in Liechtenstein and 38.1 per cent in Sweden, for example.

In sum, notwithstanding the Islamic Republic's rhetoric of having revolutionized women's status, some of the most important social and economic indicators show a discernible retrogression in women's status during the 1980s and 1990s in Iran.

The next section analyses various factors responsible for the general surge of feminine crime under the Islamic Republic. In previous chapter, we have already established the fact that the post-Islamic Revolution Iran has gone through a long cycle of over-criminalization due to a deliberate attempt on the part of the Islamic political establishment to force Iranian system of law, justice, crime and penology into a pre-capitalist and agricultural valuation system and social relations of production under the re-Islamization process.

Feminine Crime and Misdemeanours, 1970-1999

Iranian modernization efforts in the 1960s and 1970s liberated, to some extent, a segment of women belonging to the middle and upper-middle classes from the yokes of traditional gender-based restrictions in social, economic and legal affairs. Nevertheless, this liberation, whose ideological base was an externally imposed dependent capitalist division of labour, did not push women into unbridled cycles of crime and misdemeanours.

Traditional Feminine Crime and Misdemeanours

Traditional feminine crime and misdemeanours centred on prostitution coupled with illicit drug use and pushing in Iran's red light districts (e.g., Shahre-Now in Tehran). As a general rule, prostitution was tolerated by the municipal police, provided that it remained in designated areas of the urban centres; as in all traditional societies, prostitution was tolerated for its traditional function as an outlet for the sexual frustration of young men and other social categories (e.g., drafted soldiers, rural male immigrants who sought manual jobs in cities, or the so-called undesirable social elements etc.). In addition to the red light district prostitutes, there were independent madams. Through their reputation, these madams became known to their clientele, by providing relatively high-priced prostitutes who would usually participate at home parties held by young and affluent men, at which various types of illicit drugs would be provided. Most prostitutes were victims of Iran's very strict traditional view of chastity: a young woman who lost her virginity would be denounced by her family and, in most cases, subjected to the most humiliating treatment at the hands of male members of the family who could, and did, carry out honour killing. Faced with such a prospect, young women who lost their virginity would escape to large cities (usually Tehran) and then fall into the larger prostitution rings.

After the Islamic Revolution, the new regime sought to eradicate prostitution by closing down the red light districts and sending the prostitutes to re-education camps. With the onslaught of the war, this project, like other reactive and totalitarian re-Islamization projects, was shelved. The end result was the spread of prostitution, with its criminogenic results, throughout the cities.

Feminine Power-related Crimes

With the advent of Iran's industrialization process in the 1970s, educated women of the middle and upper-middle classes entered into various professions, a picture of which we presented in Chapter 6. Professions such as banking, real estate, finance and accountancy brought women closer to Iran's strictly male-controlled economic and political centres of decision-making and therefore provided some opportunities for economic and financial crimes. Women were also involved in the use and pushing of narcotics as previously documented this in Chapter 6 of this study. There was a persistent rumour that some of the Shah's courtesans and female members of the Imperial Family were involved in embezzlement, bribery and other such power-related financial crimes.

Women's Involvement in Political Crime

Like other developing and modernizing Third World countries of the 1960s and 1970s, the Iranian Penal Code, analysed in Chapter 6, had conceived of any challenge to the monarchy's power in terms of potentially anti-state and subversive acts, and therefore crimes. In democratic societies, a political crime is a misnomer. Political activities are protected by law and legitimate attempts to change a government, or to assume the highest office in the land, are allowed through various means (plebiscite, voting and general elections, political coalitions). One tangible measure of the openness of any political system is the degree to which a political system allows women to assume a position of power in the various echelons of a political establishment. Under the monarchy, and especially after the White Revolution, a number of upper-middle-class Iranian women were appointed by the shah to the Iranian senate; some others were elected to the Iranian parliament. Women lawyers were allowed to sit as judges and were licensed as practicing attorneys. Other professions were also becoming open to educated middle-class Iranian women. At the same time, there was a new cadre of high school- and university-educated women who were drawn into the realm of political dissent and even anti-state activities because there was this general perception that the shah, Muhammad Reza Pahlavi, was becoming a despot dependent on foreign powers, especially the United States. In the 1970s, the Pahlavi political establishment, strategically aligned with the United States, was fast turning Iran into one of the most dreaded police states. Horror stories of the maltreatment of political prisoners, especially women, circulated among the

Iranian intelligentsia and especially among college and university campuses throughout Iran. Women political prisoners such as Marziyeh Oskui and Ashraf Dehqani (members of the PFGOI) as well as Fatimah Amini and Ashraf Rabi`i (members of the PMOI), were looked on as symbols of highly educated women revolutionaries who had rejected the reform measures of the White Revolution and had opted instead for the pure revolutionary ideals of socialism (in the case of PFOGI) and of egalitarian Islam (in the case of the PMOI).

Because of the widespread and systematic torture of political prisoners in the 1960s and 1970s, the International Commission of Jurists, concerned over the human rights violations in Iran, commissioned William J. Butler and Georges Levasseur, two distinguished lawyers, to visit Iran in 1975 in order to obtain, in the words of the Commission, "first-hand information about the operation of the military tribunals or the organization and activities of the SAVAK security police."[3] Under the heading of "The Suppression of Political Opposition," the report gave two main periods: mass detention following the fall of Premier Dr. Muhammad Musaddiq, 1953-1959; and political trials between 1963 and 1975. In the first period, members of the communist Tudeh Party of Iran (TPI) and the National Front (NF) were persecuted resulting in:

(1) The arrest, trial and imprisonment of 500 military personnel who had connections with the TPI. Of those, 50 were executed.

(2) The arrest of "several hundred" civilians members of the TPI; some were released upon their public denunciation of the Party and the rest, comprising "an unknown number," were sentenced to prison.

(3) The arrest, trial and imprisonment of Dr. Mussadeq, Dr. Shayegan, Dr. Lutfi, and Ahmad Razavi.

(4) The arrest, trial and execution of Dr. Fatemi (Dr. Musaddeq's foreign minister) in 1954.

(5) The arrest and *in camera* trials of 471 military personnel and 6 civilians for alleged illegal political activities that supposedly endangered the state's security; of those, 27 were executed, 144 received life sentences with hard labour, 119 received 15 years with hard labour, and 165 received sentences varying from 3 to 10 years of solitary confinement.

(6) The execution of 4 military officers in 1954 for having had associations with the TPI.

(7) The executions of 5 TPI members which took place in 1955 in Tabriz.[4]

These arrests and executions took place in the aftermath of the 1953 *coup d'état* against Iran's popular and democratically elected Dr. Muhammad Musaddiq, whose nationalization of Iranian oil industries had brought him face to face with the then most formidable oil ventures, the famed Seven Sisters.

With the success of the coup in 1953, the new regime moved against "undesirable" political forces and personalities in order to pave the way for Iran's entrance into an externally imposed and dependent capitalist division of labour which, among other things, required a new distribution of Iranian oil. The next waves of arrests and executions took place, argues Butler, in the period of 1963-1975 that corresponded to the implementation of a series of reforms that the shah, Muhammad Reza Pahlavi initiated in the early 1960s under the banner of the White Revolution. These reform measures aimed to facilitate the implementation of the new division of labour's infrastructure. This scheme, of course, necessitated modernizing Iran's social relations including, among other things, a shift in the gender relations within the context of laws and social participation. Following the anti-regime nation-wide mass demonstration in June 1963, the next wave of arrests and detentions covered the following (according to Butler's report):

(1) The mass detention, summary trials and execution of unknown numbers; the report argued that "an estimated 1000 deaths in Tehran alone" took place.[5]

(2) The detention of 3 members of Iran's Liberation Movement (Nehzat-e Azadi Iran); another eight members in May 1963, and a trial in January 1964.

(3) The arrest and trial of 4 members of the Socialist Society of Iran (Jameeh-e Susiyalisthay-e Iran) in September 1965.

(4) The arrest and trial of 14 intellectuals charged with conspiring against the state and plotting to kill the head of state (some were given short sentences and 2 were given life sentences) in 1965.

(5) The arrest and trial of 55 members of the Islamic Nation's Party in February-March, 1966.

(6) The arrest and trial of 7 members of the TPI in April-May, 1966.

(7) The arrest and trial of 14 intellectuals and students between December 1968 and January 1969.
(8) The arrest and trial of 18 students between December 1970 and January 1971.
(9) The arrest and trial of 100 persons between January and March 1972.
(10) The arrest and trial of 12 writers and artists in January 1974.

Representatives from the International Association of Democratic Lawyers were allowed to attend some of the trial proceedings and received complaints from defendants (including some women) about having been tortured, not having been allowed to examine the charges against them, and not having been accorded a host of other procedural rights. The report concluded that:

> Since 1971 of the 424 known individuals who have been imprisoned for charges relating to actions against the security of the state, 75 have been executed, 55 have been given life sentences, 33 have been sentenced between 10 to 15 years of imprisonment and others have been given lesser sentences. Also 50 have been killed in skirmishes with the police, 9 have been killed in prison, presumably while trying to escape, and the opposition press has named 16 prisoners all of whom have been killed under torture.[6]

The year 1971 corresponded to the beginning of an armed struggle against the Pahlavi regime that was initiated by the Marxist-Leninist PFGOI. The struggle began in the Siyahkal region of Mazandaran Province in Northern Iran. The Siyahkal became a symbol of Iranian guerrilla forces' readiness to challenge the shah's much dreaded army-SAVAK, anti-terror apparatus that had been installed with the help of American military advisers stationed in Iran. The Siyahkal event was to be followed by another city guerrilla group, the PMOI, a radical and yet modern Muslim group of young and educated revolutionaries who waged armed struggle against the Pahalvi regime in the 1970s. Up until then, the reformist movements led by a coalition of bourgeois-democratic forces represented mainly by the National Front, had been crushed by the shah, argued these guerilla forces. From 1971 to 1979, the armed struggle was to provide, in the words of Massud Ahmadzadeh, one of the ideologues of the PFGOI, a new strategy and a new tactic.

Because the armed struggle became the main tactic of the revolutionary forces in the 1970s, it was these revolutionary forces who became the main concern of the shah's police, army, gendarmerie and security forces. For the first time, young and university-educated Iranian women entered the rank and file of both the PFGOI and PMOI as revolutionaries bent on toppling the Pahlavi monarchy and replacing it with alternative regimes that were to be revolutionary, progressive, anti-imperialist and non-aligned. These women revolutionaries, once captured by the SAVAK and army intelligence units, were subjected to severe treatment in such notorious prisons as Qezel Qaleh, Qasr, Evin and Gohar Dasht in Tehran, or similar ones in other large urban centres built for warehousing political prisoners.

The Pahlavi regime, as oppressive a police state as it had become in the 1970s, followed, nonetheless, a relatively modern and rational theory of economics that allowed the regime to create a vast infrastructure for an externally imposed process of economic differentiation and development. It also structured a constructive international diplomacy and was accorded a certain division of labour in the world capitalist system. The regime, under the shah, Muhammad Reza Pahlavi had shifted its Third World dependent status from Britain to the United States of America especially after the inauguration of the White Revolution principles in 1963. This reform programme, as I have argued elsewhere,[7] was to sever the social and political umbilical cord of the *coup d'état* regime of 1953 from British imperialism and transform it into a dependent-capitalist formation within the world capitalist system under its hegemonic power, the United States of America. Within the context of this transformation, the laws and the judiciary had to have some semblance of modernity. This premise is not to absolve the shah, Muhammad Reza Pahlavi and the United States from their grave mistakes in launching the illegal coup against the only viable democratic regime that Iran's post-Second World War generation experienced under Dr. Musaddeq. Neither is this premise to absolve the shah for having illegally, indeed criminally, crushed the remnants of those democratic forces that believed in a parliamentarian form of opposition but were systematically neutralized through the criminalization of political dissent. What is certain is that the Pahlavi regime's development and modernization efforts took place at the expense of democracy and the democratic institutions that Dr. Musaddeq had tried to install in Iran during his brief tenure (1951-1953). One ideal of the Iranian Revolution in 1979 was to make Iran a democratic society whose social, economic and legal progress was to be harmonious with Iran's internal priorities. Political crime, torturing of political opponents and political prisons were to be the heritage of the despotic Pahlavi monarchy.

Feminine Crime in the Post-Islamic Revolution Period, 1979-1999

For the first time in Iran's modern history, a large number adults and young women have been involved in the commission of both traditional and political "crimes," all of which, except prostitution, have historically been associated with men. Under the previous regime, the reasons for the commission of non-traditional feminine crimes could be explained by Freda Adler's famous "liberation" hypothesis – namely, that the liberation of women from traditional social, political and economic bondage is bound to have a discernible impact on the commission of crime. But this hypothesis cannot explain feminine crime under the present Islamic regime. In fact, based on the Islamic Republic's ideological rationale that women's place is in the home, the surge in feminine crime has to be explained by the combined impacts of: the feminization of poverty, and a feminine social reaction to Iran's Sharia Law-based social and legal status, including the Islamic criminal justice system's treatment of women. The next section substantiates this argument through a number of tables created from different official and semi-official data in order to make a comparison between the pre- and post-Islamic Revolution periods in terms of feminine crime.

Feminine Violent Crimes

Tables 7.8 and 7.9 pertain to arrests for homicide, injury, battery, threat, and intentional poisoning, as reported by the Islamic Republic's municipal police and categorized by sex and age (1985-1990).

Table 7.8's data shows a fluctuating arrest rate for five serious crimes for the general population, for males and for females during the 1985-1990 period. Another set of official data released by the Statistical Centre of Iran (SCI), pertains to the above category of violent crimes between the 1995-98 period as depicted in Table 7.9.

Year	1985	1986	1987	1988	1989	1990
Population (million)	47.82	49.44	50.67	51.92	53.14	54.47
AARMF*	42,029	45,640	41,711	45,668	55,240	44,596
18 yrs of age and less	6,908	7,680	6,174	7,401	8,076	6,689
19-30 yrs of age	20,925	22,754	20,480	23,840	28,478	22,662
31 yrs of age or more	14,196	15,206	15,057	14,427	18,686	15,245
AAR* per 100,000 general population	88	92	82	88	104	82
Male	36,723	39,638	36,129	39,787	48,703	39,895
18 yrs of age and less	5,886	6,163	5,381	6,516	7,186	5,963
19-30 yrs of age	18,184	19,921	17,555	20,811	25,026	20,259
31 yrs of age or more	12,689	13,554	13,193	12,460	16,491	13,673
Female	5,306	6,002	5,582	5,881	6,527	4,701
18 yrs of age and less	1,022	1,517	793	885	890	726
19-30 yrs of age	2,777	2,833	2,925	3,029	3,452	2,403
31 yrs of age or mor	1,507	1,652	1,864	1,967	2,195	1,572
AR* per 100,000 males	77	80	71	77	92	73
AR per 100,000 females	11	12	11	11	12	9

Source: Adapted from *Saalnaameh Aamaari-ye Keshavar* (Iran Statistical Year Book 1370 (March 1991-March 1992), Table 8.11, p. 233.

The original data set does not show aggregate arrest rates which I have added to the table.

AARMF*=aggregate arrest rate for males and females.

AAR*= aggregate arrest rate.

AR*=arrest rate.

Table 7.9 Aggregate arrest statistics for five crimes (murder, assault, battery, threat and willful poisoning), 1995-1998

Gender and age groups	1995-96	1996-97	1997-98
Male and female	*50,244	*51,662	*54,145
17 years and under	4,285	4,094	4,291
18-24 years	17,136	17,847	17,090
25-34 years	18,039	18,454	20,708
35 years and over	8,441	8,982	9.924
AARMF per 100,00 general population	84	85	88
Male	*42,135	*43,330	*44,214
17 years and under	3,407	3,301	3,504
18-24 years	13,975	14,650	14,075
25-34 years	15,327	15,453	15,980
35 years and over	7,381	7,806	8,693
AR per 100,000 males	70	71	71
Female	*8,109	*8,332	*9,931
17 years and under	878	793	787
18-24 years	3,161	3.197	3,015
25-34 years	2,712	3,001	4,728
35 years and over	1,060	1,176	1,231
AR per 100,000 females	13.50	14	16

Source: Adapted from *Markaz-e Aamaar-e Iran* (Statistical Centre of Iran) at http://www.sci.irannet/english/se1/lif11.htm

*Differences between total and sum of parts is [sic] due to inclusion in total of the number of persons whose age groups were not stated."

AARMF=aggregate arrest rate for males and females.; AAR=aggregate arrest rate; AR=arrest rate.

In reading Table 7.9, it should be noted that these rates are based on arrest rather than actual crimes committed in this period (1995-98). The actual figures for these five violent crimes were 65,500 for 1995-96, 63,531 for 1996-97, and 69,591 for 1997-98 according to statistics provided by the same source.

A comparison with the pre-Islamic Revolution period Table 7.8 becomes more meaningful when compared and contrasted with comparable data on similar crimes categorized by gender and age for a similar period in terms of duration. I have already designed some tables pertaining to the aggregate arrests for the whole country during the 1970-1975, period as well as those pertaining to 36 types of serious crimes as reported by the municipal police of the Central Province. Table 7.10 depicts the combined data set.

Table 7.10 Offenders apprehended for 36 crimes or misdemeanours, 1970-1975

Year	1970	1971	1972	1973	1974	1975
Population in million	28.66	29.93	30.76	31.62	32.50	33.37
Total arrestee	158,787	155,169	173,219	187,162	220,152	203,387
AAR per 100,000 GP	554	518	563	592	677	609
Male	36,723	39,638	36,129	39,787	48,703	39,895
18 yrs of age and less	5,886	6,163	5,381	6,516	7,186	5,963
19-30 yrs of age	18,184	19,921	17,555	20,811	25,026	20,259
AAR per 100,000 GP	554	518	563	592	677	609
Male	36,723	39,638	36,129	39,787	48,703	39,895
18 yrs of age and less	5,886	6,163	5,381	6,516	7,186	5,963

Table 7.10 continued

19-30 yrs of age	18,184	19,921	17,555	20,811	25,026	20,259
31 yrs of age or more	12,689	13,554	13,193	12,460	16,491	13,673
Female	5,306	6,002	5,582	5,881	6,527	4,701
18 yrs of age and less	1,022	1,517	793	885	890	726
19-30 yrs of age	2,777	2,833	2,925	3,029	3,452	2,403
31 yrs of age or more	1,507	1,652	1,864	1,967	2,195	1,572
AR per 100,000 males	77	80	71	77	92	73
AR per 100,000 females	11	12	11	11	12	9

Source: Adapted from the United Nations Criminal Justice Information Office's *Profile on Iran* and from *Aamaarnaameh Ostan-e Markazi, Tir 1352* (The Statistical compendium of the Central Province, April 1974, Table 86, pp. 122-123).
AARMF=aggregate arrest rate for males and females.
AAR=aggregate arrest rate.
AR=arrest rate.

Comparing Tables 7.8 and 7.9 with Table 7.10, we may reach the following conclusions concerning the feminine commission of violent crime and misdemeanours in the post-Islamic Revolution period: first, if both adult and young women have been involved in the commission of five types of serious crime (homicide, injury, battery, threat and intentional poisoning), they must have committed other, lesser serious ones with a higher frequency, a conclusion substantiated by the aggregate arrest data of Chapter 6. The high arrest rates pertaining to the general population, coupled with those pertaining to both adult and young women, give an indication of the magnitude of the over-criminalization process in the post-Islamic Revolution period.

Second, Iran's post-Islamic Revolution data on the feminine commission of the five violent crimes makes Iran one of the most violent Islamic countries both in terms of female arrest rates and rates of commission. No other Islamic country comes even close to Iran's rates.

Third, the statistics given by Table 7.9 are based on arrests for five serious crimes. Based on the actual commission, the aggregate rates for both males and females rise. In addition, the data pertains to the municipal police, which is one among a multitude of law enforcement agencies that operate in Iran and are authorized to arrest or detain suspects. The others are as follows:

(1) The revolutionary committees (*Komiteha-ye Inqilab-e Islami*)
(2) The moral police (*Nahaiyan Munkarat*)
(3) The paramilitary units *(Basij-e Mustazafan)*
(4) The Revolutionary Guards of the Islamic Revolution (*Pasdaaran-e Inqilab-e Islami*)
(5) The city patrol units (*Gasht-e Thar Allah* etc.,)
(6) The court police (*Zabetin-e Dadgustari*)
(7) The secret police (VEVAK formerly SAVAK)
(8) The paramilitary units of the Ummat-e Hizbullah and Ansar-e Hizbullah
(9) The NOPO (The Special Forces Loyal to the Jurist Council)
(10) The gendarmerie of the Islamic Republic.

Based on the large number of enforcement agencies, the data of Table 7.8 should be adjusted within the context of the overall arrest capabilities of the above agencies.

Feminine Narcotics-related Crimes

For the first time in Iran's modern history, a large number of adult and young women have been involved in both the use and pushing of illicit drugs. Besides the official data disseminated by various organs of the Islamic criminal justice system, some of which we have used in this and the previous chapter, there are other sources that can be considered as semi-official because they are based on the print and communication networks that are under the strict control and censorship of the state. The number of persons arrested for drug and auxiliary crimes is usually in several hundreds as reported in the semi-official dailies. For example: "...143 suspicious persons were arrested near Bazzar Safviyeh and Park Mellet," reports the daily *Keyhan* adding that "a large number of expensive cars" were confiscated from these persons.[8] The daily *Jumhuri Islami* quoting Mr. Hishmati, the Prosecutor General of the Islamic Revolution, reports the arrest of 1,500 persons for having opened dens of corruption in the Sistan and Baluchistan provinces. Among the arrested, tens of young girls and boys are reported as being used for prostitution and/or for drug pushing by their addicted parents.[9] In one incident, 2,096 smugglers were reported as having been arrested with 3,300 kilos of different narcotics.[10] To curb the spread of drugs, drug traffickers may face stiff sentences ranging from long jail sentences to public executions. *Jomhur Islami*: "179 drug smugglers were executed on the conviction of thousands of kilos of illicit drugs." It gives the name and their prior "smuggling" records and of the executed including women convicts. The *Keyhan* reports that "The names of 56 convicts executed in provincial towns were released" and again the list includes the names of women convicts executed for dealing in illicit drugs.[11] *Resalat* reports: "The execution of 11 smugglers in Tehran, Arak, Rasht and Waramin." These arrests were carried out by a combined police, military and paramilitary forces.[12] This in itself is an indication of the extensive use of illicit drugs in Iran that in turn can give an indication of other auxiliary types of crime that take place around illicit drug use and pushing, such as theft and prostitution.

The official data The official data in Table 7.11 agrees with the semi-official data in regard to feminine narcotics-related crimes and arrests in the post-Islamic Revolution years of 1983-1990.

Table 7.11 Narcotics amount and related arrests as reported by the municipal police, 1983-1990

Year	Population	Total	M	F	MAR per 100,000 general population	FAR per 100,000 general population
1983	42.07	15,460	14,478	982	34.41	2.3
1984	43.41	14,900	13,845	1,055	32	2.4
1985	47.82	7,373	6,935	438	14.5	0.9
1986	49.44	5,541	5,265	276	10.64	0.6
1987	50.67	6,446	6,025	421	11.89	0.83
1988	51.92	4,284	3,963	321	7.63	0.62

Table 7.11 continued

1989	53.14	2,448	2,231	217	4.19	0.408
1990	54.47	2,005	1,867	138	3.42	0.25
Averages	**49.11**	**7,307**	**6826**	**481**	**16**	**1.03**

Source: Adapted from *Saalnaamehe Aamaari-ye Keshwar 1370* (Iran Statistical Yearbook, March 1991-March 1992, Table 17-8, p. 239).
P stands for population, M for male, F for female.
MAR=male arrest rate.
FAR=female arrest rate.

As Table 7.11 indicates, although there was a steady increase in the population from 1983 to 1990, there was a systematic decrease in narcotics arrests for both males and females. This declining arrest rate, of course, seems very positive but is misleading for two reasons. First, according to the official data, Iran has become a major market for the consumption, or a transit route, of narcotics and, second, the rate of addiction has skyrocketed in comparison to the pre-Islamic Revolution period. Table 7.12 gives a longitudinal picture of the amounts of the narcotics disclosed by the municipal police during the Iranian calendar years 1362-1369 (1983-1990).

Table 7.12 Narcotics disclosed as reported by the municipal police, 1983-1990

Year	**Narcotics (Kg)**						
	Total	**Heroin**	**Opium**	**Opium ashes**	**Hashish**	**Others**	**Pills**
1983	6,508.8	361.0	3,423.3	255.3	239.0	2,230.3	2,71
1984	3,073.7	230.5	1,732.0	81.0	799.1	231.1	6,295
1985	3,702.4	76.1	1,499.5	55.5	1,574.7	496.6	249
1986	1,330.7	191.1	474.2	93.8	61.4	510.2	11,588
1987	660.3	77.5	309.4	59.0	213.0	1.5	1,188
1988	808.9	90.4	556.2	59.6	44.1	58.6	233
1989	958.4	38.4	523.2	74.6	45.5	276.7	904
1990	708.7	108.6	521.5	24.0	51.3	3.3	533

Table 7.12 continued

Total	17,751.9	1,182	9,039.4	702.8	3,028.1	3,808.3	23,761
Average	**2,219**	**147.75**	**1,130**	**88**	**379**	**476**	**2,970**

Source: Adapted from *Salnameh Aamaari-ye Keshvar 1370*, (Iran Statistical Year Book, March 1991-March 1992, Table 8.16, p. 238).

Based on Table 7.12 data, the average narcotics disclosed by one, among a multitude, of the anti-narcotics law enforcement agencies operating in post-Islamic Revolution Iran was more than two tons (2,219 kg) and around three thousand pills. It should be noted that Table 7.12 shows a declining trend in the disclosure of the narcotics corresponding to a declining trend in the number of narcotics-related arrests by the same law enforcement unit as depicted in Table 7.13 below.

Table 7.13 Narcotics-related arrests categorized by gender as reported by the municipal police, 1983-1990

Year	**Total narcotics-related arrests**	**Male**	**Female**
1983	15,460	14,478	982
1985	7,373	6,935	438
1986	5,541	5,265	276
1987	6,446	6,025	421
1988	4,284	3,963	321
1989	2,448	2,231	217
1990	2,005	1,867	138
Grand total	58,457	54,582	3,848
AA per yr by MP	**7,307**	**6,823 (93.37%)**	**481 (6.58%)**

Source: Adopted from *Saalnaamehe Aamaari-ye Keshvar, 1370* (Iran Statistical Year Book, March 1991-March 1991, Table 8.17, p. 239).

AA=average arrest.

MP=municipal police.

The data of Tables 7.12 and 7.13 can be interpreted in the context of the municipal police's efficacy in fighting against narcotics, provided that one could show an improvement in addiction treatment programmes and facilities. The sad reality is that Iran's post-Islamic Revolution addiction rate has dramatically risen at the same time that Iranian general health and health-related services have deteriorated. In addition, what makes the efficacy of the police argument questionable is the sheer volume of narcotics disclosed by other law enforcement agencies, and yet illicit drugs are widely circulated in both urban and rural parts of Iran in spite of the fact that the penalty for drug smugglers is death.

Tables 7.14 and 7.15, on the other hand, pertain only to the amount of narcotics disclosed by the Islamic Republic's gendarmerie and revolutionary committees respectively. The period covered in Table 7.14 pertains to the post-Islamic Revolution years of 1983-1990.

Table 7.14 Narcotics disclosed by the Islamic Republic gendarmerie, 1983-1990

Year	Narcotics (Kg)						
	Total	**Heroin**	**Opium**	**Opium ashes**	**Hashish**	**Others**	**Pills**
1983	11,074	360	9,048	88	1,578	------	------
1984	15,888	1,394	13,422	65	1,007	------	------
1985	11,212	1,088	9,313	80	714	------	------
1986	NA	NA	NA	NA	NA	NA	NA
1987	14,531.5	670.0	11,029.6	155.2	2,676.6	------	------
1988	7,508.7	523.3	5,942.1	10.6	1,032.7	------	------
1989	7,830.1	454.9	5,502.6	6.5	1,866.1	------	------
1990	1,769.2	80.5	1,247.7	1.5	439.5	------	------
Total	69,814	4,571	55,504	407	9,314	------	------
Average	**7,748**	**571**	**6,938**	**51**	**1,164**	------	------

Source: Adapted from *Saalnaameh Aamaari-ye Keshvar 1370* (Iran Statistical Year Book, March 1991-March 1992, Table 8.18, p. 240).

In reading Table 7.14, it should be noted that no data for the year 1986 have been given, neither have any data been provided for "other" and "pill" categories without any explanation. One could surmise that narcotic pills, because they are used in urban areas, have a lesser chance of being disclosed by the gendarmerie which operates in the rural areas as the main law enforcement agency. The same rationale may apply to the "other" category, considering that this category may include various non-traditional types of illicit drug that are attractive to the urban, rather than to a rural, populace.

Table 7.15 Narcotics disclosed by the revolutionary committees, 1983-1990

	Narcotics (Kg)						
Year	**Total**	**Heroin**	**Opium**	**Opium ashes**	**Hashish**	**Others**	**Pills**
1983	NA	NA	NA	NA	NA	NA	NA
1984	NA	NA	NA	NA	NA	NA	NA
1985	13,486.3	707.0	6,821.2	1,249.1	2,730.8	1,978.2	NA
1986	27,519.3	1,071.5	10,701.3	12,141.1	2,437.5	1,167.9	NA
1987	20,020.7	971.9	12,153.6	5,046.7	1,618.6	2,29.9	NA
1988	31,063.2	1,326.2	21,082.3	5,060.7	3,209.0	385.0	NA
1989	22,766.3	744.7	14,962.6	4,304.0	2,013.1	741.8	NA
1990	27,366.6	1,385.9	14,234.6	3,103.0	3,126.5	5,516.5	NA
Total	142,222	6,243	79,956	30,905	15,136	10,019	NA
Average	**23,704**	**1,041**	**13,326**	**5,151**	**2,523**	**1,670**	**NA**

Source: Adapted from *Saalnaameh Aamaari-ye Keshvar 1370* (Iran Statistical Year Book, March 1991-March 1992, Table 8.19, p. 241).

The data of Tables 7.12, 7.14 and 7.15 when juxtaposed together give the figure of 33,671 kg (around 34 tons) representing the yearly average amount of narcotics that has been disclosed by three law enforcement agencies (municipal police, gendarmerie and revolutionary committees) during 1983-1990. This, of course, is the tip of the iceberg considering that disclosure does not correspond to the actual amount of illicit drugs that are being consumed in Iran. In addition, the narcotics data disclosed in the 1990s shows that there is a huge amount of narcotics that is regularly being disclosed. Although the data of Table 7.16 depict this picture pertaining to the second half of the 1990s, there is no doubt that, in comparison to the 1980s, the use of illicit drugs went through a dramatic surge.

Table 7.16 Narcotics disclosed by the disciplinary forces of the IRI, 1995-1998

Year and Province	Total	Heroin	Morphine	Opium & opium liquid	Hashish	Other
1995-96	189,267	5,331	23,465	127,561	24,319	8,591
1996-97	162,694	1,232	6,170	144,608	10,432	253
1997-98	156,082	2,455	13,728	*130,702	*8,941	255

Source: Adapted from Statistical Centre of Iran website at http://www.sci.irannet.net/english/se!/lifl1.htm

*Including 898 kilograms of opium and 82 kilograms of hashish discovered by the general department for the anti-drug campaign.

Comparing Table 7.16 with 7.15, the yearly average amount of narcotics disclosed by the combined forces of the Islamic Republic has gone up from 34 tons (pertaining to the 1980s) to 169 tons (169,348 kg). Again, one can argue that this shows the efficacy of the anti-narcotics campaign in Iran. Alternatively, one could also explain this in the context of the spread of addiction among the general population and especially among Iranian youths that the dignitaries of the Islamic regime warn has reached the status of a national calamity.

Feminine Political Crimes

Iranian women, from the time of the Constitutional Revolution (1906-1911), to the time of the Islamic Revolution (1979), to the present (2000), have been involved in social protest movements. With the establishment of the Islamic Republic, women have been involved in both pro- and anti-state activities. The protagonists of the Islamic regime are known as the Sisters of the Community of the Party of God (*Khaharan-e Ummat-e Hizbullah*); the antagonists have belonged to a wide spectrum of ideologies and political parties. Some of these groups are in exile and some others are of an underground nature, conducting armed struggle against the central government. The most disciplined among these is the PMOI with its cadre of women fighters and political agitators in Europe and North American societies.

The Data on Feminine Arrest and Execution

Since the inception of the Islamic Republic in 1979, waves of executions have taken place. One document depicting the executions of 12,028 persons (belonging to 34 political groups and parties among whom the execution of juveniles and pregnant women were recorded) was published in 1986 (in both Persian and English) by the PMOI, and was widely circulated among various human rights organizations around the world. The list, in the form of a 426-page booklet, contains several hundred pictures of executed adult and young women (and men), including scenes of public hanging, as well as pictures of tortured and mutilated bodies of the opponents of the regime. Another complementary list of executions published by the same group contains the specifications of 2,000 executed during the mid-1980s.[13] The first list gives the following statistical information about those executed in this period, and I quote directly from the document:

(1) For the 7,448 martyrs whose ages are given, the average age (at the time of execution) is 23 years 5.5 months; 599 were under 18; 91 were over 40 and 27 were infants.

(2) Of the 7,407 martyrs whose education was specified, 51.6 per cent were university and school students, 37.4 per cent were high-school graduates or had diploma degrees, 6.3 per cent were university graduates and 1.7 per cent held MA, MS or doctoral degrees.

(3) Of the 2,433 martyrs whose occupations were specified, 26.6 per cent were in the teaching profession, 25.5 per cent were workers, 12.4 per cent were office employees, 10.2 per cent were armed forces and police personnel, 10.7 per cent were merchants and traders, 6.2 per cent were engineers and 3.6 per cent were doctors and medical professionals.

(4) Of the 10,722 martyrs whose circumstances of martyrdom have been recorded, 71.5 per cent were executed. At least 361 of these martyrs (3.4 per cent) died under torture and 250 (2.3 per cent) were hanged.

(5) 45 martyred women whose names appear on the list were pregnant at the time of their execution. The real figure of executed pregnant women is far higher.

(6) There are some 130 families on the list who have lost at least three of their members in executions since 20 June 1981.

(7) Of the 7,394 martyrs whose marital status is given, 1,664 (22.5 per cent) were married and the rest were single. In at least 300 cases both the husband and the wife have been martyred.

(8) There is a supplementary list of 26 mothers or fathers who have died of heart attack or shock upon receiving the news of the martyrdom of their loved ones. Their names have been listed separately.[14]

Table 7.17, representing the above data in tabular form, is designed to give some indication of the extent of the criminalization of political dissent under the Ayatullah Khumaini's tenure (1979-1989) as well as under his successors.

Table 7.17 Social and economic status of 12,028 persons executed for political crimes, 1981-1986

Age	Education	Political Group	Occupation	Marital Status	Punishment
Average 23.5 at execution	HS	PMOI	Teaching	Married	Executed
KN 6,471	KN 2,860	KN 11,128	KN 647	KN 1,644	KN 7,666
>18 years of age	UG	Others	Workers	Single	Other forms of execution
KN 599	KN 596	KN 900	KN 630	KN 5,750	KN 4,362
<40 years of age	Unknown	-------	Professionals	-------	-------

Table 7.17 continued

KN 91	KN 4,975	-------	KN 541	-------	-------
KN executed 7,448	KN executed 7,407	KN executed 12,028	KN executed 2,433	KN executed 7,394	------
U 4,580	U 4,621	U 0	U 9,595	U 4,634	-------
Total 12,028	**Total 12,028**	**Total 12,028**	**Total 12,028**	**Total 12,028**	**Total 12,028**

Source: Adapted from the People's Mojahedin Organization of Iran's document titled *List of Names and Particulars of 12,028 Victims of the Khomeini Regime's Executions*, (PMOI, np., 1986).
HS= high school.
UG= university/college graduates.
GS= graduate school.
KN= known number.
U= unspecified

In reading Table 7.17, it should be noted that the data set contains a large number of adult and young women who have been executed. In fact, item 7 of the statistical list gives the number of 1,644 married persons who have been executed which means that at least 822 women were executed during the 1981-1986 period. This means a yearly execution of 165 Iranian adult and young women, which is unprecedented in the world annals of executions. Iranian dissident groups have argued that execution has been utilized extensively in penalizing political dissent in Iran from the time of the Islamic Revolution in 1979. For example, the PMOI argues that the data set has been gathered clandestinely by the PMOI resistance units in Iran under the threat of arrest and immediate execution by the state because the Islamic regime does not want the data be disclosed to the world public opinion and especially to the Human Rights groups (e.g., Amnesty International, United Nations, Pax Christi, etc.). The grand total number in Table 7.17, the data set maintains, does not reflect the actual number of executions that have taken place. The PMOI estimates that a total of 120,000 executions took place in the 1980s and 1990s. Table 7.17 gives the reader an idea about the intensity of the political struggle in Iran since the Islamic Revolution. At the same time, the PMOI has argued that this data set is being continuously updated as the spate of political killings and disappearances continues. Even under the moderate President Muhammad Khatami, the spate of summary executions and disappearances has not stopped. The PMOI has documented another 266 political killings since Khatami took office in June 1997.

As a result of its policies, the Islamic Republic of Iran has been condemned 45 times since 1980 by the United Nations General Assembly and UN Sub-Committee on Human Rights. This unprecedented number of condemnations has been on the grounds that Iran's Islamic system of justice does not differentiate between political and non-political crimes; moreover, adjudication standards are arbitrary and do not conform to internationally recognized standards of fair treatment and due process. This is despite the fact that the Islamic Republic's Constitution recognizes the principles of due process.

Dissident groups in exile have also disseminated a wide range of documents on what the world media has termed as "state-sponsored terrorism," including the extra-judicial and extra-legal killings of Iranian dissidents in Europe, Asia and the Middle East. Table 7.18 gives an idea about the Islamic regime's involvement in the extra-judicial and extra-territorial execution of dissidents, including women.

Table 7.18 Extra-legal executions of Iranian dissidents, 1980-1995

Year	Total	Foreign Targets	Dissidents	PMOI	KG	Other
1980	3	0	0	0	0	3
1981	6	0	3	2	0	1
1982	13	0	5	7	0	1
1983	6	5	1	0	0	0
1984	4	2	0	1	0	1
1985	11	5	0	2	0	4
1986	10	3	1	3	0	3
1987	17	5	4	3	0	5
1988	9	2	3	4	0	0
1989	10	3	0	2	2	3
1990	8	1	1	3	2	1
1991	19	9	1	1	5	3

Table 7.18 continued

1992	32	5	7	13	4	3
1993	19	3	3	9	4	0
1994-1995	25	4	1	13	7	0
Grand Total	**192**	**47**	**30**	**53**	**24**	**29**

Source: Adapted from the National Council of Resistance of Iran website: http://www.iran-e-azad.org
KG=Kurdish groups.

In another data set, we come across the names of foreign countries in which these extra-legal executions and felonious assaults on Iranian and foreign nationals have been carried out by the Islamic Republic's secret services and agents (see Table 7.19).

Table 7.19 Extra-territorial executions of political dissidents, 1979-1996

Number	**Country**	**Date**	**City**	**Description**
4	Austria	1987-1989	Vienna	AS
3	Dubai	1986-1992	Unspecified	AS
11	France	1979-1996	Paris	AS/AgA
40	Germany	1982-1993	Unspecified	AS/AgA
30	India	1982	Unspecified	AS/AgA
22	Iraq	1989-1996	Solyemaniyeh, or Baghdad, or Kurdish regions of Iraq	Assassination/ Bombing/ Grande Launchers
3	Italy	1989-1993	Rome	AS/AgA
1	Netherlands	1992	Unspecified	Assassination Attempt
16	Pakistan	1982-1996	Karachi and unspecified	AS/AgA

Table 7.19 continued

5	Philippines	1982-1983	Manila	AS/AgA
6	Sweden	1981-1993	Stockholm and unspecified	AS/AgA
14	Turkey	1984-1996	Istanbul, Ankara and unspecified	AS/Kidnaping
4	United Kingdom	1986-1987	London and unspecified	AS/Bomb injury
3	U.S.A.	1980-1992	New Jersey, Oklahoma, and Dallas	AS/AgA

Source: Adapted from the National Council of Resistance of Iran website: http://www.iran-e-azad.org
AS=assassination, AgA=aggravated assault

Iranian dissident groups have also compiled a list of many unofficial prisons and houses of detention that operate independently of official correctional institutions. These extra-legal centres, a number of ex-political prisoners have argued, are operated clandestinely by various secret service organizations whose exact number is unknown but are rumoured to number around twenty, ranging from paramilitary groups called the Hizbullah, the Ansar-e Hizbullah, the Basij-e Mustazafan, to highly organized units of the Revolutionary Guards. Table 6.11 gives an idea about many prisons and unofficial detention centres that the Islamic regime has built since 1979, an indication of the retrogressive criminalization process there. The document gives the names and the addresses of 298 prisons and detention centres built during the tenure of the Ayatullah Khumaini (1979-1989). We have already discussed these in Chapter 6.

In sum, under the present Islamic regime, like its predecessor, political dissent is criminalized. Unlike its predecessor, whose rationale for the criminalization of dissent was the security of the state and of the monarchy, the Islamic regime's rationale is much wider entailing the state, the Islamic Revolution and Islam. Therefore any type of dissent that is deemed "un-Islamic" has been criminalized despite the fact that the Constitution of the Islamic Republic provides for dissent provided that such does not conflict with the so-called Islamic criteria (*mawazin-e Islami*). These are very vague criteria that to this date have not been defined, let alone been institutionalized. Because of these criteria, pre-Revolution political parties and revolutionary groupings have been banned since the early 1980s. These include:

(1) PMOI: People's Mojahedin Organization of Iran
(2) NFI: National Front of Iran
(3) KDPI: Democratic Party of Iranian Kurdistan
(4) IPFG: Iranian People's Fedai Guerrillas
(5) UCL: United Council of the Left
(6) UIC: Union of Iranian Communists
(7) Peikar: The splinter group from the PMOI in 1975
(8) KOMALA: A Kurdish group that follows Maoism
(9) Razmandegan: a leftist group that advocates a type of Third World socialism
(10) Ranjbaran: A Maoist group composed of university educated intellectuals
(11) Worker's Way: A communist group that advocates "true" Marxism-Leninism
(12) Aarman Mostazafan: An Islamic leftist group with a radical view of Islam based on political economy
(13) Revolutionary League: A Marxist group composed of university-educated intellectuals
(14) Forghan: A radical Islamic group at the beginning of the Islamic Revolution, which took this Qur'anic name for itself and was involved in some executions of Islamic dignitaries such as the Ayatullah Morteza Motahhari and Brigadier General Qaranei, the first Army Chief of the Staff under Premier Bazargan
(15) Red Star: A communist group of writers and intellectuals
(16) Toofan: A communist group aimed to attract Iranian proletariat to its cause and organization
(17) Independent Labour Movement: A group of communist intellectuals aiming to attract the Iranian proletariat to its cause and organization
(18) Union of Communist Militants: A group of communist intellectuals who advocate revolutionary and armed struggle against the Islamic regime
(19) Ershad: A group of bazaari and Muslim intellectuals with a radical view of Islam and state and economy.

The following groups, as the supporters of the Islamic regime, are allowed:

(1) Ansar-e Hezbollah
(2) Mojahedin of the Islamic Revolution

(3) Muslim Students Following the Line of the Imam
(4) Islamic Coalition Associations
(5) Hezb-e Kargozaran
(6) Hezb-e Kar-e Islami
(7) The Combatant Clerics.

These latter groups are not political parties in the context of democratic parties and political affiliations that operate in modern democratic societies; instead, they represent powerful partisans composed of both religious and the so-called Hizbullahi political dignitaries of the Islamic political establishment. They have shown their loyalties to the present political establishment and to its central doctrine, the *Wilayat-e Faqih*, whose meaning and range of powers I explored in Chapter 6. Even these loyal political groups are not allowed to oppose the state in the manner that democratic societies allow. Therefore, political activities whose aim is to change the state have taken an underground and clandestine form. Some political groups have engaged in armed struggle, such as the PMOI, KDPI, KUMULAH, KEHBAT. The Nehzat Azadi-ye Iran belonging to the first premier in 1980, Mr. Mahdi Bazargan, and the National Front have chosen non-confrontational forms of existence. Both types of movement are invariably depicted as "agents" of the United States, Israel, Britain, France, Soviet Union, Iraq and a host of other world and regional powers. Any secular and democratic political opposition is deemed as "destroying" Islam, the Islamic Revolution, the Islamic Republic, the heritage of the Imam Khumaini, and the Community of the Party of God. Even under President Khatami, this view prevails. The Islamic political establishment has categorized Iranians into two distinct categories of people: those belonging to the inner circle (*khodi*) and those belonging to the outercircles (*ghay-re khodi*). The inner circles cluster around the *Wilayat-e Faqih* doctrine that I outlined in Chapter 6. The outercircle is any political group or philosophy deemed anti-*Wilayat-e Faqih*. Political activity belongs to the inner circle, provided that the principle of the *Wilayat-e Faqih* is not undermined.

In sum, to achieve the above goal, the Islamic political establishment has relied excessively on its revolutionary committees and tribunals, and its partisan penal system. The suppression of political dissent has been legitimated by the political regime's attempts to resurrect an imaginary ideal Islamic order based on an ideal version of the Twelve Imami Sharia Law. It is through the idealization of an undifferentiated Islam and of Sharia Law that the political regime has tried to suppress political dissent by arguing that there is only one version of Islam that ought to be followed and implemented. From its earliest inception to the present, the political regime has insisted that the judiciary and penology are the exclusive province of the Twelve Imami Shii men of the cloth and has urged that the religious judges to be vigilant in dealing with these foes, regardless of what these foes profess, what kind of activities they engage in, what kind of methods they use, or what kinds of evidence the judges may muster. The punishment ought to be swift, and as prescribed by the appropriate religious codes. In practice, however, punishment, whether intended to be of general or specific deterrence, is arbitrary. For example, in its 1989 Annual Report Amnesty International (AI) maintains that "More than 1200 political prisoners have been executed some of whom are said to have had been condemned to prison terms only."[15] It adds further that: "Thousands of others, including unspecified numbers of prisoners of conscience still remain in prisons."[16] Insofar as torture and arbitrary punishments are concerned, the following picture is presented in the report:

> Torturing the political prisoners, in an extensive fashion, has been continued and persons suspected of political opposition to the state, following an unjust prosecution, have been condemned to prison terms or execution. Lashing, as punishment, has extensively been used for different types of offenses sometimes being added to other punishments....[17]

In addition to the systematic use of torture in prisons and detentions centres, arrest has become the *modus operandi* of the Islamic regime in suppressing any type of dissent, be it civil or political.

In Chapter 8 I explore women's "moral" crimes and other aspects related to the Islamic regime's treatment of women's crimes and misdemeanours.

Notes

1. See the "Economic activity by sex, 1995" on the United Nations website at htpp://www.un.org/Depts/unsd/gender/5-lasi.htm

2. See the "Percentage of government positions occupied by women, 1996: Asia and Pacific"on the United Nations website at http://www.org/Depts/unsd/unsd/gender/6-2asi.htm

3. *Human Rights and the Legal System in Iran: Two Reports by William J. Butler, Esq. and Professor Georges Levasseur*, (Geneva, Switzerland, International Commission of Jurists, 1976), Preface.

4. *Ibid.*, pp. 7-8.

5. *Ibid.*, p. 8.

6. *Ibid.*, p. 13.

7. See Hamid R. Kusha, "Iran: The Problematic of Women's Participation in a Male Dominated Culture" *Working Paper*, no. 136, published by Office of Women in International Development, Michigan State University.

8. *Keyhan*, 17 Aban 1368/8 November 1989, cited in *SHOWRA*, no. 50, December, 1989, p. 79.

9. *Jomhuri Islami*, 23 Aban/ 14 November 1368, cited in *SHOWRA*, no. 50, December, 1989, p. 80.

10. Reported by Radio Iran, 3 Ordibehesht 1369/23 April 1990, cited in *SHOWRA*, no. 53, May, 1990, p. 127.

11. *Keyhan*, 27 Bahman 1367/16 February 1989.

12. Radio Iran, 18 Farvardin 1369/ 7 April 1990, cited in *SHOWRA*, no. 53, May 1990, p. 126.

13. The People's Mojahedin Organization of Iran, *Gerami Baad Khaatereh-e Taabnaak-e Shohada-ye Mojahed-e Khalq Parchamdaaraan-e Javidan-e Azaadi wa Enqelab-e Nowin-e Iran: Asaami wa Moshakhasaat-e 2000 Tan Digar az Shahidan-e Mojahed-e Khalq*, (Salute to the Glorious Memories of People's Mojahed Martyrs the Eternal Bearers of Freedom and New Democratic Revolution of Iran: The Names and Particulars of Another 2000 People's Mojahed Martyrs), (PMOI, np., 15 Sharivar, 1366/20 June 1987).

14. The People's Mojahedin Organization of Iran, *List of Names and Particulars of 12,028 Victims of the Khomeini Regime's Executions*, pp. 5-6.

15. 1988 Amnesty International Report cited in *SHOWRA*, no. 50, p. 141. The Persian text.

16. *Ibid.*

17. *Ibid.*

8 The Sharia Law and Female Victimization in Iran

The Islamic Republic's attempts to stamp out crimes in Iran has led to nowhere other than a high rate of female victimization at the hands of Iran's oppressive criminal justice system. Among a multitude of law enforcement agencies involved in victimizing women, the moral police plays a significant role. Composed of a multitude of ramshackle forces that are known as the *Munkirat*, the main concern of the moral police has been to control a category of "crime" that is based on the Islamic judiciary's view of gender and sexuality, and can be characterized as female provocative crimes. These "crimes," accordingly stem from the manner in which adult and young women appear and conduct themselves in public in order to provoke young and adult men's sinful desires. Therefore, these provocative female schemes have to be brought under control. The state's concerns have been expressed in the Constitution under the so-called *Mawazin-e Islami* (Islamic criteria). In this chapter I explore these Islamic criteria in the Constitution by means of which Iranian women have been victimized at the hands of the state and its criminal justice agencies.

Islamic Criteria in the Constitution

The Constitution of 1979 maintains that the general status of women is based on the "Islamic criteria". These criteria, accordingly, converge "...the cultural, social, political, and economic institutions of Iranian society on the basis of Islamic principles and norms, which represent the earnest aspirations of the Islamic *Umma*."[1] The key word here is the *Umma*, a Qur'anic term generally understood to represent a supra-class, supra-national, and religious entity. The aim of the Constitution of the Islamic Republic is to reconstruct an Islamic *Umma* whereby the social and the legal status of women can be framed within the confines of an ideal Islamic *Umma*.

To achieve this pre-capitalist notion of an ideal order, the new Islamic political establishment, under the guidance of the Ayatullah Khumaini, set upon a rediscovery of the traditionalist Twelve Imami Shii jurisprudential texts with regard to women's social and legal status. For example, Article 8 of the Constitution aims to institutionalize the Qur'anic concepts of *maaruf* and *munkar,* in respect of dissent and conflict resolution.

The Maaruf and the Munkar Criteria

As we have already discussed, Article 8 of the Constitution has established the principle of the *maaruf* and *munkar*, one of the main constitutional principles with which to transform Iranian society into an ideal Islamic *Umma*. I have already cited the article in full above, but for the sake of the flow of the argument, I quote the part of the article which reads:

> In the Islamic Republic of Iran, *al-amr bi'l-ma`ruf wa al-nahy `an al-munkar* is a universal and reciprocal duty that must be fulfilled by the people with respect to one another, by the government with respect to the people, and by the people with respect to the government. The conditions, limits, and nature of this duty will be specified by law. [2]

The operative clause here is law – namely, the conditions and limits of this criterion shall be established by law. Of especial importance is the notion that this principle is of a reciprocal nature, governing the affairs of the governor and governed. This premise implies that in the ideal Islamic Republic: (1) it is law that specifies the nature and scope of the *maaruf* and *munkar* and (2) that as the state has the right to enjoin its citizens from wrongful acts, so does the average citizen enjoy the right to warn the state against its unlawful acts without fear of reprisals. First, we have to consult the text of the Qur'an about this criterion.

The maaruf and munkar in the Qur'an Both of these are Qur'anic terms, expressed in the Madinan chapter *al-Imran*. Verse 104 maintains: "And let there be from you a nation who invite to goodness, and enjoin right conduct and forbid indecency. Such are they who are successful."[3] Verse 111 in the same chapter maintains that: "...you enjoin what is good and forbid what is evil and believe in Allah...."[4] Further, verse 115 there maintains that: "They believe in Allah and the Last Day, and enjoin what is good and forbid evil, and hasten, vying with one another, to good works. And these are among the righteous."[5]

All reputable classical and post-classical Shii and Sunni commentators of the Qur'an have agreed that *maaruf* pertains to a good deed and *munkar* to an admonished deed, as for instance in Muhaqih Hilli's juristic vernacular.[6] These commentators have argued that, in Islam, calling the believers to good deeds and admonishing them of evil ones is a religiously sanctified (*waajib*) reciprocal duty. Some post-classical jurists, like Hilli, have divided *maaruf* deeds into sanctified (*waajib*) and non-sanctified (*mustahab*) ones, but not the *munkar*. Simply put, the principle maintains that there are deeds whose performance is imperative, there are deeds whose performance is not imperative, and there are deeds whose performance is forbidden. This classification, of course, is a medieval one categorizing social acts into *mala in se* and *mala prohibita* (their counterparts in Western criminology); therefore, this categorization is subject to time and social conditions. Insofar as women's social and legal status under the Islamic Constitution is concerned, it is constructive to give one example of the manner in which this Qur'anic principle has been interpreted with regards to the veiling (the *hijaab*).

Veiling as an Application of the Maaruf and Munkar in Iran

According to the Qur'an, and Hadith, it is better for Muslim men and women to be modest in their attire. The word *hijaab* has customarily been translated as a coverage for women as they appear in public. This covering, throughout centuries, and in different Islamic societies, has taken various forms and shapes, ranging from the Iranian *chador*, to the Turkish *charshaf*, to the Indo-Pakistani *prudah,* to the Persian Gulf Sheikdom's *neqab*.

Hijaab is a Qur'anic term. As observed by some modern commentators, such as Fatima Mernissi, it means "'curtain - descended,' not to put a barrier between a man and woman, but between two men."[7] Mernissi's rational for this anti-traditionalist designation of *hijaab* is relevant to our discussion. She argues that verse 53 of the Chapter 33 in the Qur'an was revealed to the Prophet Muhammad on the occasion of his marriage to Zaynab Bint Jahsh in 627, a point agreed upon by all classical commentators of the Qur'an. To paraphrase Mernissi, the occasion of the revelation is that after eating the ceremonial meal, some male guests did not leave the Prophet's house and occupied themselves in idle talk. The Prophet was anxious to attend his newly wedded bride, but, as the revelation points out, his gentle manners did not allow him to ask these guests to leave. The verse was revealed accordingly:

> O ye who believe! Enter not the dwellings of the Prophet for a meal without waiting for the proper time, unless permission be granted to you. But if ye are invited, enter, and, when your meal is ended, then disperse. Linger not for conversation. Lo! that would cause annoyance to the Prophet, and he would be shy of [asking] you [to go]; but Allah is not shy of the truth. And when ye ask of them [the wives of Prophet] anything, ask it of them from behind a curtain. That is purer for your hearts and their hearts.[8]

Mernissi first takes the verse within its jurisprudential significance and writes that:

> The fuqaha speak of "the descent of the hijab." This expression in fact covers two simultaneous events that take place in completely different realms: on the one hand, God's revelation to the Prophet, which is in the intellectual realm; and on the other hand, the descent of a cloth hijab, a material object, a curtain that the Prophet draws between himself and the man who was at the entrance of his nuptial chamber.[9]

This said, there is no doubt that this and some other verses in the Qur'an have led to the imposition of the *hijaab* on women in Islamic societies, an imposition that requires women to cover their hair, bosoms, arms and thighs by a garment. There is nothing unusual in this coverage. However, in the Qur'an, the lack of *hijaab* is not sanctioned as a crime. Veiling is part of customs and traditions (*urf wa adaat*). Customarily, and as a matter of tradition, women in Islamic societies have covered their bodies and their hair. In present-day Iran, under a republican form of governance and a Constitution that, on paper, guarantees every modern democratic right for its citizens, the forced veiling of women has become a main concern of the state, without any regard for the voices of millions of Iranian women. This attitude of the state, translated into concrete social policies, has led to the criminalization of women's attire and appearance in Iran, the topic of the next section.

From modesty to the criminalization of the veil Modesty in appearance has been advised in the Qur'an, and in the Prophetic Hadith. During the 1980s and 1990s, veiling went through a bizarre transformation in Iran: from imploring women to modesty in dress, a lack of modesty has regressively turned into the status of crime with gradations of punishment. On 3 March 1979 (13 Isfand 1357), the Ayatullah Khumaini, at the height of his popularity, in an audience he had granted to a number of women in the city of Qom, maintained that "women are allowed going [to continue their employment] into offices, but they should go in Islamic hijaab."[10] What this allowance entailed was not specified, but was left to speculation. Several days later, and on the occasion of the International Woman's Day on 8 March 1979, Iranian women staged a huge rally to protest against Khumaini's declaration on the issue of the veil. They chanted: "Woman's Day is Neither Eastern, nor Western, it is Global"; "In the Dawn of Freedom, Freedom is Missed"; "Freedom, Equity, Our Absolute Right"; "Freedom has no Ifs and Buts."[11] Some counter-demonstrations took place by the emerging, pro-state Hizbullahi groups against women's demonstrations.[12] Two days later, another such demonstration was staged by various women's organizations in front of the Ministry of Justice. The following declarations were issued. After some preliminary remarks, it reads:

> (1) We the women who perform our social duties toward the country shoulder to shoulder with men and carry the responsibility of upbringing the future generations are mature enough being cognizant of protecting our dignities, personalities and honour. With firm belief in the necessity of protecting the dignity of women, we believe that woman's honour is not incumbent upon a certain form of appearance and coverage. And the customary garb of women based on customs and social proclivities ought to be left to their own decisions.
> (2) The right of enjoying equity in civil rights ought to be recognized and every discrimination in this and the laws related to family rights ought to be discarded.
> (3) Women's political and social and economic rights ought to restitute without any discrimination.
> (4) Complete security of women in enjoying their rights and freedoms ought to be guaranteed.
> (5) True enjoyment of principal rights, freedom of pen, freedom of speech – freedom of opinion, freedom of occupation, and the freedom of congregation for women and men of the country ought to be guaranteed.
> (6) Every type of inequality among woman and man in the

> country's laws including the Work Law and the State Employment Codes ought to be discarded.
> (7) The present employment position of women ought to be preserved.
> (8) Agreeing and acknowledging the state's decision in restitution and implementation of the Family Protection Law, the shortcomings of this Law ought to be addressed so as to reclaim women's discarded rights. We implore the Provisional Government of his excellency Mr. Bazargan to express their views on this declaration and its items thereof.[13]

These demands were directed to the then Prime Minister, Mahdi Bazargan. Two days later, on 10 March 1979, and in response to another huge women's gathering at the University of Tehran, followed by a rally to Freedom Square, Bazargan declared that the veil was not going to be mandatory.[14] However, Bazargan could not make good on his promises, for he resigned his post when he found that he could not expel the occupiers of the American Embassy on 4 November 1979.

A Critique of Veiling and of its Criminalization

Now, I would like to submit that a correct reading of the Qur'anic principles of *maaruf* and *munkar*, in this day and age, should imply the establishment of democratic structures in which citizens should be able to direct their concerns and criticisms against the state and those in charge of state policies. Put simply, this Qur'anic premise should be looked upon as an attempt to found democratic dialogue between the governor and the governed. This premise implies that, in an ideal Islamic government, enjoining good and forbidding evil is of a reciprocal nature between the governor and the governed. As this principle applies to the issue of veiling, the drafters of the Constitution would have been obliged to take Iranian women's demands into consideration. In other words, it is not enough to state in the Constitution that the *maaruf* and *munkar* principle implies reciprocity between the affairs and duties of the governor and governed, it ought to be practised: the many rallies, demonstrations, declarations, sit-ins, appeals to the Ayatullahs (Khumaini, Hussain Ali Muntazari and Mhamud Taleqani) by Iranian women who played a crucial role in the success of the "Islamic Revolution" ought to have satisfied the reciprocity clause in the Constitution.

In Islamic societies women have traditionally been veiled; however the Qur'anic stress on *modesty* in this day and age ought to imply something different from that of medieval Shii and Sunni jurists. In addition, forcing millions of women to wear the veil runs against the famous Qur'anic principle that the affairs of religion can not be compelled upon believers by compulsion (*la ikraha fi-al-Din*), not to mention the fact that the text does not make veiling mandatory let alone non-veiling as a crime with all gradations of punishment. In the medieval view of the Sharia Law, veiling became mandatory under the so-called *Hadd-e Shari* criteria, which required the covering of the face (*qurs-e surat*) – with the exception of the eyes and nose – the neck (*gardan*), shoulders (*shaneh*), bosoms (*sineh*), arms, legs and buttocks. Modesty in dress and in appearance has always been observed in Iranian society as a matter of tradition and culture; therefore, Iranian women, by and large, were cognizant of the fact that to choose veiling was part of their basic human rights. There is yet another aspect of forced veiling – the procedural laws.

The procedural laws with regard to veiling The Islamic judiciary's view of procedural laws with regard to veiling is of interest here because women's non-observance of veiling or what the authorities consider as "mal-veiling" (*bad -hijaabi*) has assumed the status of a serious law-infracting (munkar) behaviour in the eyes of the state and law enforcement agencies. This exclusively feminine law-infracting behaviour in turn, has put the majority of Iranian women at odds with the state and its Islamic criminal justice system. This situation, as I shall explore shortly, has led to an intense process of female victimization in the 1980s and 1990s in Iran; at the same time, because non-veiling or mal-veiling has assumed the status of an indexed crime, the anti-veiling law and its enforcement have deeply intruded into the Islamic criminal justice system.

The enforcement of veiling Very early on in the course of the new Islamic state's and of its criminal justice system's formation, Iranian society witnessed the rise of the so-called *chumaqdari* or club-wielding. Club-wielders were mainly supporters of the new Islamic regime of the Ayatullah Khumaini and of his partisan clerics who used this "para-legal" means to disrupt political gatherings that were deemed "un-Islamic" in their political affiliations. With the passage of time, these groups became more organized and more violent; they especially terrorized unveiled women, chanting the slogan of either veil or club (*ya rusari ya tusari*). Although the government, because of the new

Constitution, was duty-bound to intervene and put a decisive stop to these types of disruptive and usually criminal behaviours, it refrained from its constitutional duties. In the early 1980s, it became apparent to a large number of political observers and women's organizations that this was a tactic endorsed by the government.

The use of force in this fashion not only ran against the ideals of the Revolution (freedom, independence and Islamic government), it also ran against Articles 22, 23, 26, 27 and 39 of the Constitution; the use of force also ran counter to the very famous Qur'anic premise that Islam, as a faith, is against compulsion as previously mentioned – a premise that the Ayatullah Khumaini used, time and again, as he was vying for power in exile and especially during his short stay in Paris. At the same time, and from a purely Sharia-Law perspective, this enforcement ran against the Shii jurisprudential perception of *the munkar*, to be critiqued below. To refresh the reader's memory, *munkar* is an act whose commission is not desirable or is forbidden in the Sharia Law. We have to explore the meaning of the term *munkar* in the Shii view of the Sharia.

Munkar in the Shii fiqh Muhaqiq Hilli, one of the most respected post-classical Shii jurists centuries before the Ayatullah Khumaini, and writing on the *munkar* principle, maintains that for this principle to become operative it has to satisfy four conditions. First, one who is enjoining others of a certain act has to have a thorough knowledge about the nature of that act. Second, enjoining of a certain act must be based on reasonable premises so that enjoining does not become ineffective. Third, if one who in the past has been insistent on the commission of an act which is considered of an enjoined nature but starts showing signs of abandonment, the act of enjoinment is no longer necessary. Fourth, imploring others against the commission of a certain is not corrupting. In the words of Hilli, "Thus if it were to be suspected that a damage were to befallen upon one, or one's belongings, or to a Muslim due to imploring and its rejection, imperative becomes defunct."[15]

Hilli's rationale is simple: *maaruf* and *munkar* should not be turned into a socially disruptive and corrupting endeavor. Nevertheless, in Iran, after twenty years of trial and error, the state seems unable to define once and for all what it considers to be acceptable veiling. This inability of the state, as the enforcer of its notion of veiling, has been compounded by the fact that no state authority can tell Iranian women to which organ of the state the responsibility for defining adequacy in veiling has been regulated. For example, the Ayatullah Khumaini, as we previously discussed, argued that veiling ought not to be mandatory. Later, the issue of an acceptable style of veiling was passed on to the parliament, then to the Office of the Jurist Council, then to the Guardian Council, then to the revolutionary committees. None of these, to this date, has been able to come up with one definition of acceptable veiling. From a purely jurisprudential perspective, this inability of the state has rendered the imperativeness (*wujub*) of the prohibition defunct, in accordance with the first condition of Hilli. In other words, from a traditional Shii jurisprudential perspective, the Islamic Republic's notion of *munkar*, as it relates to veiling, is defunct because those in the position of authority cannot define what principle of the Sharia Law it is that women are ignoring in their daily dress and in the coverage of their bodies.

The second condition of Hilli – namely that one should be reasonable in order for imploring to be effective – is not adhered to; in the absence of such reasonableness, the imploring is not imperative. The futility of forcing veiling is best exemplified by the phenomenon of mal-veiling (*bad-hijaabi*). A mal-veiled (*bad-hijaab*) woman is one whose veil supposedly does not cover her adequately. Mal-veiling has become an epidemic for the very simple reason that Iranian women, excepting Hizbullahi women, have resisted forced veiling through ingenious stratagems.

Women's resistance to forced veiling These resistance tactics have ranged from total defiance – i.e., non-veiling irrespective of its dire penal consequences – to the aforementioned mal-veiling, to turning the veil into a provocative means of flirtation. By half covering, half exposing their faces, hair, necks, bosoms and legs in a teasing fashion, women send an endless array of provocative messages to the opposite sex. This practice not only empowers women, it also challenges the state's puritanical values and in fact mocks them. The dignitaries of the Islamic regime have called such stratagems as women's "thumbing their nose" at the Sacred Order of the Islamic Republic. What seems to be ignored is that by over-criminalizing mundane behaviour, the Islamic regime has opened itself up to a wide range of challenges, undermining the regime's legitimacy in the eyes of the average citizen and especially among women.

To combat mal-veiling, different authorities from the Ayatullah Khumaini to the President of the Republic, to Islamic judges, to Islamic prosecutors, to prominent religious figures and jurists have started to proclaim a multitude of strange, confusing, contradictory and outright absurd definitions of veiling and mal-veiling that they demand to be enforced both in public and in the workplace. An example is the "Regulatory Code for Executing the Law with Respect to Non-veiling and Mal-veiling and Vulgar Dress" (*Ain-nameh-e Ijraiy-e Mawadd-e Qanuni dar Rabeteh ba Bi-hijaabi wa Bad-hijaabi wa Lebaashaay-e Mubtazal*):

> Article 1: Categorization and definition of types of mal-veiling (*bad-hijabi*) that would engender arrest (*jalb*) and arraignment before judiciary authorities (*maqamat-e qazai'*): A. Unveiling related to head (*bad-hijabiy-e sar*), 1-showing part of the hair in a theatrical (*namayeshi*) and vulgar (*zanandeh*) manner; 2- facial make up with lipstick, eye shadow in a vulgar fashion. B. Unveiling related to trunk and legs: 1- Wearing dresses that would not cover parts of the body; 2- Wearing net-like and transparent dresses; 3- Wearing dresses that would be provocative (*tahrik-aamiz*) by showing the curvatures of the body; 4- Wearing tight pants without a tunic (*manto*); 5- Wearing leg transparent knit stockings without pants or tunic; 6- Wearing dresses that carry signs, pictures and vulgar writings contravening Islamic morals.[16]

These articles are followed by "clarifications" on the tradition-based manner and appearance in public that supposedly emanate from the Sharia Law:

> Clarifications: 1- The Shari limit in coverage (*hadd-e pushish-e shari*) is the coverage of whole body other than the facial round (*qurs-e surat*) and hands up to wrist; 2- this is applicable to men too, wearing vulgar dress contravening public morals (*iffat-e umumi*) expressing vulgar culture (*farhang-e ibtizal*). Cases that would engender warning (*tazakkur*) and imploring (*irshaad*) and finally written reprieves (*tahhud-e katbi*) are as follows: A. Showing of hair other than those in Article 1; B. If the length of the hair makes it apparent from under head-cover; C. If various bodily movements (*harakat-e mukhtalifih-e badani*) were to cause unveiling; D. Unbuttoning were to expose parts of the body.[17]

This "regulatory code" was enacted in the spring of 1989. The fact that in 1989, after almost a decade of trying to force the veil on women, the state had to criminalize women's style of dress, hair, make-up and even walking in public indicates that the Qur'anic principle of *al-amr-e bil maaruf wa an-nahy min al-munkar* is a general principle that does not lend itself to a literal interpretation. At the same time, it is absolutely positively criminogenic and anti-Sharia Law to ignore tens of millions of Iranian women's wishes in regard to their dress code (veiling, or non-veiling).

Based on published documents, the Islamic regime has used a combined strategy of threat of force coupled with the actual use of brutal force from 1980 to the present (2000) in implementing the principle of the *munkar and maruf*. As a result, mal-veiled women have systematically been arrested in the streets, at work, and at public and private transportation venues; moreover, mal-veiled women are systematically stopped and lectured by the armed, and mostly illiterate, paramilitary groups known as the *Basiji*. These units have been empowered to arrest and/or to lecture mal-veiled women in the streets of Teheran and other large cities of Iran. These arrests are absolutely against the Qur'anic exhortation of modesty in appearance as well as against the Constitution's third section that covers the "Nation's Rights."

The Islamic Judiciary's View of the Substantive Law

Under the new Islamic justice system, we come across two types of substantive laws: (1) the Islamic Civil Code and (2) the Islamic Criminal Code. Both are based on the Twelve Imami Shii version of Sharia Law and legitimated by the Constitution. Both have led to women's victimization at the hands of the state and criminal justice agencies.

The Islamic Civil Code and Women

The new Islamic Civil Code known as the *Majmueh-e Qavaanin-e Kanevaadeh*, which translates into the Compendium of Laws of Family, was ratified by the Islamic Consultative Assembly in 1980 and reconsidered in 1989.[18] This Compendium takes the family as the most important social unit in the context of women's status (rights and responsibilities). As usual, the Compendium has a dual basis: the Islamic Sharia Law and the Constitution of the Islamic Republic. A synopsis of both documents is presented below.

The Civil Code states that because Article 10 of the Constitution views the family as the most basic social unit, the state is duty-bound to provide all means necessary for the enhancement of the family based on

Islamic laws. The Civil Code then cites Article 21 of the Constitution which stipulates that:

> The state is obligated to safeguard woman's rights in every respect based on Islamic criteria and perform the following:
>
> (1) Taking appropriate measures for the growth of woman's personality and revitalize her tangible and moral rights.
> (2) Protection of mothers, especially during pregnancy and custody of children, and custody of parentless children.
> (3) Establishment of a mediation court for the preservation and sustenance of the family.
> (4) Creation of insurance for widowed women, the elderly and women without family.
> (5) Custodial rights of children to those deserving mothers in order to upgrade them and in the case of the lack of a religiously prescribed custodian.[19]

Following this rationale, the Civil Code in Chapter One (and through this Chapter's 38 sections), expounds on the establishment of:

(1) Family mediator and divorce courts
(2) Religious minorities and the family affairs courts
(3) Family protection laws
(4) Marriage laws
(5) Laws on Iranian women's marriage to foreign citizens
(6) Laws to protect women and children who lack proper custodians.

Chapter Two covers laws concerned with familial matters that ought to be notarized (e.g., birth, death, marriage, divorce, death and various punitive measures in case such were not properly notarized).

Chapter Three covers 27 articles of the Civil Code regarding the dynamics of the family and its rights. Some of these are of interest to our argument and are to be dealt with later in this chapter.

Chapter Four is about the laws concerning the power of attorney with regard to the family.

Chapter Five is about work laws and their relationship with the family.

Chapter Six is about the laws of social security and their relationship with the family.

The central problem with these laws is that they reflect a legalistic reasoning whose social and economic contexts no longer exist. This problem is elaborated in the marriage and divorce laws, the subject of the next sub-section.

The Islamic Civil Code on divorce, custodial rights and marital provisions
The thrust of the Code is that divorce is a disruptive process in the life of the family. Divorce ought to be the last resort only after attempts at mediation (informal and formal) have failed. After reiterating this premise, the Code details the various Sharia-based factors that the two parties ought to observe so that an Islamically legitimate divorce may proceed. What are these factors? First, during the separation period, women ought to reside in husband's domicile and observe the period of *uddah* that the Qur'an has prescribed and sanctioned by the Sharia Law. This period commences from the last copulation between the couple and continues for a period of three months. The rationale for this stipulation has been that (1) either of the two parties may decide against the divorce and want to return *(rija)* or (2) the observation of the *uddah* not only allows for the return, it is also a precautionary practice considering that, during the initiation of the divorce, the wife may be pregnant without the knowledge of the husband, or the wife may not have yet detected her pregnancy. Refraining from any sexual activities during this period may help the foetus and may allow the parties to go through a cooling-off period to reconsider reunion. From a purely theoretical perspective, this is sound. The problem is that in present-day Iran the feminization of poverty has reached crisis proportions, manifested in the rise of widespread prostitution, feminine suicide and an alarming rise in female crime. Consequently, these types of cautionary practice are violated by married men who want to divorce their wives and marry younger ones who avail themselves to any economically viable suitors. Second, the husband is required to provide for his wife and children during the separation period. This has also been sanctioned by the Qur'an and the juristic texts. The rationale has been that attempting to divorce does not negate a husband's obligations towards his spouse(s) or offspring. A spouse is not allowed to abandon his family because he is divorcing his wife. This protective measure of the Qur'an, of course, is very important and gives an indication of the Qur'anic stress on believers' responsibilities towards one another within a family structure. Again, the feminization of poverty has negatively influenced the overall social and political structure that existed in

pre-Revolution Iran and which allowed for a more rational divorce process and support for divorced women.

Third, the Civil Code provides for various scenarios under which a divorcee can be remunerated for the services that she has rendered in her husband's domicile provided that: (a) she is not the initiator of the divorce; (b) has not refrained from performing her conjugal responsibilities; and (c) has not committed "immoral" acts. Once the family court is assured of these, then it may determine the amount of monthly monetary provision that a husband has to provide for the ex-spouse. This amount depends on the number of years of married life, the kind of works that the wife has performed in the domicile, and the husband's economic position.[20]

There is no problem so far and, in fact, the Civil Code seems to provide some protective measures for divorced women. The problem emerges when we deal with specific articles of the Code. For example, Article 1105 maintains that: "In the conjugal relations, assumption of the position of the head of the family is one of the characteristics of the husband."[21] In other words, the assumption of the head of family is like an inborn and biologically determined "characteristic" of the husband. This is sexist and misogynous, denying women of their deserved position in the family. Articles 1106 and 1107 outline the wife's rights to maintenance (*nafaqah*), provided that she performs her responsibilities towards her husband, in accordance with Article 1108.

Article 1109 is quite of a medievalist nature, stipulating that (1) maintaining a returning divorcee woman in the period of *uddah* is incumbent upon the husband provided that the divorce has not been due to the *nushuz*, a Qur'anic term, translated variously as conjugal rebelliousness. This means that a man can divorce his wife by alleging *nushuz* on the part of his wife in order to deprive her of the provision to which she is entitled.

Article 1113 is about temporary marriages (*aqd-i inqitaa*). This is a practice that almost all modern Islamic societies have abolished, including Iran, under the monarchy. Under the Islamic Republic, this practice has been resurrected in full force. In the simplest terms, it is the practice of concubinage that is known as the *mutah* in Sunni jurisprudence and as the *sighah* in Shii jurisprudence. It has a long and controversial history, and we have already touched upon its foundation in Chapter 4 of this study. In modern Iran, it has been looked as semi-prostitution usually carried out by socially and economically indigent women. With the rise of the Islamic Republic, this practice has been acclaimed as Islam's solution to men's so-called "insatiable" desire for sex even though the majority of Islamic societies have denounced this practice as beneath Muslim women's dignity and their exalted station of life in the Qur'an and in the Prophet Muhammad's Tradition.

Article 1132 is one of the most misogynous articles of the Islamic Civil Code: it maintains that "Man is allowed to divorce his wife any time he wishes."[22] This right does not apply to women.

Through Articles 1143 and 1145, the Code elaborates two general types of divorce, *Baain* and *Rijii*. The former is a type of divorce that, if initiated, does not allow for a reconsideration (the so- called *rijat*), whereas the second type of divorce allows for such reconsideration.[23]

Article 1145 defines *Baain* if the following conditions apply: (1) a divorce initiated prior to intercourse; (2) divorce of a woman in menopause (*yaisah*); (3) divorce on *khal* and *mubarat* provided that woman has not appealed for her Sharia-based right to compensation (4) divorce that has taken place after three consecutive remarriages (to the same spouse) whether due to reconsideration or due to remarriage. These are medievalist practices whose social and economic rationales do not exist any more.

Through Articles 1150-1157, the Civil Code explores the meaning of the *uddah,* a cautionary practice in which divorcing women should refrain from sexual intercourse for a certain period of time.[24] This is due to the possibility that prior to divorce the female spouse may have been impregnated by her husband. By refraining from sexual activities, not only is the physical well-being of the foetus guaranteed, but reconsideration (*rija*) between the two parties is possible. This cautionary practice has a cherished place in both Sunni and Shii juristic texts, some of which I have already dealt with in Chapter 4 of this study.

The problem with the Islamic Civil Code is that, besides being out of touch with the realities of the modern world, its articles apply only to women. As a result, the husband is almost free of the many Qur'anic restrictions placed on both husband and wife. Divorce has become a powerful controlling mechanism in the hands of husbands.

Through Articles 1158-1194, the Civil Code explores the situation of the children in the family by resurrecting a manifestly medievalist patrilineal regime with regard to the position of children in the family.[25] These articles (1157-1167) explore the so-called *nisba* of the newly born child (the child's genealogy traced to the father), what happens if a child is born after a divorce has taken effect (again, the new-born belongs to the father provided that the divorced wife has not remarried, which is quite unlikely considering the length of the *uddah* period specified in the Civil Code), under what conditions a father is allowed to denounce his lineage to a newly born child (*dawi nafi wald*), and under what conditions a newly born child can be considered as illegitimate (*namashru*).

Through Articles 1168-1179, the issues of the child's upbringing are discussed in the Civil Code. Although both parents are charged with this responsibility (Article 1168), other articles give priority to the father, as for instance, Article 1169 which maintains that, until age two, a child is under the care (*hizanat*) of the mother. After that age, a male child becomes the ward of the father. In the case of a female child, she becomes the father's ward after age seven because the Civil Code extends a female child's maternal care as far as age seven.

Other articles of this section contemplate scenarios concerning the issue of child custody. In case of the father's death, the mother assumes the custody of the children (Article 1171). If both parents are unfit morally the custody can pass on to close relatives based on legal action taken on behalf of the children (Article 1173). Other articles of this section explore the child's rights and responsibilities in the family.

In short, the Islamic Civil Code has resurrected the centuries-old system of marriage, divorce, child custody and family structure that reflects an agricultural valuation system whose social relations of production no longer exist any more. To appreciate these points, the next section is devoted to a comparison between the Islamic Civil Code's view of family protection with its secular predecessor under the monarchy.

The Family Protection Acts of 1967 and 1975

According to the British Parliamentary Human Rights Group that has conducted extensive research on the situation of Iranian women under the Islamic regime of the Ayatullah Khumaini and his successors: "Under the Shah, the Family Protection Acts of 1967 and 1975 had radically improved the situation of married women."[26] The pamphlet elaborates by arguing that: (1) the Acts put a decisive end to husband's ability to unilaterally divorce his spouse at will; (2) the Acts increased the legal age of marriage for both women (to 18), and men (to 20); (3) the Acts improved women's custodial rights; and (4) the Acts gave the authority for granting divorce to family courts. With the Islamic regime, however, the group concludes: "All this was swept away seven months after the mullah's revolution, and the Family Courts were replaced by Special Civil Courts presided over by Islamic judges."[27]

On the other hand, exploring various articles of the Islamic Civil Code, the group cites a number of studies to reach the conclusion that the Civil

Code represents the Sharia Law which is "based on an ideology of male dominance."[28] The result has been controversial. Assessing the impact of the Islamic Revolution on family structure, Jaquiline Rudolph Touba argues that: "Before the Revolution, it was believed that Western industrialization had penetrated the Iranian culture and affected the family according to the Western model. This assumption now appears to be incorrect."[29] Touba makes three claims that have been supported by anecdotal, rather than hard-core, data: (1) the family has remained strong and intact; (2) a "limited" number of opportunities have been created for the development of a gender-based egalitarian attitude due to revolutionary activities; and (3) the institution of family has been strengthened by strengthening women's traditional status in the family.[30]

In a more systematic study, Valentine Moghadam gives a more sophisticated and detailed view of women's status in Iran after the Revolution.[31] The data covers economically active male and female populations, as well as the distribution of male and female governmental employees in selected industries in the pre- and post-Revolution periods. She concludes that during the first stages of the Revolution (1980-1989), women's status, in terms of education and employment, deteriorated because of the revolutionary turmoil. Under the Ayatullah Khumaini's successors, the situation has stabilized, and women's status has undergone a steady improvement. Moghadam is among very few Iranian women scholars who have reached this conclusion. Her data have been attacked by a number of Iranian feminist scholars who have observed that she has relied too much on official data disseminated by the Islamic regime.[32]

In sum, it is difficult to see how a small number of scholars have reached the conclusion that women's status has improved, considering the large amount of unofficial data that give a different picture. For example, the British Parliamentary Human Rights Group, citing Homa Omid's study, reports "Between 1976 and 1986, the number of women in employment declined from 14 per cent of the labour force to 9 per cent, and in 1990 the level of women's participation in the labour market ranked 108 in the International Labour Organization's study of 110 countries."[33] The Group also cites the following from a BBC report on 6 April 1993: "...[A] decade after the revolution the female population has risen by ten million while the number of jobs for women has not only not increased, but has decreased from 1.2 million in 1977 to 975,000 in 1987...."[34] More important is the Islamic Penal Code that has become operative since the early 1980s in Iran as a main instrument in victimizing women, the topic of the next section.

The Islamic Penal Code and Women

To further comprehend the Islamic Republic's treatment of women's law-infracting behaviour, we now turn our attention to the *Matn-e Kaamel-e Qaanun-e Hudud wa Qisaas wa Muqarrarat-e Aan* (The Compendium of the Law of Retribution and Boundaries and its Ordinances). This Compendium was later amended to the *Qaanun-e Mujazaat-e Islami: Hudud, Qisaas, Diyaat, Taziraat.* (The Islamic Penal Code: Boundaries, Retribution, Compensation, Corporal Punishments). This Penal Code was ratified by a clergy-dominated Iranian parliament in 1982 and amended in 1992; it gives the reader another example about the Islamic judiciary's view of substantial law based on the Shari`a. In its original version (*Matn-e Kaamel,* unless stated otherwise), it has two sections: *Qisaas* and *Hudud.* Both concepts are borrowed from the Qur'an. The term *Qisaas* applies to retribution in punishment. The term *Hudud* applies to a number of prohibited acts, the commission of which necessitates appropriate punishment. The so-called Hudud-Allah (God's boundaries, singular, *Hadd*) comprise punishments that Muslim jurists have categorized in juristic texts. I have already given a synopsis of these terms and their meanings in previous chapters.

For example, in Malik ibn Anas's *al-Muwatta,* the section on *Hudud* covers acts for which *Hadd* applies (e.g., homicide, robbery, adultery, theft, slander, etc.) as well as acts for which *Hadd* does not apply (e.g., a man's intercourse with a slave-girl to whom she has become religiously sanctified, *halaal,* etc.). A variety of such scenarios can also be found in the classical Shii texts.[35]

The purpose of the present Islamic penal code is to institutionalize such prohibitions and punishments. The preamble to the Code maintains: "Qisaas is a punishment that a criminal is adjudicated with, and it must carry equity [equity between crime and punishment], covering two types of qisaas: qisaas-e nafs [retributory death penalty] and qisaas-e uzw [bodily retribution]."[36] We first analyse the Qisaas part of the Code, which comprises five chapters with eighty articles.

Retributory capital punishments Qisaas is of two types – that which applies to capital punishment (*qisaas-e nafs*), and that which applies to injury-related punishments (*qisaas-i uzw*). Chapter One of the Code, composed of seven articles (and various clarifications) makes the Code discriminatory, a point to be explored shortly.

Article 1 is about intentional murder (*qatl-e amd*). Intentional murder is subject to retribution whereby the so-called legal "guardians of the murdered person's blood" (*ulia-ye dam*) are allowed to exact retribution on the convict provided that they acquire the consent of the Guardian of the Muslims (*Wali-ye Muslimin*), or his representative, and by following the prescribed norms (as specified). The Guardian of Muslims means the highest authority in the Islamic Republic which is Ali Khamenehi, who has assumed the Office of the Jurist Council, without whose consent no punishment can be meted out, at least theoretically.

Article 2 explains the conditions under which murder can be categorized as intentional murder, whereas Article 3 divides murder into intentional, and pseudo-intentional (*shebh-e amd*), and negligent (*khataa*). This categorization is based on a traditional jurisprudential categorization of murder, covered in both Shii [37] and Sunni sources.[38]

Article 4 explores the impact of duress in murder, maintaining that one should not commit murder based on duress, but does not define duress.

Article 5 maintains that if a Muslim were to be killed, the killer is to be reattributed, implying that the Islamic state takes the issue of murdering of a Muslim very seriously.

Articles 6 and 7 interject gender, opening the gates for the brutalization of women.

Article 6 maintains that: "If a Muslim man wilfully murders a Muslim woman [he] is subject to retribution in kind with the proviso that the guardian of the [murdered] woman ought to pay half of compensatory blood money to him."[39] Based on this article, which transparently reflects the drafters' Sharia Law-based agriculturalist valuation system, when a Muslim male murderer is to be executed, half of his blood money ought to be paid to the murderer's family by the guardian of the female victim. Why? Because a Muslim male's blood, even when he is a murderer, has value. However, the opposite does not hold true. The Penal Code does not apply the same principle to a Muslim female murderer. Why? Because a female murderer's blood has less value than that of a Muslim male murderer; therefore, she can be executed without having her blood compensated for.

This disparity in the valuation system is found in medieval juristic texts, but it is not found in the Qur'an. The same discriminatory valuation system is found in Article 7 of the Penal Code. It states:

> If a protected infidel wilfully murders another protected infidel [he/she] is subject to retribution in kind even though

> they may be followers of two different religions and if the murdered is a woman protected infidel her guardian has to compensate the protected infidel man with half of compensatory blood money. [40]

The drafters have definitely applied the same discriminatory valuation system to the so-called "zemmi infidels" who live in Iran as Iranian citizens, whatever their religious affiliations. The Penal Code has not provided a clue in the text as to the principle of adjudication upon which it has reached the conclusion that females, whether Muslim or non-Muslim, have a lesser value in so far as their blood money is concerned.

A Critique

The Islamic judiciary maintains that retribution in kind is a Qur'anic concept which of course is true. There is no doubt that the Prophet Muhammad and "the Four Rightly Guided Caliphs" applied some aspects of the retributory penology, a fact validated by both Sunni and Shii texts. Questionable is the idea that the present judiciary applies its version of retributory punishments based on the Prophet Muhammad's rationale which was progressive for his time; he applied retributory punishments without regard for the offender's power or social standing. Under the present judiciary, the Code penalizes the socially disenfranchised (women, social and economic indigents), but leaves the powerful unmolested.

The Qur'an's View on Compensation of Blood Money

In consulting the Qur'an concerning the principle of compensation for blood money when capital crimes are committed, the following picture emerges. First, verse 93 in chapter *al-Nisa* explores various situations concerning unintentional murder. It reads:

> It does not become a believer to kill a believer unless it is by mistake. And he who kills a believer by mistake shall free a believing slave, and *pay* blood-money to be handed over to his heirs, unless they remit it as charity. But if *the person slain* be of a people hostile to you, and be a believer, then the *offender* shall free a believing slave; and if he be of a people

> between whom and you is a pact, then *the offender* shall pay blood money to be handed over to his heirs, and free a believing slave. But whoso finds not *one*, he shall fast for two consecutive months – a mercy from Allah. And Allah is All-Knowing, Wise.[41]

Reading this verse and comparing it with the Islamic Penal Code under the present judiciary makes it obvious that the drafters of the Code have utilized this verse in the adjudication of such murders. However, the drafters have completely ignored the fact that the verse intends to put a believing Muslim on par with those under Islam's protection (the *zemmi)* by requiring two things in the case of a *zemmi* being unintentionally murdered: (1) the payment of blood money to the *zemmi's* heirs; (2) the freeing of a believing slave (a slave who has converted to Islam and therefore has to be given free status).

Since slavery does not exist in any Islamic society, the practice of freeing slaves is out of question, making this part of the clause procedurally and substantially irrelevant to the adjudication process. Instead, a correct reading of the verse requires the drafters of the Code to consider a non-Muslim Iranian citizen *absolutely equal* to a Muslim Iranian citizen, whether male or female. This legal egalitarianism would have made the judiciary truly Islamic, in accordance with the humanitarian and egalitarian thrust of Islam. In turn it would have resonated harmoniously for a state that is a signatory to various international non-discriminatory conventions. A move towards the Prophetic model of adjudication would necessitate a move in the direction of equality rather than reinstating a medievalist discriminatory valuation system in the judiciary.

The next verse in *al-Nisa* is about intentional killing, and it states: "And whoso kills a believer intentionally, his reward shall be Hell...."[42] There is a Hadith on the authority of Said bin Jubair that the people of Kufa had a dispute over the interpretation of this verse. Consulting with Ibn Abbas, one of the most respected authorities on the issue, Said bin Jubair reported: "He said, 'This Verse:- "And who ever kills a believer intentionally..." was revealed last of all (concerning premeditated murder) and nothing abrogated it.'"[43] The verse and the Hadith were to perhaps warn the degree to which murder is detested in the eyes of Allah, especially the murder of a believing Muslim, whether male or female. The idea that a female Iranian citizen's blood money, whether a Muslim or a *zemmi*, is worth less than that of a male citizen's blood money, whether Muslim or *zemmi*, is patently anti-Qur'anic and has little to do with Prophet Muhammad's model; it is a post-Prophet Muhammad assertion, most probably started with the onset of Islam's feudalization process.

Insofar as females are concerned, (ii: 179) maintains that:

> O ye who believe, *equitable* retaliation in the matter of the slain is prescribed for you; the free man for the free man, and the slave for the slave, and the female for the female. But if one is granted any remission by one's brother, then pursuing *the matter for the realization of the blood-money* shall be done with fairness and *the murderer* shall pay him the blood money in a handsome manner. This is an alleviation from your Lord and a mercy. And whoso transgresses thereafter, for him there shall be a grievous punishment.[44]

The drafters of the Penal Code have followed the male for male equity clause of this verse, applying to it both believing Muslim and *zemmi* males. However, they have completely misconstrued the female-for-female equity clause, surmising that only a female murderess can be subjected to the punishment of retribution for a female murdered; in the case of a male murdering a female, the murderer can only be subjected to the punishment of retribution *only* if his blood were compensated by the guardians of the murdered female. Why? Because in terms of human value, Iranian females count as half insofar as human life is concerned in the eyes of the present judiciary in Iran.

The drafters of the Penal Code have completely misconstrued the historical context of the above verse. First, in medieval agricultural societies women were generally valued less than men for obvious reasons: although they worked at home and in the fields, they were not considered as the breadwinners of the family; neither were they allowed to go to war or to participate in many social, political and economic affairs. Women were less in danger of being murdered, and they had fewer chances to murder others.

Second, in the Arab *Jahiliyah* tradition, baby girls, if unwanted, were allowed, by tradition, be buried alive in the desert, whereas baby boys brought joy and pride to the parents and the tribe. In addition, Arab tribes were renowned for their blood feuds that could take generations to settle. In these feuds, it was mostly the men of the tribe who got entangled in fights and the blood feuds that subsequently ensued, resulting in the loss of life, limb and property. When we put these historical facts together, the above Qur'anic verse gives some semblance of order to these gendered aspects of the *Jahiliyah* tradition. The verse provided symmetry in compensation for the spilled blood of free man, female and slave. It also prevented the arbitrary killing of an innocent person (e.g., the murder of the female relatives of a male murderer by the wronged party's relatives).

This verse is irrelevant to a conception of human value in modern theories of adjudication for one obvious reason: in modern civil societies, men and women are born equal in the eyes of the law, and are treated equally. However, the novelty of the above scenario is not so much in seeing "infidels" in a culturally and ethnically heterogeneous society such as Iran, but that in the eyes of the present judiciary, and two hundred years after the French Declaration of Universal Human Rights, a woman, whether Muslim or non-Muslim, is worth half a man, dead or alive. And yet the Constitution of the Islamic Republic speaks of social progress, modern technology, the Iranian nation, equity before law and freedom.

Within the Penal Code, Articles 8 through 14 explore various procedural scenarios concerning one's participation in murder. Article 8 pertains to Muslim men, and the clarification (*no.2*) of this article is about protected infidels (*kaafar-e zemmi*).[45] Other articles of this section provide various compensatory scenarios in case of murder. Most of these scenarios pertain to agricultural societies and are irrelevant to the dynamics of social entanglements and crime in modern Islamic societies, including Iran.

Conditions of Retributory Punishment in the Penal Code

Chapter Two of the Penal Code, composed of eight articles (15 through 22), explores the conditions of retributory punishment by inserting medievalist notions, making adjudication quite arbitrary and at times almost impossible procedurally.

Article 22 maintains that: "Murder is subject to retribution in kind provided that the murdered victim were not to be death deserving from the perspective of the Sharia and if the [murdered] victim were to be deserving death the murderer has to prove victim's deserving in court."[46] The general thrust of this article is understandable, considering that adjudication is the very process through which the guilt or innocence of the accused is determined in modern criminal justice systems. Therefore, a defendant's punishment ought to be legitimated through adjudication. What is problematic here – besides the terminology that reflects the medievalist mind set of the judiciary – is a very distinct discriminatory practice in the application of the article. For example, how does a judge determine equity in justice if a Muslim believer is found guilty of the murder of an atheist? Does this mean that the life and limb of a non-believer is valueless?

Chapter Three of the Penal Code, composed of four articles (23 through 26), explores the conditions under which murder and murder-related grievances are allowed to be brought before the court. [47]

Rules of Evidence and Witness in the Penal Code

Chapter Four of the Penal Code, composed of fourteen articles (27 through 42) and a number of clarifications, explores the rules of evidence, rules of witness and proof in court. These are: (1) confession, (2) witness, (3) oath and (4), judge's knowledge. These rules, based on the Islamic judiciary's notion of procedural laws, manifestly express a medievalist conception of the rules of evidence, and of proof. For example, Article 33, clarification 1, maintains: "Intentional murder is provable based upon two just men's witnessing."[48] Who is a "just man"? How do we determine this vague criterion? There is no mention of this condition in the Penal Code. However, one could surmise that Penal Code's sections are based on traditional Shii juristic texts as, for example, Shaykh al-Taifa's *Al-Nihayah*, cited above. For example, chapter eight of *Al-Nihayah* explores witnessing, including a just witness; whereas chapter nine explores adjudication and its regulations. A witness, accordingly, ought to satisfy the following conditions in order to be considered a just witness: (1) transparency in belief; (2) being known; (3) being known for righteousness; (4) good mannerisms; (5) God-fearing; (6) non-abusive language; (7) good deeds; (8) being not a drunkard; (9) being not an adulterer.[49]

The same conditions apply to women witnesses provided they personify "ideal wives". Witness of the following are not to be accepted: (1) enemy; (2) traitor; (3) mercenary; (4) those involved in lascivious acts unless they witness against themselves; (5) those involved in theatrical performance; (6) those who use profane language; (7) those who gamble; (8) those who accept bribes in adjudication; (9) those who are illegitimate although they may be known as just persons, etc.; (10) those who are *qazaf* (e.g., one who uses abusive language against others' sisters and mothers); however, if a *qazaf* were to repent, his witness can be accepted; (11) those who are robbers. The list is a long one.[50]

What emerges from this and similar medieval juristic texts is a picture of crime and its dynamics that made sense in medieval agricultural societies with their relatively small populations, low crime rates, and their mechanical type of social control mechanisms and norms that Emile Durkheim attributed to pre-industrial agricultural societies and to their notion of social solidarity. Naturally, some of these conditions apply even today. In modern theories of adjudication, the reputation and credibility of the witness are important factors. However, a good number of these conditions and norms do not apply in modern adjudication. One cannot be denied testimony because of his/her birth conditions (illegitimacy), profession, or involvement in pre- and extramarital sexual activities. Most important, one's religious affiliation cannot be taken as the standard of denial or admissibility of testimony and witness.

What is more problematic is that the present judiciary has taken for granted that these conditions apply to a country with a population that exceeds sixty-five million and with one of the highest rates of unemployment (around 25 per cent) in the world. Faced with huge economic problems, social upheavals, and a corrupting and criminogenic judiciary, the idea that in criminal proceedings positive proof can be established through the testimony of "just" men and "just" women is problematic and has led to miscarriages of justice, especially in the case of indigent persons.

Article 33, clarification 2 of the Penal Code is also of interest to us. It states: "Pseudo-intentional murder or negligent is proven through the witnessing of: two just men, or one just man and two just women, or one just man and oath of the plaintiff."[51] Insofar as oath is concerned, Article 38 of the Penal Code maintains that:

> In cases of contestation firstly, the plaintiff is asked to provide reputable witnesses and if no witness were available, plaintiff can produce forty-nine men from his family members whom are knowledgeable about the murder and together with him take oath in order to prove their case, and in case they have less than the prescribed number repeat the oath so that [number] fifty is reached and if the plaintiff has no relatives or his relatives have no knowledge [of the event] the plaintiff can take fifty oaths in order to prove his case.[52]

Again, notwithstanding the fact that the Prophet Muhammad and his deputies applied some of these measures, the above is out of context: the number of "knowledgeable" witnesses who take an oath on behalf of the plaintiff relates to the fact that in tribal/agricultural societies, murder was hardly an individualistic act. In tribal and medieval societies, every person was protected by extended family, kin groups and tribal affiliations, and clan members. In such a social medium of protection, a person could not be murdered and left alone to decompose in his/her quarters – a situation that we witness in modern urban societies where the social bond is more of vertical affiliation, rather than both horizontal (family) and vertical nature (tribal).

The nuclearization of families in modern times has lessened the protective horizontal nature of social affiliation, allowing urban individualism to emerge. This has transformed murder from a communal into an individual act. Not to mention the fact that in many urban societies, including present-day Iran, professional killers can eliminate one's prospective enemy without one's involvement. The absurdity of this article hardly necessitates the force of criminological logic. Suffice it to say that in Iran the security of property, reputation and life of an accused citizen is contingent upon the number of oaths that an economically or socially strained loner is willing take in front of judges. However, one of the most disturbing is retribution in kind applied to organ-related injuries, the subject of the next section.

Organ-related Retributory Punishment in the Penal Code

This type of retributory punishment is explained as follows in Article 55 of the Penal Code: "Cutting of bodily organ or its injury if were to be intentional is subject to retribution in kind and the wronged party is allowed for retribution against the criminal based on the prescribed norms and religious judge's decree."[53]

Article 56 of the Code defines the cutting and injury of organs as intentional, quasi-intentional and accidental; these require the application of organ-related retributory punishments, the so-called *qisaas-e uzw*.

Article 57 defines three types of intentional cutting or injury as follows: (a) when the criminal intends to inflict such a cut and/or injury by the commission of a certain act whether that act results in a cut and/or injury; (b) when the criminal intentionally commits an act that somewhat results in a cut and/or injury although this were not intended to cut and/or injure; and (c) when the criminal does not intend to cut or injure an organ, and his act does not effectuate that result, but, due to advanced age and/or infancy, the act effectuates the severance or injury of organs and is known to the criminal.

Article 58 provides for equity in organ-related retributory punishments. In the organ-related retribution in kind (*qisaas-e uzw)*, not only must the conditions of murder-related retribution *(qisaas-e nafs)* be observed, but the following also must be met: (1) equity in the health of the organs; (2) equity in originality of the organs (i.e., not being artificial); (3) equity in the place of injury; (4) that retribution be not fatal; and (5) that retribution be not more injurious than the crime.[54]

Article 59 provides for equity in punishment. It reads:

> In the organ related retribution in kind, woman and man are equal and a male perpetrator who inflicts bodily injury or a wrong on woman is subjected to organ related retribution in kind. Unless the compensation of the injured organ [of woman] is one third or more than one third of complete compensation whereby woman can inflict retribution if one half compensatory value of that organ is paid to man.[55]

This article implies that, although equity in punishment applies, some organs of women, when injured by men, carry less value than those of men. Again, the claim is that the Islamic judiciary is following verbatim the Qur'an and Prophetic traditions. Let us explore this claim now.

The Qur'anic Notion of Equity in Punishment

The Qur'anic stance on equity in punishment pertains to murder (*qisaas-e nafs*), an extension of which applies to punishment in organ-related injuries (*qisaas-e uzw*). Verse 179 of *al-Baqarah* that we cited above is the appropriate starting point for this consideration. One of the earliest interpretations of this verse has been provided by Ibn Abbas. He argues that the term *al-qisaas* mentioned in this verse is to remind Muslims that retribution was a form of punishment that Moses prescribed for the ancient Hebrews (Israelites in the vernacular of the Qur'an); whereas blood money (*diya*) is a compensatory device that the Qur'an has prescribed in Islam as a humanitarian step:

> Narrated Ibn 'Abbas...: The law of Qisas (i.e. equity in punishment) was prescribed for the children of Israel, but the Diya [i.e. blood money (was not)]. So Allah said to this Nation (i.e. Muslims):- "O you who believe! The law of Al-Qisas (i.e. equity in punishment) is prescribed for you in cases of murder....But if the relatives (or one of them) of the

> killed person forgave their brother (i.e. the killer) something of Qisas (i.e. the acceptance of blood money in the case of intentional murder)--then the relatives (of the killed person) and the killer must pay with handsome gratitude...." [56]

From this narration, it is apparent that blood money (*diya*) is a humanitarian compensatory device whose intention was to improve the prevailing penological philosophy; this measure naturally pertains to both murder and organ-related injuries, a device that, next to retaliation, has been prescribed in case of murder. As such, it applied to both murder and injury-related prosecutions, covering both males and females during the era of the Prophet Muhammad.

The Notion of Equity in Prophet Muhammad's Tradition

The following Hadith from Malik ibn Anas's *Al-Muwatta*, lends support to my argument:

> Yahya related to me from Malik from 'Abdullah ibn Abi Bakr ibn Muhammad Amr ibn Hazm from his father that in a letter which the Messenger of Allah, may Allah bless him and grant him peace, sent to Amr ibn Hazm about blood money, he wrote that it was one hundred camels for a life, one hundred camels for a nose if completely removed, a third of the blood money for a wound in the brain, the same as that for a belly wound, and five for a head wound which laid the bone bare.[57]

There is no mention of gender-based differences in both murder and organ-related retribution in kind in the above Hadith. What is interesting is the fact that early jurists recognized that the instruments of compensation had to be based on the compensatory measures that were available to both tribal people and settled people. Malik ibn Anas reported: "The generally agreed on way of doing things in our community is that camels are not accepted from people of cities for blood-money nor is gold accepted from desert people...."[58] City people could not be asked to provide camels as a compensatory measure because they were not in the camel grazing profession, neither were tribal people expected to have gold, or recognize the quality of various gold and silver coins that were in circulation during the time of Malik ibn Anas (d.

795). In addition, Malik reports various Hadiths concerning the blood money of women, foetuses and organs. Some of these Hadiths provide equity. For example, the following Hadith relates both equity and inequity:

> Yahya related to me from Malik from Yahya ibn Said that Said ibn al-Musayyab said, "The blood-money for a woman is the same as for a man up to one-third of the blood money. Her fingers are like his finger, her tooth is like his, and her head wound which splinters the bones is like his." [59]

Giving equity in the organ-related retribution in kind, this Hadith reflects the Maliki school of jurisprudence, whereas the present judiciary in Iran follows the Twelv Imami Shii school, systemized by the Sixth Shii Imam, Jafar al-Sadiq. As previously mentioned, al-Sadiq was legendary for his knowledge of the Qur'an, Hadith and Shii Imam's Khabars and, most importantly, for his impeccable sense of justice. Next section describes the Shii notion of equity in punishment.

The Notion of Equity in the Classical Shii Juristic Sources

In consulting the reputable classical Twelve Imami Shii juristic sources, all of whom followed Imam Jafar al-Sadiq's jurisprudential reasoning and rationale, we see the following picture emerge:

> If a man were [to be found guilty in the] murder of a woman intentionally and the guardians of the woman attempt to kill him in retribution it is incumbent upon the guardians to pay that which is in excess of woman's blood money and that is half blood money [equal to] five thousand Dirhams [silver coins] or five hundred Dinars [gold coins] or fifty camels or five hundred sheep or hundred cows....If this which we said were not to be given they cannot kill in retribution under any circumstance[;] therefore if they demand blood money they should demand full compensation in blood money that is one of those which we have said....[60]

In the case of a woman found guilty of having intentionally murdered a man, she was to be subjected to murder-related retribution in kind (according to Shaykh al-Taifa), but the guardians of the murdered man were not obliged to pay the guardians of the murderer. There is unanimity among classical Sunni and Shii jurists insofar as murder-related retribution in kind is concerned: men, whether murdered or murderer, had more value than women murdered or murderer. This inequity, as we have already mentioned, reflected a medieval agricultural valuation system, to be critiqued shortly. In so far as the equity in organ-related retribution in kind is concerned, Shaykh al-Taifa provided for the following procedure in compensation:

> Women and men[,] were they [having had] straight [teeth broken,] a tooth for a tooth (*dandani be dandani*) and finger for finger (*angushti be angushti*) and injury to injury (*jarahti be jarhati*) until woman's [injuries?] exceeds two times the blood money of man and if this were to happen woman's [compensation] is to be as explored below....[61]

In so-far as organ-related retribution in kind is concerned, Shaykh al-Taifa did not discriminate between the value of women's and men's organs. The equity thrust prevailed. However, in the present Islamic judiciary we find a gender-based, retrogressive valuation system towards women.

Institutionalized Cruelty and Violence against Women

The present judiciary has also come up with punishments that are cruel and unusual. These include:

(1) Public lashing (*jild*)
(2) Stoning to death (*rajam*) for adultery
(3) Amputation (*qat*) of fingers for theft
(4) Gouging of eyes, smashing bones and cutting of limbs as organ-related retribution in kind.

These punishments are carried out arbitrarily, usually inflicted upon indigent persons (both men and women) with total disregard for the due process that traditional Shii and Sunni jurists followed meticulously. Again, one has to consult the Qur'an and the Prophetic Hadith to critique the discrepancies between these aspects of the Penal Code and the original source of the Sharia Law.

The Qur'anic Punishment for theft The Qur'anic stance on punishing thieves can be found in the chapter *al-Maidah* (v), and in verse 38: "As for the thief, both male and female, (*al-saariq wa al-saariqa*) cut off their hands (*fa qatawa iydihum*), it is the reward of their own deeds...." [62] The next verse implores for leniency if the wrongdoers repent. Two points emerge from the verse when put in the context of the circumstances surrounding the verse's revelations. First, it was revealed very close to the end of the Prophet's tenure, and by that time Muslims believed that he had established a model and just Islamic society. Naturally, in such a model Islamic society presided over by Muhammad, thievery was a grave transgression against Allah's *Hudud* as well as the communal sense of righteousness and solidarity. Therefore, the punishment had to be swift, certain and consistent. This was, one might surmise, an Islamic precursor of a Beccarian rationale in punishment. Second, some Hadith give the impression that the above verse was directed against those who stole weapons (swords, shields, lances, bows and arrows etc.) that could threaten the peace and security of the newly established Community of Believers under the Prophet Muhammad's leadership. Therefore, the cutting of the fingers rendered the would-be enemy-thief ineffective in using any type of weapons, thereby reducing a threat from malcontents. For example, the following Hadith lends support to my assertion: "Narrated Ibn Umar...: Allah's Apostle...cut off the hand of a thief for stealing a shield that was worth three dirhems."[63] There are other, similar Hadiths to this effect.

The Prophetic model The Qur'an does not discriminate between males and females involved in thievery. In fact, when we explore a famous Hadith concerning a theft committed by an apparently rich and powerful lady of the Quraish tribe (Muhammad himself was from the same tribe), we find a patently anti-discriminatory application of the law by the Prophet:

> Narrated Aisha...: The Quraish people became very worried about the Makhzumiya lady who had committed theft. They said, "no body can speak [in favour of the lady] to Allah's Apostle...and no body dares to do that except Usma who is the favourite of Allah's Apostle....[64]

The Hadith continues, depicting one person (Usma) pleading with the Prophet who apparently received the following response:

> Do you intercede [with me] to violate one of the legal punishments of Allah?" Then he got up and addressed the people, saying, "O people! The nations before you went astray because if a noble person among them committed theft, they used to leave him, but if a weak person among them committed theft, they used to inflict the legal punishment by him. By Allah, if Fatima, the daughter of Muhammad committed theft, Muhammad will cut off her hand! [65]

This Prophetic utterance on the importance of consistency in applying punishment being the case, the only explanation for a gender-based asymmetry in the present Criminal Code is located in the drafters' medievalist agricultural valuation system in interpreting Sharia Law.

Now, going back to the above Hadith, the Prophet is narrated to have stipulated the cutting off of a thief's hands as required by Allah's Boundaries, the so-called *Hudud-Allah*. The drafters of the Penal Code claim that they have followed this designation with one strategic exception. The Prophet, reports the same Hadith, took an oath that he would have Fatima's hand cut off if she committed theft. The record of the Islamic criminal justice system in Iran hardly resonates harmoniously with what it purports to emulate: Muhammad's and Ali's model of law, justice and penology. For example, on 2 May 1990 the daily *Resalaṯ* revealed that the Hujjat al-Islam Hadi Ghaffari, a junior cleric and a member of parliament, was in possession of millions of dollars of ill-begotten public funds.[66] The daily declared that these funds were misappropriated by Ghaffari through a non-profitable foundation (Bunyad-e Al-Hadi) under his general directorship. Responding to the daily, 143 MPs retorted back that the charges were baseless and the *Resalat* attempted to badmouth the parliament, the state and its organs on behalf of the anti-revolutionaries and the so-called economic terrorists. The daily, in turn, responded to these charges by naming a number of prominent officials such as the Ayatullahs Burghehi and Muhammadi Gilani, as well as naming the then Minister of Economics, Dr. Muhsin Nurbaksh, who, accordingly, were aware of Ghaffari's ill-gotten wealth.[67] Ghaffari, like many other high dignitaries of the regime who have been implicated in a mind-boggling variety of financial corruptions was never fully investigated, let alone had his hands cut off in public. This relaxed attitude of the judiciary persists despite the fact that financial corruption, maintain these dignitaries, is a form of "terrorism" (*terorizm-e iqtesadi*) punishable by various forms of fines, imprisonment and even death. Who are these terrorists? Why has a state that credits itself with following the Prophet Muhammad's model in applying God's laws never brought these economic terrorists to justice at a time that, based upon the words of the high dignitaries of the regime, corruption and illegal expropriation of public funds has reached unprecedented dimensions? For example, the Ayatullah Karrubi's words are interesting. In a speech delivered on the occasion of the 21 of Ramadan, he reiterated that economic terrorists ought to be prosecuted because:

> In the same manner that we do not say "go and advise the smugglers [to come to straight path]...but we say get them...and execute them." Why we do not say "get the Munafiqin in order to advise them" [to come to straight path]? Now that this issue [economic terrorists] is raised we say "execute not." I have done some research and I tell you to know...This much has been hoarded in these years, this much thievery has taken place, not one single person we have given two years of imprisonment....[68]

The above is self-explanatory. Karrubi is not an "anti-revolutionary," in "cahoots" with the forces of "Global Arrogance" (*Istikbar-e Jahani*) that defame the Islamic regime. He is one of the most powerful and influential clerical figures and a staunch supporter of the *Wilayat-e Faqih* doctrine and form of governance.

The proposal of the Ayatullah Karrubi has been "let us do something" against economic corruption that is the province of the powerful in the Islamic Republic – a proposal which remained a pure empty rhetoric. However, the judiciary is eager to cut off the fingers of petty and indigent thieves on a regular basis. The daily *Jumhuri Islami*: "Ahwaz – Three convicts charged with more than 15 thefts were sentenced to amputation of four fingers in public." To the question of what happens after the amputation, the Ayatullah Muqtadai, the President of the Supreme Court, gave the following response:

> There was a discussion recently about whether or not the thief should immediately be transferred to the operating room after the amputation to have his fingers sewn back....A thief's hand must stay mutilated for ever. It is not a question of his suffering during the execution of the sentence; others witness it and take a lesson. [69]

Again, when we compare persons whose hands were to be chopped off under the Prophet Muhammad with those whose hands get chopped off under the present regime in Iran, one wonders whose model of justice is being followed?

In the Islamic Penal Code, Articles 60 through 80 follow the same medievalist scenario, giving all kinds of absurd notions about retaliatory measures if one were to injure another person's eyes, ears, legs, hands, tooth; how to measure the length, depth, place of injury in order to crush bones, cut limbs, extract teeth, gauge eyes, etc. All these possibilities, unlikely as they are, give the impression that the drafters of the Penal Code live in quite a different time.

Again, when we consult various authentic Prophetic Hadiths, we find that, except for cases of murder, organ-related injuries were settled by compensatory measures. An example may clarify this point:

> Narrated Anas that his aunt, Ar-Rubai broke an incisor of a girl. My aunt's family requested the girl's relatives for forgiveness but they refused, then they proposed a compensation but they refused. Then they went to Allah's Apostle...and refused every thing except Al-Qisas [i.e., equity in punishment]. So Allah's Apostle...passed the judgement of Al-Qisas....Anas bin Al-Nadar said, "O Allah's Apostle! will the incisor of Ar-Rubai be broken? No, by Him Who sent you with the Truth, the incisor will not be broken." Allah's Apostle...said, "O Anas! The prescribed law of Allah is equality in punishment [i.e., Al-Qisas]." Thereupon those people became satisfied and forgave her....[70]

The implication of this authentic Hadith is obvious: although the thrust of the Qisaas is equity in punishment, forgiveness and compensation should also be sought. Even though the above Hadith gives the impression that forgiveness was not granted, the fact that the Prophet agreed to *al-qisaas* might have persuaded the wronged party that the law applied to weak and strong, poor and wealthy alike, and therefore the wronged party decided to forgive and settle for compensation. It is also constructive to remember that all reputable Shii and Sunni jurists have stressed the importance of compassion, forgiveness and leniency, before allowing retaliatory punishment. Most importantly, the Sharia Law was applied regardless of the social, economic and political stature of the defendant. In present-day Iran, as we explored above, the Criminal Code generally applies to indigent persons, leaving the powerful unharmed.

Hudud and its Regulations

The second part of the Islamic Penal Code is devoted to *Hudud* (punishments) and its regulations. Composed of three chapters and a number of clarifications, this part of the Code defines various sex-related crimes such as adultery (*zinaa*), male homosexuality (*lawaat*), female homosexuality (*musahiqa*), and prostitution (*qawaadi*). There are also various articles related to drinking (*muskar*), and sex-related libel (*qazaf*), and their appropriate punishments. Sex-related crimes are of special interest here because the Islamic criminal justices system's arrest and punishment mechanisms are thoroughly geared towards controlling and suppressing sexuality, a process that has proven criminogenic insofar as the social reaction to the suppression of sexuality is concerned. The section of the Penal Code on adultery is explored below.

Adultery (Zinaa) in the Islamic Penal Code

This section of the Code covers 42 articles and clarifications (81 through 112). The section is divided into four sub-sections: (1) the punishment of adultery; (2) proving adultery in court; (3) various punishments for adultery; and (4) the execution of punishments.

Every society needs codes of conduct, morality, and laws. Every religion has addressed these issues, including Islam. What is peculiar about this section of the Penal Code is that the drafters follow the same medievalist conception with regard to crime and the etiology of crime. As a result, the Code follows a rationale whose social basis no longer exists. For example, Articles 81, 82, 83 and 84 define adultery and various scenarios under which adultery becomes punishable. However, as one explores the articles, one finds that women are treated as absolutely passive objects for the sexuality of men, a premise that reflects, like other parts of the Code, a medievalist conception of sexuality. For example, Article 81 maintains that: "Adultery is copulation of a man with a woman to whom [she] is not religiously prescribed ...."[71] Article 82 again speaks of man as adulterer (*zaani*), while no mention is made of woman as an adulterer (*zaaniya*). The article reads:

> Adultery is subject to punishment provided that the adulterer satisfies the following conditions: puberty, rationality,

> choice, and knowledge. Thus the adultery of [one who is] below puberty and mentally deficient and under duress and one who mistakenly copulates with a woman or marries a woman without knowing the appropriate religious code with whom marriage is not religiously prescribed and copulates with that woman is not subject to punishment. [72]

The opposite scenario is not codified for a very obvious reason: in medieval agriculture-based social relations, sexual activity was a prerogative of the male. Females were receivers and not initiators of sex. In modern industrial societies, this scenario no longer applies, not to mention the fact that codified adultery is increasingly restricted to married couples, and not to singles.

More problematic than a definition, however, is the procedure through which the commission of adultery is proven. Article 85 maintains that: "If a man or a woman confesses to adultery in four sessions [he/she] would be subjected to punishment and if [he/she] confesses less than four times [he/she] is subjected to corporal punishment." [73] Considering the sorry state of affairs of justice under the present Islamic criminal justice system in Iran, one wonders under what rational conditions a would-be adulterer/adulteress would confess to such a "crime," subjecting him or her to the most humiliating types of punishment that the Criminal Code has institutionalized. Ironically, Article 86 makes the acceptability of confession contingent upon the following conditions: puberty, rationality, choice and intent;[74] when put together these conditions make such a voluntary confession impossible. Article 87 maintains: "Confession must be explicit or apparent so that it would not be against rationality (*ihtemal-e aql-e khalaf*)."[75] Based on these, one has to be mentally deranged or insane to confess to adultery under a judiciary that has tried to legalize morality with a medievalist view of sexuality and punishment. Articles 88 through 90 forsee various scenarios in which adultery can be confessed to, and repented of. Article 90 maintains: "If a woman who does not have a spouse is to become pregnant she would not be punished based on the fact of pregnancy unless through one of the ways provided in this Law adultery be established." [76]

This apparently "liberal" view inserted into an otherwise medievalist conception of sexuality, can perhaps be explained by the drafters' reasoning that accidental pregnancy is possible as, for instance, in public bath houses whereby ovulating women could, by accident, come in touch with men's semen in the washing pool (*khazinah*). In the past, when public bath houses functioned, they served men and women at separate hours. However, the bathing water of the pool would not be changed, allowing for such accidental circumstances to occur. This article apparently provides an answer for such eventualities. More importantly, the Criminal Code's proof mechanism is of interest to our argument. Article 91 maintains: "Adultery is proven through witness of four just men or three just men with two just women. Whether [the proof] requisites the punishment of *jild* (lashing) whether the punishment of *rajam* (stoning)." [77]

Article 92 establishes proof for the punishment of *jild* (lashing) through confession. Again, a gender-related asymmetry in valuation system arises. The article reads: "In cases that adultery only requires the punishment of *jild* (lashing) it is proven by the witness of two just men and four just women." It makes the following clarification: "Witnessing of women alone or in addition to witnessing of one just man does not prove adultery but subjects the witnesses to punishment of sex related accusatory words *(qazaf)*."[78]

Articles 93 through 98 speak of the quality of witnessing, the manner of witnessing, the agreement between time and place whereby witnessing has taken place, and the immediacy of the punishment. Ironically, although these articles are manifestly misogynous, in consulting the Qur'an, we find quite a different tone and rationale.

Adultery in the Qur'an

Adultery is mentioned in *al-Asra* (xvii) a Maccan revelation, as well as in *al-Nur* (xxiv), a Madinan revelation. Verse 32 of xvii reads: "And come not unto adultery. Lo! it is an abomination and an evil way." [79] The verse is directed towards the "children of Israel" and is preceded by Allah's reminder to the Jewish believers that they once received Allah's Commandments but went astray. The preceding verses advise believers not to slay their children, fearing that they may fall to poverty. It then advises them not to commit adultery. However, it is in (xxiv, 2-3 and 4-10) that punishment for both adulterer (*zaani*) and adulteress (*zaaniya*) is advised. Verse 2 reads:

> The adulterer and adulteress, scourge ye each one of them (with) a hundred stripes. And let not pity for the twain withhold you from obedience to Allah, if ye believe in Allah and the Last Day. And let a party of believers witness their punishment. [80]

The thrust of the verse is equity, to be posited within the ease with which marriage is formed in Islam, a point I critiqued in Chapter 4 on women's legal status in the Qur'an. Verse 3 is an ominous prediction: "The adulterer shall not marry save an adulteress or an idolatress, and the adulteress none shall marry save an adulterer or an idolater. All that is forbidden unto believers."[81] Again, the symmetry prevails: the marital fate of an adulterer is linked to that of an adulteress.

Verse 4 mandates scourging (eighty stripes) for those who accuse honourable women without bringing four witnesses. The testimony of such persons shall not be accepted once they have been found guilty of slander, and the verse characterizes them as evil-doers (*al-faasiqun*).

Verse 5 should be read in conjunction with verse 4 because it allows repentance of those who amend their evil deeds after being punished.

Verses 6, 7, 8 and 9 are complementary to one another. These verses concern a husband's accusation of adultery. Reading the verses, we find a definite picture of the equity between a husband's words against a wife's words. Verse 6 reads: "As for those who accuse their wives but have no witness except themselves; let the testimony of one of them be four testimonies, (swearing) by Allah that he is of those who speak the truth;" verse 7, on the other hand, reads: "And yet a fifth, invoking the curse of Allah on him if he is of those who lie."[82] Notice that there is no mention of punishment. The verse speaks of a husband accusing his wife of adultery without any proof other than himself as a witness.

Verses 8 and 9 establish equity. Verse 8 maintains: "And it shall avert the punishment from her if she bear witness before Allah four times that the thing he saith is indeed false;" verse 9 reads: "And a fifth (time) that the wrath of Allah be upon her if he speaketh truth."[83]

In the Islamic Penal Code in Iran, it is obvious that the drafters' notion that adultery is established by confession is out of context and has nothing to do with the Qur'an. Secondly, it is obvious that the drafters of Penal Code, following the traditional Islamic juristic notion of testimony, have applied, out of context, the idea that two "just" (whatever this means) women's testimony is worth one "just" man's testimony in adultery. This application, out of context, runs even against the main Shii tenets of jurisprudence as, for instance, the Shaykh al-Taifa who follows the Qur'anic injunctions as described above and not the notion of the drafters of the Law, a point I have already critiqued in previous chapters. In present-day Iran indigent men and women have been stoned to death based on published documents. Table 8.1 depicts this disturbing picture.

Table 8.1 Indigent females and males stoned to death in Iran, 1980-1997

Year	Number	Crime	Gender	Source
13 July 1997	1	Murder, adultery	M	*Keyahn*, daily
26 October 1997	6	Not specified	3 M, 3 F	*Slaam*, daily
8 June 1996	2	Murder, adultery	1 M, 1 F	*Hamshahri*, daily
14 July 1995	3	Not specified	1 M, 2 F	*Jomhuri Islami*, daily, Amnesty International
7 December 1994	2	Murder, adultery	1 M, 1 F	*Hamshahri*, daily
16 November 1994	3	Adultery, rape	2 M, 1 F	*Abrar*, daily
1 March 1994	1	Not specified	F	*Resalat*, daily
1 February 1994	1	Incest	F	*Keyhan*, daily
1 November 1992	1	Not specified	F	1993 UN Report on Iran
5 November 1991	1	Immoral relations	F	*Abrar*, daily
21 August 1991	1	Adultery	F	*Keyhan*, daily
16 January 1990	1	Not specified	F	*Ressalat*, daily
5 January 1990	2	Not specified	F	*Ettelaat*, daily
2 January 1990	2	Not specified	F	*Jomhuri Islami*, daily
31 July 1989	6	Adultery, moral corruption	F	*Keyhan*, daily
17 April 17 1989	10	Prostitution	F	*Keyhan*, daily
6 March 6 1989	1	Adultery	F	Tehran Radio
4 October 1986	1	Not specified	F	*Keyhan*, daily
17 April 1986	1	Not specified	F	Eyewitness, word of mouth
July 1980	4	Not specified	F	Eyewitness, word of mouth
Total	50	-------	9 M, 41 F	------

Source: http://www.iran-e-azad.org/stonning/women.html

As Table 8.1 clearly indicates, during a seventeen-year period (1980-1997), 2.9 persons have been stoned to death each year since the establishment of Iran's Sharia Law-based justice system. Whereas only 18 per cent of the victims of this cruel and unusual punishment were indigent males a huge 82 per cent were indigent women. Some of the reported cases border absurdity as, for instance, the following as reported by the *Jomhuri Islami* daily on 11 March 1991:

> ...Bamani Fekri, child of Mohammad-Isa, guilty of complicity in first-degree murder, adultery and incineration of the victim's body was sentenced to stoning, retribution, blinding of both eyes and payment of 100 gold dinars. After the announcement of the verdict, she committed suicide in prison.[84]

The absurdity of these types of punishment is compounded by the fact that guilt is established mostly on coerced confession usually in the absence of defence lawyers. Where legal representation is allowed, the defence attorney is barred from questioning the religious edict's applicability to the case. For example, nowhere in the Qur'an is it stated that stoning to death is the proper punishment for adultery; the proper punishment is flogging. The defence attorney is therefore not allowed to question those aspects of the Sharia Law that are known as the unchangeable truths (*musallamaat*), such as stoning to death. Therefore, a coerced confession to adultery seals the fate of indigent victims. Where the judge is challenged on the matter of law, the recitation of a Hadith by the judge constitutes proof that judge is right and appeal is denied by the appellate court whose religious judges follow the same rationale.

The Agricultural Valuation System in the Islamic Penal Code in Iran

The present gender asymmetry in the Penal Code of the Islamic Republic's judiciary – outrightly discriminatory and, in most cases, non-transparent as it is now – is harmonious with the aims of medieval juristic texts' view of women's value. In other words, the combined social, political and economic basis of the present Penal Code's approaches to the issue of the human worth no longer exist. This basis once existed and was dynamic and vibrant under the Abbasid caliphate and its successors in the Near East, North Africa and the

Indian sub-continent until perhaps the nineteenth century. Both the classical and post-classical Twelve Imami Shii canon and their intertwined versions of the Sharia Law, a product of this long gestation period, naturally utilized this valuation system in the adjudication process. In the same manner that in pre-industrialized agriculture-based societies women were valued less than men, their organs had less value than those of men.

The above examples reflect a medievalist valuation system. Once we ascend to modern industrial and post-industrial societies, the articles cited from the Penal Code become "Islamic" only if we "regress" to medieval agricultural societies and force women into the status of second-class citizens. The Constitution of the Islamic Republic, nonetheless, speaks of modern technology, progress and human rights, all concepts that make such regression to a medieval system and rationale of adjudication nearly impossible. In addition, in modern industrial societies women are in job markets; they constitute a very important part of the labour force; and they compete with men in social, political and economic arenas. Therefore, women should not only be considered as equal to men in every respect; in fact, their organs should carry more value than men's organs, considering that women contribute more to wealth formation through their domestic and market-related contributory impacts. This said, in any modern or would-be democratic Islamic society, the above practices ought to be abolished once and for all, considering that the Qur'an itself allows, through the abrogating (*nasikh*) and abrogated (*mansukh*), the discontinuation of such practices.

In sum, it can be argued that the change from a secular and modern criminal justice to one based on the Islamic Sharia Law not only has failed to ameliorate the strategic problem of modern Iran's criminal justice system – namely, its lack of consistency and of equity in the application of law – but in fact this change has led to the deepening of this crisis. As I have shown in this study, Iranian women have suffered tremendously under the new Islamic system.

Notes

1. Said Amir Arjomand, "Clerical Authority in the Constitution of the Islamic Republic of Iran" *in Authority and Political Culture in Shiism*, (Albany, NY, SUNY Press, 1988) p. 371. The emphasis is in the original.

2. *Ibid.*, p. 376.

3. Mohammad M. Pickthall, *The Glorious Qur'an*, (New York, Mostazafan Foundation of New York, 1984), p. 60. For a somewhat different translation of the term *umma* that Pickthall has translated as "nation" see the same verse in Mirza Tahir Ahmad *The Holy Qur'an* vol. 2, (Surah Al-Imran-Surah Al-Tauba), p. 434.

4. Ahmad, *The Holy Qur'an*, p. 437.

5. *Ibid.*, p. 438.

6. Muhaqiq Hilli, "Kitab-e Amr-e be-Maaruf wa Nahy az Munkar..." in *Tarjumeh Sharayi al-Islam*, vol. 2, p. 137.

7. Fatima Mernissi, *The Veil and the Male Elite: A Feminist Interpretation of Women's Rights in Islam*, (New York, Addison-Wesley Publishing Company, Inc., 1991), p. 85.

8. *Ibid.* Mernissi cites the verse from Pickthall, *The Glorious Qur'an*, p. 305. Parentheses are in the original.

9. *Ibid.*

10. See "Kronolodhi 'Nimeye Digar'" in *Nimeye Digar*, vol. 1, no. 1, Spring 1984, p. 105.

11. *Ibid.*

12. See for instance Bakri (no fn), "Bahar-e Azadi" in *Nimeye Digar*, no. 10, Winter 1990, pp. 112-117; see also Eliz Sanasarian, *The Women's Rights Movement in Iran: Mutiny, Appeasement, and Repression from 1900 to Khomeini*, (New York, NY, Praeger Publishers, 1982), pp. 124-131.

13. "Kronolodhi 'Nimye Digar'", pp. 106-107. Translated from Persian into English by this author.

14. *Ibid.*, p. 107.

15. Muahaqqiq Hilli, *Terjumah Sharayi al-Islam*, (Tehran, Iran, Intesharat-e Daneshga-e Tehran, 1364/1985), vol. 1, p. 137.

16. Maryam Matindaftari, "Piramun-e Aain-nameh-e Ijraai-ye Mubarezeh baa 'Bad-hejaabi''' (Concerning the Executive Code in Combating "Malveiling"), p. 31 in *Azadi: Wabastih be Jebhy-e Demukratik-e Melliy-e Iran*, no. 9, Spring 1989, pp. 30-43. The English translation of these codes belongs to this author.

17. *Ibid.*, p. 32.

18. Houshang Naserzadeh, *Majmueh-e Qavaanin-e Khanevaadeh* (The Compendium of Family Laws), (Tehran, Iran, Inntesharat-e Khorshid, 1377/1998).

19. *Ibid.*, p. 5.

20. *Ibid.*, pp. 7-11.

21. *Ibid.*, p. 149.

22. *Ibid.*, p. 154.

23. *Ibid.*, p. 155.

24. *Ibid.*, pp. 156-157.

25. *Ibid.*, pp. 157-162.

26. The Parliamentary Human Rights Group, *Iran: The Subjection of Women*, (np.), November 1994, p. 6.

27. *Ibid.*

28. *Ibid.*

29. Jaquiline Rudolph Touba, "Effects of the Islamic Revolution on Women and the Family in Iran" pp. 131-147 in Asghar Fathi (ed.), *Women and the Family in Iran*, (Leiden, E.J. Brill, 1985), p. 131.

30. *Ibid.*, p. 132.

31. Valentine M. Moghadam, *Modernizing Women: Gender and Social Change in the Middle East*, (Boulder, CO, Lynne Rienner Publishers, 1993). See the chapter on Iran.

32. See for example Haideh Moghisi, *Populist Feminism and Islamic Feminism: A Critique of Neo-Conservative Tendencies Among Iranian Feminists in the West*, (North York, Ontario, Afra Publishing Co., 1998), pp. 43-50.

33. The Parliamentary Human Rights Group, *Iran: The Subjection of Women in Iran*, p. 13. The report cites this information from Homa Omid, *Women and the Post-Revolutionary State*, (New York, St. Martin's Press, 1994), p. 191.

34. *Ibid.*, p. 13.

35. For example in Shaykh al-Taifa's *al-Nihaya*, or in Hurr al-Amili's aforementioned *Wasail*. See volume 19 under the general title of Al-Diyyat in *Wasail al-Shia*. This volume covers

various injunctions of the Qisas and Diyyat (various forms of blood money).

36. *Matn-e Kaamel: Qaanun-e Hudud wa Qisaas wa Muqarrarat-e Aan* (Complete Text: The Law of Hudud and Qisas and Their Ordinances) (Tehran, Iran, Intisharat-e Pezeshkan Nejad wa Pesaran, Azar 1361/1982), p. 5.

37. See for example Shaykh al-Taifa's *Tarjumeh Al-Nihayah*, vol. 2, p. 498.

38. See for example Malik ibn Anas, *Al-Muwatta*, pp. 344-352 and pp. 358-370.

39. *Matn-e Kaamel*, p. 6.

40. *Ibid.*, p. 6.

41. Ahmad, *The Holy Qur'an,* vol. 2, p. 550. The italics are in the original.

42. *Ibid.*, p. 551.

43. Imam Bukhari, *Sahih al-Bukhari*, vol. 6, (Beirut, Lebanon, Dar al-Arabiyah), p. 93.

44. Ahmad, *The Holy Qur'an*, vol.1, p. 229.

45. *Matn-e Kaamel*, pp. 7-8.

46. *Ibid.*, p. 8.

47. *Ibid.*, pp. 8-9.

48. *Ibid.*, p. 10.

49. Shaykh al-Taifa, *Tarjumeh Al-Nihayah*, vol. 1, p. 217.

50. *Ibid.*, pp. 217-218.

51. *Matn-e Kaamel*, p. 10.

52. *Ibid.*, p. 11.

53. *Ibid.*, p. 13.

54. *Ibid.*, pp. 13-14.

55. *Ibid.*, p. 14.

56. Imam Bukhari, *Sahih al-Bukhari*, vol. 6, p. 22. Parentheses are in the original.

57. Malik ibn Anas, *Al-Muwatta*, p. 358.

58. *Ibid.*,

59. *Ibid.*, p. 360.

60. Shaykh al-Ta'ifa, *Tarjumah Al-Nihayah*, vol. 2, p. 508. Brackets and translation (from Persian to English) belong to this author.

61. *Ibid.*, pp. 508-509.

62. Pickthall, *The Glorious Qur'an*, p. 107.

63. Imam Bukhari, *Sahih al-Bukhari*, vol. 8, Hadith no. 789, p. 516. Similar Hadiths: nos 785 through 791.

64. *Ibid.*, vol. 8, Hadith no. 779, pp. 512-513.

65. *Ibid.*, vol. 8, p. 513.

67. Cited in *SHOWRA*, no. 53, March-May 1990, p. 140.

68. *Ibid.*, pp. 141-42.

69. The speech of the Ayatullah Karrubi cited in *SHOWRA*, no. 53, March-May1990, pp. 138-139.

70. Based on an interview given by the Ayatullah Muqtadai to Radio Tehran on 27 May 1990.

71. Imam Bukhari, *Sahih al-Bukhari*, vol. 6, Hadith no. 27, pp. 23-24.

72. *Matn-e Kaamel*, p. 17.

73. *Ibid.*, p. 17.

74. *Ibid.*, p. 18.

75. *Ibid.*

76. *Ibid.*

77. *Ibid.*

77. *Ibid.*

78. *Ibid.*

79. Pickthall, *The Glorious Qur'an*, p. 281.

80. *Ibid.*, p. 359.

81. *Ibid.*

82. *Ibid.*, pp. 359-360.

83. *Ibid.*, p. 360.

84. *Jomhuri Islami*, 11 March 1991 cited in Iran-e-Azad website at http://www.Iran-e-Azad.org.

9 Conclusion

The central claim of the Sharia Law, from its inception to present, has been that Islam's divine law serves the cause of justice because the Sharia Law is not an instrument of power *per se*, but one that seeks to serve the common good. Historically, it has been this aspect of the Sharia Law that has made it anti-criminogenic. For the Sharia Law to function in its anti-criminogenic capacity, however, it needs enhancement through believers' adherence to the Law's injunctions. In particular, family, religious and educational systems enhance the Law's basic values by inculcating morality, self-worth and fear of transgression in believers. Next to these primary social institutions of informal control, the state and its organs are also responsible for the Law's equitable application, only achievable through the just and moral conduct of judges, police and correctional institutions. Theoretically, these factors allow the Sharia Law to inhibit the commission of crime. I have tried to show that the Sharia Law is a complex body whose evolution as a system of conflict resolution covers a long and detailed history. Like all other systems of law and conflict resolution, it has its ideal norms in terms of how to administer justice, how to punish criminals, and how to interpret its injunctions.

I have also tried to show that, in Islam, there is the notion of an ideal Sharia Law-based criminal justice system that, if institutionalized, is capable of deterring crime provided that its organs (police, courts and correctional institutions) are created through non-coercive measures and step-by-step in a community of believers which is sound in terms of social and economic foundations. This presumed ideal Islamic criminal justice system can only be built in an ideal Islamic community where individual, as well as communal, efforts have been undertaken in order to uphold Islam's central values. It is in such a social medium that the Sharia Law is capable of deterring crime to a good extent. That is why, in Islam, the Prophet Muhammad is believed to have created such an ideal social medium through the establishment of a model governance and a model of justice in the city of Madina whose temporal and epistemological bases were harmonious with the nascent Sharia Law, later systematized under his successors.

A return to this ideal model has now been politicized by Islamic revivalist forces throughout the Islamic world. This is one reason why the end result of Iran's Sharia Law-based criminal justice system is of interest to the fields of comparative criminology and victimology, for the dignitaries of the

Islamic Republic argue that they are following the Prophet Muhammad's model of justice which is preserved in classical juristic texts. In particular, they argue that women's treatment in the Islamic criminal justice system is an exact iteration of the Prophetic model. Whatever the merits of these claims, what is certain is that post-Islamic Revolution Iran suffers from a long cycle of over-criminalization. As I have shown in Chapters 6 and 7, the victimization of Iranian women has reached a scale that is unprecedented in Islam's, and in Iran's, long histories.

Lessons for Comparative Criminology

The Iranian experience with the Sharia Law can provide valuable lessons for the field of comparative criminology. The first lesson is that any totalitarian attempt to institutionalize a system of law and penology (e.g., the present Sharia Law-based system) is bound to lead to anomic results at best, or to extensive criminogenic results at worst. For example, the Qur'an, as the primary source of the Sharia Law, states categorically that no divine injunction should be coerced on believers, let alone on non-believers. In contemporary Iran, believers and non-believers alike are subjected to the will of one male cleric, the so-called Jurist Council, who has a constitutional mandate with regard to social, economic and legal affairs of the society. As a result of this mandate, the Jurist Council has been empowered to render semi-legal and religious opinions that are enforceable. This unprecedented range of legalistic power, guarded jealously by the political establishment, and enforced by official and paramilitary law enforcement organizations, has made Iran one of the most oppressive Islamic states in the world. The end result has been the long cycle of crime, economic corruption and suicide by young women, from the early 1980 to the present.

The second lesson is that any system of law, justice and penology is only "sacred" when it is at the service of common good. The idea that the Sharia Law is "sacred" is only meaningful when it is subjected to this yard-stick rather than to its divine nature. Believers claim that the Qur'an is God's Word, but the text warns believers that some verses are of an everlasting validity (*al-Muhkamaat*), whereas some others are of an allegorical (*al-Mutishabihaat*). If one were to argue that the Sharia Law in its totality is of everlasting validity and therefore is immune to time and culture, then, such a proponent has to accept the premise that the Law's categorization of crimes and punishments are also valid eternally. This conclusion means that Islamic societies ought to follow all procedural nuances of the juristic texts verbatim, which in essence means a retributory type of punishment regime: an eye for an eye and a tooth for a tooth. In reality, however, the absolute majority of Islamic societies do not adhere to the Sharia Law, let alone to a retribution-based penology that is cruel and unusual by any modern standard of justice. Only Saudi Arabia, the Islamic Republic of Iran, Sudan (for some time in the early 1980s), and the Taliban regime in Afghanistan adhere to a Sharia-based penology. The inevitable question arises: why have all other Islamic societies decided against a Sharia system? The answer can be found in the overall complexity of the Sharia Law, which makes it almost impossible to institutionalize in the context of modern capitalist social and legal relations. Having gone through the profound changes that modern capitalism has wrought, most Islamic societies have adapted their system to modern secular laws especially in relation to crime, justice and penology.

Ironically, when one compares the Saudi system's application of the Sharia Law with the Iranian application of it, one discovers that there are both qualitative and quantitative differences between the two. Whereas the Iranian application has been criminogenic, leading to a long cycle of over-criminalization and female victimization, the Saudi system has been, by and large, anti-criminogenic, leading a discernible general deterrence in crime commission as shown by both Freda Adler's[1] and Sam Souryal's[2] studies. The differences between the two systems' end results can hardly be explained through denominational adherence; namely because the Saudis adhere to a Sunni brand of Islam (*Wahhabi*), such deterrence is achieved. Conversely, because Iranians' adhere to Shiism, the system has failed. In fact, as I have explained elsewhere,[3] the only viable explanation for this difference has to do with the fact that the Saudi system has been built upon a socially organized economic infrastructure and a stable political regime that has been able to deliver goods and services on a regular basis notwithstanding its undemocratic structure of governance. By providing education, health care and a stable internal market economy, the Saudis have enjoyed a social structure that has brought the etiology of crime under control, allowing the Sharia Law-based system to operate in a socially organized medium. The Iranian system, on the other hand, has been imposed through force and intimidation during a decade of revolutionary turmoil, war and population dislocation. In addition, the imposition has been of a totalitarian nature, imposed upon an ancient and complex culture and society that has gone through several decades of modernization and development; worse yet, the Islamic regime's purely instrumentalist view of the Sharia Law has led to the exact opposite of the

Law's historical legacy. Finally, while the Taliban regime's application of the Law has yet to be researched systematically, horror stories of miscarriages of justice already have emerged.

The third lesson for comparative criminology is that any system of law, justice and penology has its historical legacy encapsulated in the persona of that system's founder, be it temporal or divine. For example, the American Constitution is a profoundly complex legal document whose historical legacy is encapsulated in the concepts of life, liberty and property; added to the complexity of the American Constitution is the Bill of Rights whose motto is life, liberty and the pursuit of happiness. Naturally, we tend to believe that the Founding Fathers of the American Constitution and of the Bill of Rights by and large, believed in these mottos and seldom contravened these basic values. The same goes for those who wrote the French Declaration of the Universal Human Rights, who ought to have been cognizant of the fact that universal human rights would only make sense if it transcended national boundaries; the intrinsic value of humankind is not based on race, class, gender or ethnicity, but in those sublime values for which we strive. One such value is the notion of social justice that is inseparable from equity. In other words, any system of law that alleges to be concerned with justice ought to provide an answer for issues of equity in the application of law. The more equitable a system is in the resolution of conflicts the more just, progressive and legitimate the system is in terms of its end products.

Approached from this perspective, what is the historical legacy of the Sharia Law? This is a tough question that does not lend itself to easy answers. There is no doubt that Prophet Muhammad's approach to legislation was piecemeal as he gradually received the revelations of the Qur'an upon which the Law's genesis was formed, always acting as the exemplar of a believer who adhered to the Law's injunctions and basic values. The same adherence applies to his four deputies who succeeded him. Even among the Umayyad caliphs, there were caliphs such as Umar Ibn Abad al-Aziz, who tried to emulate Muhammad's style of just resolution of conflicts based on equity. In other words, for both lay and intellectual Muslims, the historical legacy of the Sharia Law, as an instrument of justice and equity, has been enhanced by a view of history that looks to Muhammad's tradition as a living heritage. Those who politicize this heritage, as in contemporary Iran, are duty-bound to create a system that at least resembles this history.

In present-day Iran, we have the exact opposite of the Prophetic model that Islam maintains is just and equitable: during the 1980s and 1990s, the political establishment of the Islamic Republic, composed of a minority of the Shii men of the cloth and their core support group, the community of the Party of God (*Ummat-e Hizbullah*), have remained almost immune to the injunctions of the Sharia Law. Besides the prevalence of predatory crimes, I also have given examples of unprecedented economic corruption, in which the high dignitaries of the regime have been implicated time and again. None has been punished according to the Islamic Penal Code's severe punishments such as amputation of fingers for theft. Such contradictory examples abound, some of which I have documented in this study.

Lessons for Victimology

Iran's experience with the Sharia Law-based system of criminal justice can provide valuable lessons for victimology, which is a new field in criminology. As I have shown, Iranian women, especially those belonging to the lower classes, have been the biggest victims of the present system. This victimization covers a wide range of social, political and psychological realms covering every aspect of feminine life in Iran. Thanks to modern feminism, in democratic societies women have strived for social, economic, political and legal equity with men. As I showed in Chapter 4, the Qur'an, as the primary source of the Sharia Law, has recognized a wide range of rights and responsibilities for women. These rights and responsibilities, however, are now being challenged by a formidable force, the Islamic revivalist movements whose motto is a return to a "pure" Islam of the *time* of the Prophet Muhammad. My stress is on the time because a believing Muslim would have no difficulty in accepting that Muhammad's application of the Law was just and equitable. By insisting that we should go back to the Prophet's *time*, the revivalist forces give in to a literal interpretation of the time and heritage of the Prophet Muhammad. The Iranian experience has been a valuable lesson for women in general and women in modern Islamic societies in particular. Women are potentially the primary victims of this return to the "pure" Islam of the Prophet Muhammad's time. Those concerned about improving women's status should recognize the fact that Islam is not a monolithic construct represented by so-called fundamentalists forces. There are other views of Islam, the Qur'an and the Sharia Law that are different from fundamentalist views. A synopsis of these forces' arguments is provided.

The Traditionalist's View of the Sharia and of Women's Status

Women, argue the traditionalists, are not equal to men because the Qur'an, and the Prophet's Traditions have advocated this inequality between the sexes, an inequality ordained by Allah. Women, accordingly, "need" men's constant supervision over their affairs because in God's eternal wisdom, women are created for one central purpose: procreation. Based on this traditional premise, women's social and legal status is based on a functionalist view of the Sacred Law which, by necessity, is based on a centuries-old notion of the viability of sexual division of labour. The supporters of tradition argue that Islam's Sacred Law has provided believing women (*al-muminat*) with a set of rights and responsibilities, giving believing Muslim women a certain status in the family provided that women remain dependent on, and subservient to, men. The traditionalists perpetuate patriarchal structures that dominate the social, economic and political institutions in modern Islamic societies.

What about non-Muslim and atheist women? How are we to determine their status in modern Islamic societies? The traditionalists argue that the Sacred Law protects religious minorities whom the Qur'an characterizes as the People of Scripture, a designation that applies traditionally to Jews, Christians, Zoroastrians and Saabiin. The People of Scripture are free to conduct their religious affairs as they see fit and are accordingly protected by the Islamic state. The issue of atheism is much more difficult to address, considering that atheism has always existed on the fringe of medieval Islamic societies as it existed in medieval Christian Europe. It is only with the rise of modern communism that atheism, as a social phenomenon, has entered into the political discourse. In any case, traditionalist forces take the challenge of a communist-inspired atheism quite seriously when it is in the form of a political movement, but not when it is of an academic nature and especially if it has a feminine voice.

It is plausible to argue that the traditionalist view of the Sacred Law does not accord women equality because gender equality is a modern concept and is automatically anti-traditionalist. It has been suggested by radical feminists, however, that the traditionalist reading of the Qur'an and the Sharia Law is absolutely correct because Islam is a patriarchal religion with the Qur'an as its ideological blueprint. There is no doubt that there are various injunctions in the Qur'an that give this distinct impression. In fact, one could show that the traditional view of the Qur'an, and the Prophetic Tradition enhanced, in no uncertain terms, all kinds of patriarchal institution. Naturally, the traditional view of the Sacred Law, as it was devised by the medieval

Muslim jurists, could hardly go against its agriculturally-based rationale, and the male-dominated social and political institutions that gave the Muslim jurists their power base. The question confronting traditionalists is this: can the current state of affairs be justified in modern Islamic societies?

The Fundamentalist's View of the Sharia Law and of Women's Status

The position of fundamentalists is that women's social and legal status ought to be determined by a return to the *time* of the Prophet Muhammad so that the Sharia Law can be adhered to in its totality. In this determination, the question of what constitutes the *time* as well as the "totality" of the Sharia is as important as the question of "who" determines this *time* and totality. Although these are not new questions, and, in fact, one could show various such movements that preceded modern fundamentalism (e.g., Wahhabism in Saudi Arabia, Mahdisim in Sudan, Bahism in Iran, Ahmadisim in Pakistan, etc.), with the rise of the Ayatullah Khumaini a new trend of fundamentalist movements has come to the fore of politics with regard to the Sharia Law and its treatment of women, based on the claim of a strategic return to the time of the Prophet Muhammad.

The Modernizing Reformist View of the Sharia Law and of Women's Status

The position of modernizing reformists is that women's status can be improved only if the Qur'an is open to interpretive nuances. Except for those Qur'anic verses that are "eternally valid" (*Muhkamaat*), others are "allegorical" (*Mutishabihaat*). Women's social and legal status derives not from the former, but the latter. These modern reformers consider Islam as a dynamic religion, open to reform and reconsideration. They argue that Islam is not a dogmatic, closed system based on blind adherence to its principles, but that the very text of the Qur'an and the Prophet's Tradition encourages believers to enquire about various aspects of the faith and its teachings. For reformers, Islam is not based on coercion; it is a faith that is based on reason, understanding, compassion and righteousness.

The Western Feminist View of the Sharia Law and of Women's Status

Western-educated feminist scholars in many Islamic societies argue that Islam is a sexist, misogynist, patriarchal system that has historically allowed man to dominate woman, to economically use her, to psychologically abuse her, and to socially brutalize and marginalize her. From their perspective, the Sharia Law has legitimated all these in the past and has become totally irrelevant to improving women's social and legal status in Islamic societies and therefore has to be abandoned altogether. Some feminist scholars give credit to some Qur'anic injunctions as they relate to women's general status in Islam (when comparing Islam with Judaism and Christianity). The majority, however, argue that women's status has to be based on secular law. The reformers reject this view of Western educated feminists as linear and based on a selective reading of the text ignoring text, sub-text, context and immanent critique of Islam as a living dynamic religion.

Islamic Feminism

There are modern Islamic movements and political activists who now speak of a gender egalitarianism that they believe is in the Qur'an and the Prophetic Hadith. Women, in many Islamic societies, have become the victims of a literal and reactionary reading of Islam's primary sources with regard to their social and legal status; these forces and political activists argue that women in Islamic societies face double exploitation, First, they are deprived of a certain amount of egalitarianism that modern secular laws have provided for women in advanced industrialized societies. Second, they have also been deprived of even those rights that traditional Islam and the Sharia Law have delegated to them.

Muslim feminists propose a new reading of the primary sources to improve women's legal status. As I explored in some detail in this study, the thrust of this new reading is, by necessity, anti-traditionalist and anti-fundamentalist. In rejecting any such thought of egalitarianism, both traditionalists and fundamentalists argue that one cannot pick and choose from the Sharia Law because it is a totality requiring total adherence to its injunctions, despite the fact that the history of the Law belies this position. For example, all Islamic societies have abolished slavery even though slavery occupies a place in the Qur'an and in the Sharia Law. The same abandonment goes for child labour, child marriage, cruel and unusual punishments and polygamy. The Sharia Law is simply not as monolithic as both the traditionalists and the fundamentalists want us to believe. If slavery and polygamy can be abolished without adversely affecting the integrity of the Law, why not rescue the Law from gender-based inequities?

The issue of women's status in the eyes of the Sharia Law is by far one of the most complex issues modern Islamic societies now face. Each constituent of the Law has a history behind its canonization; the traditional notion of women's status in the Sharia Law has been entrenched, supported and eulogized by a very technical, arcane and legalistic literature. One cannot simply ignore this structured notion of the Law in improving women's status and opt for a preconceived model of secularization of law, hoping that traditional social relations will automatically follow suit. One can, however, effectively challenge gender-based inequalities through a systematic approach to the issue of totality in the Sharia. Is the Sacred Law of Islam applicable in its "totality" in this day and age? As this study has established, the answer to this question is "No".

Lessons for Islamic Societies

Any Islamic society that wants to establish a Sharia Law-based justice system faces a formidable challenge. First, there are the concrete realities of the modern world, including a globalized economy. The challenge can be summarized by the following question: can the world of Islam live in harmony with the rest of the modern and industrialized world within the context of a globalized economy whose social and legal relations are based on secular laws, and, simultaneously adhere to a centuries-old, traditional view of Sharia-based social and legal relations? In other words, since crime and justice are profoundly social products, there has to be a harmonious relationship between a modern concept of property and the system of law and justice that safeguard this notion. At the same time, modern concepts of property inaugurate modern concepts of crime and penology, which apply to contractual obligations, tort and crime. Naturally, accepted versions of modern property, prevalent even in Islamic societies, have economic, social and legal foundations within the context of capitalism, the hegemonic system of production and reproduction throughout the world.

The disjunction between the modern capitalist notion of property and traditional Sharia Law views of property is so profound that it is almost impossible to operate within a modern capitalist system and regulate the social and legal relations based on a Shari` system of conflict resolution.

There is no doubt that there are also profound differences between the two systems' view of law and of the administration of justice. Theoretically, the Sharia system views law as an instrument at the service of the common good, arguing that justice ought to be administered in the most equitable manner regardless of extraneous variables such as class, race and gender. In reality, however, the Iranian Sharia Law system has administered justice in the exact opposite of this ideal. The modern secular system, although giving lip service to the ideal of equity, administers justice institutions of power, especially in adversarial systems of conflict resolution. By abandoning the Sharia Law system, most Islamic societies have opted for secular laws, realizing that entrance into modern capitalist relations requires the adoption of secular laws as the base of conflict resolution and administration of justice. The problem is that this entrance into modern capitalist relations has been arduous, leading to widely divergent results. A return to Islam's fundamental values has become a solution for those who have not benefited from this long and still unfolding process of social and economic transformation.

The Challenge of Puritanical Model Building

As shown in the first four chapters above, the Prophet Muhammad left a legacy of using nascent Sharia Law to serve the cause of justice in Madina based on the premises that: equity in justice is paramount in the eyes of God; that justice is a sensitive issue whose administration has to be based on strict moral grounds; and that true faith in Islam means belief in the just resolution of conflicts. One can argue that this Islamic notion of justice has a universality that is historically transcendent. Throughout history, all systems of conflict resolution have asserted that the legitimacy of the system is based on the degree to which a system of law and conflict resolution has abided by principles of equity. In fact, one can argue that the fall of Soviet communism had a lot to do with the legitimacy crises that surrounded, among other things, its administration of justice.

As indicated in the introductory chapter, with the rise of the Ayatullah Khumaini in Iran, the Islamic revivalist forces proposed the supremacy of a Sharia Law-based system of justice and conflict resolution, arguing that the main problem of Islamic societies is that they all have abandoned the Islamic Sharia and instead have adopted secular laws and non-Islamic penology. The remedy is a "total" return to the Sharia, a system based on the Prophet Muhammad's model of governance and administration of justice. This return not only ought to be total, but one that has to follow Muhammad's procedure exactly. For example, in present-day Iran, judges have decreed that defendants compensate their victims with Yemeni gold coins called Yemeni Dinar, or with cattle, and even with milch camels because the Prophet did so. The same goes for the retributory kind of punishments that, as I explained in Chapters

6 and 7, include bone crushing, gouging of eyes, amputation of fingers and stoning. The problem is in the concept of "return" to Prophet's model, which is impossible, but in fact goes against the text of the Qur'an that advises Muslims to always look forward and raise their conscience in harmony with the desirable aspects of time and culture. The Qur'an claims that Islam's Sacred Law enhances the positive aspects of both Judaism and Christianity, at the same time that it improves the notion of justice and equity by improving upon procedures that I covered in some detail in Chapters 2 and 3. One example concerned the capital punishment of murder; another concerned the punishment for adultery.

This total return is also impossible because, as I have shown above, successive generations of Muslim jurists idealized Muhammad's model of administration of justice. The same proposal has been made about Muhammad's deputies, the "Four Rightly Guided Caliphs". However, this ideal model's procedural laws reflected the social and legal realities of the then prevailing agricultural system and its etiology of crime and penology. It is not the procedure, but the spirit, of the Law that must be emulated. The spirit of the Law is an even-handed administration of justice. This serves the high ideals of the Sharia Law.

I also provided pertinent examples from both Sunni and Shii juristic texts to argue that the ideal of equity in the administration of justice through a Sharia Law-based system has a long and cherished history. In practice, of course, the Islamic world has produced some fine judges, as well as some notoriously cruel and corrupt ones. In fact, in Islam's history, the reigns of dynasties, more often than not, have come to an abrupt end because the common populace revolted against cruel and corrupt judges, governors and even caliphs who abused the Law. The Qur'an charges believers with the duty to observe Allah's boundaries and punishments, while at the same time resisting cruel judges and rulers. In both Sunni and Shii versions of the Sharia Law, the cause of justice has been paramount. Those who opt for a total return to the Prophet's procedures can hardly explain why we are in a better position to adhere to his exact Procedure than those who were centuries closer to the Prophet's time. For example, are we better equipped to follow Muhammad's Procedure than Umar, or Ali? Are we more justified in applying punishments, which Muhammad may not have applied (e.g., stoning to death that I explored in some details in this study)? In particular, should cruel and unusual punishments be applied to indigent and socially disenfranchised women in Iran?

The Challenge of Sacredness

From the mid-nineteenth century to the present, the world of Islam has faced powerful multifaceted challenges to its social and legal institutions. Among these challenges, modern Europe's system of conflict resolution, based on secular laws, has played a significant role in shattering the traditional norms of social and legal conflict resolution in many Islamic societies. Unlike traditional Sharia Law, modern secular laws are of more temporal nature, proposing that men and women are equal in the proverbial eye of the law. Unlike traditional Sharia Law, modern secular laws do not purport to be sacred or unchangeable. As a result, modern systems of conflict resolution are much more flexible and, therefore, more in tune with the social changes that occur on a national and global basis. The world of Islam is not immune to these changes, and most Islamic societies have opted for modern secular laws and systems of conflict resolution in facing these challenges.

Iran's Experience with the Secular and Sharia Law: Durkheimian Anomie in Action

Iran, one of the oldest human civilizations, constitutes one of the most important Islamic societies. There is a school of thought that argues that the primordial Islam was internationalized through Iran's contribution to Islam, a contribution that covered every conceivable realm from the Qur'anic exegesis, to positive sciences. In particular, it is Shiism that has been characterized by a good number of Western and Iranian scholars as an Iranian version of Islam.

As I have shown in this study, Iran, under the Pahlavi Dynasty, adopted modern secular laws, court systems and penology between 1925 and 1979. As I explored in Chapters 6 and 7, the Pahlavi shahs' modernization efforts were of an externally imposed nature designed to provide Iranian economy with yet another externally imposed division of labour in the world capitalist relations of production. This division of labour necessitated the adoption of modern civil, administrative and criminal laws and penal codes as well as a court structure whose substantive and procedural laws were harmonious with the agenda of modernization efforts – namely, that the legal system has to reflect a notion of society and economy whose idealogy is premised on modern capitalism. The main problem of the Pahlavi modernization scheme was that it was of an externally imposed and dependent nature because the Pahlavi political establishment had also been imposed on the Iranian polity. The two Pahlavi shahs were brought to power not based on Iranian popular will, but through foreign interventions. In addition, the second Pahlavi, Muhammad Reza Shah, never succeeded in resolving his legitimacy crisis in the face of his collaboration with foreign powers in deposing the democratic regime of Dr. Muhammad Musaddiq, whose demise occurred at the hands of the CIA and its Iranian collaborators in the infamous *coup d'etat* of 1953.

In the 1960s and 1970s, however, Iran entered into a general cycle of prosperity, economic differentiation and industrialization, allowing for a notable and mechanical control of predatory crimes. Women's social and legal status improved through various reforms. At the same time, Iran became a dreaded police state because dissent was criminalized. This was one phase of what I consider a Durkheimian anomie in the making. Durkheim argues that as societies go through successively more complex divisions of labour, they may reach a temporary stage of anomie characterized by formlessness, or confused mores, laws and values. Although modern institutions and infrastructures are created, they are not accompanied by the requisite social and legal relations. For example, although motor vehicles are used, traffic regulations are ignored because adherence to such regulations engender a view of social relations that has to be to be inculcated in society at large. Under the Pahlavi shahs modern institutions were created without the requisite social and legal relations. The general prosperity, coupled with the regime's brutal suppression of dissent, created anomic values wrapped in political and intellectual confusion. A centuries-old tradition based Islamic society like Iran, having gone through several decades of modernization in social and economic realms, was becoming more and more alienated from the political establishment that had made such prosperity and superficial modernity possible in the first place.

This state of affairs was anomic because although general prosperity is, by and large, anti-criminogenic, a retrogressive process of criminalization of dissent alienated the Pahlavi political establishment from the common people in the midst of economic prosperity; at the same time, the criminalization of dissent was rightly conceived as one of the main sources of Iran's backwardness in the areas of conflict resolution and administration of justice. The remedy was sought in various forms of political ideologies that ranged from communism, to socialism, to Islamism, all of which had their intellectual circles, proponents and agitators during the twentieth century.

Living in Iran in the decade of the 1970s as a college-aged student, I believed, as did a generation of college-educated cohorts, that Iran deserved a democratic system of governance rather than a regime whose secret police could, and did, arrest anybody, at any place and at any time, to take them to secret houses of detention, interrogation and torture. As a graduate from one of the most prestigious colleges in Iran, Abadan Institute of Technology, that trained engineers and business managers for Iran's huge oil, gas, and petrochemical industries, most of us in that college were arguing that any regime would better serve the causes of democracy and rule of equitable law in Iran than the Pahlavi regime. This view, of course, was another sign of Durkheimian anomie in action: young, college-educated middle- and upper-middle-class Iranians (male and female) were being alienated from the political regime that had provided general prosperity at the expense of democratic institutions, yet the political alternative was sought outside the monarchy. This was not anomic at first glance, but it was anomic because the Iranian intelligentsia, including myself, never realized the depth of the political void that the Pahlavi regime had created through its systematic uprooting of every vestige of democracy and democratic institutions in order to reach a certain level of general prosperity. As a result of this policy that had led to the creation of the political void, the Iranian intelligentsia could not fathom the idea that such a void couldn't be filled with democracy overnight once the political regime was overthrown. For this reason, the 1979 Revolution, as glorious as it was, was not in a position to transform Iranian society into a democracy, especially when the leadership of the Revolution was gradually assumed by a cadre of the Shii men of the cloth under the guidance of the Ayatullah Khumaini.

Enter the Islamic Revolution: Intensification of the Anomie

Two of the main slogans of the Iranian Revolution in 1979 were democratic freedoms (*Azaadi*) and independence (*Istiqlaal*). Iran has never been colonized, in the manner of a number of African and Asian societies, during her long historical evolution that spans twenty-five centuries of written history. From the mid-nineteenth century to the time of the Islamic Revolution, "independence," by and large, has meant political independence from Western (and later from American) hegemony. The Iranian laity and intellectuals alike believe that this independence is the first step necessary towards real social and economic progress. Political independence would also enable Iran to assume a non-aligned foreign policy in the world political arena, which in turn would enable the would-be national government to steer Iran's democratization into its proper channels. In particular, it has always been assumed that the cause of justice would improve dramatically because the whole system would be put at the service of the people, rather than at the service of a minority and its political establishment. In this manner, the Durkheimian anomie would be resolved because dissent would automatically be democratized. No longer would the political establishment be at the service of foreign but national interests. In other words, by replacing the monarchy with a democratic and non-aligned regime, the Iranian government would initiate the process of democratization. In the face of the systematic elimination of modern political forces and parties in Iran under the Pahlavi shahs, however, the only viable force to challenge the might of the monarchy was Shii Islam that, because of its historical legacy, was assumed to be able to achieve all of these Herculean tasks.

Thus, in the mid-1970s, the idea of a return to an egalitarian form of Islamic governance was already being circulated in Iran's mosque-bazaar religious circles as well as in colleges and universities. The rise of the Ayatullah Khumaini can in part be explained by the shah's anti-democratic disposition. The shah's secret police, SAVAK had created a political void by systematically eliminating all modern political parties and movements through its criminalization of dissent. Khumaini's political rhetoric, wrapped in common parlance and popular slogans such as "Freedom" and "Independence," had nonetheless a subtle message that was not appreciated by the Iranian intelligentsia, let alone by the common people. A return to Islam meant a return to Khumaini's version of Islam that he had formulated in his treatise called *Islamic Government* written during the reign of the Reza Shah Pahlavi. In this treatise, Khumaini developed the concept of the Jurist Council (*Wilayat-e Faqih*) that is now inserted in the Islamic Republic's Constitution.

According to Khumaini, a total return to Shii Islam's fundamental values has to take place within the confines of this doctrine – namely, that Iran has to be re-Islamized under the total control of one religious figure, the so-called Jurist Council. It is only through this re-Islamization that Iran will be transformed into a model Islamic society, in which the cause of justice would be served by a Sharia Law-based justice system. This system has to emulate the Prophet Muhammad's and First Shii Imam, Ali Ibn Abi Talib's, models of governance and administration of justice.

In addition, it was presumed that, by a total return to Khumaini's Islam and its re-discovered fundamental values, women's social and legal status would be determined under the guidance of the Jurist Council, providing for women an ideal Sharia-based place in society. Iranian women, who under the secular laws were becoming corrupted by the intrusion of

Western values and therefore were being dragged into crime and prostitution, would now be transformed into Latter Day Fatimas acting as upright, moral and pure women revolutionaries as well as model wives, daughters and mothers spreading Khumaini's revolutionary Islam throughout the Islamic world. All these ideals would become concrete realities under an Islamic Republic that Khumaini and his lieutenants promised to be democratic, independent and pluralistic.

Islam and Democracy

The Ayatullah Khumaini believed that the Islamic society he envisioned, because it was based on Sharia Law, would become anti-criminogenic. Khumaini also believed that his version of Islam would be inclusive of a set of values that he argued were far superior to democratic values because Islam, in comparison to democracy, is more inclusive and unimpeded by extraneous variables, such as class, gender, race and ethnicity. An Islamic Community of Believers that Khumaini wanted to create in the context of an *Umma,* is ideally based on piety, moral values, fear of Allah and responsibility towards the disenfranchised, ideally creating a crime-free society. Democracy, on the other hand, argued Khumaini, is a Western and corrupt class ideology that stratifies whole categories of people, giving them unequal access to wealth, prestige and power. An Islamic *Umma* is anti-criminogenic, whereas crime is a central feature of class societies, went the argument of Khumaini and his partisans as they re-Islamized Iran during the 1980s and 1990s. Therefore, establishment of democratic institutions was never taken up by the political establishment that took over the reins of power from the monarchy. Instead, a total re-Islamization of Iranian society became the mandate of the Islamic Revolution. In the course of this total re-Islamization effort by the new regime, it soon became clear to Khumaini that this was a futile effort. The social and political reaction was intensely against Khumaini's argument that he wanted to take Iran back to the time of the time of the Prophet Muhammad. Instead of opting for a strategy based on consultative and inclusive practices, Khumaini chose a totalitarian re-Islamization strategy at the expense of his phenomenal popularity and democratic ideals of the 1979 Revolution.

With the establishment of the Islamic Republic in 1979, Iranian society and economy have gone through a profound re-Islamization process. This process, as I have shown, besides being chaotic, has been totalitarian, leading to a long cycle of over-criminalization and intensifying Durkheimian anomie. Not only has Iran's general prosperity of the 1960s and 1970s not been repeated, but in fact Iran has entered into a long process of social disorganization and poverty expressed, among others, by an unprecedented rate of female victimization at the hands of a regime whose criminal justice system claims adherence to Qur'anic injunctions. The reader may recall that these injunctions are very sensitive to the issue of equity in the administration of justice, reminding believers that Allah watches over those who sit in judgment of others' guilt. I have explored the manner in which justice is administered in Iran: the Sharia-based system is utilized as a political instrument to brutalize the socially disenfranchised, as well as to intimidate into submission and obedience the opponents of the Islamic regime. Dissent has now been thoroughly criminalized and its boundaries have been extended to a much wider realm of social actions.

The sorry state of affairs in Iran has led scholars to raise serious questions about Islam in general and the Sharia Law in particular. I have re-examined some of these questions in this study. I have tried to show that the complexity of the Sharia Law makes it almost impossible to institutionalize in this day and age, based on Khumaini's strategy: total submission to the will of one central figure, the Jurist Council (*Wali-ye Faqih*). In addition, the abject failure of the present system of justice in Iran is due to the fact that the social, economic and political conditions of a globalized economy, of which the pre-Revolution Iran was an important constituent, makes this application of the Sharia Law an impossible endeavour. It is impossible to force a sophisticated culture and a differentiated modern economy such as Iran's into a pre-capitalist agricultural society so that agriculturalist social and legal relations can be re-institutionalized. This incompatibility between form and content has led to the system's abject failure in the administration of justice, which in turn has led to a long cycle of over-criminalization and female victimization.

Notes

1. Freda Adler, *Nations Not Obsessed With Crime*, (Littleton, CO, Fred B Rothman & Co., Chapter 9, pp. 80-91.

2. Sam Souryal, "The Role of Shariah Law in Deterring Criminality in Saudi Arabia" in *International Journal of Comparative and Applied Criminal Justice* vol. 12, no. 1, 1988, pp. 1-25.

3. Hamid R. Kusha, "Revisiting the Islamic Shariah Law in Deterring Criminality: Is there a

Lesson for Western Criminology?" in *Crime and Justice International*, vol. 14, no.15, 1998, pp. 24-26.

Index

For Product Safety Concerns and Information please contact our EU representative GPSR@taylorandfrancis.com
Taylor & Francis Verlag GmbH, Kaufingerstraße 24, 80331 München, Germany

www.ingramcontent.com/pod-product-compliance
Ingram Content Group UK Ltd.
Pitfield, Milton Keynes, MK11 3LW, UK
UKHW022116190926
475702UK00013B/1468
* 9 7 8 1 1 3 8 2 6 8 8 8 3 *